USING the PAST
to SERVE
the PRESENT

Contemporary China Papers
Australian National University

Series Editor: Jonathan Unger, Australian National University

DIRECTORY OF OFFICIALS AND ORGANIZATIONS IN CHINA
A Quarter Century Guide
Malcolm Lamb

USING THE PAST TO SERVE THE PRESENT
Historiography and Politics in Contemporary China
Edited by Jonathan Unger

THE PRO-DEMOCRACY PROTESTS IN CHINA
Reports from the Provinces
Edited by Jonathan Unger

Contemporary China Papers
Australian National University

USING the PAST to SERVE the PRESENT

Historiography and Politics in Contemporary China

JONATHAN UNGER, editor

An East Gate Book

M. E. Sharpe
Armonk, New York
London, England

An East Gate Book

Copyright © 1993 by M. E. Sharpe, Inc.

All rights reserved. No part of this book may be reproduced in any form without written permission from the publisher, M. E. Sharpe, Inc., 80 Business Park Drive, Armonk, New York 10504.

Library of Congress Cataloging-in-Publication Data

Using the past to serve the present :
historiography and politics in contemporary China /
Jonathan Unger, editor.
p. cm. — (Contemporary China papers)
Includes bibliographical references.
ISBN 0-87332-747-0 (cloth). — ISBN 0-87332-748-9 (pbk.)
1. China—Historiography.
I. Unger, Jonathan.
II. Series.
DS734.7.U83   1993
951'.0072—dc20
93-15256
CIP

Printed in the United States of America

The paper used in this publication meets the minimum requirements of
American National Standard for Information Sciences—
Permanence of Paper for Printed Library Materials,
ANSI Z39.48–1984.

BM (c) 10 9 8 7 6 5 4 3 2 1
BM (p) 10 9 8 7 6 5 4 3 2 1

Contents

Acknowledgements	vii
Contributors	ix
Introduction *Jonathan Unger*	1
Tom Fisher, 'The Play's the Thing': Wu Han and Hai Rui Revisited	9
Rudolf G. Wagner, 'In Guise of a Congratulation': Political Symbolism in Zhou Xinfang's Play *Hai Rui Submits His Memorial*	46
David Holm, The Strange Case of Liu Zhidan	104
Ralph Croizier, Qu Yuan and the Artists: Ancient Symbols and Modern Politics in the Post-Mao Era	124
Susanne Weigelin-Schwiedrzik, Party Historiography	151
Lawrence R. Sullivan, The Controversy over 'Feudal Despotism': Politics and Historiography in China, 1978-82	174
Tim Wright, 'The Spiritual Heritage of Chinese Capitalism': Recent Trends in the Historiography of Chinese Enterprise Management	205
Michael R. Godley, Socialism with Chinese Characteristics: Sun Yatsen and the International Development of China	239
Geremie Barmé, History for the Masses	260
Index	287

Acknowledgements

Over the past decade, *The Australian Journal of Chinese Affairs,* of which I was editor, has published a considerable number of stimulating papers on the politics of historiography in China. Each paper depicted an important facet of the topic, and by happy coincidence, over time the papers began to form a coherent whole. What has emerged is a series of nuanced, interrelated perspectives into the complexities of politically-charged historiography in China. And repeatedly, history-writing *has* been politically charged – especially given the Chinese tradition of envisaging the past as a mirror in which the present, by analogy, can be viewed.

For this book, almost all of the papers have been rewritten and re-edited so as to integrate them yet better into the common overarching theme. Geremie Barmé has contributed an excellent final chapter especially for the volume in order to round out this theme, by examining post-Mao 'history for the masses' up through the first half of 1992. For this contribution he is owed a special debt of gratitude.

Elizabeth Kingdon, the Assistant Editor of the *Journal*, copy-edited and proofread the manuscript and provided the Index. Dianne Stacey, the *Journal*'s Production Manager, took responsibility for the volume's layout and production. Without them this book would never have appeared.

J.U.

CONTRIBUTORS

Geremie Barmé is a Research Fellow in the Division of Pacific and Asian History at the Australian National University. His most recent book is *New Ghosts, Old Dreams: Chinese Rebel Voices* (co-edited with L. Jaivin).

Ralph Croizier is Professor of History at the University of Victoria in Canada. His books include *China's Cultural Legacy and Communism* and *Art and Revolution in Modern China*.

Tom Fisher is a Senior Lecturer in History at La Trobe University in Melbourne. He has contributed major articles to *The Harvard Journal of Asiatic Studies* and to Chinese scholarly collections on Qing history and to *China's Establishment Intellectuals* (Hamrin and Cheek, editors).

Michael Godley is a Senior Lecturer in History at Monash University in Melbourne. His publications include *Mandarin-Capitalist from Nanyang*.

David Holm is Professor of Chinese at Macquarie University in Sydney. He is the author of *Art and Ideology in Revolutionary China* (1991) and is currently working on ritual theatre and peasant drama troupes in the Chinese countryside.

Lawrence R. Sullivan is Associate Professor of Political Science at Adelphi University and a Research Associate at the East Asian Institute, Columbia University. He is co-editor of *Beijing Spring 1989: Confrontation and Conflict, The Basic Documents* (M.E. Sharpe, 1990) and of *China's Search for Democracy: The Student and Mass Movement of 1989* (M.E. Sharpe, 1992).

Jonathan Unger is head of the Australian National University's Contemporary China Centre. His eight books include *Education Under Mao: Class and Competition in Canton Schools* and, most recently, *Chen Village Under Mao and Deng* (co-authored with Anita Chan and Richard Madsen, 1992) and, as editor, *The Pro-Democracy Protests in China* (M.E. Sharpe, 1991).

Rudolf G. Wagner is Professor of Sinology at the Institute of Chinese Studies, University of Heidelberg, Germany. His books include *The Contemporary Chinese Historical Drama: Four Studies*; *Inside a Service Trade*; and *Studies in Contemporary Chinese Prose*. He is currently finishing a book on the 3rd-century philosopher Wang Bi.

Susanne Weigelin-Schwiedrzik holds the Chair for Contemporary Chinese Studies at Heidelberg University, Germany. She specializes in modern Chinese intellectual history and politics. Currently she is conducting research on the beginnings of Marxism in China, focusing on the period between 1898 and 1924.

Tim Wright is Associate Professor of Chinese History at Murdoch University, Western Australia. His publications include *Coal Mining in China's Economy and Society, 1895-1937* and *The Chinese Economy in the Early Twentieth Century: Recent Chinese Studies* and a number of related articles on modern Chinese social and economic history. He is currently working on the impact on China of the 1930s world depression.

USING the PAST
to SERVE
the PRESENT

INTRODUCTION

Jonathan Unger

The recording and interpretation of history has, for the past two millennia, contained a special significance in China. More than in most other countries, history was and is considered a mirror through which ethical standards and moral transgressions pertinent to the present day could be viewed. This perspective on history was based in Confucian doctrine, which admonished followers to plumb the past for such lessons. It became a method of commentary about contemporary times that members of the literati class learned how to manipulate, sometimes as a means of flattering an incumbent emperor and government – but sometimes as a stratagem for chastising the imperial court. After all, in a centrally controlled empire it was always safer to place one's criticisms in a past age than to write directly about the present court. Well aware of this potential for allegory, suspicious emperors and their entourages kept a watchful eye open for subversive intent in the historical treatises of the literati. Repeatedly, purges and persecutions in imperial China were rooted in alleged 'historical' aspersions, real or imagined, against the imperial majesty.

The historical essays that were most prone to be riven with political analogies were those that dealt directly with the inner imperial courts of past dynasties. The upper reaches of the Chinese state had been divided into an outer court of literati officials who had been selected through examinations and, countering their power, an inner court of eunuch officials beholden only to the emperor. It was the literati who traditionally wrote China's history books, and they sometimes were tempted to paint the inner court of fallen dynasties as a not-entirely-moral sphere of government – as a cauldron of corrupt sycophants, scheming empresses, the ambitious relatives of concubines, and weak and vain emperors – versus 'good' officials of the outer court. It was a perception that entered into Peking operas and the popular imagination. The plots of two very famous historical dramas of Mao's era, which are discussed in this book by Tom Fisher and Rudolf Wagner, followed this time-worn popular scenario of a 'good' literati official and his travails at the hands of a vain emperor and/or the families of unjust powerholders with ties to the emperor. The Communist government, akin to its imperial forebears, had to face the question as to whether such portrayals were innocently and harmlessly historical – or whether subversive political metaphors might be involved.

Even more so than the emperors, the Party leaders who entered the former imperial capital in 1949 were determined to control the messages imparted in works of history – to bend those messages in ways favourable to official policy lines and to extirpate any manifestation of dissent or opposition that might be hidden within historical allegory. They were particularly determined because the traditional desire to police historical references had been reinforced and overlain by a newer, imported credo. This of course was the Leninist/Stalinist doctrine, which argued the revolutionary need for an all-powerful Party to push forward Communist social values and attitudes by controlling and reshaping both intellectual discourse and public sentiment. Given the importance of images of history in shaping both intellectual and popular thought in China, special attention was to be focused on ensuring that the proper line was followed by historians.

A new type of history-writing was introduced, to define for the Chinese a new set of paradigms through which they were to view the world and the ongoing flow of history. As always, orthodoxy was to be laid down from the centre, but orthodoxy of an altogether new kind.

Confucian historiography, as noted, had devoted great attention to emperors and high officials and their moral qualities; whilst Marxist historiography, as we all know, instead places considerable emphasis upon economic and social history. Marxist historiography, moreover, repudiated the Confucian concern with harmony in social relations. The new historiography instead placed a premium upon 'class struggle' as the motor of history and as the fulcrum for determining the moral or immoral tenor of historical personages and events. And whereas traditional historiography had posed recorded history as essentially cyclical, turning upon the rise and fall of successive dynasties that each flowered and then degenerated in turn, Marxist historiography posited a progressive march forward in history.

The premises of this new historiography were not exclusively the property of the Marxists, to be sure. From before the turn of the century, Chinese historians had borrowed from Western historians and Social Darwinists the clear notion that history progressed. And some of the 'bourgeois' historians of the May Fourth generation, again borrowing from the West, or indirectly from the West by way of Japan, had been concerned with economic and social history as explanatory factors in this historical progress.

The Marxist historiography added two important ingredients to this extant recipe. First was the notion that Chinese history necessarily had to fit into a schemata of historical stages quite precisely drawn up by Marx and Engels: from primitive communism into slave society, and onward to feudalism, capitalism and the inevitable glorious march into socialism. The second essential ingredient was the signal position given to 'class struggle'. And here, peasant rebellion was to take a central place in Chinese historiography, to be popularized and glorified: not the traditional elite but the 'masses' had made history. This perception of peasant rebellion helped the regime to get the Chinese to think in a new way that legitimized the government and legitimized ongoing 'class struggle' in the PRC against the retrograde classes. James P. Harrison, in a book about the Party-sponsored historiography on peasant rebellions, noted that 'the millions of words devoted to the subject of the peasant movements provide the historical documentation for the most massive attempt at ideological re-education in human history. The aim is nothing less than the transformation of the world view of the world's largest people'.[1]

The historians, in short, were to serve as handmaidens to the Party propagandists. A huge quantity of stereotypic writing on peasant rebellions was duly produced, with the details duly filled in, but the larger answers were already known, already dictated by the guardians of Party ideology. So, too, a vast amount of time and intelligence was wasted by historians upon a search for the exact timing of each of the stages of history, to fit the preconceived notions handed down to them by the Party leadership.

Try as the Communist authorities might, though, they were never entirely able to dictate the ways in which the Chinese people turned to history for lessons and for political analogies. As but one example, when interviewing respondents from China in the mid 1970s, I could not help but notice how frequently interviewees' discussions of current politics

---

[1] James P. Harrison, *The Communists and Chinese Peasant Rebellions: A Study in the Rewriting of Chinese History* (New York: Atheneum, 1971), p.15. Harrison concluded that this barrage of popularized history-writing was successful: 'there is no doubt that the average reader in communist China sees them in terms of class struggle, believing that the Chinese peasantry struggled for thousands of years against the abuses of the governing class and that ultimately their "liberation" had to await communist leadership'. (p.272).

turned toward historical analogy – and almost always within the terms of the *traditional* genres of political allegory. Interviewees were apt to refer to Mao's unpopular wife Jiang Qing and Mao's closest followers, for instance, in phrases that conjured up the stereotypically scheming inner-court courtiers and imperial consorts – who so often in the histories and operas had illegitimately taken advantage of an aging emperor's dotage to usurp power. Playing upon such feelings, within months of Mao's death in 1976 and the coup against the 'gang of four', the official mass media itself was similarly dressing up contemporary politics in the clothes of the past. The just-widowed Jiang Qing was presented to the Chinese people as the modern counterpart to the Empress Lu, one of the great villainesses of popular lore, who had usurped power in the Han dynasty.

The first half of this book focuses on several case studies that illuminate the interplay in the PRC between Party politics and this *old* genre of popular historiography. The ins and outs of the *official* Party-sponsored historiography under Mao's rule have already been very ably analysed by seventeen historians in a volume edited in 1968 by Albert Feuerwerker, *History in Communist China* (Cambridge, The MIT Press), and a new exegesis of this official Mao-era historiography does not warrant priority status here. Instead, the focus is on the often tense relationship between Party rule and popular historiography. The first three chapters examine the ways in which popular works about famous historical personalities became *causes célèbres* during Mao's reign – leading in all three cases to the imprisonment of the offending authors. And a fourth chapter examines how the legendary poet-scholar Qu Yuan was appropriated in art to exemplify the particular political visions of painter-intellectuals under first Mao and then Deng.

The first two chapters examine the most famous of all the political uproars that erupted under Mao over historical interpretation: the two historical dramas from the early 1960s, already noted above, that Tom Fisher and Rudolf Wagner separately examine. Both plays dealt with the 'good' Ming dynasty official Hai Rui, and in 1965-66 both of the dramas came under scathing attack by Mao's entourage in a salvo that ignited the Cultural Revolution. (The Cultural Revolution derives its title, in fact from the initial attack against Wu Han, the author of one of these Hui Rui plays, and his closest colleagues.)

Tom Fisher suggests that this barrage of criticism against Wu Han might have been misplaced – that Wu Han was a scrupulously rigorous historian who, granting the need for a bit of dramatic license in writing a play, had nevertheless fairly accurately portrayed one of the most famous episodes in the career of Hai Rui. Taking a different tack, Rudolf Wagner argues that Zhou Xinfang's contemporaneous play about Hai Rui contained a rich repertory of encoded political messages aimed directly against Chairman Mao and the Great Leap Forward, using scathingly witty analogies that his audience was culturally conditioned to look for and appreciate. In effect, Wagner is implying that similar metaphors must have underpinned a number of the other historical drams of the time, including Wu Han's play about Hai Rui. The first two contributors, Tom Fisher and Rudolf Wagner, thus take different stances in what amounts to an implicit debate in the pages of this book.

David Holm, in the third chapter of the book, does not directly address this debate, but he weighs in with a topic of some relevance to it: a major purge of officials in the early 1960s based on charges laid against an historical novel, *Liu Zhidan*, about a leading 'revolutionary martyr' of the Yenan era. Holm argues that the accusations against the novel had been drummed up for machiavellian reasons – that those purged were innocent victims of a plot that took advantage of the age-old suspicions that political messages are apt to lurk within the pages of historical works. In short, Fisher and Holm separately argue that even when writings on historical themes were *not* necessarily intended to impart contemporary political messages, they were *assumed* to do so by the top leadership, with frightening consequences.

Ralph Croizier's paper involves artists, not writers, but his theme is parallel to those of the first chapters, in that he shows how modern portraits of the ancient poet-official Qu Yuan (whose legendary suicide through drowning inspired China's Dragon Boat Festival) have depicted moods and poses of contemporary political import. Croizier traces how, over time, painters this century have depicted Qu Yuan in political allegories portraying the role of intellectuals in relation to the state. In most cases, artists in the PRC could only depict Qu Yuan in officially-approved ways, or not at all – though it became possible from exile, as with the famous artist Huang Yongyu, to employ the Qu Yuan theme in 1989 to denounce the government with devastating effect (on this, see the conclusion to Croizier's chapter).

Among the artwork that Croizier examines, one particular political interpretation of Qu Yuan that deserves mention here was obliquely expressed only by the daring Huang Yongyu in a 1978 painting. It was a theme which did get alluded to repeatedly, though, in writings by Chinese intellectuals in the late 1970s. Qu Yuan had committed suicide because he had loyally sought to serve a king but had been rejected, and many intellectuals in the late 1970s sought to depict this plight as analogous to their own collective circumstances under Mao. Akin to Qu Yuan, they too were patriotic scholars, who during the 'ten lost years' had sought to use their intellectual skills on behalf of the nation and government but cruelly had been denied the chance.[2] The Qu Yuan story fulfilled both halves of the intellectuals' claim: their heated effort to assert that, like Qu Yuan, they *had* been devoted to serving the state (a claim which the Maoists in the 1970s had disputed); and the claim of maltreatment, of wastage of talents, as seen in Qu Yuan's famous, still lamented death. Theirs was not an official Party-sponsored analogy, but neither was it subversively dissident.

If the great bulk of the historians under Mao's rule had sought to please the political 'throne' by writing precisely what they were expected to write, so too under the new post-Mao dispensation they loyally and meekly served their political masters. When the ship of state under Deng's helmsmanship cast off from its prior ideological moorings, historians were aboard as ever-obedient oarsmen, awaiting orders. There was a palpable difference from earlier years, though. Under Mao, they often had had to promote ideas and interests antithetical to their own, whereas now they were generally in sympathy with the premises that they were paid to support.

This was certainly the case when a new Party 'Resolution' on the Party's own history was drawn up in 1981. As Susanne Weigelin-Schwiedrzik explains in her chapter on Party historiography, there had been two major Party resolutions on Party history: the first in 1945 that established Mao as the moving force in Party history, and now this 1981 Party congress 'Resolution' that opened up Party history to encompass events in which Mao did not play a signal role, highlighting past leaders other than the Great Helmsman. For obvious political reasons, the writers of Party history have generally been kept on an even shorter leash than the historians of other topics and periods, and as expected they loyally depicted the new Party line. But as Weigelin-Schwiedrzik shows, this new Party line also gave the historians greater room to *be* historians, to try to depict what had occurred in the Chinese revolution in a more 'balanced' fashion, inserting the details of Party history that a Mao-centred hagiography had rendered taboo.

So, too, the politically obedient historians could now explore the previously taboo topic of capitalism's role in China, as Tim Wright and Michael Godley show in their respective chapters on the revised

---

[2] This complaint was also the theme of much of the 'scar literature' of the late 1970s, and of Bai Hua's officially-condemned film *Bitter Love*.

perspectives on early to mid 20th century capitalists and on Sun Yatsen's promotion of foreign finance. Before, under Mao's rule, capitalists had been irremediably retrograde; the only progressive force of Chinese history had been the peasantry, joined this past century by the industrial working class. In the 1980s, allusions could begin to be made to the potentially progressive role of capitalism (which, of course, was in line with Marx's own writings on capitalism). An implicit debate ensued in China. As the historian David Buck has noted, as of the 1980s 'the lines are clearly drawn between those who emphasize the role of the peasantry in modern history and those who would give greater weight to the bourgeoisie'.[3] The historians whom Tim Wright analyses are the champions of the latter perspective. More than that, as Michael Godley shows, even the international financiers of the imperialist powers could be shown to have played a potentially progressive role for China. The parallels to present-day policy under Deng could not be more obvious; but for the slow of mind and hard of hearing, China's historians hammered home the points loud and clear. Both Godley and Wright bring out in delicious detail this latest ironic effort of a Party-led state to 'use the past to serve the present'.

At the very same time, in the 1980s and 1990s the officially-sanctioned histories have not always been uniform in their appraisals of the past. Disagreement within the leadership is tolerated, and so too historians can serve one political mentor or another, and one or another line of political thought. They can use the now-wider parameters of what is permissible to debate one another, and in so doing can push what presumably are genuinely their own views. Paul Cohen and Merle Goldman have noted this Deng-era trend:

> It is clear that modern history still serves politics in China. However, there is a difference between a situation – such as prevailed during the Cultural Revolution and even before – in which historians are told by the political leadership what to study, how to study it, and what conclusions to reach, and one in which historians, although consciously or unconsciously responsive to shifting political and ideological winds, are relatively free to look at the evidence and draw conclusions on the basis of what they find. It

---

[3] David D. Buck, 'Appraising the Revival of Historical Studies in China', *The China Quarterly*, no.105 (March 1986), pp.140-41.

seems evident to us that Chinese historians have broken out of the first situation and are moving toward the second.[4]

Lawrence Sullivan's chapter discusses one important example: the politically charged historical debate in the first half of the 1980s over the role of despotism in Chinese history.

In short, the historians of the post-Mao era who have turned to political analogy have not just been acting at the service of the state (though many were: *vide* Wright and Godley) or as dissidents seeking to discredit the government and past Party policies (see examples in Geremie Barmé's chapter). *Some* (*a la* Sullivan's chapter) were becoming increasingly autonomous as historians, arguing not specifically on behalf of or against the political authorities, but rather staking out their own political ground *vis à vis* colleagues in the profession.

Geremie Barmé, in the book's final chapter, brings out yet another dimension of this growing semi-autonomy in interpreting history. Popular culture no longer is under such tight political wraps, and popular fiction, movies, TV docudramas and even soap operas nowadays purvey their own versions of history, in ways that consciously or unconsciously sometimes move beyond the parameters of Party orthodoxy. A fitful tug-of-war has ensued, as the Party erratically bans work that it deems overstep the line of what is permissible. (See, e.g., Barmé's description of the ostensibly historical, deliciously subversive TV series *Tiananmen* that was banned in 1991).

That famous phrase by Mao about 'Using the past to serve the present' remains a double-edged sword so far as the Party's leaders are concerned. They continue to wield it for their own purposes, but it is a blade that can cut both ways, at times in a fashion that undermines the Party-sponsored interpretations of history or that sabotages the Party's latest political line. This book examines the changing nature of this clash between an ever-shifting orthodoxy and alleged subversion, from the late 1950s through the early 1990s. It is a chronicle that has not yet ended. Each new year can be expected to bring new shifts, new episodes, new clashes over interpretations of history, and sporadic official crackdowns.

---

[4] Paul A. Cohen and Merle Goldman, 'Modern History', in Anne F. Thurston and Jason H. Parker (eds), *Humanistic and Social Science Research in China* (Social Science Research Council, New York, 1980), p.52.

'THE PLAY'S THE THING': WU HAN AND HAI RUI REVISITED

Tom Fisher

The opening shot of what became the Great Proletarian Cultural Revolution was an attack by Yao Wenyuan, one of the so-called 'Gang of Four', on the play 'The Dismissal of Hai Rui'. The play's author was Wu Han, an eminent authority on Ming history and deputy mayor of Beijing. Wu died in October 1969, apparently the victim of a savage beating administered in a Beijing prison. Ten years later, however, the Communist Party of China (CCP) had not only rehabilitated Wu's reputation but had lauded him as a model intellectual for post-Cultural Revolution China.[1]

By the end of 1979 the Chinese press had praised his biography of the first emperor of the Ming dynasty. 'The Dismissal of Hai Rui' had been restaged and republished, and an impressive range of Party officials had attended a memorial service for him and his wife, who also had died in horrifying circumstances during the Cultural Revolution.[2]

Blame for the misguided attack against 'The Dismissal of Hai Rui', according to the *People's Daily,* should be laid squarely at the feet of Jiang Qing, who was said to have been responsible for a 'literary inquisition' unsurpassed in history. While acknowledging that Wu Han had used the story of Hai Rui (1514-87) to comment on current politics,

---

[1] I have also written a more general appraisal of Wu Han's work and rehabilitation that places relatively more emphasis on the political context. I see him as an 'establishment intellectual', working within boundaries prescribed by the CCP, or at least the Beijing leadership, rather than a 'dissenter' outside of the system. [See Tom Fisher, 'The "Upright Official" ' as a Model in the Humanities', in Carol Lee Hamrin and Timothy Cheek (eds), *China's Establishment Intellectuals* (M. E. Sharpe, Armonk N. Y. and London, 1986), pp.155-84.] However, I make no claim to take historical plays of the 1960s in general 'at face value and read them as disquisitions on history with only marginal political implications', as claimed by Rudolf Wagner in the chapter that follows, 'In Guise of a Congratulation'.

[2] Wu Han, *Hai Rui baguan* (The Dismissal of Hai Rui) (Beijing, 1979); *Guangming ribao*, 31 December 1978. For a more detailed discussion of the biography, see my 'Wu Han, The Cultural Revolution, and *The Biography of Zhu Yuanzhang*: An Introduction', *Ming Studies* 11 (Fall 1980), 33-44.

the paper denied that he was referring to Peng Dehuai, a charge specifically made by Mao Zedong.[3] Moreover, in a belated eulogy, Wu was praised as a 'good member of the Chinese Communist Party (CCP) and a staunch revolutionary fighter'.[4] It is thus a fitting time to re-examine the case of Wu Han and his use of the model Ming dynasty official, Hai Rui.

Purpose and Methodology

As an historian of the early Qing dynasty, I became interested in Wu Han for reasons quite unrelated to the politics of the Cultural Revolution and the Ming context of Hai Rui.[5] But in reviewing both what Wu Han wrote and what earlier Western political analysts had written about Wu Han, I was struck by two things. The first was the near unanimous support given by Western scholars to the basic charges levelled against Wu by Yao Wenyuan and Mao Zedong at the start of the Cultural Revolution. The second was their lack of attention to Wu Han as an historian. Western literature on the Cultural Revolution generally gave the impression that Wu Han was an 'anti-Maoist satirist' who seized on the symbol of Hai Rui to write allegorical historical polemics against specific policies of the contemporary CCP.[6] Some writers even accused him of purposely distorting history to accomplish these ends.[7]

---

[3] *Renmin ribao*, 1 February 1979.

[4] *Renmin ribao*, 15 September 1979. Similarly, *Notes on the Three Family Village*, to which Wu Han was a contributor, has been republished with a laudatory preface.

[5] I was asked to review two English language translations of 'Hai Rui Dismissed from Office' for the journal *Ming Studies*.

[6] I have gained this picture from what I hope is a representative selection of works published to date in the field. They include Clive Ansley (trs. and ed.), *The Heresy of Wu Han: His Play 'Hai Jui's Dismissal' and Its Role in China's Cultural Revolution* (Toronto, 1971); Ansley's review of Pusey's book (see below) in *The China Quarterly*, no.45 (January-March 1971), 182; Bill Brugger, *Contemporary China* (London and New York, 1977); Parris H. Chang, *Power and Policy in China* (University Park, Pa. and London, 1975); Lowell Dittmer, *Liu Shao-ch'i and the Chinese Cultural Revolution* (Berkeley, Los Angeles and London, 1974); Jürgens Domes, *The Internal Politics of China, 1949-1972*, trs. Rüdiger Machetzki (Sydney, 1973); Hong Yung Lee, *The Politics of the Chinese Cultural Revolution: A Case Study* (Berkeley, Los Angeles, and London, 1978); James R. Pusey, *Wu Han: Attacking the Present Through the Past* (Cambridge Mass., 1969); and Edward E. Rice, *Mao's Way* (Berkeley, Los Angeles and

Western scholars in general have seen in Wu Han's play criticism of Maoist policies in 1958-59, especially the treatment of Peng Dehuai and the commune programme of the Great Leap Forward. For example, we are told by one writer, 'the reader easily recognizes in Hai Rui the Peng Dehuai whose rehabilitation Wu Han had pleaded for in his play',[8] and by others that 'Peng Dehuai was dramatized as the contemporary Hai Rui'[9] and the play was a 'defence of Peng'.[10] Still other analysts have discovered implied criticism of the people's communes in the play's oft-repeated slogan 'return the land' (*tuitian*).[11]

In what follows, I wish to re-open the issue of Wu Han's 'Dismissal of Hai Rui'. I shall first evaluate the usefulness and nature of those explanations that have been put forth already and then offer a descriptive analysis that suggests a multi-dimensional approach to the problem. At the outset, however, we should consider the type of historical data at hand and evolve satisfactory strategies for dealing with them. Since the data that concern us are found in a literary text, we must answer the question of how best to deal with a piece of linguistic evidence to arrive at historical understanding.

London, 1972). The term 'anti-Maoist satirist' comes from Dittmer, p.69. More recent works, which I read only after completing the early drafts of this article, show greater sensitivity; see Peter R. Moody, *Opposition and Dissent in Contemporary China* (Stanford, 1977) and Frederick C. Teiwes, *Politics and Purges in China* (White Plains, N.Y. and Folkestone, Kent, UK, 1979).

[7] For example, see Qi Benyu (Ch'i Pen-yü), 'The True Reactionary Nature of "Hai Jui Scolds the Emperor"' and '*The Dismissal of Hai Jui*', *Chinese Studies in History*, vol.3, no.1 (Fall 1969), pp.4-33, and Guang Feng and Lin Jie, '*Hai Rui ma huangdi*' he '*Hai Rui baguan*' shi fandang fan shehui zhuyi de liang zhu daducao ('Hai Rui Upbraids the Emperor' and 'The Dismissal of Hai Rui' are Two Great Poisonous Weeds Opposing the Party and Opposing Socialism), *Hongqi* [Red Flag], no.5 (May 1966). The accusations are picked up by Pusey, p.16, and J.D. Simmonds, 'Peng Te-huai: A Chronological Re-examination', *The China Quarterly*, no.37 (January-March 1969), p.133. All three Chinese critics were close associates of Yao Wenyuan. See Moody, pp.199-200.

[8] Domes, p.125.

[9] Chang, p.137.

[10] Brugger, p.232.

[11] The point is put forth most forcefully by Pusey, especially pp.31-33; it is echoed by D.W.Y. Kwok in his introduction to *Hai Jui Dismissed from Office*, trs. C.C. Huang (Hawaii, 1972), pp.19-21, and Roxanne Witke, *Comrade Chiang Ch'ing* (London, 1977), p.297.

The central problem is uncovering the significance of Wu Han's words on the subject of the Ming official Hai Rui. We know, first of all, that Humpty Dumpty in *Through the Looking Glass* was wrong when he said 'When I use a word, it means what I want it to mean, neither more nor less'.[12] There is in fact no exact congruence between a linguistic sign (a word) and what it signifies: language is arbitrary. Moreover, it is affected by a variety of non-linguistic factors, like the social biographies of both author and audience, the tone in which words are uttered or written, and the intentions of both parties. Meanings are verbalized and apperceived in mediated forms, rather than through a one-to-one pairing of signs and meanings.[13] Or, to put it differently, in the use of language there are inbuilt frictions between the intention of the author and the performance of the linguistic act, for the latter requires an audience to assimilate the words employed.[14]

There are of course a number of significances that can be found in the words of Wu Han. From the point of view of understanding the Cultural Revolution perhaps the most important one is the one assigned by the Maoists. This significance, however, is not to be confused with the significance of the author's words to himself. It is this latter significance I wish to explore by re-examining the context of Wu Han's writings on the subject of Hai Rui.

In such an endeavour the English historian Quentin Skinner urges us to set up a kind of dialectic between the text itself and the historical and linguistic contexts of its writing, especially in the case of what he labels a 'heteronomous' text, or one 'that points outwards towards some other points of reference' (as opposed to an 'autonomous' text). From an examination of the text itself we should, Skinner tells us, arrive 'at an interpretation which serves to suggest what contexts may most profitably be examined as further aids to interpretation'. From the text we thus move outward towards the context, but we must also reverse the direction to bring the context back to bear on the text. In so doing, we thus trace a 'hermeneutic circle', which is done 'by placing the text to be interpreted within a field of assumptions and conventions to which it contributes and from which it derives its distinctively meaningful

---

12 J.G.A. Pocock, 'Verbalizing a Political Act: Towards a Politics of Speech', *Political Theory*, vol.1, no.1 (February 1973), pp.33-34.

13 Hansfried Kellner, 'On the Cognitive Significance of the System of Language in Communication', in Thomas Luckman (ed.), *Phenomenology and Sociology* (Harmondsworth and New York, 1978), p.336.

14 Pocock, p.35.

character'.[15] In this manner we end up not with an explanation of historical certainties, but a multi-layered description that elucidates the text on its own grounds, even if it may not definitively recover the author's intentions.

Most previous interpretations of Wu Han and Hai Rui have not followed such a strategy. First, in general they appear to have started not from the text itself but from the later vantage point of the Cultural Revolution. The basic interpretations of 'The Dismissal of Hai Rui' thus echo charges first laid by Yao Wenyuan and Mao Zedong. At the time of the script's publication in an internationally circulated Chinese literary journal we have no published accounts that grasped the play's 'allusions to recent politics' which 'were all too clear' to students of Chinese politics, who, like 'the sophisticated theatre-goers...were sure to see...the parallel case of Peng Dehuai'.[16] The fact that contemporary observers did not see such meaning in the play until after the Maoists interpreted it that way in 1965 does not of course rule out the possibility that Wu Han intended it in this manner.[17] But such conclusions are clearly methodologically suspect, even if they are somewhat bolstered by Wu Han's well-deserved pre-Liberation reputation for 'pointing at the mulberry to revile the ash', using historical allegory to criticise contemporary policies, a potent weapon in the arsenal of Chinese social thinkers since at least the time of Confucius.

It was in late 1965 that Wu Han's play about the Ming official Hai Rui, first performed in early 1961, was publicly attacked. The offensive began on 10 November with the publication in the Shanghai-based *Wenhuibao* of an article by Yao Wenyuan that, according to Jiang Qing, took seven months of secret work to prepare and revise[18] and evidently had the approval of Chairman Mao himself.[19] Yao's article thus was the

---

[15] Skinner, 'Hermeneutics and the Role of History', *New Literary History* 7 (1977), *passim*. For a penetrating critical look at the mishandling of ideas in history, see Skinner, 'Meaning and Understanding in the History of Ideas', *History and Theory 8* (1969), pp.3-53.

[16] Witke, p.296.

[17] Teiwes also notes the lack of contemporary awareness of the message presented by the Cultural Revolution critics. See *Politics and Purges*, p.477.

[18] Witke, p.296.

[19] Brugger, p.282; Chang, p.162; Dittmer, pp.62-63.

spearhead of a carefully orchestrated campaign that kicked off the Cultural Revolution.[20]

Yao criticized Wu Han for portraying Hai Rui as a model official acting heroically on behalf of the peasants, who themselves are depicted as passive beneficiaries of his reforms. Moreover, argued Yao, Wu Han's Hai Rui is 'fictitious': 'The Hai Rui in the play is fabricated by Comrade Wu Han to publicise his own point of view.' To substantiate this contention Yao went into a fairly detailed examination of mid-Ming land-holdings patterns of the area in which Hai served, the fruits no doubt of research team activity during those seven months. Yao Wenyuan proceeded to raise questions about how much land actually was returned to peasants through Hai Rui's intervention, and to whom it was returned, concluding that the peasants did not benefit from Hai's policies, which were designed simply to make the system work more efficiently.[21]

After dealing with several other historical points, Yao attacked Wu on theoretical issues. He castigated Wu Han for failing to show his protagonist acting in the interests of his own class and therefore perpetuating the 'antiquated' point of view of the landlord class and bourgeoisie.[22] Finally, Yao queried what there is to learn from the play.

> Should we follow the example of 'return of occupied land'? Our villages have realized the socialist system of collective ownership and established the great people's communes. Under these circumstances, who is to 'return the occupied land'? The people's communes? On the other hand, to whom should the land be returned? To the landlords? Or to the peasants? Is that what the 500 million peasants who are advancing with determination along the socialist road should 'learn' such 'return of occupied land'?[23]

Yao concluded that the play was part of a hopeless effort to combat the inevitable direction of socialist development in China and that it should thus be labelled a 'poisonous weed'.[24]

Despite the vehemence of this attack, Chairman Mao felt that Yao had not gone far enough. It was Mao, not Yao or later political analysts,

---

20 Lee, ch.1; Brugger, p.282.

21 Yao Wenyuan, 'On the New Historical Play *The Dismissal of Hai Jui*', *Chinese Studies in History and Philosophy*, vol.2, no.1 (Fall 1968), pp.13-43. A translation also appears in *Current Background* 783 (1966), pp.1-18.

22 Yao, pp.28-32.

23 ibid., 36.

24 ibid., 40.

who introduced the analogy of Peng Dehuai. At the end of the following month he gave a speech in Hangzhou in which he touched on Yao's polemic:

> Its defect is that it did not hit the crux of the matter. The crux of *Hai Rui Dismissed from Office* was the question of dismissal from office. The Jiajing [Chia-ching] Emperor dismissed Hai Rui from office. In 1959 we dismissed Peng Dehuai from office. And Peng Dehuai is Hai Rui too.[25]

Wu Han responded on 30 December with a 'self-criticism' published in the *People's Daily*. He acknowledged several factual errors, while defending with great erudition much of the historical context with textual references. He did admit, however, that 'I had forgotten the class struggle' and that the play had serious theoretical mistakes.[26] The attack against Wu Han lasted until early May 1966, when it switched to other prominent intellectuals associated with the Beijing administration and with whom Wu had close ties.[27] From there Mayor Peng Zhen was implicated, and eventually President Liu Shaoqi was brought down. Wu Han was later arrested, tortured, and subjected to a public 'struggle' rally. He died on 11 October 1969 after almost two years' imprisonment and further physical abuse.[28]

Drawing on such material, it was not difficult for Western observers of China to substantiate the Maoist critique of Wu Han and reduce to a

---

[25] Stuart Schram (ed.), *Chairman Mao Talks to the People* (New York, 1974), p.237.

[26] 'Self-Criticism on *Dismissal of Hai Jui*', *Current Background* 783 (1966), pp.28-51.

[27] The campaign is set out by Pusey, ch.7. Neither he nor Dittmer sees evidence for a conspiracy linking Wu Han through Peng Zhen to Liu Shaoqi, though Dittmer, like others, sees a close connection between 'revisionist intellectuals' like Wu, Deng Tuo and Liao Mosha and the Beijing Municipal Party Committee (Dittmer, pp.67-68).

[28] A fairly full and seemingly accurate account of the tragic fate of Wu Han and his family is Han Jian, 'Wu Han de beiju' (The Tragedy of Wu Han), *Lianhe bao*, 1 March 1979, p.12. It appears to be based on a letter from Wu's son, which is also cited in abbreviated form in 'Kunning jiulu' (Old Partner from Kunming), *Wu Han Yuan Zhen sinan jishi* [A True Record of the Political Deaths of Wu Han and Yuan Zhen], *Ming bao*, 27 November 1979, p.3. For the struggle rally, see Rice, p.274. For accounts of the deaths of Wu, his wife, and daughter, see Anne F. Thurston, *Enemies of the People: The Ordeal of the Intellectuals in China's Great Cultural Revolution* (Harvard University Press, Cambridge, Massachusetts and London, 1988), p.134.

single dimension the complex mind and many-sided personality of Wu Han.

The Writer

Prior to 1949 Wu Han had combined serious historical scholarship with independent political commentary as a leading non-aligned academic. He had done his university work and early teaching at Qinghua, then closely allied with American educational interests, and favourably impressed such eminent liberal scholars as Hu Shi, Gu Jiegang and Jiang Tingfu. An astute textual scholar, he made an important contribution to Ming history in 1934 with the publication of his first major work, in which he demonstrated that charges laid by the government in an early Ming purge were political fabrications. Over the next three years he published 'standard references' on several aspects of Ming history. After the Japanese invasion in 1937 he moved to Kunming, where he became professor of history at Southwest Associated University. While there he wrote the first edition of his biography of Zhu Yuanzhang, the founder of the Ming dynasty, which has been considered by many scholars as 'the best biography written in modern Chinese'.[29] At the same time Wu used his vivid and incisive prose in the service of historical allegory to comment in newspapers on the political state of China in the 1930s and 40s.[30]

After returning to Beijing in 1946 as professor of history at Qinghua University his attacks against the government became more outspoken. At this time he became a member of the Standing Committee of the

---

[29] Chaoying Fang, 'Hai Jui', in L. Carrington Goodrich and Fang (eds), *Dictionary of Ming Biography,* 2 vols (New York and London, 1976), vol.1, no.4, p.478.

[30] Howard Boorman (ed.), *Biographical Dictionary of Republican China,* 4 vols (New York and London, 1967), vol.3, p.246. Hereafter referred to as *BDRC*. *BDRC* contains the best English language biography of Wu Han (3:425-430). More complete is Li Youning, *Wu Han zhuan* [Biography of Wu Han], (Hong Kong, 1973). A recent biography is Jin Ruonian, '*Wu Han tongzhi shilüe*' [Biographical Sketch of Comrade Wu Han] in Wu Han he 'Hai Rui baguan' [Wu Han and 'Hai Rui Dismissed from Office'], (Beijing, 1979), pp.114-38. The most complete biographical works appearing since the original publication of this article are those by Su Shuanghi and Wang Hangzhi mentioned in Fisher, 'Upright Officials', no.1, pp.156-57. Their *Wu Han zhuan* (Beijing) was published in 1984.

China Democratic League.[31] Within the university he was a leading member of a reform group of Young Turks and also helped students escape into communist-held areas, where he eventually followed them in late 1948.[32] He continued to combine his scholarly and political interests, publishing, among others, an important article on the political oppressiveness of early Ming education.[33]

In 1949 he returned to Qinghua as head of the History Department and Dean of the Arts Faculty, and in October of that year he was appointed deputy mayor of Beijing, the most important of a variety of positions and honours that stretch to over three columns in the pages of *Who's Who in Communist China*.[34] He became a tireless promoter of historical and other cultural and educational activities in Beijing, often acting as a bridge between the scholarly and political worlds.[35] He was also elected to the National People's Congress in each of its pre-Cultural Revolution sittings and continued to play a major role in the Democratic League, although in 1957 he joined the CCP.[36] During the anti-rightist campaign that followed the Hundred Flowers, Wu Han came down squarely on the side of intellectual constraint with an attack against his fellow Democratic League leader, Luo Longji.[37] Though originally

---

[31] Union Research Institute, *Who's Who in Communist China*, 2 vols (Hong Kong, 1969), vol.2, no.7, p.18.

[32] Wu Han, 'Qinghua zayi' [Memories of Qinghua (University)], *Chuntian ji* (Spring) (Beijing, 1961), pp.36-48.

[33] *BDRC* 3:426.

[34] *Who's Who*, 2: 717-719. *BDRC* dates Wu's gaining the post of deputy mayor as 1952, unlike Hong Kong and Taiwan sources. *Renmin ribao*, 15 September 1979, confirms the earlier date.

[35] For accounts of Wu's multifarious activities, see Xia Nai, 'Wo suo zhidao de shixuejia Wu Han tongzhi' [Comrade Wu Han, the Historian I Knew], *Shehui kexue zhanzian* 2 (1980), pp.24-39, and Jin, pp.135-37.

[36] *Renmin ribao*, 15 September 1979. There has been confusion about Wu's Party status in earlier western analyses. It now seems clear that he did join the CCP in 1957, but his membership may not have been publicly disclosed at the time. See Zhang Youren, 'Lieshi danxin, shijia bense: shenqie huainian Wu Han jiaoshou' [Loyal Heart of a Martyr, True Qualities of an Historian: Profoundly Cherishing the Memory of Professor Wu Han], *Shehui kexue zhanxian* 2 (1980), 34.

[37] Roderick MacFarquhar, *The Origins of the Cultural Revolution. 1: Contradictions among the People 1956-1957* (New York, 1974), pp.271, 276 and 278. Pusey finds this piece written in an uncharacteristic style (p.11). Luo's

uneasy with the intellectual world of Chinese communism, in 1950 he published an account of how he had overcome his 'supra-class' viewpoint.[38] He published little history during the first decade of the new regime, but around the time he joined the Party he was able to reissue a collection of pre-1949 articles entitled *Notes on Reading History (Dushi zaji).*[39]

In 1959, however, he bounced back into print with both a slightly revised collection of earlier essays previously entitled *History as a Mirror (Lishi de jingzi)* and a spate of popular articles. *History as a Mirror,* as Wu himself acknowledged, contained much historical material that was critical by analogy of the Kuomintang regime then in power. The collection was given the new name *Spear-throwing (Touqiang ji)* the target of which was never specified.[40] His essays covered a wide range of periods and subjects, combining historical erudition with the fast-paced and simple writing style characteristic of the *zawen* genre. In 1960 and 1961 he published two collections of these articles, *Under the Lamp-light (Deng ia ji)* and *Spring (Chuntian ji),* the latter of which includes some non-historical literary essays.

His Beijing opera 'The Dismissal of Hai Rui' appeared in print in January 1961 and was performed on stage the following month. In 1961 and 1962 Wu collaborated with Beijing literary figures Deng Tuo and Liao Mosha in writing a series of short satirical pieces that appeared under the title *Notes from a Three-Family Village (Sanjiacum zhaji).* He was also involved in a printed debate in which he favoured the resurrection of selected values from the 'feudal' period and was chief

---

'confession' is translated in *Communist China 1955-1959: Policy Documents with Analysis* (Cambridge, Mass., 1965), pp.331-337.

[38] *BDRC* 3:427, Pusey, pp.8-9.

[39] *BDRC* states that 'prior to 1957, he confined himself to scholarly pursuits', but mentions only two publications, both dealing with the 'sprouts of capitalism' controversy. One is a report to the History Department at Beijing University and the other is a substantial research article. A colleague of Wu Han informed me privately that Wu had been steadily engaged in an on-going project using the Korean Li Dynasty Veritable Records *(Lichao shilu).* According to Xia Nai, he had begun this work while still a student in Beijing. See Xia, p.27.

[40] There is of course speculation that the new target was the CCP. See Pusey, pp.12-13.

editor of several series of multi-volume works popularizing aspects of Chinese culture, a task he took very seriously.[41]

The Text

Though Wu Han was a gifted writer, he was not a playwright, a fact seized upon by some political analysts. 'I do not understand drama and I do not go to the theatre either', Wu begins in his preface to the play. 'This is especially true with regard to Peking opera... However, I have not only written a drama, but have written a Peking Opera. Isn't this terribly strange?'[42] He goes on to say that after he had begun some research on Hai Rui and written a few articles about him in 1959, Ma Lianliang consulted him on writing an opera on the same subject. Ma, who also is said to have died during the Cultural Revolution, at that time was a highly paid leader of the Beijing Opera Troupe (of Beijing), one of the few remaining such groups that had not been nationalized.[43] With the encouragement and help of friends in the troupe, Wu eventually undertook to write the opera himself, a task that required seven drafts over a year before he was able to satisfy the dual historical and dramatic aspects of the job. He deliberately avoided writing about Hai Rui's famous memorial criticizing the Jiajing Emperor (r. 1522-66) because it had been the theme of another play, and concentrated instead on the upright official's short tenure in Nanjing, during which he 'suppressed the local tyrants and returned the land seized by them to the people'.[44]

'Dismissal' is a morality play in which the outgunned good guy, the reformist official Hai Rui, confronts the bad guys, the local landlords

---

[41] These included two historical series: *Zhongguo lishi xiao congshu* [Small Collectanea of Chinese History] and *Zhongguo lishi changshi* [A General History of China]. For an account of his work as a populariser, See Zhang Xikong, '*Yiwei rexin puji gongzuo de lishixuejia*' [An Historian Who Worked Enthusiastically at Popularization], *Wu Han he 'Hai Rui baguan'*, pp.73-84.

[42] I follow Huang's translation, p.30. This work henceforth will be abbreviated *Dismissal*.

[43] On Ma, see Colin Mackerras, *The Chinese Theatre in Modern Times* (London, 1975), pp.164 and 192; and Richard F.S. Yang, 'The Reform of Peking Opera under the Communists', *The China Quarterly*, no.11 (July-September 1962), p.137. Ma also played the leading role in the play. See 'Zi Ling' and 'Zi Zhen', 'Wu Han he "Hai Rui baguan" ' [Wu Han and 'Hai Rui Dismissed from Office'], in *Wu Han he 'Hai Rui baguan'*, p.5.

[44] *Dismissal*, pp.30-33. The other play is, of course, *Hai Rui Submits His Memorial*, which Rudolf Wagner analyses in the volume.

with official ties (*xiangguan*), and gets cashiered for his efforts. The action is set in Songjiang in 1569-70 and focuses on the brutalization of a peasant family by a son of the retired Grand Secretary Xu Jie (1503-83) and the rectification of the situation by Hai Rui, who has just taken over as governor. Firmly siding with the victimized peasants against the exploitative landlords and their hireling local officials, Hai Rui executes the younger Xu and only then gives up his seal of office to an emissary from the capital who has been sent to replace him as governor at the urgent demand of Xu Jie and the *xiangguan*.[45]

The play met with critical acclaim in some circles of the Beijing intelligentsia when it was first performed in February 1961.[46] It seems to have enjoyed a successful run at a dozen or more venues until September 1962 when it closed, perhaps due to criticism from Jiang Qing.[47] The entire script was first printed in a January 1961 issue of *Beijing Literature and Art (Beijing wenyi)* and then published separately as a book about half a year later.

The relationship of history to the theatre was one of Wu Han's major preoccupations during the period 1959-62,[48] and in 'Dismissal' he attempted to attain a balance between the demands of the two media. Later, during the Cultural Revolution, he was accused of deliberately distorting historical texts, and in the play historical distortion does take place in a minor way in the plot and characterization of the protagonists, both of which were highly simplified to suit the stage. The specific incidents of abuse of the peasantry by the third son of Xu Jie are

---

[45] The two complete translations of the play available in book form are Huang and Ansley. I have reviewed them in *Ming Studies*, no.8 (Spring 1979), pp.23-25.

[46] Though I can find no review of it in the leading theatre journal *Xijubao*, favourable comments evidently were published in *Beijing wenyi* and *Beijing wanbao* [Beijing Evening News]. See *Studies in Chinese History and Philosophy*, vol.2, no.1 (Fall 1968), p.41n. Concerning the suspension of the play, neither Pusey nor Kwok provides any reference to the number of performances of it that were given. A *Xijubao* interviewer of Wu Han in May 1961 refers to it as having occasioned 'a great interest' (Lu Mei, *Wu Han tongzhi tan lishijui* [Comrade Wu Han Talks About Historical Plays], *Xijubao* 9-10 (1961), 23). A standard history of Chinese communist drama, however, describes it as not very good theatre (Zhao Cong, *Zhongguo dalu de xiju gaige* [The Reform of Chinese Drama on the Mainland] (Hong Kong, 1969), p.154).

[47] *Beijing xin wenyi* [New Beijing Literature and Art], 8 June 1967. I am indebted to Roderick MacFarquhar for bringing this and other Red Guard sources to my attention.

[48] See below.

fictitious, as are the punishments dealt to local officials who co-operated with the *xiangguan* and, so too, is the play's execution of Xu's son. Moreover, the censor Dai Fengxiang did not replace Hai as governor. On the other hand, Hai did specifically criticize the behaviour of Xu's sons, though ultimately it was Xu's old rival Gao Gong (1512-78) who punished the younger Xus, and Dai was instrumental in Wu's impeachment process.[49]

The portrayal of Hai Rui is recognizable as the official *Ming History* stereotype and makes no attempt to deal with the very real problem of the accuracy of this characterization.[50] The tone of this portrait is captured by the following excerpt from the *Ming History*:

> Subordinate officials all feared his sternness; some corrupt ones excused themselves and left. Influential families of the area who had their gates painted a bright vermilion colour changed it to a gloomy black when they heard of Hai Rui's impending arrival. A eunuch who was the superintendent of the [imperial] textile factories reduced the number of his sedan-carriers [to feign austerity]. Hai Rui was firmly determined to promote [new useful projects] and to reform old evils. He instituted the dredging of the Wusong River and the Baimao River so they could drain freely into the sea. The populace depended on the effectiveness [of this drainage system]. He persistently opposed annexation of property by the large land-owners; he forcefully restrained the rich and mighty and cared for the poor and weak. He took back land that had been transferred to the rich and returned it to the poor farmers. Dismissed Grand Secretary Xu Jie had retired to his native village [in Songjiang] under Hai Rui's jurisdiction. Hai Rui submitted even [so powerful a family as Xu Jie's] to investigation to ensure that no [unjustified] leniency was shown towards them. He issued orders which were sharp and harsh. His subordinates carried out the orders in great fear [lest disciplinary action befall them]. Some of the powerful and mighty sneaked away to hide in other provinces, while some bad elements exploited the opportunity to lay [unwarranted] charges against old families and big clans. There were instances of false accusations and of injustices being suffered [as a consequence].
>
> Hai Rui reduced and abolished unnecessary expenses in connection with the courier service. Higher officials were no more to be supplied with free lodging. This caused much resentment. A certain Shu Hua, a chief supervising secretary, criticized Hai Rui for being an impractical

---

49 Chaoying and Lienche Tu Fang, 'Hsü Chieh', in Goodrich and Fang, vol.1, pp.574-75.

obstructionist who lacked comprehension of the essence of government administration. He suggested to dispose of him by giving him an important high-ranking office in Nanking. When the emperor was then still praising Hai Rui in a favourable edict, a supervising secretary, Dai Fengxiang, impeached Hai Rui for protecting evil doers and for oppressing officials and the gentry merely in order to build up a reputation for himself while throwing the administration into confusion. As a consequence, Hai Rui was transferred and placed in supervision of the Nanking granaries. Hai Rui had been governor of the Wu area for only half a year, but when the common people [of the area] heard that he was about to leave, their wailing and crying filled the streets. In their homes they performed sacrificial rites [prayed for his welfare] before his portrait. When he was about to proceed to his new official post, Gao Gong, head of the ministry of personnel and a long time opponent of Hai Rui, had the position abolished by combining it with the ministry of revenue's Nanking office. Hai Rui subsequently submitted his resignation on the pretext of sickness.[51]

In the play virtually all these points are mentioned and there also are references to his renowned frugality and filial piety, as well as to his famous remonstrating memorial to the previous emperor. Moreover, the author's concern with authenticity of tone is demonstrated by little touches, such as setting the opening abduction of the peasant girl at the Qingming festival, which was one of the few times a year young women were allowed out of the house and thus subject to the scrutiny of the local young rakes.[52] Similarly there are allusions to pre-modern beliefs, like predestination,[53] and at one point an opponent of Hai Rui hurls at him the imprecation 'death to you and annihilation to your clan'.[54]

Historical veracity (and the Cultural Revolution perspective) aside, the symbolism of Hai Rui was a powerful one in traditional terms. An eminent authority on Ming history summarizes Hai's popular reputation:

> When his body was being transported from Nanking to the river, the funeral procession...is said to have been participated in by people from miles

---

[50] I touch on some issues in my *Ming Studies* review. For a critical appraisal of Hai by another Ming historian, see Ray Huang, *Taxation in Sixteenth Century Ming China* (Cambridge, 1974), pp.187 and 312.

[51] Ernest Wolff, 'A Preliminary Study of Hai Jui: His Biography in the *Ming-shih*', *Journal of the Oriental Society of Australia* vol.7, no.1-2 (December 1970), pp.158-59.

[52] See for example Herbert A. Giles (trs.), *Strange Stories from a Chinese Studio*, 2nd ed., rev. (London, 1909), pp.116-17, 141-42.

[53] *Dismissal*, p.106.

around... Admirers bought prints of portraits to worship at home. Shrines were erected at the places where he had held office... Hai was likewise celebrated in legend and folk literature, one piece being the fictionalized account of his life and the proceedings of his court and his pronouncement [sic] of judgement...printed in 1606. In the Ch'ing period several novels were written about him and also the drama *Sannü qiangban*...[55]

It is clear that in pre-modern times, at any rate, Hai Rui was regarded by many with almost religious feeling as a saviour of the people and dispenser of justice.

In direct symbolic opposition to the upright official is not the reigning emperor, who is barely mentioned in the play, but the *xiangguan* and the local officials who co-operate with them. Hai Rui says, 'The people have suffered more than they can bear, because the *xiangguan* are cruel and lawless'.[56] And the local magistrate remarks, 'This is a tough case, involving beating and open abduction. I am merely a bean-sized official; how would I dare offend Prime Minister Xu by trying to settle it according to the law of the land?'[57] There is no protest against government policy, only against its lack of implementation.

The peasants are depicted as generally acting within the cultural confines of pre-modern rural life. They are victims, but not passive, for if anything they are uncharacteristically active in their quest for justice from officialdom. 'The despots are fiercer than tigers and wolves', remarks one. 'To redress our grievances we must go to the court.'[58] Later, after Hai Rui has announced he is ready to receive complaints, a *xiangguan* complains, '[W]icked people by the tens of thousands have brought false charges against us *xiangguan*. The subordinates are rebelling against their superiors. What kind of world is this?' Nevertheless, after failing to get a fair hearing from local officials, the peasants do turn to Hai Rui to act on their behalf.[59] In turn, he sees himself in quite paternalistic Confucian terms. 'Now that I am governor of this region, the commoners will be treated as my own children.'[60]

---

54 ibid., p.146
55 Chaoying Fang, 'Hai Jui', in Goodrich and Fang, vol.1, pp.477-78.
56 *Dismissal*, p.106.
57 ibid., p.63.
58 ibid., p.59.
59 ibid., p.83.
60 ibid., p.84.

Dismissal from office and return of the land, the two symbols that attracted most of the Cultural Revolution invective, are used in ways that are not unambiguously political. The term 'dismissal from office' appears of course in the title, but does not play a major role in the action. It is the theme only of the highly dramatic final act, which in fact represents a decrease in its importance from earlier drafts.[61] Aside from asking the grounds for his removal from office, Hai Rui does not protest, nor does he in any way criticize imperial policy. Furthermore, rather than have Hai Rui supported by an outpouring of popular sentiment, as he had earlier planned,[62] Wu Han closes the play simply with Hai's order to execute Xu's son and his offer to transfer his official seal to his stunned replacement. Only after the curtain falls does the chorus sing:

> Heaven and earth are freezing,
> And the piercing wind is howling;
> The thought of Hai Rui's departure,
> Has plucked ten thousand heartstrings.
> As the elder must return home,
> There's no way to detain him;
> So every household his incense lit,
> And hands up his portrait for worship.[63]

'Return of the land' *(tuitian)* is a much more prominent theme, despite Wu Han's claim to have relegated it to a secondary position.[64] In the first act the Xu family is accused of having confiscated peasant land, and when Hai Rui takes up office he issues the following statement;

> [R]egarding the question of giving back the land to its lawful owners; the *xiangguan* and other ferocious despots have, in the past, seized many people's land. Consequently, the peasants have become unemployed and live miserable lives. The law demands that all the land thus seized must be returned to its lawful owners...[65]

As stated in his official biography, Hai did in fact 'persistently oppose the annexation of property by the large land-owners'. Moreover, his collected correspondence contains a short letter to Xu Jie complaining that to date the latter has returned far too little land, the

---

61 ibid., pp.36-37.
62 ibid., pp.37-38.
63 ibid., p.147.
64 ibid., pp.33-34.
65 ibid., p.12.

blame for which Hai Rui lays on his sons.[66] Even the exact term *tuitian* occurs in the letter, clear testimony to its historical authenticity. Moreover, there is no threat of rebellion, as alleged in at least one analysis of the play.[67]

Political Contexts

The writing of 'The Dismissal of Hai Rui' did not take place in a cultural vacuum. Characteristics of the text suggest various contexts in which it may be placed to contribute to our understanding of the writer's intentions.

There are actually two political contexts to consider. The first of course is the one in which Wu Han wrote the play. The other, though it does not relate directly to the text, is the political context of the attack against Wu Han, for we have seen how influential that particular context has been on other understandings of Wu Han's intentions. I do not propose to devote much space to either, as detailed accounts about both already exist.

In mid-1959, as Wu Han was beginning to work on Hai Rui, the Party was in the grip of a major crisis centring on the Great Leap Forward. Moreover, the years 1959-62 were marked by a dramatic worsening of Sino-Soviet relations and three disastrous harvests. The period coinciding with Wu's interest in Hai Rui thus was one full of unprecedentedly sharp policy debates in China.

One of those most dissatisfied with the Great Leap Forward was Peng Dehuai, the outspoken Minister of Defence, who was critical not only of military modernization policy but, more importantly, the general thrust of economic planning and its political implications. In May-June 1959 he toured the Warsaw Pact countries. A month later at a Politburo meeting at Lushan convened to prepare for the coming 8th Plenum he

---

[66] *Hai Zhongjie gong quanji* [The Complete Works of Hai Rui] (Taibei, 1973), 5:38, p.448. This does not indicate that Wu did not oppose policies of The Great Leap Forward (see below), but that he was not being historically irresponsible in his choice of words.

[67] It is alleged that on p.27 of the original Beijing edition the following words appear: '...The people are impoverished and the national economy is in jeopardy... Unless the seized land is returned [your rule] will not last long'. See Merle Goldman, 'The Unique "Blooming and Contending" of 1961-62', *The China Quarterly* 37 (January-March 1969), p.76. This does not seem consistent with the Chinese text. Nor do either of the translations use anything remotely similar to the English rendering above.

circulated a memo that was critical of Great Leap policies. At the time of the Plenum a major campaign against 'right opportunists' that was to last into November was underway. The substance of his points, the manner in which he raised them and the pointedly-timed interference of Khruschev (whom Peng had just visited in Moscow) in the internal affairs of the CCP combined to place Peng in an untenable position, and decisions taken at the Plenum during the first half of August declared Peng's political demise.[68] During the Lushan Plenum, it was later alleged, Peng had equated himself with Hai Rui, and three years later when he attempted to reverse the Plenum's verdict against him he is said to have declared 'I could no longer remain silent. I wanted to be Hai Rai'.[69]

Yao Wenyuan's attack on Wu Han in late 1965 was, as we have seen, the culmination of many months of research. Its roots, however, can be traced back at least as far as early 1962 when Jiang Qing started to become politically influential in the post-1949 world of the arts. The 10th Plenum, held in September of that year, affirmed a commitment to expose bourgeois tendencies in the cultural sphere and included Jiang Qing's 'May Sixteenth Circular'. Around that time she also turned to the reform of Beijing Opera and even wished to attack Wu Han.[70] The subsequent purge in 1966 of dominant cultural figures was directed not only at Wu Han and his immediate associates, but at many other 'monsters and demons' and 'black gangsters', including at least one other author of a play about Hai Rui, Zhou Xinfang, as well as writers, performers and scholars. Many were accused of 'crimes' similar to those alleged against Wu, though few were subject to such intensive and widespread campaigns.[71]

---

[68] Simmonds, pp.120-38. See also David A. Charles, 'The Dismissal of Marshall P'eng Te-huai', *The China Quarterly* 8 (October-December 1961), pp.63-67. Teiwes' account in Chapter 9 now seems to be the fullest and most judicious available in English.

[69] Xuan Mo, *Zhonggong wenhua dageming yu zhishifenzi* [The Great Cultural Revolution of the Chinese Communists and Mainland Intelligentsia] (Taibei, 1973), p.85; 'Peng Teh-huai's Testimony', in Union Research Institute (ed.), *The Case of Peng Teh-huai, 1959-68* (Hong Kong, 1968), pp.120-21.

[70] Witke, ch.12; Chang, pp.157-58; and Byung-joon Ahn, 'The Politics of Peking Opera, 1962-1965', *Asian Survey*, vol.12, no.12 (December 1972), pp.1068-69.

[71] For a list of such people and some of their works, see Asia Research Centre (ed.), *The Great Cultural Revolution in China* (Rutland, Vt. and Tokyo, 1968), pp.116-

Chronological Context

The chronological proximity of the dismissal of Peng Dehuai and Wu Han's publications on Hai Rui has been a major factor in upholding the Maoist interpretation of the historian-playwright's intention. It has not, however, been subject to close scrutiny, though the dating of Wu's interest in Hai Rui is crucial to our understanding of his intentions.[72]

Wu Han's first published reference to Hai Rui occurs on 15 June 1959, just two days after the return of Peng Dehuai from Europe and the USSR and two weeks after Tao Zhu's public call for bolder discussion of the Great Leap.[73] On face value the point of this article was to condemn the convoluted language of bureaucratism, and the historian mentions a peasant-born dynastic founder Ming Taizu (not unlike Chairman Mao perhaps as a model for straight talk).[74] On the next day the *People's Daily* printed Wu's famous 'Hai Rui Upbraids the Emperor' in which he approvingly cites the example of the upright Ming official castigating the Jiajing emperor for inattention to public affairs and self-indulgence.[75] Both articles relied heavily on colloquial translations of classical texts that were not difficult to find, but the references attested to a well-prepared piece of writing. Furthermore, the first must have been given to the newspaper no later than 14 June to have been published the following day. The corpus of Wu Han's popular writings on historical subjects published in 1959 and 1960 manifests enormous knowledge of a stunning variety of sources and the ability to write quickly, but it is debatable whether even he could have produced these early articles on Hai Rui at such short notice.

Both these articles, as noted, were written within one or two days of Peng's return, but about a month before the initial confrontation between Peng and Mao in the secret pre-Plenum meeting and three months before any public announcement of Peng's purge. Whereas there

---

206. The other play referred to is '*Hai Rui shangshu*' [Hai Rui Sends a Memorial], which is discussed below.

[72] Simmonds (p.133) points to certain chronological discrepancies in the accusations, but these are relatively minor.

[73] Brugger, p.202.

[74] 'Fandui fanwen' [Oppose Excessive Verbiage], reprinted in *Chuntiar ji* (Spring) (Beijing, 1961), pp.1-4.

[75] Interestingly, this article was not reprinted in either of Wu's collections of articles from this period. It does appear in a collection put out by the Hong Kong monthly *Ming bao, Hai Rui baguan ji qita* ['Hai Rui Dismissed from Office' and others], (Hong Kong, 1966).

may have been indications that Peng was in political hot water during his trip and even before his departure, we simply do not know how widespread the signs of his downfall were prior to mid-July and how much Wu Han could have known about impending events at the core of the national Party organization.[76] Red Guard sources allege that Hu Qiaomu, at that time an alternate secretary of the Central Committee secretariat and senior propaganda official, informed Wu Han that the name of Hai Rui had come up several times at Lushan,[77] but the fact that Peng may have referred to himself as a Hai Rui at Lushan and again three years later invites the interpretation that he followed Wu Han, not *vice versa*.[78] Moreover, it has been universally overlooked in the West that in 1962 Wu Han published an authoritative edition of Hai Rui's collected writings, which included as a preface one of Wu's 1959 articles.[79] It is therefore logical to interpret Wu Han's interest in Hai Rui as serious and sustained, having begun some time prior to 15 June 1959 and lasting until the completion of a major piece of scholarship in 1962.

Historiographical Context

The play 'Dismissal' was written by a recognized historian and deals with verifiable historical figures and events. We should therefore consider the play within both the context of its Ming dynasty symbolism and the practice of history in China around 1959. Though the Ming is well known for the 'despotism' of its imperial politics, it was also a period famous for outspoken remonstration by courageous officials against various rulers, most notably the Jiajing emperor. In the mid-1540s, for example, there were at least half a dozen notable cases of torture, imprisonment and killing of censors and other officials who

---

[76] Teiwes, who disagrees explicitly with Simmonds, argues that Mao was taken by surprise by the depth and style of Peng's criticism at Lushan. See Teiwes, ch.9. More recent information cited by Wagner indicates that Peng had criticized Mao at a Work Conference in Shanghai in late March or early April and that a number of writers had been writing about Hai Rui since the beginning of the year, thought not in Beijing. See Rudolf Wagner, 'In Guise of a Congratulation' Political Symbolism in Zhou Xingang's play *Hai Rui Submits His Memorial, Australian Journal of Chinese Affairs*, no.26 (July 1991), pp.101-103, 107.

[77] *Beijing xin wenyi,* 8 June 1967.

[78] Indeed, This seems to have been the case. See Moody, *Opposition and Dissent,* pp.168-69.

[79] *Hai Rui ji* (Beijing, 1962).

directed criticism at the emperor and his favourites.⁸⁰ Hai Rui thus was but one of numerous officials who risked their lives as critics of government administration, a fact appreciated by historically knowledgeable Chinese readers.

The theoretical cornerstone of post-1949 historiography has been Mao's famous dictum 'make the past serve the present' (*gu wei jin yong*), which bears some resemblance to the Confucian approach to history as a mirror for contemporary times. Though in the debate over 'historicism' (*lishizhuyi*) versus 'class viewpoint' (*jieji guandian*), the historicists sought to emphasize the historical perspective of their evaluations of the past, even they acknowledged the present in the study of the past.⁸¹ During the Great Leap Forward the CCP attempted to muster politically mobilized historians around the country by questioning the utility and direction of their productivity.⁸² A shift in policy became apparent by mid-1958, when the leading historical journal *Lishi yanjiu* published writings by an influential array of leading historians to illustrate the new call to 'emphasize the present and de-emphasize the past' (*houjin bogu*).⁸³ Accompanying this historiographical campaign was a movement to reverse the judgement of major political figures from the past who had suffered unsavoury Confucian reputations. Cao Cao (155-220) was the first such person to attract attention, and others like Empress Wu (r. 690-705) soon followed.⁸⁴

---

80   Lienchu Tu Fang, 'Yang Chueh', in Goodrich and Fang, vol. 2, pp.1506-08.

81   Arif Dirlik, 'The Problem of Class Viewpoint Versus Historicism in Chinese Historiography', *Modern China*, vol.3, no.4 (October 1977), pp.465-88.

82   Cliff Edmunds, 'Politics and Historiography after the Great Leap: The Case of Chien Po-tsan' (paper prepared for the Mid-Atlantic Regional Meeting of the Association for Asian Studies, 30-31 October 1976, and forthcoming in revised form in F. Gilbert Chan and Harlan W. Jenks (ed.), *Maoism and Revisionism in China: 1949-79*), pp.11-16.

83   For generally unsympathetic reviews of Chinese historiography see Albert Feuerwerker, 'China's History in Marxian Dress', *American Historical Review*, vol.66, no.2 (January 1961), which is reprinted in Feuerwerker (ed.), *History in Communist China* (Cambridge, Mass., 1968), pp.14-44, and Feuerwerker and S. Cheng, *Chinese Communist Studies of Modern Chinese History*, Harvard East Asian Monographs 11 (Cambridge, Mass., 1961), ix-xxvii.

84   Feuerwerker, 'Marxian Dress', pp.39-43; Edmunds, p.17. See *Cao Cao lunji* [Collected Articles on Cao Cao], (Beijing, 1960).

Around March 1959 Wu Han, who had been virtually silent as an historian and writer since 1949, began publishing a substantial number of newly written articles on historical subjects. A colleague of his has suggested in private conversation that his going public at this time was related to his shock at discovering the havoc wrought by the Great Leap Forward in the countryside, and there is some other evidence to support this view.[85] His historical writings of 1959 and 1960 were not like the scholarly essays of the pre-Liberation period, but were short newspaper pieces each centring on a primary text that Wu translated into the vernacular and upon which he commented. These articles displayed an impressive range of topical and chronological diversity, misleading subjects like the origins of Chinese commerce, overseas trade, early agricultural texts, cotton production, techniques and strategies in pre-modern warfare, clothing, terminology for the common people, the cost of books, lower-class movements, and a number of pieces discussing historical dramas and personalities.[86]

Despite this varied output, Wu Han's historical concerns centred on three themes: the relevance of the past, especially the pre-modern past, to the present; the evaluation of 'progressive' figures from the ruling class in traditional times; and the relationship of historical plays to historical reality.

In the 'Foreword' to his 1960 collection of writings, he acknowledged their miscellaneous nature, but pointed out that all relate to history. He claimed that prior to the revolution he wrote history out of a sense of outrage, but that now his goal was to enrich popular historical understanding through the use of easily comprehensible language. He also expressed his uneasiness with the lack of historical education gained by contemporary youth, a concern he set out to deal with not only by writing, but also by acting as editor of two series of popular

---

[85] This explanation was suggested privately by a senior Chinese historian who was a colleague of Wu Han. It seems borne out by an account by a young acquaintance who saw Wu shortly after the latter's return from a visit to his native place in Zhejiang, though the acquaintance dates this event in the 'early 1960s'. Fang Mu, 'Wu Han de beiju' [The Tragedy of Wu Han], *Guanchajia* 50 (January 1979), p.35. It is interesting that slightly earlier Deng Tuo reissued his respected *History of Famine Relief in China* (*Zhongguo jiuhuang shi*). See Timothy Cheek, 'Deng Tuo: Culture, Leninism and Alternative Marxism in the Chinese Communist Party' (unpublished seminar paper), p.9.

[86] See *Dengxia ji* (Beijing, 1960).

histories.[87] The medium he employed as an historian thus was a function both of the types of audience he wished to reach and also of the demands of his administrative life, which probably made sustained work difficult.

Wu Han dealt most systematically with the issue of relevance in a medium-length essay discussing the two historical slogans 'emphasize the present and de-emphasize the past' and 'make the past serve the present'. They are, he argued, two sides of the same coin, for though contemporary history (i.e., since the May 4th era) is more important, even Mao argued that China's pre-modern past should not be neglected. Previous historical eras cannot simply be denied but must be interpreted according to the dictates of historical materialism to put them in the service of present concerns.

After vaguely praising the history profession for its contributions to the Great Leap Forward, he addressed himself to three issues that clearly disturbed him as an historian of pre-modern society. First, he attacked those who wished to omit the study of the past altogether or to study only the actions of the masses. Such an approach, Wu stated, ignored the background of the eventual victory of the masses and the internal contradictions within the ruling classes of earlier times, as well as the efforts of individuals. Secondly, he criticized those who simplistically applied the standards of today in treating the past and who, erroneously, concluded by totally affirming the present and negating the past (*shijin feigu*). Third, he expressed disapproval of mechanically attempting to relate everything to practice, to force relationships where they were inappropriate.[88]

Wu Han's concern with the relevance of the pre-modern past to the present is well illustrated by his attempts to formulate an approach for evaluating outstanding figures from those times. In the preface to his second collection of recent articles, *Spring,* he supported his interest in such figures for reasons, he wrote, both substantive and methodological: to acquaint his countrymen with models from the past and to formulate a method of historical judgement.[89] Even if the actors in many of the great phenomena of history were drawn mainly from the labouring classes, he argued elsewhere, leadership functions were performed by members of the feudal elite. Even Mao's poems, he noted, dealt with figures like the

---

[87] 'Qianyan' [Foreword], *Dengxia ji*, pp.1-9. Also see note 40.

[88] 'Houjin bogu he gu wei jin yong' [Emphasise the Present and De-emphasise the Past and Make the Past Serve the Present], *Dengxia ji,* pp.61-67.

[89] 'Xu' [Preface], *Chuntian ji,* p.2.

First Emperor, Emperor Wu of the Han, and the founders of the Tang and Song dynasties. Their membership in the ruling class did not negate their contributions to China.[90]

Mass action in traditional times, like peasant uprisings, usually failed or did not alter the system, Wu pointed out. There was no reason to beautify such acts, for it is from their failure that we can understand the success of the masses under the leadership of the CCP.[91] Because of the emphasis on class activity, some historians, Wu asserted, were afraid to mention individuals. But history ceases to exist without individuals: the problem is to judge them according to the nature of their contributions to progress in their own times.[92]

Aside from Hai Rui, the two major figures to whom Wu Han devoted most attention were Cao Cao and the Empress Wu, both of whose previously negative reputations were then being revised by other Chinese historians as well. Wu Han began his own re-evaluation of Cao Cao by relating previous judgements to the culture-bound criteria of traditional historians. He then went on to enumerate Cao Cao's virtues, which included capabilities as a general administrator and poet. On the other hand, it certainly was true that he had helped suppress the Yellow Turban popular uprising, which was consistent with his class background, and was responsible for a great deal of killing.[93] Wu's writings and lectures on Empress Wu dealt with her popular support, her administrative accomplishments, and her suppression of the nobility, all of which contributed to a peaceful and prosperous reign. Yet she too had a darker side of wholesale execution that should not be hidden.[94]

In October 1959, Wu Han attempted to systematize his thoughts in a paper entitled 'Preliminary Ideas on the Evaluation of Historical Figures', in which he formulated eight guiding principles. These included the figure's contributions to the majority of the people or general level of culture; the sentiments of the masses (not just of historians, who came from the landlord class); the individual's personal

---

[90] Lu Mei, '*Wu Han tongzhi tan lishiju*' 26-27.

[91] ibid., p .28.

[92] 'Cong Cao Cao wenti di taolun tan lishi renwu pingjie wenti' [Discussion on the Question of the Evaluation of Historical Figures Prompted by the Question of Cao Cao], *Dengxia ji*, pp.138-39.

[93] 'Tan Cao Cao' [On Cao Cao], *Dengxia ji*, pp.120-29.

[94] 'Lun Wu Zetian' [On Empress Wu], *Chuntian ji*, pp.130-36. See also C.P. FitzGerald, 'The Chinese Middle Ages in Communist Historiography', in Feuerwerker (ed.), *History in Communist China*, pp.134-35.

development within his class background (i.e., whether he was a progressive in the context of his society); and his public, not private, achievements. Other considerations were the inappropriateness of modern terms of judgement, like 'democratic', to pre-modern situations; the avoidance of exaggeration; the utility of the past to the present; and the cumulative contribution to later generations of actions not welcomed by the people of the original period, such as the construction of the Grand Canal.[95] Wu Han's approach in Hai Rui thus was part of a more generalized concern in making the past useful to the present and in locating individual models in that past to serve contemporary society. It is interesting, though, that Hai's historical reputation, unlike those of Cao Cao and Empress Wu, had been overwhelmingly positive.

Wu Han's specific interest in Hai Rui, however, was stimulated by non-historical considerations. The role model of Hai Rui apparently first was raised publicly by Chairman Mao himself at a Shanghai Central Work Conference in early 1959.[96] And it appears that a 'comrade with central-level responsibility' (now known to be Hu Qiaomu) personally suggested the topic of Hai Rui to Wu Han.[97]

In mid-June 1959, accordingly, Hai Rui appeared in an article by Wu Han entitled 'Hai Rui Upbraids the Emperor', which praised the official's frank remonstration to the Jiajing emperor as a model for official behaviour. Wu Han skilfully translated into colloquial Chinese extracts from Hai Rui's famous memorial reprimanding the emperor for inattention to the affairs of state and listening to flatterers while punishing critics. Although Hai Rui was an official of the feudal period, wrote Wu Han, his example is relevant today because of his ability to

---

[95] 'Guanyu pingjie lishi renwu de yixie wenti chubu' [Preliminary Ideas on the Evaluation of Historical Figures], *Dengxia ji, pp.*186-200. The principles are well summarized in *BDRC*.

[96] *Renmin ribao,* 23 October 1979; 'Zi Ling' and 'Zi Zhen', p.2.

[97] 'Zi Ling' and 'Zi Zhen', p.2; Jin, p.137. A Taiwan account states Wu was following Mao's orders. See Han Jian. 'Wu Han de Beiju [The Tragedy of Wu Han], *Lianhe bao,* 1 March 1979. I am grateful to Bruce Jacobs for pointing out this article to me. See also Fisher, 'The "Upright Official" ' p.159, no.7. Red Guard sources indicate that the Propaganda Department of the Central Committee, under Lu Dingyi and Zhou Yang authorised the new edition of Hai Rui's collected writings (*Hai Rui ji*), a task that was entrusted to Wu Han. See *Beijing xin wenyi,* 8 June 1967.

discern right from wrong and to fight against the 'powers of darkness'. That had been the cause of his great popularity among the masses.[98]

'On Hai Rui' appeared in *People's Daily* three months later and contained a much more detailed portrayal of the official, clearly set within confines of a 'feudal' period that he did not transcend. The historian pictures Hai Rui as siding with the people against the exploitative bureaucracy and the large landlords, but still as a patriotic official loyal to the emperor. His life, wrote Wu, was one of continual struggle in which he represented the left against the right within the context of his day. His position in history is important because he was lauded by the people of his times, and thus he can serve as a model for today. However, cautioned Wu, in what seems to be an explicit attempt to distance himself from the 'rightists' then under attack, there are those today who claimed to be like Hai Rui and who formed an opposition without aligning themselves with the people.[99] This article was later reprinted as the introduction to Wu's edition of Hai Rui's collected writings.

In November 1959 Wu Han published a collection of some of his writings on Hai Rui, including 'Stories of Hai Rui' and 'Incorruptible Hai Rui' (*Qingguan Hai Rui*). 'Stories' comprises three separate sections: the leading problems of the times in the lower Yangzi area (excessive property held under the designation 'government-owned land', corrupt local administration, and the incursions of 'Japanese pirates'); Hai Rui's reforms at Chun'an; and his tenure in and dismissal from Nanjing. Wu includes vernacular (*baihua*) translations of Hai Rui's letter to the retired Grand Secretary Xu Jie about the behaviour of his sons and the need to return the land to its original owners and also of his memorial to the emperor, defending Hai's punishment of the local bureaucratic-landholders. Hai Rui is praised once again for being a model official who served the people in an uncompromising way.[100] 'Incorruptible Hai Rui' concentrates on traditional popular stories about the official's frugality and plain living.[101] In mid-1960 Wu Han compared the career of Hai Rui with those of two other famous Ming

---

[98] 'Hai Rui ma huangdi' [Hai Rui Upbraids The Emperor], *Renmin ribao*, 16 June 1959; reprinted in the *Ming bao* edition of *Hai Rui baguan*, pp.12-15.

[99] 'Lun Hai Rui' [On Hai Rui], *Dengxia ji*, pp.146-68.

[100] 'Hai Rui de gushi' [Stories of Hai Rui], reprinted in the *Ming bao* edition of *Hai Rui baguan*, pp.2-9.

[101] 'Qingguan Hai Rui' [Incorruptible Hai Rui], reprinted in the *Ming bao* edition of *Hai Rui baguan*, pp.10-12.

reformers, showing that while the actions of the latter two actually benefited the great landlords, those of Hai Rui did not. Thus the other two were greatly honoured by the court, while Hai lost his position.[102] Towards the end of 1961 Wu finished the play 'The Dismissal of Hai Rui', and at the end of the following year, as noted, his scholarly edition of the *Collected Writings of Hai Rui* was published. Wu Han's work on Hai Rui, completed over a period of more than three years, though done as popular writing and theatre as well as scholarly compilation, seems informed by the logic of the historian's own concerns about the writing of pre-modern history in communist China. It was certainly not just a spur of the moment concern.

Some Textual Questions

Wu Han's approach to Hai Rui's historical texts was no more irresponsible than his handling of the major themes in the Ming official's life. Much of the force of his treatment of Hai Rui relies on his translations of Hai Rui's classical prose into contemporary *baihua,* a point on which he was attacked during the Cultural Revolution. Textual criticism of Wu Han focused on his *Renmin ribao* article 'Hai Rui Upbraids the Emperor', perhaps because of the political implications of remonstration with an emperor. Hai Rui's memorial had been written at the end of the Jiajing period, a reign renowned in Chinese history for the emperor's lack of personal involvement in governmental affairs. It followed the spate of remonstrating memorials that had brought so much grief to officials in the mid-1540s and is straightforward to the point of bluntness. The memorial naturally outraged the emperor, who, according to the standard biographies, was then told that Hai Rui had prepared himself by already having bid farewell to his family and having ordered the construction of his coffin. The emperor later commuted Hai's original death sentence to flogging and had him put in prison, where he remained until the emperor died some months later. The new emperor released Hai Rui and allowed him to continue his career.[103]

In 'Hai Rui Upbraids the Emperor', Wu Han takes key passages from the Ming official's 'Memorial on Peace and Order' (*zhi' an shu*) and links them together with an historical commentary. With the exception of the striking pun mentioned below, Wu Han followed the

---

102 'Hai Rui', *Chuntian ji,* pp.228-37.
103 Chaoying Fang, in Guodrich and Pang, vol.1, pp.477-78.

order of the original, but abbreviated the lengthy memorial and failed to include ellipses or provide any other indication of where he had omitted portions of the Ming text. For purposes of evaluating his textual accuracy I shall compare some random examples of both the original and Wu Han's *baihua* rendering of them, using the rather awkward medium of English.

Wu Han begins by retelling the famous pun on the emperor's reign title that Hai Rui writes was current at the time:

> Wu Han's translation into modern Chinese: 'Jiajing, all empty, all houses [or families] are so poor that they are completely cleaned out and have no money to use'.[104]
>
> Hai Rui's original text: As for [the reign title] Jiajing, [people] say, 'All houses are empty [jiajia jie jing] and there is no wealth to use'.[105]

Hai Rui castigates the emperor for his inattention to the affairs of state, dallying instead with the palace women and devoting himself to the cultivation of the occult.

> Wu Han's: 'You should know that Daoist self-cultivation has no benefits and should immediately come to your senses and attend court every day and study national policies and the livelihood of the people. You should repent of your decades of impropriety and give a little consideration to benefiting the people.'
>
> Hai Rui's: 'Your Majesty really knows that occult self-cultivation has no benefits... You should turn over [a new leaf] and awaken from your sins. You should hold formal court every day and see the various ministers [these are listed]. You should explain and discuss what is beneficial and what is harmful to the empire and cleanse yourself of the decades of impropriety in the way of the ruler'.[106]

There is no evidence in these passages of any misleading translation from the classical Chinese to the modern colloquial of Hai Rui's extremely blunt and sometimes sarcastic criticism of the emperor.

Nevertheless, there is some substance in the specific textual criticism levelled against Wu Han by his Cultural Revolution attackers, though they were ultimately guilty of some of the same faults that they

---

[104] This and subsequent citations from 'Hai Rui Upbraids the Emperor' are from *Renmin ribao,* 16 June 1959, p.8.

[105] Chen Zilong (ed.), *Huang Ming jingshi wenbian* [Collection of Statecraft Essays from the Ming Dynasty] (1638; Taiwan reprint, 1964), 309:3b; Wu Han (ed.), *Hai Rui ji* 1:218.

[106] Chen, 309:6b-7; *Hai Rui ji* 1:220.

attributed to the historian. In a major *Hongqi* article Guan Feng and Lin Jie charged Wu Han with, among many other things, inserting several lines in his translation that were not present in the original memorial and citing others out of context. The authors correctly note that in his *People's Daily* article Wu Han criticized the *Ming History* excerpt of Hai Rui's memorial for omitting key passages and claimed to cite instead a version found in *Mingshan cang,* a major private history by the Ming scholar He Qiaoyuan (1558-1632).[107]

The two critics demonstrate that in the following passage the italicized sections cannot be found in *Mingshan cang*: 'How do you compare with Han Wendi [Emperor Wendi of the Han]? *A few years ago you did a few good things. What about recently?* All you've done is talk about occult self-cultivation...*and excessively grant official positions to people.*'

Questions regarding traditional Chinese texts are notoriously tricky to deal with, especially when they concern edited texts such as this one, for, as the critics point out, the *Mingshan cang* version is itself incomplete. There are often several variants of a given text, for without copyright protection an author's works could be reproduced without his having control over new editions, the accuracy of which depended on the integrity of the new editor. It thus was possible that Wu Han and his critics had used different editions of the rare *Mingshan cang*.[108]

There is, however, a more probable explanation. In his *People's Daily* article, Wu Han's reference was to 'He Qiaoyuan's *Mingshan cang* 23, biography of Hai Zhongjie gong' [referring to Hai's posthumous name of respect]. Now, only the first forty-five chapters of *Mingshan cang* are numbered, and the biography of Hai Rui appears well towards the end of the 100-plus chapter work.[109] Moreover, the title refers to him simply by the name 'Hai Rui', without honorifics.[110] On the other hand, the biography of Hai Rui found in Li Zhi's *Xu cangshu*, which Wu Han also consulted, does appear in chapter 23, the heading of which contains the official's posthumous name.[111] Wu Han simply appears to have made a mistake here, though the *Xu cangshu* biography

---

107 Wolfgang Franke, *An Introduction to the Sources of Ming History* (Kuala Lumpur, 1968), p.47.

108 At that time there were known to be only a few copies in China. See Franke, p.47.

109 This is true in the reprint edition and is confirmed by Franke, p.47.

110 He, p.4717.

111 Li Zhi, *Xu cangshu* (reprint Beijing, 1959), p.471.

does not contain much of the memorial. If the two critics had wished to consult the complete memorial as reproduced in Wu Han's scholarly 1962 *Hai Rui ji,* they would have found that all the 'fabrications' they attribute to Wu Han have a sound basis in that text, which itself accords almost exactly with an authoritative version in a collection of statecraft essays edited by Chen Zilong (1608-67).[112] Clearly, despite what he wrote in the *People's Daily,* Wu Han was not relying exclusively on the truncated *Mingshan cang* version seen by Guan and Lin.

A second type of allegation raised by Guan Feng and Lin Jie, following an earlier comment on the same passage by Qi Benyu, is that Wu Han completely misconstrued the meaning of an important phrase. Qi had written that Wu Han's 'story of Hai Rui is full of exaggerations and fabrications... He even invented such a statement as 'You think you are correct and reject criticism'. In a footnote Qi somewhat clarified the issue by stating that though there are such words in the memorial, 'The persons whom Hai Rui scolded here were the "various ministers", not the Emperor'.[113] Guan and Lin reiterate this point and conclude that Wu had taken this phrase out of context, thus 'stealing the sky and putting up a sham sun'.[114]

The phrase in question appears in the middle of a long passage critical of both the emperor and his officials, the theme of which is succinctly summarized in the sentence 'When Your Majesty commits improprieties, your ministers follow in impropriety, and no one will talk straight to Your Majesty'.[115]

> Your Majesty deludes his mind by his whole-hearted preoccupation with occult self-cultivation. Your Majesty prejudices his sentiments by his excessively harsh judgements. It is said that Your Majesty has no regard for his family. Is this [in accordance with] human nature? Your ministers think only of themselves and their families.[116] When they obtain an office they frequently fail because of cheating, stealing or inattention to affairs.... Occasionally the ideas of the ruler and his ministers are different, *so they say Your Majesty follows only his own ideas and rejects criticism.* They take the appearance of one or two of Your Majesty's improprieties and apply them to the totality of the hundreds and thousands of affairs [undertaken by

---

[112] For a judgement on Chen, see Franke, pp.123-24.

[113] Qi, pp.6, 31-32. Pusey (p.16) seems to follow Qi's criticism without taking into account the footnote.

[114] Guan and Lin, pp.21-22.

[115] Chen, 309:4; *Hai Rui ji,* 1:218.

[116] Here I follow Chen, 309:4, rather than *Hai Rui ji,* vol.1, p.219.

Your Majesty], charging that Your Majesty's errors are so great as to make recovery impossible. The crime of ministerial deception of the ruler is great.[117]

In the context of this larger passage it is clear that the phrase about the emperor's rejection of criticism can be attributed to what Hai Rui is saying about certain ministers. It also is evident, however, that the attempt by Guan Feng and Lin Jie to portray this as Hai Rui's support for the emperor is equally out of context, for the root of the problem is the behaviour of the superior, which engenders similar actions on the part of his subordinates. By saying that the emperor has become victimized by bad officials, Hai Rui of course was attempting to pave the way for the ruler to listen to his own remonstration. Wu Han thus may be faulted for a limited amount of sloppiness in his reference to *Mingshan cang* and his contextual handling of one phrase, but by and large his handling of Hai Rui's text is quite consistent with the original.

Context of Contemporary Theatre

At the time of the writing of the 'Dismissal of Hai Rui' there was an especially close connection between the discipline of history and the theatre.[118] Moreover, both Wu Han's concerns about the utility of the pre-modern past and the role of the hero in history were central topics in this relationship. As in pre-modern times the government was concerned about the effects of plays upon popular behaviour and thought.[119] Even before Jiang Qing's advent it attempted to lay down guide-lines for the reform of drama in the service of a revolutionary society. Some of these had serious implications for the popular perception of the pre-modern past.

As a result of such policies there emerged a new genre of drama known as 'new historical plays' (*xin lishi ju*), which took their themes from history, but which were written to serve contemporary society. During the late 1950s and early 1960s more than a dozen such plays

---

117   Chen, 309:4a-b; *Hai Rui ji*, 1:219. Emphasis added.
118   The noted historian Hou Wailu also makes this point in his eulogy of Wu Han. See 'Daonian Wu Han tongzhi' [Grieving for Comrade Wu Han], in *Wu Han he 'Hai Rui baguan'*, pp.24f. I have dealt with this subject in a cursory way in my 'Newly Arranged Historical Plays in the Light of "The Dismissal of Hai Rui, 1979-82"', in Marlis Thiersch (ed.), *Chinese Theatre in the Twentieth Century*, (Potts Point, NSW, 1983), pp.69-92.
119   Mackerras, p.92.

were staged by major companies. Authors of these plays included not only well-known writers like Tian Han and Cao Yu, but also the president of the Academy of Sciences, Guo Moruo. Some of their themes were quite clearly related to the debates then current among historians, for they included works on Cao Cao and the Empress Wu. Others used traditional stories as the basis for their plays, such as those about the Song general Yue Fei and the revenge of the King of Yue against the state of Wu at the end of the Spring and Autumn period.[120] Both of these subjects may have drawn inspiration from the deteriorating relations between China and the USSR, for Yue Fei was famous for his single-minded pursuit of an aggressive policy against the northern barbarians, and the King of Yue 'slept on firewood and tasted gall' (*woxin changdan*) for ten long years while preparing to overthrow his feudal masters in Wu.[121]

Historians very quickly were involved in discussions about the new plays. In October 1959 a conference was convened in Beijing to discuss a play about the Empress Wu.[122] Attending it, in addition to Wu Han, were scholars like Jian Bozan, a senior professor of history at Beijing University; Shang Yue, principal exponent of the 'sprouts of capitalism' theory; and Lu Zhenqu, a leading Marxist theoretician and social historian.[123] A play written by members of the Chinese navy about the Sino-Japanese War (1894-95) became the focal point of another conference on history and drama the next year.[124] 'Historical truth and artistic truth' was the heading of an on-going series of articles in China's leading theatre journal *Xijubao* during the latter part of 1959.[125]

The issues that dominated the controversy about theatre and history were not very different from those under consideration by historians. Discussion focused on questions like the proper use of the past, criteria for the evaluation of 'feudal' ruling-class heroes, and the portrayal of the

---

[120] Zhao, esp. pp.147-62.

[121] Yue Fei was featured in '*Manjiang hong*' [River Red with Blood], and several plays were written on Yue-Wu rivalry. See Zhao, pp.158-60.

[122] Wu Han, 'Lishi de zhen shi yu yishu de zhenshi' [Historical Truth and Artistic Truth], *Dengxia ji*, p.140.

[123] *Xijubao* 20 (1959), p.5.

[124] Editors of *Xijubao*, *Lishiju lunji* [Collected Articles on Historical Plays], vol.1 (Shanghai, 1962)., p.1.

[125] *Xijubao*, nos 10, 11, 15, 20, 21, 22 (1959).

masses.[126] The editorial board of *Xijubao* was concerned that historically responsible plays continue to be produced, in addition to modern plays. These should include revised versions of traditional plays, which were products of their own times, but also completely new attempts to find examples of the past relevant to the problems of the present. Such plays, the journal's 'commentator' argued, should fulfil both the requirements of historical materialism and dramatic art. Imagination was of course called for, but it must be used within the parameters of the class structure of the period about which the plays were written. The plays should not be attempts to impose current values on figures of the past. Among the plays lauded by *Xijubao* in late 1960 was one by editor Tian Han about the playwright Guan Hanqing (ca. 1220/30-1300/10), who was punished for refusing to alter the text of a play critical of the repressive Yuan government. The journal, on the other hand, criticized other writers for making 'arbitrary changes' in history by incorporating in their plays phenomena that could not have occurred at the historical time in which they were set.[127]

Among the heroes of feudal times portrayed on stage prior to the production of Wu Han's 'Dismissal' was, of course, Hai Rui. Not only was there 'Hai Rui Sends a Memorial by Zhou Xinfang's Shanghai group, but the Shenyang Beijing Troupe produced 'Hai Rui Hauls The Boat (*Hai Rui beiqian*), which was based on a traditional romance about Hai Rui's exploits as a district magistrate, and two other regional theatre groups staged plays about the Ming official.[128]

Wu Han was not only active in writing his own play, but entered into the debate on historical drama both as a theatre critic and as a theorist by presenting papers at the major conferences and contributing reviews, articles and an interview to the periodical press. Next to his writings on heroes in history, his publications on the subject of historical plays were most prolific. As a critic of specific plays Wu Han

---

[126] Lu Mei, 'Guanyu lishiju wenti de zhengming' [Controversies About the Question of Historical Plays], *Lishiju lunji,* pp.353-75. Reprinted from *Xijubao*.

[127] 'Ji yao shenghuo de jiaokeshu, ye yao lishi de jiaokeshu', [Textbooks Should Be Both Lively and Historical], *Xijubao* 22.

[128] *Chinese Studies in History and Philosophy*, vol.2, no.1, 1968, 42n; *Cultural Revolution in China*, pp.128, 202. Photos of the former appeared in no.20 (1959), p.20. and no.5 (1961), cover; photos of the latter appeared in no.1-2 (1961). The latter play was reviewed by Lu Mei, Xijubao, no.3 (1961), pp.11-13. This was the time when Wu Han's play was being performed, but there is no review of it. Xuan Mo, no.29, p.92.

demonstrated concern for both the historical and artistic dimensions, though he concentrated much more heavily on the former.¹²⁹

Wu Han's strongest criticism was directed against a play called 'Women Generals of the Yang house' (*Yangmen nüjiang*), a story of female patriotism and martial endeavour set in the Song dynasty and the focus of controversy in the current press. He pointed not only to historical inaccuracies, such as the invention of characters, but dwelt also on the historical nature of much of the behaviour and thought in the play. These historiographical weaknesses, he hastened to add, do not mean that the play is no good. It simply cannot be called an 'historical play'. Wu then proceeded to establish categories that were helpful in analysing their content. Plays like 'Women Generals of the Yang House', though they dealt in part with figures from the past, should be termed 'story plays'. This terminology, Wu stated, is not meant to be judgemental, but descriptive.¹³⁰ Much more license can be granted to authors of story plays, for they are not bound by the constraints of fact and can draw on the rich storehouse of traditional popular tales. Historical plays, however, must be rooted firmly in verifiable historical texts.¹³¹

Despite his concern with the scholarly rigour of historical plays, Wu Han recognized that theatre is not history. Whereas purely historical works should be comprehensive, plays can only be selective, dwelling on one or two aspects of a topic and relying on the judgement of the historian for matters of interpretation. In terms of popular education about China's past, plays reach a far wider audience than history books and thus are important tools in raising the cultural level of the masses and youth. It is of course important that they employ the techniques of the medium to 'heighten reality', but 'artistic realism ought to respect *(fucong)* historical truth'.¹³²

---

129 For example, he criticized 'Empress Wu' (*Zetian huangdi*) for dwelling on her failures rather than her successes, as well as having too broad a scope in time and dramatic events. In addition he found that 'The War of 1894' concentrated too much on the naval battles and does not deal sufficiently with the fragmentation and corruption of the late Qing administration.

130 *Tan lishiju* [On Historical Plays], *Chuntian ji*, pp.142-47 and *Lishiju lunji*, pp.265-70; 'Zai tan lishiju' [More on Historical Plays], *Chuntian ji*, pp.148-60, and *Lishiju lunji*, pp.276-88.

131 Lu Mei, 'Wu Han tongzhi', p.118.

132 ibid., 25.

Wu Han argued that playwrights must portray their characters within the confines of the spirit of times in which their plays are set, not the spirit of contemporary times. Thus, he pointed out, the Song general Yue Fei (1104-42) cannot be depicted in terms of the People's Liberation Army. Nor should pre-modern peasant rebellions be shown carrying out a programme of equal land distribution, for that is a phenomenon occurring in Chinese history only with the advent of the CCP.[133] The historian also stressed the relevance of leading figures from the feudal ruling class, for some of them displayed virtues applicable to the problems of today, like martial courage and perseverance in the pursuit of goals. For the latter characteristic he cited the Tang monk Xuan Zang (602-664), who brought back the Buddhist scriptures from India, and the geographical explorer Xu Hongzu (1586-1641), who travelled the length and breadth of China in search of scientific information.[134]

By reading 'The Dismissal of Hai Rui' within the context of Chinese theatre we can place it securely within the framework of contemporary events. Historians and playwrights were co-operating to a perhaps unprecedented degree, and similar problems regarding the nature of history and its relationship to present society were on the minds of both groups. Foremost among these concerns were problems posed by 'making the past serve the present' and 'emphasizing the present while de-emphasizing the past'. These two slogans were clearly focused on the problem of portraying the feudal ruling hero on the contemporary stage.

Wu Han's own treatment of Hai Rui was informed both by what other playwrights had already done with Hai Rui and by his own approach to the marriage of history and theatre. By reviewing other historical plays Wu had recognized the impossibility of treating the life of a model figure in its entirety and thus sought a single dramatic focus. The most dramatic events in Hai Rui's public life were his memorial of remonstration to the Jiajing emperor and his dismissal from office. Since the former had been the theme of the play 'Hai Rui Submits His Memorial', Wu Han elected to concentrate on the latter. Avoiding the historical irresponsibility of those whose plays he had criticized, Wu derived the great bulk of his stage material from standard historical sources, while distorting history to a minimal degree to attract the interest of his popular audience. Despite earlier policy guide-lines to

---

[133] ibid., 23.

[134] ibid., *24.*

avoid the 'backward gestures' of pre-modern times, his references to cultural beliefs and acts were carefully placed within the Ming context he knew so well.

Historical Description: Some Concluding Thoughts

The nature of historical explanation has bedevilled historians and philosophers alike, for though it may share characteristics with other disciplines and everyday life, it is also quite different. It is impossible to demonstrate rigorously cause and effect in historical situations or to 'prove' a relationship between historical phenomena in the same way that articulates the congruence of two triangles. Nevertheless, the past is recoverable to an extent that depends on the perspicacity and methodological awareness of the historian. Rather than forego analytic rigour in despair of finding historical certainties, we must redouble our self-consciousness in the pursuit of the past. Our goal becomes both more modest and more sophisticated: to describe the past rather than re-create it.

Historical description at this level has much in common with the 'thick description' of the ethnographer Clifford Geertz. Rather than attempt to be 'experience-near' emphatic observers of the past, we should distance ourselves with our rich variety of materials and analytic tools and sort out the various 'structures of signification'.[135] By crudely applying Skinner's model of the 'hermeneutic circle', I have tried to recover Wu Han's intentions in writing the play 'The Dismissal of Hai Rui'. Starting with the text itself I have endeavoured to identify contexts in which it can be usefully examined and then returned to the text armed with the added insights of these contexts. I have not succeeded, it must be admitted, in definitely or fully recovering what Wu Han meant. I hope, however, I have contributed to an historical understanding of what was going on by uncovering a series of meaningful structures in terms of which the dimensions of 'The Dismissal of Hai Rui' can be contextually situated.

Dissatisfaction with the Great Leap Forward provided an overall context for Wu Han's work on Hai Rui, but there is no demonstrable link between it and Peng Dehuai, at least in its inception. Wu responded to a generalized call by Mao to imitate 'the spirit of Hai Rui' and to a

---

135 Clifford Geertz, 'On the Nature of Anthropological Understanding', *American Scientist*, vol.63, no.1 (January-February 1975), pp.47-53; and 'Thick Description: Toward an Interpretive Theory of Culture', in his *The Interpretation of Cultures* (London, 1974), pp.3-30.

specific request by a leading Party member to begin work on the Ming official. Despite the anti-rightist campaign, he continued for about three years with the support of Party circles in Beijing, who at the very least gave him time and encouragement.[136] During this period he produced historically verifiable work in genres ranging from the popular essay and Beijing Opera to academic scholarship. Aside from Jiang Qing's carping in 1962, there appears to have been no major criticism of his work. Neither he nor other authors who wrote on Hai Rui were punished until the Cultural Revolution, which broke out more than six years after Wu's initial publications on Hai Rui.

Wu Han's creation of a play about Hai Rui was but one aspect of his deep-seated and wide-ranging interest in the pre-modern past and its utility in the contemporary world of Chinese society. His preoccupation with Hai Rui, though stimulated from the outside, mirrored wider concerns of the Chinese cultural elite in the fields of history and theatre at the time of the Great Leap Forward and shortly thereafter. Wu seems to have perceived the 'de-emphasis' of the past and of its chief actors as potentially an even greater distortion of history than its traditional Confucian bias, a distortion that would render history completely useless to revolutionary China. Wu Han certainly did not believe in history for its own sake, but saw it as a medium for raising social and political consciousness, especially in its more popular forms. In sustaining Hai Rui as a major focus of his work, Wu Han raised from the past to contemporary awareness the example of a loyal, but outspokenly critical, member of the Chinese cultural and political elite bent on reforming administration from within. He thus articulated a Party consensus that remonstrating officials in the Ming mode were still needed in revolutionary China. Ironically, Wu Han came to the same end as many such spirited spokesmen did in the faction-ridden politics of 16th century China.

---

[136] Wu's relations with the Beijing Party establishment are detailed in conspiratorial terms in *Beijing xin wenyi,* 8 June 1967.

'IN GUISE OF A CONGRATULATION': POLITICAL SYMBOLISM IN ZHOU XINFANG'S PLAY *HAI RUI SUBMITS HIS MEMORIAL*

Rudolf G. Wagner[*]

When rehabilitation of the intellectual victims of the Cultural Revolution began in 1978, the leadership had to decide on what basis they should now be praised. Some of the most prominent had been attacked by Red Guards and Kang Sheng's machine for disagreeing with Mao Zedong or even openly criticizing the Chairman. Should the historian Wu Han, the dramatists Meng Chao and Tian Han, the essayist Deng Tuo, or the actor Zhou Xinfang be rehabilitated as people who dared to speak up when the common people were in distress during the Great Leap years, as people who stood up to the strong and mighty, as courageous defenders of civil liberties whose emulation would be the best defense against a recurrence of a Cultural Revolution?

A great chance for setting new political standards was to be missed and the new leadership lived up to its reputation. Speeches, books, and articles praised the Wu Hans and Tian Hans in unison for their utter obedience to orders from the Party leadership. Why then, had they become victims of the Cultural Revolution? Because, according to the new dispensation, this social conflagration had arisen exactly through

---

[*] This study grew out of my *The Contemporary Chinese Historical Drama: Four Studies* (University of California Press, Berkeley, 1990). It was first presented at a conference on Chinese drama and film in Oslo in 1988. Much of the background is given there and will not be repeated here. I owe much gratitude to Ms Marion Betz from the University of Heidelberg for her research assistance. The German Research Foundation (DFG) made possible the visit to Shanghai with its archives and opportunities to interview actors, cadres and scholars involved in the writing and performance of the play. This support which is graciously acknowledged was crucial for assembling an unusually rich documentation.

reckless criticism directed at Party leaders. The rehabilitated intellectuals were presented as victims of their obedience, not of their daring outspokenness.[1]

Of course, there was some double talk involved. These intellectuals had been linked to now-rehabilitated political leaders. In their outspoken criticism of certain Party leaders and their policies before the Cultural Revolution, they had all too often obediently followed directives given to them by their elders. As these leaders were now back in power and as their opponents were dead or jailed, there was no further need for daring and outspoken critics, and the now praiseworthy virtue of these intellectuals was their continuous obedience to orders from the right people.

In actuality, their obedience had not been restricted to the now restored leaders, nor their criticism to Mao Zedong and his associates. They had had their own reasons to do each other in, their own trivial squabbles; the media and genres they used had their own laws and restrictions, and the actual record of their lives would probably rather land them in Dante's messy Limbo than in the neatly defined realms of Paradise or Hell.

Background

The Anti-Rightist Campaign which began in June 1957 eliminated from the literary scene the bulk of the prose writers affiliated with the Communist Youth League, such as Liu Binyan, Wang Meng, Liu Shaotang and Gao Xiaosheng.[2] Their criticism of bureaucratic abuse was termed 'anti-socialist', and their advocacy of greater leeway for intellectuals 'decadent'. Prose lost its critical potential as well as its promoters. The role models of these young authors, the engagé journalistic writers from the Soviet Thaw like Ovechkin, Nikolayeva, Ehrenburg, and Dudintsev, became unlivable and unquotable.

The acceleration of rural collectivization in early 1958, which resulted in the establishment of People's Communes as well as the

---

[1] John Israel makes this point in his Introduction to Carol Lee Hamrin and Timothy Cheek (eds), *China's Establishment Intellectuals* (M.E. Sharpe, Armonk, 1986), p.xviii. For Zhou Xinfang, this argument is made by Xu Siyan, 'Wei Hai Rui shangshu wenziyu bianyuan, [Against the Unjust Banishment of 'Hai Rui Submits His Memorial' into the Literary Prison], *Jiefang ribao*, 3 January 1979.

[2] I have dealt with them and this period at greater length in my *Inside a Service Trade: Studies in Contemporary Chinese Prose* (Council of East Asian Studies, Cambridge, in press), chs. 1 and 2.

attempts to achieve a Great Leap Forward in production through a militarily organized production campaign, exacerbated the inherent problems of one-Party leadership. The abrogation of individual economic prerogatives together with the political Anti-Rightist Campaign combined to increase the powers of the cadres and to close the avenues of [open] talk (*yanlu*). The ensuing marked increase in cadre abuses of power was accompanied by an equally marked decrease in the options available to ward them off. Lower level cadres ceded to higher level pressure to come up with inflated 'Great Leap Forward' production targets, and squeezed the amounts of grain required for sale to the state from the defenseless peasants. This resulted in the by far largest man-made famine in this century.[3]

The 'new historical drama' of the period 1958 through 1963 provided the principal medium to depict the Great Leap, to analyse who was responsible for its failings or achievements, and to suggest remedies to overcome the crisis or to bring the slanderers to order. The authors were not young men from the Youth League but older cultural leaders like Tian Han, Zhou Xinfang, Meng Chao, Guo Moruo or Wu Han. Their public were not the traditional Peking Opera *aficionados* from the lower orders. The plays were new or radically rewritten, and comprehension of their message required a substantial knowledge of *wenyan*, of history, and of top-level contention within the Party's leadership. Their intended audience comprised the senior members of the political class.

The historical drama traditionally deals with the Centre, the court, and not with the common folk, the *laobaixing*, as had the reform prose of the preceding years. It was thus able to portray indirectly the struggles at the very centre of power, which had been removed from the corpus of legitimate literary topics at the very moment when these internal political debates assumed an unprecedented importance for the fate of the country.

The new historical drama inherited elements from the rewritten historical drama of the early Fifties. At that time, scores of popular operas had been rewritten to conform to new educative purposes. *Qin Xianglian* now appeared on stage as a public warning to the cadres not to change their wives as their social status rose. The Monkey King now ends his *Great Uproar in Heaven* in victory, because the revolution with which this uproar had been equated had been victorious. There was a

---

[3] B. Ashton et al., 'Famine in China, 1958-1961', *Population and Development Review*, vol.10., no.4, 1984, pp.614 ff.

shared understanding that these restaged old works directly referred to contemporary things. Works where no such echo with the present was found were not performed.[4]

The new historical drama also inherited a rich tradition dating from its use in the battle against the Guomindang. Most of the senior figures in drama, including Wu Han, Guo Moruo, Tian Han and Meng Chao, had experience in using historical drama for indirect criticism of contemporary politics from pre-1949 times.[5] This was true, too, for the author of the play studied in this paper, Zhou Xinfang. He had reacted to every one of the major political developments since the May 4th period by selecting and reworking historical pieces in a fashion that joined the contemporary fray.[6] The implication of the renewed use of historical drama since 1958 was that times were again such as to leave no other avenue of discourse open.

The Hai Rui Model

A small number of *qingguan*, pure officials, had been waiting for their time in the wings of the opera houses during the first half of the Fifties, especially Bao Cheng, the Song Dynasty judge. During the Hundred Flowers period, some quite critical Judge Bao plays had been performed. He was eventually joined by the Ming official Hai Rui, who became his 'southern' counterpart.

Jiang Xingyu, a member of the Shanghai Cultural Office, began work on his biography *Hai Rui* in 1955.[7] The biography eventually came out in September 1957[8] after two substantial revisions, and nearly landed the author in the position of a 'Rightist' during the 'Anti-Rightist Campaign' that had just begun.[9] The book ran through five printings until 1962 and remained the main source for public information on Hai Rui during these years. Jiang Xingyu greatly praised Hai Rui for his

---

[4] Zhao Cong, *Zhongguo dalu de xiju gaige 1942-1967* (Zhongwen daxue Publ., Hongkong, 1967).

[5] For Guo Moruo, cf. my 'The Chinese Writer in His Own Mirror: Writer, State and Society', in Merle Goldman (ed.), with T. Cheek and C. Hamrin, *China's Intellectuals and the State* (Harvard University Press, Cambridge, 1987), p.186.

[6] Tao Xiong, 'Zhou Xinfang', in *Zhongguo da baike quanshu. Xiqu, quyi* (Zhongguo da baike quanshu chubanshe, Beijing, 1983), p.611.

[7] Interview with Jiang Xingyu, Shanghai, 21 May 1989.

[8] Jiang Xingyu, *Hai Rui*, (Shanghai renmin chubanshe, Shanghai, 1962).

[9] ibid., postface p. 129, and interview, 21 May 1989.

defense of the 'interests of the peasants and small landowners', and for his outspoken criticism of corruption and misrule in the Centre. He rejected as being 'all too one-sided' the argument proffered by 'some people' that Hai Rui's 'progressive measures' only softened the class contradictions and deferred revolution.[10] In this way Hai Rui became a possible behavioural model for the present. The key terms used later for Hai Rui, i.e., his 'daring to act', (*ganzuo ganwei*), were not now in political fashion when Jiang Xingyu wrote the book. Jiang Xingyu's Hai Rui, with his popular and upright stand and brave battle against bureaucratic abuses of power, was very much a hero of the Hundred Flowers period.

A few months later, in mid-1958, Hai Rui was joined by Guan Hanqing, the Yuan Dynasty playwright. A decision at that time by the World Peace Council to elevate Guan to the level of a world cultural giant provided Tian Han with the opportunity to write a play ostensibly about Guan Hanqing.[11]

Tian Han's *Guan Hanqing* operated as a guide for the reading and appreciation of the new historical drama, written by none other than the head of the Dramatists' Association himself. Tian Han was composing a drama about a 13th century playwright who, unable to write about the Yuan court, i.e., the present, writes a historical play so as to indirectly attack the chief villain at the Yuan court, Kubilai Khan's confidant Ahmad. Two problems plague the country, both caused by this Ahmad. He controls the law courts so that no justice can be done and no one can speak out, and his henchmen take people's land away. These themes were echoed and reinforced in 1958 by the restaging of Guan Hanqing's outcry against injustice, *Dou E yuan*, in tandem with Tian Han's new *Guan Hanqing*.

By mid-1958, the historical drama had become the only arena of public discourse in which, albeit in a very indirect manner, the political and social problems of the country could be aired before a rather restricted elite. The stage was in no way monopolized by critics of the

---

[10] ibid., p.125.

[11] Tian Han, *Guan Hanqing*, *Juben* 1958.5. For a detailed study of this play see my *The Contemporary Chinese Historical Drama*, ch.1, 'A Guide for the Perplexed and a Call to the Wavering: Tian Han's *Guan Hanqing* (1958) and the New Historical Drama'.

Chairman or of the Great Leap; Mao's acolytes like Guo Moruo responded in kind and scene to the charges made by critics.[12]

Late in 1958, Zhou Xinfang, the star actor of the Shanghai school of Peking Opera, came out with a play on another unflinching critic of tyrannical rule, Bi Gan, entitled *Hatred at Deer Terrace (Lutai hen)*.[13] The play deals with loyal minister Bi Gan who bitterly remonstrated with Zhou, the notorious 'bad last emperor' of the Shang Dynasty, for which the Emperor had Bi Gan's heart cut out. In the play, the people resent the huge army maintained by the Emperor as well as his tyrannical cruelty. The social situation of the country is summed up in the phrase 'loyal words grate on the ears of the tyrant and irritate him; all over the countryside moaning and weeping fills the air'. The people remember the virtues of the Shang dynasty, but when Bi Gan's heart is pulled out, it is clear that the dynasty is beyond redemption. Under headings like 'in the name of the people, attack the guilty' and 'turn the spears against the tyrant', the play subsequently depicted the rebellion of Wuwang together with 800 feudal vassals, which eventually put an end to Zhou's rule and the Shang dynasty altogether.[14] The play was performed only a few times in early 1959 and must have run into political trouble, for it focused the attack on the highest political leader, and brought out the uprightness and popularity of the remonstrator in the figure of Bi Gan.[15]

By January 1959, the troubles of the Great Leap Forward had been exacerbated to such a degree that a historical echo of the present was found in the bleakest periods of the past, and even the time of the

---

12 Guo Moruo, *Cai Wenji* (Wenwu chubanshe, Beijing, 1959). Id. *Wu Zetian*, *Renmin wenxue wiuxue*, 1960, no.5. Zhejiang sheng wenhuaju Sun Wukong sanda baigujing zhengli xiaozu (ed.), *Sun Wukong sanda baigujing* (Zhejiang renmin chubanshe, Zhejiang, 1979). cf. *The Contemporary Chinese Historical Drama*, op. cit., p.247 ff.

13 The play had been rewritten from the third section of the long play *List of Enfeoffed Gods (Fengshen bang)*. To my knowledge it has not been published but was dug up by Zhou Xinfang's critics during the Cultural Revolution.

14 Wang Jiaxi, '*Lutai hen* shi Zhou Xinfang xumou fandang de youyi tiezheng [*Lutai hen* is a further iron proof for Zhou Xinfang's premeditated opposition to the Party] *Jiefang ribao*, 24 June 1966.

15 The *Wenhuibao* only carried advertisements for performances on January 12, 13, and 14. The unique feature of these advertisements was that they carried the slogans mentioned above, a practice I have not found elsewhere and which, given the potentially inflammatory meaning of the slogans, permits educated guesses as to the political problems the play ran into. I have not found reviews.

notoriously bad last Shang Emperor Zhou. In these plays, public opinion is stifled to a degree that a superhuman remonstrator is needed who is willing to give away his life to speak out for the people.

Hai Rui himself had already made it onto the stage in 1958. Guan Hanqing's *The Injustice Done to Dou E which Moved Heaven and Shook the Earth* (*Gantian dongdi Dou E yuan*) had been rewritten for the Guan Hanqing anniversary, with Hai Rui entering at the end to set things right again.

Hai Rui moved to centre stage in January 1959 with *Tablets of Life and Death* (*Shengsi pai*).[16] The performance by a troupe from Mao's home province was attended by the Chairman himself, Tian Han, Mei Lanfang and others.[17] Hai Rui intervenes here in the last scene to save an official and three young women from disaster at the hands of a bully who was in league with Yan Song, the notorious Prime Minister of the Jiajing Emperor's earlier years, but the Jiajing Emperor neither comes on stage nor is he directly attacked.

At the Shanghai Work Conference (24 March through 4 April 1959), Peng Dehuai charged the Chairman with flouting Party rules and running the place as if the other members of the Standing Committee of the Politburo did not exist, and this in a situation where the country was wracked with grave problems.[18] After having seen *Tablets of Life and Death*, Mao Zedong had now read Hai Rui's biography in the *History of the Ming Dynasty*.[19] There, Hai Rui's harsh remonstrance with the Jiajing Emperor is quoted at length, but he is also depicted as being loyal to the emperor. Although the Emperor immediately had sentenced Hai Rui to death for his criticism, Hai Rui is moved to tears when the announcement of the Emperor's death reaches him in prison and he spits out the food he had just eaten by way of a hangman's supper.[20] At the meeting, Mao Zedong suddenly praised Hai Rui and 'someone' there,

---

16 Wu Shaoqiang, adpt., *Shengsi pai* (Renmin meishu chubanshe, Beijing, 1962).

17 Guo Xinghua, '*Hai Rui baguan* shi zenyang xiechulai de' (How was *Hai Rui Dismissed From Office* Written). *Wu Han xueshu shengya* (Jiangxi remin chubanshe, Jiangxi, 1984), p.112.

18 Union Research Institute, *The Case of P'eng Te-huai* (Union Research Institute, Hongkong, 1989), p.204.

19 *Ming shi*, quoted here from the edition in Chen Yizhong, *Hai Rui ji* (Zhonghua shuju, Beijing, 1962), vol.2, p.525ff.

20 ibid., p.528.

probably Qian Junrui, a Vice-Minister of Culture, coined the slogan that one should 'learn from the spirit of Hai Rui'.[21]

Mao then proceeded in his usual manner, by sending the *Ming shi* biography of Hai Rui to none other than Peng Dehuai for his perusal.[22] This implied an offer to Peng Dehuai that his remonstrance would be accepted as being motivated by loyal concerns, but did not exclude the possibility that the Chairman might persecute him, as the Jiajing Emperor had done with Hai Rui. Mao might have felt that many leaders harboured unspoken resentment against his policies, and may have been trying to drag them into the open. As is well known, Peng accepted the offer and donned the oversized coat of the Ming official at the Lushan meeting later that year.

It would seem that Mao, in playing upon Hai Rui, was reacting to a Hai Rui wind that was already blowing in the literary and cultural spheres, rather than creating it. In fact, the Beijing Opera Troupe (*Jingjutuan*) had just performed a play about Hai Rui, *Da hongpao* (Great Red Honorary Robe),[23] and the Huangpu Peking Opera Troupe had written and produced a Peking opera, *Hai Rui*.[24]

In terms of values, the Hai Rui figure stressed the need for indomitable, fearless and outspoken characters among the Communist officialdom. More important, however, was the potential to define the present period as akin to that during which this Ming official lived.

There were other, and better known, candidates for the role of the upright official, but they had lived under other and less suggestive circumstances. Hai Rui was first introduced as 'Judge Bao of the South', but the celebrated Judge Bao had lived under much easier circumstances. His emperor was willing to listen to his remonstrance, there were no special police to watch over officials, and the economic situation of the land was not too bad. Wei Zheng, the minister under the

---

[21] Guo Xinghua, 'Hai Rui baguan', p. 112.

[22] Guo Xinghua, '*Hai Rui baguan* shi zenyang xiechulai de', in *Wu Han xueshu shengya*, (Jiangxi renmin chubanshe, Jiangxi, 1984), p.112.

[23] Compare Zong He, 'Nan Bao gong Hai Rui' (Hai Rui, the Southern Judge Bao), *Beijing ribao*, 15 May 1959. A summary of the play is in *Hai gong xiao hongpao* (Baowentang shudian, Peking, 1987), p.268f.

[24] This had been honoured at the Shanghai Theatre Gathering which ended on 21 March 1959. 'Shanghai xiju wutai fan hua si jin' [The Shanghai Stage is Colourful like Brocade], *Wenhui bao*, 22 March 1959. A summary of the play is in *Hai gong xiao hongpao*, p.276. In terms of plot, this play is similar to *Hai Rui beiqian* [Hai Rui Pulls the Rope].

Tang founder Li Shimin, lived under similarly benign conditions. Being himself the role model for Judge Bao, he joined the 'pure officials' on stage in 1962 with a play *Li Shimin yu Wei Zheng*, written by none other than Jiang Xingyu.[25] Other 'pure officials' to come on stage during the early 1960s included Jie Fangping from Pu Songling's *Liaozhai zhiyi*.[26] To survive and be effective under the 'present' circumstances more than an iron mien was required. Tactical wit and shrewdness were needed together with the willingness to throw in one's life. This combination was what the Hai Rui figure could offer.

By not writing at this time about such other upright officials, the point could be made that the present corresponded best to Hai Rui's particular circumstances. Under Jiajing, remonstrators were routinely beaten to death or exiled, the special police sent terror into the hearts of the officials, the government was for all practical purposes inoperative for decades, and problems piled up in the country. The potential of the Hai Rui figure to define, in historical terms, the peculiar features of Mao, the Anti-Rightist Campaign, the Great Leap, and the situation in the political centre was considerable, and it was eagerly tapped. This potential of the Hai Rui figure was not lost on the political class and on the writers at the time. In an interview in May 1989, Jiang Xingyu explicitly mentioned that Judge Bao had been 'in a much better situation under Renzong than Hai Rui under the Jiajing emperor'.[27] Once people started to read up on historical materials about Hai Rui, the surprising potential of their assignment to write about him gradually became clearer. There can be much freedom in assignment literature. Dr Tom Fisher has suggested that we should take these plays at face value and read them as disquisitions on history with only marginal political implications. The record of Zhou Xinfang's *Hai Rui Submits His Memorial* does not make this hypothesis very plausible – although the argument can also be properly made that the political implications of these plays as well as the books and articles on which they drew in no way exclude interesting historical interpretations.

The Hai Rui figure is thrown into relief by another character much discussed in early 1959, Cao Cao, the historical figure who featured as

---

[25] Compare Jiang Xingyu, *Mingren yishi*, (Zhongzhou guji chubanshe, Chengzhou, 1988), p.135 ff. In an interview on 21 May 1989 Jiang Xingyu stated that this play was also written on assignment, this time from the editor of the *Jiefang ribao*.

[26] Interview with Jiang Xingyu, 21 May 1989.

[27] Interview with Jiang Xingyu, 21 May 1989.

one of the contending rulers in *The Romance of Three Kingdoms*. Guo Moruo's *Cai Wenji* on this theme had just come out and its story was serialized in the *Wenhui bao*. The discussion about Cao Cao concedes weaknesses in this character who was much admired by Mao Zedong, but otherwise serves the purpose, as Guo Moruo said, of 'reversing the verdict on Cao Cao'. The situation in the country is compared to that after the collapse of the Han Dynasty, and Cao Cao competently restores order and prosperity, while living modestly himself. The Hai Rui figure contrarily operates at a time of an incompetent and ruthless emperor, unable to reform himself and administer the country. All hopes of the 'people' focus on the loyal remonstrator from among the officials, to reprimand the emperor and restore law and order in the land. The battle between these two radically different assessments was on, and it was carried out by both sides on the vast grounds of history.

After the Shanghai Work Conference, Qian Junrui transmitted leadership approval for the propagation of the Hai Rui theme to the appropriate departments. Zhou Yang, the vice-head of the Party's Propaganda Department in charge of literature, was dispatched to Hainan Island to collect materials on Hai Rui in his birthplace. On 19 April, he met with the director of the Shanghai Peking Opera Theatre and the most famous Peking Opera actor of the South, Zhou Xinfang, in the Jinjiang Hotel in Shanghai.[28] He asked him to write a play about Hai Rui for the occasion of the 10th Anniversary of the PRC on 1 October 1959, an anniversary which eventually was celebrated under the grand slogan of Zhou Enlai's report 'Ten Great Years'.[29] Zhou Yang is quoted by Red Guard sources as having said during this meeting: 'One should put together a play about that indomitable (*liaobuqi*) Hai Rui and should

---

[28] Shanghai shi Hongdaihui (chou) Wenyijie gaoju Mao Zedong sixiang hongqi, pipan wenyi heixian lian'gezhan, jingju fenzhan [Peking Opera Branch of the Liaison Station for Raising High the Red Banner of Mao Zedong Thought and Criticizing the Black Line in Literature and the Arts of the Red (Guard) Delegate Assembly (Preparatory) and the Literary and Arts Circles of the City of Shanghai] (ed.), *Piping jingju wenyi heixian ziliao xuanji* (2) (*Zhou Xinfang fan dang fan shehuizhuyi fan Mao Zedong sixiang zuixing cailiao zhi yi* [A Selection of Materials to Criticize the Black Line in Peking Opera Literature and Arts] (2) (Materials on Zhou Xinfang's Anti-Party, Anti-Socialism, Anti-Mao Zedong Thought Crimes 1), Shanghai 1966, p.1. Others present at the meeting with Zhou Yang were Shi Ximin, the head of the Shanghai Party Propaganda Department, and Liu Housheng, the head of the Literature and Arts Section of the Shanghai Cultural Office.

[29] Zhou Enlai, *Weida de shinian* [Ten Great Years], *Renmin ribao*, 6 October 1959.

perform it... Since the Anti-rightist campaign nobody dares to talk, therefore it is necessary to perform such plays'.[30] By this time, however, Zhou Xinfang, who had played Hai Rui already in his youth, and had much experience playing another upright official, Judge Bao,[31] had already made up his mind to fan the Hai Rui wind by writing a new Hai Rui play.

Cultural Revolution rebels stressed the link between top government leaders like Zhou Yang and Zhou Xinfang's work saying that Zhou Yang in fact gave the 'assignment' to write the play to Zhou Xinfang.[32] However, Tao Xiong, who was part of the writing group, claims that 'in March 1959, the [Shanghai] Peking Opera Company established a group for the creation [of *Hai Rui Submits His Memorial*], and by early April, Xu Siyan, who 'held the pen', had already written a first draft outline.[33]

---

[30] Shanghai jingjuyuan 'Wuchanzhe' lianhe zhandoudui [United Combat Brigade 'The Proletarian' of the Shanghai Peking Opera Company], *Dadao Zhou Xinfang, xijujie de nan batian* [Down with Zhou Xinfang, the Southern Overlord of Drama Circles] (Shanghai jingjuyuan, Shanghai, July 1967), p.1.

[31] Zhou Xinfang played Hai Rui in 1920 in *Hai Rui can Yan Song* [Hai Rui Impeaches Yan Song] and in 1922 in *Zhu lian xiang cai yuan* cf. *Haigong xiao hongpao quanjuan* (Baowentang shudian, Peking, 1987), p.264 and 278. For a list of the roles staged by Zhou Xinfang see Shanghai Jingjuyuan 'Wuchanzhe', *Dadao Zhou Xinfang, xijujia de nanbatian*, Shanghai, July 1966, p.28 ff.

[32] Shanghai jingjuyuan, 'Wuchanzhe', *Dadao Zhou Xinfang*, p.1; Shanghai shi hongdahui (chou) wenyijie gaoju Mao Zedong sixiang hongqi pipan wenyi heixian lian'gezhan, jingju fenzhan, Shanghai jingjuyuan (ed.), *Piping jingju wenyi heixian ziliao xuanji 1*, Shanghai s.d. (1966), p.1.

[33] Tao Xiong, 'Chenyuan shi'erzai de wenziyu, – tuidao 'sirenbang' dui *Hai Rui shangshu de wuhui* [A Literary Inquisition Undisclosed for Twelve Years – Reversing the Slanders of the 'Gang of Four' against *Hai Rui Submits His Memorial*] in *Hai Rui shangshu*, Shanghai, 1979, p.77. Xu Siyan himself agrees that work began in the first part of March 1959, but being intent on proving that the work was written on the basis of an assignment, argues that Zhou Yang ordered Zhou Xinfang already in early March during a visit to Shanghai to write about Hai Rui, a position shared by Liu Housheng (Xu Siyan, 'Wei Hai Rui shangshu wenziyu bianyuan', op.cit). It does not seem likely, however, that Zhou Yang should have promoted that theme before a decision had been reached after the Shanghai Plenum. In an indirect manner, even the Red Guard sources concede that work on the Hai Rui play had begun well before Zhou Yang's talk with Zhou Xinfang on 9 April 1959 by stating that a first outline had already been written by 8 April, which coincides with the date given by Tao Xiong.

Zhou Xinfang's plan was thus most probably part of a current in political opinion ante-dating the Shanghai Plenum and in fact reflected there rather than initiated. Still, Zhou Yang's intervention in April was important. It gave status to a topic with which Zhou Xinfang had failed but a few months earlier when he wrote his play on Bi Gan. As popular appeal was hardly a criterion for the political leadership when deciding which plays to stop and which to promote, the Bi Gan play must have run into foul political waters. After Zhou Yang's intervention, Zhou Xinfang reset the core features of the plot to include a conflict between the loyal remonstrator and the Emperor himself.

In the aftermath of Zhou Yang's intervention, a full-fledged Hai Rui industry sprang up in Shanghai, with half a dozen new plays commissioned and some older ones rewritten.[34] As early as May 1959, Sun Pengzhi staged *Hai Rui beiqian* (Hai Rui Pulls the Rope) in Shanghai, a play developed in Liaoning Province well before the official Hai Rui wave started.[35] Various articles appeared in the press praising Hai Rui as indomitable, and for 'cursing the dim emperor with straightforward talk'.[36] The senior editor of *Wenhuibao* claimed in May 1959 that it had much 'contemporary significance' (*xianshi yiyi*) to see plays on Hai Rui and Judge Bao.[37]

It seems surprising that Zhou Yang should turn to Shanghai and not to the capital in order to get the Hai Rui plays written. This was most likely due to particular political circumstances. The purge during the Anti-Rightist Campaign had been exceedingly severe in Beijing. The

---

[34] Compare Wagner, 'Politics', p.261 f.

[35] Xi Wen, Yang Zhixun, Xu Juhua, *Hai Rui beiqian [Hai Rui Pulls the Rope]*, in *Juben 1961. 2/3*; for a summary and analysis see Wagner, 'Politics', p.302 ff.

[36] Jiang Xingyu, 'Nan Baogong – Hai Rui' (The Southern Judge Bao – Hai Rui), *Jiefang ribao*, 17 April 1959.

[37] Wen Yibu (=Chen Yusun), 'Bao Gong yu Hai Rui', in *Wenhuibao*, 13 May 1959. The key feature of Hai Rui, he claimed, was to be 'indomitable', *gang*, which meant 'to step forward bravely for justice and truth, to have a fearless spirit completely devoted to the public good'. Such characters were admirable at all times. People would enhance and idealize their features so that they became the 'concentrated expression of closeness to the people' *(renminxing)*. Being based on an historical character, the figure of Hai Rui was 'realistic', while also 'romantic' as 'the embodiment of people's ideals'. True, he said surprisingly, 'we already live during a great period where he who speaks out is without guilt'(a reference to a Mao statement some weeks before); however 'people are nonetheless afraid of possible consequences, but this is like being afraid of ghosts. They only exist in your head'.

capital leadership (i.e., Peng Zhen) had set a goal of cleansing the capital of all 'Rightists'. Even people like Wang Meng who had never been formally made 'Rightists' lost their residence permit. Although the Shanghai mayor Ke Qingshi was a man of the left, he had been unable to push his line in the cultural circles of the city, most probably because the leadership had been installed and continued to be protected by his predecessor, Chen Yi. Compared to the neighbouring province of Zhejiang where the Cultural Bureau lost one half of its 70 members as 'Rightists' in 1957-1958, Shanghai had lost only three out of a hundred.[38] The extensive support for Zhou Xinfang's play from all sections of the city's cultural leadership supports the assumption that the climate for a Hai Rui wind was better in Shanghai than in Beijing.

The selection in Shanghai of Zhou Xinfang's troupe for the big anniversary performance indicated the importance attached to this new propaganda goal. Zhou Xinfang was the most celebrated Peking opera actor in the *qipai* or Shanghai style, and the troupe that he headed had spearheaded the drive for Peking opera reform.[39] In 1956 Zhou Xinfang had sent actors and directors to the Shanghai Drama School to learn 'Sitani', the performing technique of Soviet director Stanislawski,[40] and they were among the pioneers in the development of Peking operas on contemporary themes, many of which eventually were developed into the much-maligned but fairly popular model operas of the Cultural

---

[38] Interview with Jiang Xingyu, 21 May 1989. Jiang was a member of the Shanghai wenhuaju at the time.

[39] 'Shanghai jingjuyuan jieshao' [An Introduction to the Shanghai Peking Opera Troupe], *Shanghai jingjuyuan qingzhu jianguo shizhounian yanchu* [Performances of the Shanghai Peking Opera Troupe for the 10th Anniversary of the Founding of the Republic], Shanghai, September, October 1959, p.2. The Shanghai Jingjuyuan, Shanghai Peking Opera Theatre, had been formed in 1955 through a merger of the Huadong jingju shiyan jutuan (East China Experimental Peking Opera Troupe) and the Shanghai shi renmin jingjutuan (The People's Peking Opera Troupe of Shanghai City). The two troupes continued to coexist side by side within the new framework. The Huadong troupe mostly did new plays, the Renmin troupe traditional plays. Zhou Xinfang was head of the entire theatre, but belonged to the Huadong troupe.

[40] Interview with actors Li Zhonglin, Wang Zhengpin, and Xu Xingye, 21 May 1989, Shanghai jingjuyuan. To this day, Stanislawski has a good name among the members of the Huadong troupe.

Revolution, the *yangbanxi*, with their stress on the key hero and the main conflict.⁴¹

Once the assignment had been confirmed by Zhou Yang, who furthermore obliged by sending copies of Hai Rui's works to Zhou Xinfang,⁴² the local cultural leaders did their share. Li Taicheng, the head of the Shanghai Cultural office, Sun Jun, the Party Secretary in Zhou's Opera company, and Wu Shijian, the vice-head of the company met with Zhou Xinfang to decide that this was to be a 'play given key emphasis' (*zhongdian jumu*). This status entitled it to have extra advisers, and reports in the press, and to enjoy a fairly wide audience.⁴³ The body of advisers was made up of Jiang Xingyu, the only real Hai Rui specialist, Tao Xiong, a leading member of the Shanghai branch of the Democratic League and literary specialist in the Peking Opera Company concerned with Peking opera reform,⁴⁴ Xu Siyan, who did the actual writing, and Zhang Bingkun, who later wrote reviews under the pen name Wei Ming.⁴⁵ In the background everyone down from Zhou Yang to Zhou Enlai's former personal secretary and later Vice-minister of Culture Qi Yanming,⁴⁶ from Shi Ximin to Li Taicheng, from Liu Housheng to the playwrights Tian Han and Cao Yu gave advice.⁴⁷ The

---

41   Among the later *yangbanxi* developed here was *Hongse fengbao* [Red Storm], at the time directed by Ma Ke, the assistant director of *Hai Rui shangshu*. Interview with Ma Ke, Shanghai, 11 May 1989.

42   Zhou Yang sent the *Qiu Hai ergong wenji hebian* [Combined Works of the two Masters Qiu (Jun) and Hai (Rui)], a print of the Kangxi period, as well as the *Hai Gangfeng qi'an* [Strange Cases of Hai the Indomitable], cf. Shanghai jingjuyuan 'Wuchanzhe', *Dadao Zhou Xinfang*, p.1; Zhou Xinfang mostly used the former text, cf. Jiang Xingyu, 'Wo yu *Hai Rui shangshu*', in id., *Mingren yishi* (Zhongzhou guji chubanshe, Chengzhou, 1988), p.133.

43   Compare Shanghai shi hongdahui, *Piping jingju wenyi heixian*, p.2, and Shanghai jingjuyuan 'Wuchanzhe', *Dadao Zhou Xinfang*, p.1.

44   Tao Xiong, *Hongqushu shang* [On the Red Carpet] (Zhongguo xiju chubanshe, Peking, 1987). This is a collection of his earlier essays on opera reform.

45   Compare Wei Ming, 'Shiping Zhou Xinfang de xinzuo *Hai Rui shangshu*', *Wenhuibao*, 27 October 1959, for the identification of the pen name see Shanghai jingjuyuan 'Wuchanzhe', *Dadao Zhou Xinfang*, p.1.

46   Interview with actors Li Zhonglin, Wang Zhengpin, and Xu Xingye, 21 May 1989, Shanghai.

47   Shanghai shi hongdaihui (chou), wenyijie gaoju Mao Zedong sixiang hongqi, pipan wenyi heixian liange zhan pian, Jiangsu sheng wenyijie hongse zaofan silingbu (repr.), *Pipan jingju wenyi heixian ziliao xuanji, Zhou Xinfang fan dang*

history of the genre, the status of the theme, the experience of the authors, actors, and audience, the prominence of the troupe, and finally the growing crisis in the country, with a widening rift among the top political leaders, created an environment where no word in such a play would be perceived as innocent or accidental.

The Play

Evidently, at the centre of this study is the text of the play. It is not quite clear, however, what this text is. There are three published versions, all of which carry the same title *Hai Rui Submits His Memorial*.[48] All three are said to have been 'collectively produced, with Xu Siyan holding the pen'. In addition to these, the archive of the Shanghai Peking Opera Troupe was gracious enough to permit me to copy three handwritten versions of the play, all of which antedate the earliest printed version.[49] The last draft was finished on the very day the Resolution of the Lushan Plenum was published. Zhou Xinfang had taken things into his own hand on 20 July, and on 2 August he and Xu Siyan had gone for a retreat to Qingdao to finish the play. This draft is again written by Xu Siyan,

---

fan shehuizhuyi fan Mao Zedong sixiang zuixing (Wenyijie sanshi niandai heixian renwu pipan ziliao 3), Nanjing, October 1967, p.9.

[48] The first, dated 9 November 1959, is Shanghai jingjuyuan collective with Xu Siyan holding the pen, 'Hai Rui shangshu', *Shanghai xiju*, 1959.2. The second, in which a few changes were made, is Shanghai jingjuyuan collective with Xu Siyan holding the pen, *Hai Rui shangshu* (Shanghai wenyi chubanshe, Shanghai, 1960). The third included changes made in 1961, was printed when the play was rehabilitated in 1979 and is titled Shanghai jingjuyuan collective with Xu Siyan holding the pen, *Hai Rui shangshu* (Shanghai wenyi chubanshe, Shanghai, 1979).

[49] Originally, the writing group had set out to take stories about Hai Rui from the popular tradition and to write a 'play based on stories handed down' (*zhuanshuo ju*), while the 'Outline' already describes a 'historical play' (*lishi ju*). Compare Anon. [Tao Xiong], 'Qian ji (Foreword)', in *Hai Rui shangshu*, Shanghai 1979, p.v, originally written for *Hai Rui shangshu* (Shanghai, 1960) in December 1959. The information that Tao Xiong is the author comes from Fang Zesheng, '*Hai Rui shangshu* bixu jixu pipan' [Criticism of *Hai Rui shangshu* Must be Continued], *Gongren ribao*, 28 May 1966. The first ms, entitled 'An Outline of *Hai Rui Submits His Memorial*, is dated May 1959. It is a draft proposal (*ni*) from the hand of Xu Siyan. The second, the first draft of *Hai Rui Submits His Memorial* in 14 acts, was written between the end of May and 26 June, again by Xu Siyan. The third manuscript is entitled Second Draft of *Hai Rui – The Most Important Thing in the World*. It has 12 acts, and was completed on 27 August 1959.

but there are insertions from another hand, which 'rebels' from the Shanghai Peking Opera Troupe later identified as being Zhou Xinfang's.[50]

From Red Guard sources within the Shanghai Peking Opera Ensemble we know that previous to these, two preliminary drafts had been drawn up,[51] which are not available to me. We accordingly have in our hands six out of the nine known drafts and prints of the play.

In drama, the text used for the performance often differs from the written text, there being cuts, changes, and additions, as well as a tradition of impromptu inserts. In the PRC, furthermore, different censorship rules prevail on different media. Things can be printed that cannot be shown in a film, and things may be said on stage which will not be included in the printed version. I do not have a sound or video recording of any of the performances, but contemporary reviews, Cultural Revolution polemics, and interviews in 1989 with actors who had been part of the original cast reveal some things said and done on stage which do not appear in any printed or even handwritten version and show substantial cuts at the last minute to keep the play at manageable length.

None of the above texts can claim a monopoly as the 'true text'. In fact, this might never have been written, if by the true text is meant a version which the author would have written were he free to write without fear of persecution. As we are primarily interested here in the relationship of the play with the political and social environment at the time, we will make use of all available versions. Their differences will help us to break through the polished surface of the finished printed product, to discover the signs of stress in the crafting and recrafting of scenes and characters as well as the rejection of, or emphasis on, certain options.

According to Tao Xiong, the very first draft sketched by Xu Siyan (i.e., the one finished on 11 April) was to be based on traditional Hai Rui

---

50 Jin Juyuan (pseud. for 'someone from the Jingjuyuan, the Peking Opera Company'), 'Jiekai Zhou Xinfang zhizuo daducao *Hai Rui shangshu* de heimu', [Discovering the Background of the Big Poisonous Weed *Hai Rui shangshu* Fabricated by Zhou Xinfang], *Jiefang ribao*, 24 June 1966. This draft of the play was printed as *Hai Rui shangben* for use by the Shanghai Peking Opera Troupe, without a word being changed. (See the program notes *Shanghai jingjuyuan qingzhu jiangguo shizhounian yanchu 'Hai Rui shangben'* (Shanghai Tianchan wutai, Shanghai, September, October, 1959.)

51 On 11 and 30 April, respectively. ibid., p.2.

plays: 'but as the theme [there] was too restricted, nothing came of it. During the first ten days of May, the second draft [probably identical with the 30 April draft mentioned above] was written with the help of the Ming historian Jiang Xingyu; it dealt with Hai Rui being promoted by [Prime Minister] Xu Jie [1503-83], but acting strictly according to the public interest, keeping to the law when Xu's son bullied the common people; it elucidated the theme [that officials should act] "all for the public interest without selfish considerations" '.[52]

The episode used here later became the focus of Wu Han's *Hai Rui Dismissed from Office* (*Hai Rui baguan*). Tian Han's *Xie Yaohuan* takes up a similar topic.[53] But, continues Tao Xiong, 'during the second decade of May after many negotiations (*shangliang*) with leading cadres and professional artists it was decided to adopt [the theme] of Hai Rui handing in a memorial, and remonstrating [with the Emperor] with straight words in order to better propagate the spirit of the "five not-afraids" '.[54] While according to the second outline, the play would have come out against the patrimonial relationships prevailing among Chinese cadres and would have advocated the full use of the law against cadres and their relatives, this did not seem to be the proper focus in 1959. The new emphasis was on straight remonstrance, and this with the Emperor directly.

There is no traditional play about Hai Rui handing in the memorial.[55] What then is the basis of the plot? On the morning of 16 April, Zhou Yang had made a report to Shanghai literature and arts circles in which he promoted the Hai Rui theme. Immediately thereafter, Jiang Xingyu was called by Shanghai's *Jiefang ribao* [Liberation Daily] with a request to immediately write a Hai Rui story. The text would be picked up at noon. Jiang Xingyu instantly wrote a text of 1500 characters length, the subject matter, motif and structure were approved for publication in the afternoon, but in the evening one of the editors of the paper suggested that the plot should be further developed and that he

---

[52] Tao Xiong, 'Chenyuan shier zai de wenziyu', p.78. This line is confirmed by a similar stress in the 13 May article by the editor of the *Wenhuibao* that has already been quoted in note 37.

[53] Wu Han, *Hai Rui baguan*, *Beijing wenyi*, 1961.1; Tian Han, *Xie Yaohuan*, *Juben*, 1961.7/8.

[54] Tao Xiong, loc. cit.

[55] Lists of traditional Hai Rui plays are to be found in *Hai gong xiao hong pao quanzhuan* (Baowen tang shudian, Beijing, 1987), p.264-89, and in *Hai gong da hong pao quanzhuan* (Baowen tang shudian, Beijing, 1984), p.429-42.

should change the text into a 'short story' for publication on the next morning. The text was finished at ten in the evening.[56] This 'short story' in fact contains all the core characters and plot elements of *Hai Rui Submits His Memorial*. The way in which Jiang Xingyu's story was written illustrates well the combination of rigid 'central planning' and complete chaos in implementation which is so characteristic of modern China.

Zhou Xinfang greatly liked the story, and decided to take it as the basis for his play. Jiang Xingyu later was to pay for the work of this one day with a few dozen struggle meetings, a few years in a 7 May cadre school, and a few years as a factory hand.

The first draft of the play was finished on 26 June. On 20 July, Zhou Xinfang, as one Red Guard source put it, 'suddenly burst forth from his study' and proposed drastic changes.[57] Zhou Xinfang and some other important opera actors became Party members during this month.[58] On 2 August, the day when the Lushan Plenum started, Zhou Xinfang went with Xu Siyan to Qingdao to finalize the Hai Rui play.[59] The Plenum where defense minister Peng Dehuai donned Hai Rui's hat and criticized Mao Zedong ended on 16 August with Peng Dehuai's dismissal and replacement by Lin Biao, but the Resolution was only

---

[56] It was published as Jiang Xingyu, 'Nan Bao gong – Hai Rui', *Jiefang ribao*, 17 April 1959. Its authorship is described in Jiang Xingyu, 'Wo yu *Hai Rui Shangshu*', in Jiang Xingyu, *Mingren yishi*, p.131 f. In Beijing, similar propaganda activities got under way much later. It was not until 15 May that the first article about Hai Rui appeared in a local paper, *Beijing ribao*. The editor's preface listed a number of Hai Rui plays already being performed and referred to the 'upright' Hai Rui in *Tablets of Life and Death*. The text then gives a short summary of Jiang Xingyu's article. On 20 May, *Wenhuibao* began to serialize Hai Rui's life written by Jiang Xingyu under the pen name Bugu (Cuckoo), a bird that signifies spring, and only on 16 June did the Party's national paper, the *Renmin ribao*, carry Wu Han's 'Hai Rui Curses the Emperor' (Hai Rui ma huangdi), which deals with the very episode that had been made the focus of the Shanghai play.

[57] Jin Juyuan, 'Jiekai Zhou Xinfang zhizuo daducao *Hai Rui shangshu* de heimu', *Jiefang ribao*, 24 June 1966.

[58] Anon., *Shanghai wenyijie liangtiao luxian douzheng dashiji (chugao) 1949.3-1966.8* [Chronology of the Struggle Between the Two Lines in Shanghai Literary and Arts Circles (Draft) 1149.3-1966.8], Shanghai, 1967 ?, p.31. Compare Zhou Xinfang, 'Yongyuan wangbuliao zhe zhuangyan de shike' [I Will Never Forget This Grand Moment], *Xijubao* 1959.13.

[59] Jin Juyuan, 'Jiekai Zhou Xinfang'.

published on 27 August. In the meantime, Hu Qiaomu, who at the time acted as Mao Zedong's private secretary, had encouraged Wu Han to write another piece, 'On Hai Rui', which Hu Qiaomu himself rewrote. It was published on 21 August. Zhou Xinfang finished work on his Hai Rui play on the very day when the Resolution was published. He dispatched Xu Siyan to Shanghai to have the manuscript typeset and printed, and began rehearsals for the première, which was to be on 30 September, the eve of the 10th Anniversary celebrations.

In normal situations, a foreign literary scholar dealing with 20th century Chinese texts has only one printed version at his disposal. This version might be the product of endless revisions by the writer, which may be motivated by any number of artistic, political or personal reasons. In the case of PRC texts, there is furthermore much probability of heavy editorial interference without, as a rule, any part played by the writer in this process. The author is often confronted with a product published under his name which bears only faint resemblance to his original text or intention. The object of analysis in these cases is, *strictu sensu*, the published text, and little can be said about the author or the editor. The situation is similar to analysing a finished building. It is possible to dynamize such a static structure by inferring from the finished product the intended interaction with the environment, and by studying the clumsy corners as signs of structural stress (and I had to do this in other cases). The availability of the various handwritten and printed versions of *Hai Rui Submits His Memorial* as well as the available information on the creative process permits us for the first time to study and document the eventual 'static' outcome as the result of (or a stage in) a dynamic process. Rare are the opportunities for such a dynamic interpretation and great its potential methodological implications for the analysis of final 'static' texts. Otherwise legitimate concerns about the inordinate length of this paper should not deter us from making the best of the occasion.

I will first give a short summary of the version published in *Shanghai xiju*. Surrounded by Daoist magicians and eunuchs, the Jiajing emperor is engrossed in his pursuit of immortality. 'Magically', a peach branch appears on the Laozi altar. The emperor thereupon decides to perform the great sacrifice to Heaven suitable only for a time of prosperity and Heavenly support. Premier Xu Jie is to order all officials to write congratulatory messages for the occasion, and magician Wang Jin is to clear an area of the town for a 'Jade Mushroom Terrace' for the 769 magical plants offered to the emperor from all over the country. In the second act, officials crowd outside the palace doors with urgent news but fail to gain access to the emperor. Two ministers then withdraw, but Liang Cai, a lower official, loudly and courageously protests when a Daoist is admitted; he is instantly banished to an outlying region. Premier Xu Jie, who has witnessed the scene, proceeds to write his congratulatory message. In Act Three, Hai Rui enters on stage. He witnesses how Wang Jin evicts people from their homes in a snowstorm in order to build the Jade Mushroom Terrace on the site while pocketing for himself the funds that had been allotted to reimburse them. Hai Rui outwits Wang Jin, who withdraws with the promise to bring the money. When he sees his own subordinate Liang Cai being dragged off to exile, Hai Rui decides to ask the Premier to remonstrate with the emperor. In the fourth act, Hai Rui accuses the Premier of ignoring the plight of the country, but the latter refuses to act, arguing that this would only be suicidal. In the fifth act, Hai Rui 'stumbles through the streets' and decides to hand in his own remonstrance the next morning in the guise of a congratulatory missive. In Act Six, he writes the memorial and orders his coffin to be brought to the palace next morning. His wife fails to persuade him to put his own safety above the nation's interest, and burns the memorial. Hai Rui retreats in Act Seven to the house of his colleague He Yishang to rewrite the text. He Yishang has drowned his distress in wine but, impressed by Hai Rui's stance, smashes his wine pot. The next act, set in court during the audience, contrasts the saccharine congratulations presented by the other officials with Hai Rui's scathing memorial, which makes the emperor spit blood. Hai Rui is sent to the torture chambers in hope that his backers can be found out. He Yishang protests against Hai Rui's arrest in Act Nine, but is flogged in court and jailed. In the next scene the people who were to be evicted 'show their gratitude' and parade in front of the prison with placards and slogans asking for Hai Rui's release. In the last act, Hai Rui is offered what he thinks to be his pre-decapitation wine, but is surprised by an envoy who announces his and He Yishang's release, restoration to their original offices, and promotion. The emperor has just died and Xu Jie has persuaded his successor to make this move. The people outside the prison rejoice at Hai Rui's release. They return an umbrella Hai Rui had lent in the third act to an old woman who was being evicted. It begins to rain, and all crowd under the umbrella. With the words 'straight words are the most important things in the world – the emperor is of little avail, the people are most important' they march off stage. The light goes on again, a gigantic umbrella floats down to cover all of the people on the stage with Hai Rui holding the handle.[60]

Approach: A Political Analysis of the Play

The different drafts, editions, and reviews of the play as well as interviews with those involved in the writing and production allow us to trace the evolution of the play through the tumultuous and difficult years 1959 through 1961. To establish the main framework of the analysis, however, we will begin with analysing the play as officially printed in 1959 in the journal *Shanghai xiju*.

According to the published versions, the play is a 'collective product' of the Shanghai Peking Opera Ensemble with Xu Siyan 'holding the pen', i.e., doing the actual writing.[61] Zhou Xinfang himself rarely wrote because his eyesight had become very bad.[62] Cultural Revolution sources, however, agree with survivors involved in the original production that Zhou Xinfang guided the writing and staged the production in addition to playing the lead, i.e., Hai Rui.[63] In fact, Zhou had the choice to use one of the senior libretto writers of the Shanghai Peking Opera Ensemble like Chen Xiting to 'hold the pen'; instead he asked Xu Siyan, who had no knowledge of Ming history and furthermore was a free-lance amateur of the Peking opera.[64] He neither had the status nor the experience to challenge Zhou Xinfang on any issue. As director, Zhou chose Ma Ke, then a young man fresh from the drama school, instead of one of the more experienced older directors of the Ensemble. In an interview in May 1989, Ma Ke recalled his lowly status, which did not even allow him to ask for explanations of certain passages; and it seems that in the end Ma Ke was altogether dismissed

---

[60] Shanghai jingjuyuan jiti chuangzuo, Xu Siyan zhibi, *Hai Rui shangshu, Shanghai xiju* 1959.2, p.33-51.

[61] ibid., p.33.

[62] Discussion with Li Zhonglin, Wang Zhengpin, Xu Xingye and Ma Ke, Shanghai jingjuyuan 11 May 1989. Compare the line 'oblivious of your weak eyes and white hair, your voice reaches to the hill sides and the beaches...' in a poem by Tian Han written for the 60th anniversary of the beginning of Zhou Xinfang's professional career, *Beijing ribao*, 12 December 1960.

[63] Jin Juyuan, 'Jiekai Zhou Xinfang;' Pipan jingju wenyi heixian ziliao xuanji 2, p.1. The participants of the original *Hai Rui shangshu* production quoted in the preceding footnote confirmed this assessment.

[64] Xu Xingye interview 11 May 1989. Jiang Xingyu, interview 20 May 1989.

from his duties.⁶⁵ Zhou Xinfang put himself into a position of absolute control over all aspects of the play. According to Cultural Revolution rebels, the head of the Cultural Affairs Bureau, Li Taicheng, the Party secretary of the Shanghai Peking Opera Ensemble Sun Jun and the vice head of the Ensemble decided together with Zhou Xinfang from the outset that Zhou should 'personally take command' of the entire process of writing, staging and performing.⁶⁶

After the revision in Qingdao, Zhou sent Xu Siyan back with the manuscript to have it printed under Sun Jun's command 'without a word to be changed'.⁶⁷ Sun Jun's management implies what Jiang Xingyu confirmed in an interview in 1989, namely that Zhou Xinfang got previous approval from the Shanghai Cultural Affairs Office, from the Shanghai Propaganda Department, and from the Shanghai Municipal Committee.⁶⁸ But none of the members of the Peking Opera Ensemble got in a word, although some objections were raised. This level of control allowed Zhou Xinfang a text and an interpretation which he never had to nor did explain to other members of the Ensemble.⁶⁹

The play in its entirety was thus anything but a collective product of the Shanghai Peking Opera Ensemble. Zhou Xinfang's own attitude towards the historical drama accordingly is of some consequence. According to Tao Xiong's note on Zhou Xinfang in the *Chinese Encyclopedia*, Zhou had reacted to every one of the major political developments since the beginning of the May 4th period by selecting and reworking historical pieces in a fashion that joined the contemporary fray.⁷⁰ The play on Bi Gan discussed above continues this

---

65   Interview with Ma Ke, Shanghai, 11 May 1989.

66   *Pipan jingju wenyi heixian ziliao xuanji 2*, p.1.

67   ibid. p.2.

68   Interview with Tao Xiong, Shanghai, 17 May 1989.

69   Tong Xiangling, the actor who played Hai Rui's friend He Yishang at the première in 1959, and Shen Jinbo, who replaced him in this role in spring 1961 were among the insiders joining in the criticism on Zhou Xinfang in 1966. See Tong Xiangling and Shen Jinbo, 'Fan dang tiezheng rushan, xiu xiang menghun guoguan', *Jiefang ribao*, 3 June 1966. As a consequence of Zhou's complete control, the young actors who eventually joined the rebel groups during the Cultural Revolution were unable to dredge up any significant statement by Zhou Xinfang about the Hai Rui play.

70   Tao Xiong, 'Zhou Xinfang', in *Zhongguo da baike quanshu. Xiqu, quyi* (Zhongguo da baike quanshu chubanshe, Beijing, 1983), p.611.

tradition, and in an article in late 1959 Zhou Xinfang, who was in the midst of staging *Hai Rui Submits His Memorial* wrote:

> True, the things on stage are historical stories, but through many excellent traditional pieces as well as new historical plays one still can both reflect the historical face of a particular period and embody the spirit of the present... Most recently, I myself have created two new historical plays, namely 'With Justice Accuse Wang Kui' and 'Hai Rui Submits His Memorial'. In these two plays I made sure to take care of this point.[71]

There are thus good grounds for a hypothesis that *Hai Rui Submits His Memorial* deals not only with history but also with the present.

The Time Frame of the Plot

In the play, as noted, the officials receive orders to compose congratulatory messages for the grand ceremony of the emperor's sacrifice to Heaven, just as Zhou Xinfang's troupe had received the assignment (*renwu*) to write a play for the celebration of the PRC's tenth anniversary on 1 October 1959. Hai Rui writes his memorial for the occasion 'in the guise of a congratulatory message'[72] in order to bring the actual crisis of the country to the attention of the emperor and the court and to suggest remedies. So, too, with the 10th Anniversary of the PRC, the conflict between fact and fiction became such that the festivities commemorating the 'Ten Great Years' had to be curtailed for lack of food and money. By then, many districts were in the grip of famine. *Hai Rui Submits His Memorial* offers a sharply drawn picture of the actual conditions of the country as opposed to the fanciful miracle-stories dreamed up by the claque of the Chairman, accused of fattening themselves on the desire of their master to become 'immortal'.

The play thus accomplishes what Hai Rui's memorial is supposed to do in the text: using the opportunity of a grand festivity to get a hearing for a frank description of the actual situation in the country. The play *Hai Rui Submits His Memorial* is the present-day equivalent of Hai Rui's Ming dynasty memorial.

The political pressure from the ongoing Anti-Rightist Movement had prevented cadres from making realistic assessments of the actual

---

[71] Zhou Xinfang, 'Yuejin, yuejin, yongyuan di yuejin', (Leap Forward, Leap Forward, Eternally Leap Forward), *Wenhuibao*, 22 September 1959.

[72] *Hai Rui shangshu*, *Shanghai xiju*, 1959.2, p.40.

economic situation.[73] Any such assessment was instantly attacked as 'rightist', often followed by the dismissal of the official and his transfer to 're-education' without the right of appeal. This was the situation to which Zhou Yang referred when he said that since the Anti-Rightist movement nobody had dared to speak up.

Not only did *Hai Rui Submits His Memorial* paint a portrait similar to the circumstances of 1959. More than that, Zhou Xinfang used a strategy for getting a public hearing somewhat similar to Hai Rui.[74] The play itself announces this strategy in detail. Hai Rui sings:

> As my eyes see how the court's policies go daily more awry and how people's livelihoods become daily more meagre – how can I retreat for fear of difficulties? If I, Hai Rui, don't step forth with my body erect, who else will dare to lift his head! What a thing! To think that this Jiajing is walled up deep in his Xiyuan palace, hoodwinked on his right and left, believing that great peace reigns under Heaven; and to think the demon Daoists make him believe that there is a hope of achieving long life! Tomorrow at the great ceremony of the sacrifice to Heaven I will submit a memorial in the guise of a congratulatory message to make it clear that there is neither great peace under Heaven nor any hope in prolonging one's life, and when all the ministers proffer their eulogies and His Majesty is elated, my memorial is going to pour cold water over his head! It will, with a shock, awaken His

---

[73] R. MacFarquhar, *The Origins of the Cultural Revolution 2: The Great Leap Forward* (Oxford University Press, Oxford, 1983), pts. 2 and 3.

[74] From the very first outline, the plot was to hinge on the presentation of the memorial to the Emperor, which forms the core of Jiang Xingyu's story. According to the historical sources, however, Hai Rui had not actually personally confronted the Emperor with his memorial; but already in the 29 May Draft, the dramatized Hai Rui uses a ruse to get admitted. In the introduction of his original memorial, Hai Rui had favourably compared the Jiajing Emperor with Emperor Wen of the Han Dynasty. Zhou Xinfang followed Jiang Xingyu in interpreting this as a tactical device to ensure that the emperor would read the memorial. In the Outline, the emperor had charged all officials to present eulogies (*qingci* and *hebiao*) to him for having attained immortality and the Way. Hai Rui claims to have written such a eulogy and gains admittance despite his low rank, because the emperor is flattered that even a man known for his indomitable uprightness would congratulate him. The memorial, however, is not read in court, but in the inner chambers. In the subsequent First Draft, Hai Rui even claims to have studied techniques of immortality with a Taoist master. His prescription, he says ironically, is contained in his memorial. Finally, in the Second Draft, which was finished late in August, the historical conflict between the Jiajing Emperor and Hai Rui is exacerbated by introducing a face-to-face confrontation for 'dramatic

Majesty from decades of superstitious dreams about becoming an immortal and end the decades of distress and suffering of the common folk. And if then I should be flogged in court, be banned to exile or beheaded in the Western City I will die without regrets. Indeed![75]

While the presentation of the memorial was parallel to the staging of the play for the 10th Anniversary of the People's Republic, the remaining acts of the play revolve around speculation as to the possible fate of the cause and of the author. In the Chinese diction, this latter part would be reckoned 'romantic', as it expressed lofty aspirations and hopes for China's future. Being 'romantic', it is rather independent from the historical record, and operates with a deft admixture of symbolism. The first part, by contrast, comes under the category 'realistic' as it dealt historically with sources, and in the present with available facts. Ironically the whole play thus fits the combination of realism and romanticism advocated by Mao since early 1958 and elaborated upon by Zhou Yang and Guo Moruo later in that year.[76]

The Protagonists

That first section of the new historical drama defines the key contemporary problems of society first through the selection of a historical period and cast, and second through the particular reordering and treatment of that period and cast to fit present needs.

Stage time is set in the later years of the Jiajing Emperor. The titles of the first two acts in the printed versions deftly define the problem. The emperor is 'striving for immortality and is letting the government go to rot' while 'one word [of remonstrance] is enough to garner punishment'.

The main problem, according to the printed versions, is thus the clogging of the regular channels of administration by the favourite

---

effect'. This suggestion came from Liu Housheng. (Interview with Tao Xiong, Shanghai, 17 May 1985.)

[75] *Hai Rui shangshu*, *Shanghai xiju*, 1959.2, p.40.

[76] The structure is taken directly from Tian Han's *Guan Hanqing*, which provided the model and guide for these new historical dramas. The Shanghai Peking Opera Ensemble staged a Peking Opera version of *Guan Hanqing* for the 10th Anniversary. There, Guan Hanqing stages the historical play *Dou E yuan*, using the opportunity of the birthday performance for the mother of the Prime Minister. The play contains a 'romantic' part, namely a speculation of what might have happened to Guan Hanqing after he staged *Dou E Yuan*. (Tian Han, *Guan Hanqing, Juben*, 1958.5; cf. my 'A Guide for the Perplexed', p.3ff; p.40, rule U.)

magicians of the emperor. The phrase by Hai Rui's friend, 'If the top beam is not straight, the lower beams will be crooked',[77] attributes direct responsibility to the Emperor himself, although the Premier also places part of the blame on the magicians for 'having poisoned and bewitched his Holy Majesty'.[78] The troubles of the country are known and so are the solutions for them, and there are officials of all levels who even try to bring this to the Emperor's attention. But as the second act shows, they are not admitted into his presence, and most of them are afraid of falling into trouble.

Guo Moruo, whose historical plays at the time set out to defend the Great Leap and the Chairman, opted for other historical screens. His *Wu Zetian* (1960) is set during the height of Tang Dynasty prosperity, and Empress Wu has set up a vast secret information network to keep herself informed about the state of the country and abuses of power by officials.[79] Both features reject the implications of *Hai Rui Submits His Memorial*.

As the putative audience, we are now to identify two factors on the screen of the present, the attitude of the emperor and the officials, and the problems requiring solution. To be sure, we are not interested at this stage in the truth of the criticism encoded in Zhou Xinfang's play, but in its specific content.

In Russia, it had been a rule in Stalin's time that the highest ranking person in a literary piece should reflect on Stalin himself. This device had been imported into China with the result that, at least during the Fifties, villains were never chairmen but at best vice-heads. The Jiajing Emperor, by this device, thus could be expected to be read as Mao Zedong. Mao subsequently, in 1965, identified himself as the Jiajing figure in Wu Han's *Hai Rui Dismissed from Office*.[80] And during the Cultural Revolution, Zhou Xinfang similarly was explicitly charged with slandering Mao through his depiction of the Jiajing Emperor.[81]

---

77   *Hai Rui shangshu, Shanghai xiju*, 1959.2, p.38.

78   ibid., p.39.

79   Guo Moruo, *Wu Zetian* (Zhongguo xiju chubanshe, Beijing, 1962).

80   Stuart Schram (ed.), *Chairman Mao Talks to the People* (Pantheon, New York, 1974), p.237.

81   According to Xu Siyan, Zhou Xinfang responded to his critics at denunciation meetings during the Cultural Revolution: 'You obstinately compare the Jiajing Emperor with Chairman Mao. This means that you have very little respect for Chairman Mao'. Xu Siyan, 'Wei *Hai Rui shangshu* wenziyu bian yuan', *Jiefang ribao*, 3 January 1979.

Since the death of Stalin, the chair of the 'greatest Marxist-Leninist of our time' had stood empty. Mao Zedong certainly considered himself a candidate. By 1958, Kang Sheng declared that Mao indeed was that sage, and he consequently advocated that in the curriculum of the Central Party School the reading of the Marxist-Leninist classics be replaced by Mao's works alone as embodying their insights.[82] Moreover, the 'popular' songs from the mass poetry movement accompanying the Great Leap spoke about Mao ever more in terms of major celestial bodies like the sun eternally illuminating the world.

Mao's intense literary and philosophical activity between 1956 and 1960, when *Hai Rui Submits His Memorial* was last revised, would seem to give the appropriate contemporary resonance for the Jiajing Emperor's yearning for immortality. The Laozi image on the wall, with its white beard, is a fine pun on the omnipresent portraits of Marx, and the Emperor's self-ascribed title 'True Lord of the Miraculous One Flying Towards the Origin' plays on the hagiographical language used in the depiction of Marxist leaders, and Mao in particular. The Great Leap with its flood of reports of miraculous achievements in the countryside is reflected in the miracle plants constantly carried in by the magicians.

In fact, Mao Zedong was seen by many at the time to have surrounded himself with a personal claque of confidants who supported his claim to 'immortality' based on the triumphs of the Great Leap. These confidants superseded the regular government, a point explicitly made by Peng Dehuai at the Shanghai meeting early in 1959. The first scene of the play with the Emperor surrounded by his cronies in his immortality lab thus becomes a spicy satire on the Chairman's quest for ideological immortality and his willingness to believe the most outlandish reports of miracles as sure signs of his unfailing *youdao*, possession of the Way.

Other plays treated the Emperor quite differently. In Tian Han's *Guan Hanqing* (1958), Khubilai Khan is fooled by his favourite Ahmad, but takes proper measures once informed about the truth. In Guo Moruo's *Wu Zetian* (1960), the problems of the country are just rumours fabricated by the Empress's detractors. In Tian Han's *Xie Yaohuan*

---

[82] Compare R. Wagner, 'The Politics of Historical Drama', in id., *The Contemporary Chinese Historical Drama*, p.271.

(1961),[83] the relatives of Empress Wu Zetian conspire to hide the truth from her, but she instantly turns against them when Xie Yaohuan reveals the actual problems. These variants imply radically different assessments of the contemporary variant of the Emperor/Empress. *Hai Rui Submits His Memorial* is quite radical in its attack on the Emperor. In the play, the Jiajing Emperor in fact prides himself that the founder of the dynasty had established the *Jinyi wei*, the Brocade Uniform Brigade, as a secret police to keep the officials under control,[84] and critics are uniformly shipped to the Brigade's quarters for torture and interrogation. During the years preceding the 'present' of the stage, the notorious Yan Song had held the Jiajing Emperor's confidence by combining flattery for the Emperor with ruthless suppression of critics, and had used his power to cruelly punish his detractors like Yang Jisheng, who had criticized his usurpation of power. The officials in the play thus have an experience to go by, and they constantly quote this gruesome example to each other as a reminder of the futility of remonstrance.[85] The frequent repetition of Yan Song's example makes it mandatory to look for a contemporary equivalent. Given the harshness of the references, the option that Yan Song refers to Kuomintang policies concerning Communist critics must be considered. However, Xu Jie was operating under Yan Song, the 'dynasty' was the same, and the same Jiajing was on the throne. We are thus forced to read Yan Song as Zhou Xinfang's reference to the campaigns against Communist critics (Hu Feng) and others during the early Fifties.

The play minces no words in its description of the Emperor. In Hai Rui's statements the monarch is a 'muddled (blind, confused) prince' (*hun jun*), his government is 'without the way' [i.e., a disaster for the country] (*wu dao*); he is a 'tyrant without pity nor justice' (*gua en boyi de baojun*), who 'massacres his officials'. When the Emperor asks Hai Rui whether he has no achievements at all to show for his forty-five years of government, the following exchange occurs:

> Hai Rui: You have, you have indeed!
>
> The Ministers in chorus: His Majesty's merits surpass those of the Three Dynasties [of old when sages ruled the country].

---

[83] Tian Han, *Xie Yaohuan, Juben*, 1961. 7/8. For an analysis see my 'Tian Han's Peking Opera *Xie Yaohuan*', in R. Wagner, *The Contemporary Chinese Historical Drama*, p.80 ff.

[84] *Hai Rui shangshu, Shanghai xiju*, 1959. 2, p.46.

[85] ibid., pp.35, 39, 41, 50.

> Hai Rui: Since Your Majesty ascended the throne, you have built over a dozen Immortality Terraces! (Drum) Have enfeoffed over a hundred Daoists! (Drum) Have consecrated 769 magical mushrooms and immortality plants! (Drum) And countless Immortal Rabbits, Immortal Swans, Immortal Turtles, Deer, Drugs, and Cinnabars! (Drum)
>
> Jiajing:(In rage) What!
>
> Hai Rui: There's more! Your Majesty has given yourself the title of 'True Lord of the Miraculous One Flying Towards the Origin', to which you first added 'Immortal Senior of the Ultimate of Pureness' and then 'Emperor and Prince of Ten-thousandfold Immortality. (Drum) These indeed are Your Majesty's momentous achievements![86]

In fact, in contrast to Khubilai Khan, the Jiajing Emperor is beyond redemption. Zhou Xinfang took from Tian Han's *Guan Hanqing* the medical metaphor of 'licorice root' for the obsequious attitude of the high officials towards the Emperor.[87] From Jiang Xingyu's article he took the comparison of the medicine needed for this sick court, namely the heavy and bitter purgative *dahuang*, as a metaphor for strong remonstrance. In a deft exchange between the Prime Minister and Hai Rui, the Emperor's health is considered:

> Hai Rui: There is an adage 'strong disease requires strong medicine', I have an excellent prescription.
>
> Xu Jie : What is it?
>
> Hai Rui: The Emperor has for decades eaten licorice root so that this disease has already entered the vital region between heart and diaphragm. Therefore he has to now take *dahuang* and *batou* [two strong laxatives] so that His Majesty can have some major bowel movement and his entrails are cleaned out. Only in this way he can return from the dead to the living! *Dahuang* and *batou* can bring the desired result. Swallow the medicine and the hundred symptoms will disappear...
>
> Xu Jie : Ayaya. Your *dahuang* and *batou* are much too violent, much too violent! You! You are neither a high official nor can you cure the disease!
>
> Hai Rui: Although I am not a high official, I can still prescribe drugs to eliminate diseases.

---

[86] *Hai Rui shangshu, Shanghai xiju*, 1959. 2, p.48f.
[87] Compare my 'A Guide for the Perplexed', p.58.

Xu Jie : Perhaps you know that a body that has been sick for a long time is all exhausted; one has to use harmonizing drugs and cure gently in order to be successful.[88]

The disease has already entered the region between heart and diaphragm which means the Emperor is not curable. Consequently, the shift to the romantic part of the play comes about through his death. The hopes for a serious bowel movement by the Chairman were dim.

The Emperor is not just a Daoist adept oblivious to the duties of government. His treatment of remonstrating officials has in fact crippled the capacity of the court to handle the problems of the country. It will be recalled that Zhou Yang had complained after the Anti-Rightist Campaign that 'no one dared to speak up'. The same was most certainly true during the early Fifties. During both periods, critics had been publicly attacked as 'anti-socialist' and even counter-revolutionary, and had been shipped off to remote state farms if not imprisoned. This fate might have been less terminal than that of Yang Jisheng and Liang Cai, but it had similarly affected the articulation of public opinion.

Not all officials react alike, however, and the Shanghai troupe parades the various options on stage. The first official to appear on stage is Premier Xu Jie. He introduces himself as a slick manoeuvrer for whom survival holds top priority. Fully convinced that the Taoist promises of longevity are empty chatter, he accepts without a word of remonstrance the mandate to organize the sacrifice to Heaven and to gather congratulatory messages. The Prime Minister is not intrinsically a bad man; he recognizes talent and even indirectly intervenes for Hai Rui. In fact, the hopes of people like Hai Rui initially rest on him.

Hai Rui: As things stand now, there is only one person able to prompt the Emperor to turn over a new leaf and reform himself.

Xu Jie : Ah, who is that?

Hai Rui: Your Excellency.[89]

But when confronted by Hai Rui, Xu Jie positively refuses to take the measure of the country's plight and denounces the 'madness' of Hai Rui. From this reaction, Hai Rui learns the merits of the popular appellation of the Prime Minister as 'national champion of compromise'.[90] In the historical record, Hai Rui wrote to Xu Jie's son

---

[88] *Hai Rui shangshu, Shanghai xiju*, 1959. 2, p.39.

[89] ibid., p.39.

[90] ibid., p.40.

that the latter's father prided himself as being such a national champion of compromise, and Hai Rui had taken him to task for giving in too much and achieving too little.[91] Within the play, the expression more broadly denotes criticism of the Premier among upright low-level officials. The historical record is being rewritten to fit the needs of the present: that is, to describe Zhou Enlai.

By refusing to risk his head as an upright official and by taking charge of the solemn festivities to praise the Emperor's attainment of the Way, Xu Jie perpetuates and exacerbates the general hypocrisy. 'If you continue to seal your mouth and do not speak up people will ask what difference there is between Your Excellency and Yan Song', says Hai Rui.[92]

Next come two ministers from the cabinet. They want to hand in memorials dealing with disasters in the land. When magician Wang Jin does not admit them into the imperial presence they withdraw without objection, admonishing each other to be 'more tactful'.[93] The implied argument is that the entire top leadership in both state and Party offices do not dare to speak up to the Chairman but, like Zhou Enlai in 1959, busy themselves in the solemn celebration of fake achievements. The satirical high point of this attack on the top leadership comes on the day of the sacrifice. After having obsequiously proffered their eulogies, in which they compare the emperor to all the sage kings of antiquity, the eight top ministers eventually break into a chorus, their hips perhaps swaying in tune with their paean:

> Truly, rivers and mountains are secured for thousands and thousands of years, the altars of the nation are at peace for hundreds of millions of years.[94]

This paean mockingly parallels the congratulatory odes for the 10th Anniversary of the People's Republic in 1959, and serves as a fine counterpoint to Hai Rui's memorial, which is read in court directly afterwards. More generally, the charge implied here, that the top leadership fawns upon and flatters the Chairman, not only finds an echo in the published eulogies on the Great Leap but also in the many protocols of internal discussions during the mid- and late-Fifties among the top Party leaders that have been published during the Cultural

---

[91] Hai Rui, 'Fu Xu Jizhai shangbao shaoqing', in *Hai Rui ji*, vol.2, p.435.

[92] *Hai Rui shangshu, Shanghai xiju*, 1959.2, p.39.

[93] ibid., p.35.

[94] ibid., p.46.

Revolution. The obsequiousness of participants, including Zhou Enlai, Kang Sheng, Mao Dun and others, is painful to read. There is not a single instance available of someone directly disagreeing with the Chairman, remonstrating with him, or simply voicing a strong opinion of his own.[95]

This certainly does not imply that the top leaders always agreed with Mao Zedong. But if they had definite views of their own, they buried them deep in their bosoms and waited for an opportune moment. The play charges that their motive is fear of losing their positions, and this indeed is what the Chairman himself had said in April 1959 at the 7th Plenary Session:

> When people don't dare to speak out, it is for one of the following six reasons: fear of admonition, fear of demotion, fear of loss of prestige, fear of dismissal from the Party, fear of execution, fear of divorce.[96]

Or, in the language of Hai Rui in the 1961 version: 'To protect their families and safeguard their lives, they go through the movements of being officials at court, without in the least caring for the sufferings of the people'.[97]

General statements by Hai Rui about the top officials further stress this feature of hypocrisy originally suggested by Cao Yu to Zhou Xinfang. Hai Rui quotes a popular saying:

> The Emperor only cherishes his might and power; an open word is the harbinger of disaster; the whole lot of officials are of low calibre; they do nothing but flatter.[98]

Hai Rui himself also does not mince his words. The top officials are 'just adapting to the [Emperor's] whims and are but hypocrites' *(xiangyuan)*.[99] In fact, he tells the Emperor that with their flattery 'they commit the great crime of deceiving the Emperor and failing the state'.[100] In this harsh criticism, many of the Hundred Flowers charges against the bureaucrats find a Peking Opera translation.

---

95 Helmut Martin (ed.), *Mao Zedong Texte* (Hanser, München, 1982), vol.4, pp.111, 415.

96 *Miscellany of Mao Tse-tung Thought* (Joint Publication Research Service, Arlington, 1974), vol.1, p.176.

97 *Jingju Hai Rui shangshu*, op.cit., p.20.

98 *Hai Rui shangshu*, Shanghai xiju, 1959. 2, p.39.

99 ibid., p.39.

100 ibid., p.48.

The play not only deplores 'that there is in the entire court not a single official who dares to stick out his head and remonstrate'[101] but suggests that this prevalent attitude is the result of earlier recruitment strategies. When Yan Song ruled supreme, Hai Rui charges, 'he stressed cringing and obsequious smiles, bent heads and obedient ears as the best qualities',[102] and never remonstrated with the emperor. In a conversation with his wife, Hai Rui refers to the present high officials as *weiwei ruruo*, 'yes-men'.[103] The play challenges the recruitment policies of the past and the present which give such prominence to the quality of unquestioning obedience. This is a charge which had been made in 1956-57 by some of the more outspoken critics during the Hundred Flowers, in particular by Liu Binyan who claimed that during the early Fifties the key criterion for Party recruitment had been obsequious obedience to orders from above.[104]

The next brand of officials to appear in the play includes Liang Cai. These are minor officials, also bringing memorials that lay out the problems of the country. They have two different attitudes. One of them immediately refers to the fate of Yang Jisheng at the hands of Yan Song, and claims that for a small official it is best to keep one's mouth shut. In fact, he implies that things are still as bad as they reputedly were under Yan Song, but argues that nothing can be done about it. Liang Cai, on the other hand, a junior official from Hai Rui's *yamen*, risks his life by getting into a shouting match with Wang Jin and with a Daoist magician who has just arrived to present another miracle plant to the Emperor. Liang Cai is banished without further ado, a man who shares Hai Rui's uprightness, but not his strategic wit, a fact already noted in one early review of the play.[105] As this incident is set at the very beginning of the story's time frame, it seems to refer to the Anti-Rightist Campaign that began in mid-1957 and was mostly directed against young 'intellectuals' in the vast Party and state apparatus.

Two other options for officials' behaviour are presented by Hai Rui and his friend and subordinate He Yishang. They fully agree in their

---

[101] *Hai Rui shangshu*, Shanghai xiju, 1959.2, p.41.

[102] ibid., p.39.

[103] ibid., p.41.

[104] Compare my 'Liu Binyan and the *texie*', in id., *Inside a Service Trade* (Harvard University East Asian Monographs, Cambridge, in press).

[105] Wei Ming (=Zhang Bingkun), 'Shiping Zhou Xinfang de xinzuo *Hai Rui Shangshu*', *Wenhuibao*, 27 October 1959.

assessment of the role of the magicians at court as well as in their empathy with the plight of the common people. He Yishang, however, assumes that 'small officials like us cannot do anything about this', and when Hai Rui insists that 'regardless of whether we are high or low-ranking officials, we have to eliminate the cunning and wipe out the evil so as to help the common people in their distress', He Yishang points out where Hai Rui's argument will land him: 'All this might be true, but... in order to eliminate the cunning and wipe out the evil, you will end up having to do your wiping out [of evil] at the very top, Emperor Jiajing himself'.[106] After experiencing the fate of the common people in their eviction at the hands of Wang Jin, Hai Rui forms the plan to personally remonstrate with the Emperor. He Yishang points to the fate of Liang Cai, who is just being dragged by. Eventually, He Yishang is to drown himself in wine.

Amazingly, Hai Rui has a more optimistic perspective than He Yishang, assuming that remonstrance is Prime Minister Xu Jie's duty, and therefore deciding to visit him. Liang Cai's fate notwithstanding, Hai Rui feels that things have improved since Yan Song's times, perhaps not for the common people and the small fry among the officialdom like Liang Cai, but in terms of the capacity of a nationally renowned official like Hai Rui to speak out. Zhou Xinfang's status in the opera world made him into a natural leader, much as Tian Han's in the drama world had put the burden on him to speak out. At least, this dogged assumption that things ought to run as they should prevents Hai Rui from accepting the option of 'withdrawing into the mountains', and motivates him to use all possible channels.

Finally, there are the common people. They regularly suffer and groan, but they neither speak up nor do they rebel. Only upon Hai Rui's promise not to take revenge and to speak up for them if they have a grievance, are they willing to tell their story. They can devise quotable songs and ditties, and they may like Hai Rui a lot, but the play keeps their capacity for independent action at a very low level until Hai Rui galvanizes their support. When Hai Rui is arrested, the 'people' get a separate act to stage a rally in his support with posters, slogans and placards outside the prison.

We are thus left with Hai Rui as the only hope. Everyone above him from the Prime Minister through the entire cabinet lacks the mettle for remonstrance; everyone below him lacks the status and the strategic wit to make such an attempt successful. In this time of frenzied miracles,

---

106 *Hai Rui shangshu, Shanghai xiju*, 1959.2, p.37f.

congratulatory prose, and claims to immortality, Hai Rui is the only one with the factual knowledge, the renown, and the analytical and literary skills to serve as a spokesman for reality, realism, and popular interest. His forté is his adherence to the weakest of Chinese institutions, the law. He outwits Wang Jin with a reference to a law which makes compensation mandatory for people who are removed from their dwellings to make room for government buildings. He outwits the Emperor who arrives in court in his Daoist garb by saying that he bends the knee before Heaven, the Emperor, and his parents, but not before a Daoist. And he outwits the magicians with his memorial. As in the other Hai Rui plays, this element of strategic wit in a dense and difficult situation is always emphasized. It implies the recognition that under the particular Chinese conditions of the late Fifties and early Sixties, the obstinate defense of justice in the style of Judge Bao is hopeless unless it is linked with a strategic talent to make the point in the right time and way. The emphasis on legality and the legal struggle was no rarity at the time among those members of the political class who were critical of the extraordinary discretionary powers of the cadres since the Anti-Rightist Campaign and the establishment of the People's Communes. In 1961, Zhou Enlai himself denounced in the strongest terms this attempt to curtail the Party's powers through legal codifications. Hai Rui in fact operates in the very manner in which Zhou Xinfang proceeded, and in this sense, he echoes Zhou Xinfang himself, who, of course, played his role on stage.

Hai Rui comes onto the stage with much of the symbolic accoutrement of the writer living under conditions which were as tightly controlled under the PRC government as they had been under the Jiajing Emperor. In PRC parlance, the writer's 'realistic' descriptions of social reality were often the only way to alert the leadership to some problem. Hai Rui hands in his report on the state of the nation in a written form, which is publicly presented at the celebration meeting in a fashion similar to a theatrical drama for an audience.

Many of the plot and performance techniques of the 'model operas' (*yangban xi*) of the Cultural Revolution decade are said to have been developed at the Shanghai Peking Opera Ensemble during the late Fifties, especially in *The Red Storm* (1959) (*Hongse fengbao*).[108] Most important among these was the enormous threefold elevation of the

---

[107] Quoted in Qi Benyu, ' Hai Rui ma huangdì he *Hai Rui baguan* de fandong shizhi', *Xin Jianshe*, 1966.3 p.9.

[108] Interview with Ma Ke, the director of *Hongse fengbao*, 11 May 1989.

main hero above normal mankind (*san tuchu*). Hai Rui, although not listed in the official pedigree of these proletarian supermen, easily outdoes them as much in terms of the role he plays in the plot as in terms of the language used to characterize him. He alone represents the people's aspirations, sacrificing his career, family, and life for a lofty goal, and outwitting the powers-that-be through brilliant strategy. The people have heard of him as Hai Blue Sky;[109] he is described by his opponents as 'indomitable, [someone who] does not let things pass' and 'does what he says', 'wreaking disaster' for the officials he impeaches.[110] The Premier knows him as 'upright and exceedingly capable', and 'indomitable'.[111] His wife praises the 'wind of cleanliness in his sleeves' [his incorruptibility], and says that he 'has by nature an upright character and hates evil like an enemy'.[112] And even the prison guard knows Hai Rui is 'devoted to the state and the people'.[113]

His memorial is instrumental in bringing about the rapid death of the Emperor, and thus the ensuing 'change in the overall situation'[114] of the country is solely due to his intervention. His figure is furthermore enhanced by the fact that Liang Cai is one of his underlings, and that He Yishang, who will be the only one to protest against Hai Rui's arrest, again comes from Hai Rui's office, and has been personally inspired by his superior. We have to conclude that the core features of the proletarian heroes of the model operas were developed in the crafting of their counterparts, the pure officials.

The Process of Composition

The Outlines, Drafts and other information at our disposal allow us to trace the growth and development of the play's political critique.

---

[109] *Hai Rui shangshu, Shanghai xiju*, 1959.2, p.37.

[110] ibid.

[111] ibid., p.38.

[112] ibid., p.40.

[113] ibid., p.50.

[114] The phrase is from a comment made by Zhou Xinfang: 'Jiajing was already weakened, and he did not survive Hai Rui's attack; after his death the crown prince ascended the throne and the overall situation changed'. The phrase is quoted time and again in Red Guard sources as evidence for the counter-revolutionary purposes of Zhou Xinfang, cf. Jin Juyuan, 'Jiekai Zhou Xinfang zhizuo daducao *Hai Rui shangshu de heimu*', *Jiefang ribao*, 24 June 1966.

The Emperor's obsession with longevity, his reliance on quacks of all sorts, and his ruthless handling of remonstrators were among the earliest and most stable features of the play once the decision had been made to focus on Hai Rui's memorial. However, given the evident sensitivity of any statement about the Emperor, there is much change in the relevant passages. Only from the Second Draft (August 1959) onward is the phrase 'if the top beam is not straight, the lower ones, too, will be crooked' included, which explicitly lays the ultimate responsibility for the sorry state of officialdom at the door of the Chairman.[115] The Second Draft also had Hai Rui characterize the Emperor to his face as a 'cruel and tyrannical muddled prince' (*canbao de hunjun*),[116] which Zhou Xinfang seems to have again toughened for the premiere to the 'most tyrannical of rulers', (*cuicui bao de jun*),[117] who 'abuses his wanton powers' and is 'brutal and ruthless',[118] while the printed versions just made him a 'muddled prince without pity nor justice'.[119] Mao Zedong had stressed Hai Rui's ongoing loyalty to the Jiajing Emperor as an important feature. Hai Rui, the biography in the *Mingshi* relates, was so overcome by grief at the news of the Emperor's death that he vomited out the delicacies which he had just eaten in what he had thought to be his last meal before execution.[120] Mao's reference to this incident normally would have meant its inclusion into the play. However, as Red Guard critics were quick to point out, Zhou Xinfang did not agree to have this played according to the *Mingshi* text. The Outline had carried this scenario and so had the First Draft, but Hai Rui claimed there that he only wept because he was sorry that the Emperor had neither accepted his remonstrance nor improved his ways before dying.[121] In the Second Draft Zhou Xinfang eliminated Hai Rui's

---

[115] '*Hai Rui – tianxia diyi shi*' *ergao*, p.40.

[116] ibid. p.90.

[117] Jin Juyuan (pseud.), 'Jiekai Zhou Xinfang zhizuo da ducao *Hai Rui shangshu* de heimu', *Jiefang ribao*, 26 June 1966. This article is written by actors from the Shanghai Peking Opera Ensemble with much insider knowledge.

[118] Quoted in 'Zhou Xinfang yihuo gen 'Sanjiacun' heibang shi yi qiu zhi hao (Zhou Xinfang Is a Dog from the Same Hill as the 'Sanjiacun' Black Gang), *Tianjin ribao*, 16 June 1966.

[119] *Hai Rui shangshu*, Shanghai xiju, 1959.2, p.48.

[120] *Mingshi*, Biography of Hai Rui, here quoted from Chen Yizhong (ed.), *Hai Rui ji*, vol.2 (Zhonghua shuju, Beijing, 1962), p.528.

[121] *Hai Rui shangshu' tigang*, p.17; '*Hai Rui shangshu*' *chugao*, p.121.

vomiting altogether and had him just cry shortly, 'The Emperor, Ah'.[122] This was accompanied by '*ji sanqiang*', a musical notation used in Peking Opera to accompany someone 'writing or reading a letter or recalling something that has already been told on stage'[123] – that is, with a musical accompaniment which further undercuts Hai Rui's already meek reaction.

Still, Hai does not rejoice at the Emperor's death, nor does he advocate a change in dynasty with its very far-reaching implications for the present – namely, a change not in the Chairman, but in the system. The plot of the play, however, had this explosive potential. The state of the administration and Hai Rui's imprisonment would certainly have supported such a development in Hai Rui's thinking. Furthermore, there was the precedent of Zhou Xinfang's earlier play, *Hatred in Deer Terrace* (*Lutai hen*), where the killing of the remonstrator Bi Gan by the last Shang king was the signal for a rebellion and the establishment of the Zhou dynasty. Hai Rui's biography in the *Mingshi* links him directly to Bi Gan. After reading the memorial the Emperor is quoted as saying: 'This man might compare himself to Bi Gan, but I am definitely not [the Shang Emperor] Zhou'.[124] In the First Draft, Hai Rui sang in the streets:

> Jiajing, you muddled prince without the Way, how many officials have you massacred since you ascended the throne... You are ruthless and without pity, and since it has come to that, even [the two bad last emperors, namely] Jie from the Xia Dynasty and Zhou from the Shang Dynasty are no match for you.[125]

This reference to the last Shang emperor is taken up in the next scene, where Hai Rui writes his memorial, saying 'today I study Bi Gan's remonstrance of King Zhou of the Shang', because 'the rot of the court of the great Ming Dynasty is daily getting worse'.[126] And later, near death, the Emperor rejects Xu Jie's entreaties and decides to take Hai Rui down with him to the nether world, raging: 'Ah, this despicable swine, that Hai Rui, he compares himself to Bi Gan, doesn't that

---

[122] *Hai Rui – tianxia diyi shi' ergao*, p.105.
[123] 'Ji sanqiang', in Zhongguo xijujia xiehui Shanghai fenhui, Shanghai yishu yanjiusuo (eds.), *Zhongguo xiqu quyi cidian* (Shanghai cishu chubanshe, Shanghai, 1981), p.126.
[124] Biography of Hai Rui in *Mingshi*, ed. cit., p.529.
[125] '*Hai Rui shangshu*' *chugao*, p.46.
[126] ibid., p.53.

calumniate me as being similar to King Zhou of the Shang dynasty!'[127] To this Xu Jie assures him that he is an 'enlightened ruler in possession of the Way'. The Second Draft cut the first long statement, used Hai Rui's studying of Bi Gan, added an implicit reference to Bi Gan through Hai Rui's claim when tortured on stage that he will keep to straight talk 'even if my heart is dug out and my belly slit open',[128] and changes the dialogue between Jiajing and Xu Jie:

> The Emperor: This Hai Rui wants to be comparable to that Bi Gan.
>
> Wang Jin (interrupts): He might want to be Bi Gan, but Your Majesty is not King Zhou of the Shang.
>
> The Emperor: True. In fact, I have the true Way like [the sage emperors of antiquity] Yao, Shun, Yu and Tang.[129]

The printed versions eliminate all earlier references to Bi Gan, and just keep the last quoted lines, in which Hai Rui is not directly charged with comparing the Jiajing emperor to King Zhou. From the constant changes, which I read as signs of stress, we can infer that Zhou Xinfang was well aware of the implications of this historical precedent to Bi Gan. By eliminating Hai Rui's own references to Bi Gan, and only leaving the Emperor's, the editors of the printed versions changed its function. In the printed form, the precedent of King Zhou's killing of Bi Gan prevents the Emperor from having Hai Rui executed straight away, if only for tactical considerations. The scene thus becomes part of the 'romantic' scenario of hope, that the Chairman might deem it impractical to continue terrorizing his critics.

Although we do not know who made the decision to change the first printed version against the stage manuscript, it is probable that this attenuation was not just the result of an internal process within the Shanghai Peking Opera Ensemble. For the restaging of the play in 1961, in point of fact, Zhou Yang insisted on having Hai Rui break into a great wail, vomit and collapse into the arms of He Yishang. Immediately thereafter, another new feature is inserted; the guard exclaims that Hai Rui 'is altogether a loyal heart'. Zhou Xinfang accepted the changes but kept the music.[130] Through Peng Dehuai's identification with Hai Rui, care had to be taken to reinforce those features of Hai Rui such as his

---

[127] *'Hai Rui shangshu' chugao*, p.110.

[128] ibid., p.87.

[129] ibid., p. 95.

[130] Xu Siyan, 'Chongban houji', *Jingju Hai Rui shangshu*, p.94.

loyalty to the Emperor and the non-inflammatory nature of his actions which best coincided with the self-perception and tactics of an entire leadership group which saw itself as the embodiment of the Ming official.[131]

At the same time, though, the terror against remonstrating officials was strengthened through the course of successive scripts. In the second scene of the first Outline, a censor impeaches the Daoist Wang Jin, and is immediately jailed and flogged. In the second and fourth scenes of the First Draft, two censors suffer the same fate and four more ministers ask Prime Minister Xu Jie to hand on their memorials. In the Second Draft no higher official dares to confront the mighty Daoist any more. Only one official remonstrates against the arrest of another official, and is arrested in his turn. The Emperor bans further memorials of this kind and leaves the stage with the injunction that the festivities were to be 'solemn' (*longzhong*). In this version, Hai Rui's subordinate Liang Cai appears for the first time. Introduced here to further stress Hai Rui's grandeur, he is the only official apart from his superior who dares to confront the Emperor's sycophants, and is promptly banned. Between the first Outline and the stage draft, the portrait of the top officials gets ever darker. In the stage draft, none of them shows even an intention to remonstrate, and certainly no one dares. The experiences of summer 1959 with its quickly spreading famine and continuing official Great Leap hyperbole (especially after the Lushan Plenum, with its campaign against 'Right Opportunists') have left their traces in the text.

The same darkening can be observed in the portrayal of the Premier, Xu Jie, whose resonance with Zhou Enlai provides some idea about the leading intellectuals' views concerning the Premier's policies towards the Chairman at that time. Jiang Xingyu's story already casts a gloomy light on him. When Hai Rui inquires whether Xu Jie could be relied upon to remonstrate with the Emperor, a high friend answers: 'The old boss? He was able to survive decades with Yan Song, which certainly wasn't easy; for sure he will not take the smallest risk'.[132] According to the Outline, Xu Jie 'submitted blindly [to the Emperor] and was afraid to irritate him'[133] As noted, though fully aware that the Heavenly signs of favour for the Emperor are only a hoax, he docilely organizes the grand ceremony, and fails to intervene when a remonstrator is jailed.

---

131 R. Wagner, 'Politics of the Historical Drama', p.305 for the documentation on this group.

132 Jiang Xingyu, 'Nan Bao gong – Hai Rui', *Jiefang ribao*, 17 April 1959.

133 '*Hai Rui shangshu*' *tigang*, p.5.

Although sympathetic to Hai Rui, he warns him to wait for the right time, and continues to write his eulogy for the Emperor after Hai Rui has left. In the First Draft, Xu Jie comes to the court with four memorials from officials, announcing in his first aria that he will see how the wind blows before handing them on. After a remonstrating official is banned, Xu Jie sings, 'Firmly close your mouth, and always watch out – that already was the maxim of the sages of old; I'll just have to make sure to always go with the wind'.[134] In his confrontation with Hai Rui, Xu refuses to join in the remonstrance, but maintains that Hai has 'great talent'. Hai Rui's eventual release from prison is engineered by Xu for tactical reasons, i.e., to 'win back the heart of the people'.[135]

In the Second Draft, Hai Rui says that Xu Jie 'is much better than Yan Song', and therefore decides to talk to him.[136] But the third act had already shown Xu threatening a minister who wants to accuse the court of mismanaging the country.[137] When Xu Jie himself refuses to remonstrate with the Emperor, Hai Rui bluntly states: 'When today your Excellency [Xu Jie] locks your mouth and doesn't speak up, people will ask what difference there is between you and Yan Song'.[138] Still, Hai Rui, who owed his own promotion to Xu Jie, concedes that he is 'pliant, magnanimous and full of self-restraint, honours the worthies and lowers himself to meet the scholars, and in this shows great generosity'.[139] In the end these qualities don't count in the dramatized crisis. In the First Draft Hai Rui recalls the popular saying about Xu as the 'national champion of compromise' and concludes himself that he is just a 'Mister Fine, Fine' *(haohao xiansheng)*,[140] who agrees with everything without stating his own opinions. In the Second Draft 'Mister Fine Fine' has become a 'slick operator, fawning and flattering to all sides'.[141] And in the printed versions, he introduces himself as 'I am Xu Jie, the Prime Minister; I am good at adapting to political changes, I seal my mouth,

---

[134] *'Hai Rui shangshu' chugao*, p.27.

[135] ibid., p.112.

[136] *'Hai Rui – tianxia diyi shi' ergao*, p.40.

[137] ibid., p.23.

[138] ibid., p.48.

[139] ibid., p.50.

[140] *'Hai Rui shangshu' chugao*, p.44.

[141] *'Hai Rui – tianxia diyi shi' ergao*, p.54.

avoid expressing my opinion, and put caution first',[142] a very apt description of Zhou Enlai's attitude during this time.

The ever more gloomy light shed on the Emperor and his hypocritical courtiers in succeeding drafts and editions is replicated by the ever brighter colours given to Hai Rui. The revolutionary model operas had subhuman villains, superhuman heroes, and a waverer in the middle who would join the hero's camp. All three are present in *Hai Rui shangshu*. Hai Rui matches Bi Gan from the distant past in his daring, lives up to Wen Tianxiang, the Song loyalist, with his emphasis on the necessity of 'righteousness prevailing' (*zhengqi*), takes over the flame of upright remonstrance from Yang Jisheng, whom Yan Song had slaughtered a few years earlier, and provides the heroic model for 'waverer' He Yishang who is pulled from his drunken stupor and driven to acts of heroism and valour.

The decisive shift to the direct confrontation between Hai Rui and the Emperor from the Second Draft onward gave the ultimate lift to Hai Rui's stature. In this confrontation, it will be recalled, Zhou Xinfang had Hai Rui refuse to recognize the Emperor in his Daoist garb and to bend his knee. He thus has the upper hand from the outset. The first version of this confrontation had long satirical exchanges between the Emperor and Hai Rui, who had gained admission to the imperial presence by claiming that he himself had studied all the Daoist mysteries and had become a master in them.[143] All his statements are puns on his memorial, which he indirectly praises as the panacea for the empire. These exchanges were the drama's most lively pieces, but they were too light in view of the stature of Hai Rui. They were all cut for the performance and the printed editions.

Having elevated Hai Rui above all officialdom, on an equal footing with the Emperor himself, the Second Draft also enhanced Hai Rui's popularity. The original Outline has the inhabitants of Immortals' Lane give a happy reception to Hai Rui outside the prison when he is released. In the First Draft, they rename their lane into Sage's Lane in honour of Hai Rui,[144] but in the Second Draft the people hold a rally outside the prison and in a chorus they sing, 'He offended the Emperor and dared to speak straight words only because he loved the people like his children; to throw him into prison inverts right and wrong. On our knees we offer

---

142 *Hai Rui shangshu, Shanghai xiju,* 1959.2, p.34.

143 *Hai Rui – tianxia tiyi shi,* p.78 ff.

144 '*Hai Rui shangshu' chugao,* p.121.

incense and plead for his release'.[145] The sudden reaction of Xu Jie, who gains Hai Rui's release, is now dictated by popular pressure in support of Hai Rui. The rebellious potential of this scene, which was kept in the first printed version, is evident. The earlier play *Guan Hanqing* had included nothing less than a legitimate political assassination of the chief culprit, and popular petitions for the release of Guan Hanqing. Here, a year later, further forms of popular articulation are paraded on stage. The hero attracting this support is not a revolutionary of peasant origin, but a Confucian official who never questions the legitimacy of the existing dynasty. The Hai Rui play was developing in dangerous ways.

In a second intervention, Zhou Yang had this scene eliminated altogether for the restaging as being 'too modern'.[146] The self-assertive and independent activity of the 'people' was unacceptable, but Hai Rui remained very much the benign saviour, the 'father and mother' of the people, a role in which reform-minded officials critical of the Great Leap preferred to see themselves portrayed.

The Issue

The ineptitude of the Emperor and the obsequiousness of the officials could have been set against the background of either a hypothetical or an actual crisis in the country. In the printed edition of 1959, the moment Hai Rui first comes on stage it becomes clear that the social crisis has materialized. His first words are:

> Hai Rui (behind scene): What a snow storm! (Hai Rui and He Yishang come on stage holding their umbrellas).
>
> Hai Rui: Alas, the climes are out of harmony, the seasons are all awry.[147]

The political climate of the 'present' is defined on stage or in a story in terms of the weather or the season, a common practice in PRC literature. In *Hai Rui Submits His Memorial*, the climes and seasons are out of joint; this is a standard device of Heaven to show its displeasure with the present government. The environment of the above quote

---

[145] '*Hai Rui – tianxia tiyi shi*' *ergao*, p.99.

[146] Xu Siyan, 'Chongban houji (Postface for the Reedition)', *Jingju Hai Rui shangshu*, p.94. The reference there is to 'the leading comrade from the Propaganda Department of the Central Committee', which is the standard reference to Zhou Yang.

[147] *Hai Rui shangshu*, *Shanghai xiju*, 1959.2, p.36.

specifies the crisis. People are driven from their homes and their kitchen utensils are thrown onto the streets to make way for the Jade Mushroom Terrace, where all the auspicious plants and animals are to be kept that have been presented to the Emperor. This scene, 'The Ears Hear and the Eyes See', which shows how Hai Rui personally witnesses the plight of the people, illustrates a doggerel of Jiajing's time which had been quoted in Hai Rui's memorial and alluded to by Mao Zedong: it translates with a pun on the Jiajing emperor, 'Jiajing, Jiajing, [your name means] house after house empty and cleaned outľ'.

The 'present' echoed that of the stage. With the introduction of the People's Communes during the Great Leap, land was 'fully collectivized'. Individual housing was considered in many places a thing of the past and households were dissolved as cooking units, with their implements used as scrap for the steel drive or simply smashed.[148]

The historical situation on stage is presented as a 'present' one, and people on stage speak in the present tense to the audience about their problems. Authors remind the public of the parallelism between the stage time and their own through the use of terms like 'today', (*jintian*), 'nowadays', (*dangqian*) and others, a practice that had been popularized by Tian Han in his *Guan Hanqing*.[149] We might assume that where these terms occur, the author wants the public to be particularly intrigued by the double meaning of the play. I will now try to map out the details of the 'present situation' in the country and to specify the political 'weather'. All statements quoted in the following sections are made by Hai Rui or 'good' people associated with him and are thus, in terms of the play, 'true'.

In Hai Rui's confrontation with the Prime Minister, the situation on the land is presented as one of pressing crisis. Hai Rui asks the Prime Minister:

Hai Rui (agitated): Mr Prime Minister, but have you not seen?

Xu Jie : Seen what?

---

[148] The point has been noted by two actors from the Shanghai Peking Opera Ensemble, Tong Xiangling, Shen Jinbo, 'Fan dang tiezheng ru shan, xiu xiang menghun guoguan [Proofs for Anti-Party [attitude] Mountainhigh, Gone the Dream of Getting by Under False Pretenses], *Jiefang ribao*, 3 June 1966. Tian Han's *Xie Yaohuan* also alludes to this Great Leap feature with the scrapping of agricultural and household implements to erect a Heavenly Pillar in praise of Wu Zetian's New Zhou dynasty. Cf. my 'Tian Han's Peking Opera *Xie Yaohuan*', p.124 ff.

[149] R. Wagner, 'A Guide for the Perplexed', p.47 ff.

> Hai Rui: Natural calamities and human misery – all over the land wailing and crying.
>
> Xu Jie (shocked): Please!
>
> Hai Rui: But haven't you heard?
>
> Xu Jie : Heard what?
>
> Hai Rui: Cries of resentment fill the streets, everybody curses *the present*.
>
> Xu Jie : Stop! No further!
>
> Hai Rui: If nothing is done, people will be completely without any livelihood.[150]

In short, Hai Rui writes in a formula much used throughout this strand of new historical drama at the time: 'The social fabric is coming apart, the affairs of the state are in ruin'.[151] And He Yishang sums up when he sees the plight of the people being evicted from their homes: 'Life here is not different from hell'.[152]

In his memorial to the Emperor, Hai Rui finally writes what his friend He Yishang describes as 'words hot like peppers', *huo lala de huar*, to address the cause of all this distress: 'At present, the officials in the Empire are greedy and the cadres brutal; the taxes and corvee duties multiply; within the country there are natural calamities, and outside there is aggression. The people have nothing to live on, every member of the hundred families is full of hatred, each one of them yells and curses. Already for a long time they are not satisfied with your majesty'.[153] The 'present' here was not in the original text of Hai Rui's memorial, but added by the Shanghai troupe.[154] In terms of contemporary realities, the behaviour of the cadres in enforcing the steel drive, grain deliveries and collectivization, the natural calamities of 1959, and finally the emerging famine provide ample illustration for this text. In the corresponding passages of the original memorandum, Hai Rui deals with many more issues, like robbers and Jiajing's religious policies. As there is no contemporary echo, they have been cut out of later drafts. Whereas the historical Hai Rui does not mention external

---

[150] ibid., p.40.

[151] ibid., p.44. For the expression cf. the index of my *The Contemporary Chinese Historical Drama*, op.cit., sub 'social fabric'.

[152] ibid., p.37.

[153] ibid., p.44.

[154] Hai Rui, 'Zhi an shu', *Hai Rui ji*, vol.1, p.218.

aggression, as the Taiwan straits crisis was in progress in 1959 Zhou Xinfang added a reference.

According to the play, the present crisis is entirely a man-made disaster with the Emperor the main cause. Hai Rui exclaims:

> Jiajing hurts the people by increasing the special and ordinary taxes;
>
> Jiajing hurts the people so that their livelihood is in imminent danger.
>
> Jiajing hurts the people so that they want to weep but have no tears left;
>
> Jiajing hurts the people by indulging in extravagance and reckless use of power.
>
> Jiajing hurts the people so that they become destitute and drift from place to place;
>
> Jiajing hurts the people so that they have no home left to which they could return.[155]

Similar passages abound. Read in the contemporary context, they most certainly give some of the most harrowing and specific accounts in print of the social situation of the country in 1959.

The unwillingness of the officials to remonstrate with the Emperor is due mostly to the latter's ruthlessness, the contemporary parallel of which is stressed by further 'at presents'. He Yishang warns Hai Rui in the midst of the campaign against 'right opportunism' launched against Peng Dehuai and others after the Lushan Plenum: 'At *present* high officials are cut down like grass'[156] and adds shortly afterwards: 'At *present*, autocracy waxes ruthless and tyrannical, and the routine of killing [remonstrating officials] has become second nature'.[157]

It would seem from the text of the play that the crisis lending urgency to Hai Rui's action is a crisis ultimately of the administration *per se*. It is due to the absence of orderly government, the absence of legal protection for the critic, and recruitment policies which favour the obsequious. This assessment coincides in many aspects with that presented in *Guan Hanqing*. There, absence of legal protection and suppression of public criticism were the main issues. The earlier play already alludes to the land question, but by the time *Hai Rui Submits His Memorial* was written, things were coming to a head both politically and socially. The language denouncing the Emperor and the officials has become harsher, and so too the words dealing with the suffering of the

---

[155] *Hai Rui shangshu, Shanghai xiju*, 1959. 2, p.42.

[156] ibid., p.44.

[157] ibid., p.45.

people. In the text used for the 1961 edition, Hai Rui's dialogue with Xu Jie is changed. Hai Rui does not ask Xu Jie whether he has seen 'natural calamities and human misery – all over the land wailing and crying', but bluntly whether he has seen 'the black haired people, the Hundred Families – they have famine in their faces'.[158]

Still, the play seems to have an analytical lacuna at its core. The crisis of the land does not seem to be linked to any policy specifically mentioned in the text. When *Guan Hanqing* was written and staged, the Anti-Rightist Campaign was in full swing, which imparted to Ahmad's control of the courts and the public sphere a concrete counterpart. In *Hai Rui Submits His Memorial*, however, such a counterpart existed in the form of the Great Leap, but the play does not contain specific references to the central issue of the transfer of jurisdiction over the land to the cadres with the establishment of the People's Communes. Later, with the retrenchment of the People's Communes in 1961, demands for the 'return of the land' could be articulated. But in 1959, when the Communes were just being established with much fanfare, and when, further, the campaign against Right Opportunism was in progress, such a demand would have sounded much more inflammatory. Yet such a passage, pointing out the core problem and its core remedy, did exist. Zhou Xinfang wrote it into the Second Draft, and it was in fact used for at least the premier performance, but cut for the printed publications.[159] Speaking to the Premier, Hai Rui says:

> The imperial family and its relatives, the mighty and the nobles take advantage of their powers to monopolize farming land, the peasants have nothing to live on and as a consequence they raise the banner of revolt. As to strategies for the *present*, the only way is to return to the peasants the land grabbed by the mighty and nobles, and that will mean solving the root cause for the troubles.[160]

The 'root cause' for the troubles of the country lies in the monopolization of the land not by wealthy landlords, but by people who rely on their official powers. This type of arrogation of land fitted the modern scene best where land was 'collectivized' and put under cadre

---

[158] *Jingju Hai Rui shangshu*, p.27.

[159] Jin Juyuan, 'Jiekai Zhou Xinfang', loc.cit.

[160] *Hai Rui – tianxia tiyi shi*, p.44.

control.¹⁶¹ The 'romantic' threat included in this exchange was that the dynasty might altogether fall if it did not return the land to the farmers. Xu Jie seemingly agreed with Hai Rui, and even claimed to have submitted such a proposal himself. But in Xu Jie's statement, the grabbing of land was due to the abuses of one single prince, while Hai Rui instantly rejected this standard theory of individual abuses of power. He maintained, faithfully in view of the People's Communes, that it was an ubiquitous phenomenon.¹⁶²

The cut of these passages in the printed edition creates an odd structure for the text. It leaves a very specific lacuna, which in this case had to be filled in by the audience and readers from their own contemporary experience of land 'collectivization' and its consequences. We have singular evidence here for the argument that literary PRC texts do not only interact with social reality, but that at times the readers' own immediate experience and concerns become an essential part of the text without which the text remains incomplete.

In short, we are provided with an analysis of dynastic decline as a consequence of the monopolization of land, the corrosion of regular government with the suppression of the loyal and upright, and the instalment at the Centre of eunuchs, quacks and sycophants around a befouled Chairman who dreams about immortality while rebellion is brewing. Yet the play's depiction of both the main problem and the solution focuses simply on law and legality. The play emphasizes the loss of confidence among the populace and the officials, but it does not preach revolution. When Hai Rui witnesses the eviction of people from their houses, he does not conclude that this government has to be overthrown, but tries to secure for the people the few legal rights they have, in this case that of compensation. The Daoist Wang Jin is bad not because he evicts people, but because he breaks the law by pocketing their compensation money. Hai Rui does not become a rebel of the lakes and marshes, but uses all legal means and tricks to get a hearing with the Emperor. His demands focus on the restoration of legality and orderly government, in short the return of the Centre to its own standards. Against the constant political campaigns and the loss of even the most basic human rights in this period, in which everything was run by the leadership of the 'collective', this stress on law and legality (which also

---

¹⁶¹ Compare the index of my *The Contemporary Historical Drama*, sub 'land, grabbing of' for the sources. Since *Guan Hanqing*, many historical dramas had used this descriptive device to deal with the land policy.

¹⁶² *Hai Rui – tianxia diyi shi*, p.44.

appears in *Guan Hanqing* and was shared by quite a few leading intellectuals at the time) posed an argument that was reintroduced into the Chinese public debate only at the close of the Maoist era.[163]

The Action and the Functions of Literature

What is the function of literature in such a situation? This was a question very much on Tian Han's mind when he wrote *Guan Hanqing*, and it was a question the authors of *Hai Rui Submits His Memorial* also had to address to define their own role.

In the play, two types of literature appear. First, the *hebiao* or *qingci*, congratulatory messages, a genre which in fact flourished under the Jiajing Emperor, and consisted of grand claims of Heavenly favour for the emperor interspersed with a rich lore of Daoist references. The authors here are the *xiangyuan*, or hypocrites as Hai Rui calls them, from the Prime Minister down. Xu Jie is not happy that he has to compose them. He sings in his study:

> Ai! An essay is something that rises from one's genius. But these *qingci* and *hebiao* are nothing compared to the voice of one's heart, and if I now grudgingly oblige, the taste of the product is like wax![164]

He is writing literature, assignment literature at that, to pander to the present court. Assignment literature is a fair description of what Chinese writing was supposed to do in the PRC, and more so than at other times in 1958 and 1959. For the 10th Anniversary of the People's Republic, Premier Zhou Enlai was in charge of organizing the celebrations. Zhou Xinfang had a fine moment when he chose the notorious *qingci* and *hebiao* of Jiajing's time as symbols of present-day

---

[163] This was a charge made against the play by Cultural Revolution polemicists, cf. Qin Dezhao, 'Chuochuan hefa douzhengì de yinmou' [Expose the Dark Plan to use 'Legal Struggle'), *Wenhuibao*, 3 June 1966, see also Fang Zesheng, '*Hai Rui shangshu bixu jixu pipan*', *Jiefang ribao*, 26 May 1966. They had good ammunition to work with. In a long and fine satire from the First Draft, which like other passages of this kind was probably cut because it gave too much satirical lightness to a plot ever more designed to create a very high pedestal for Hai Rui, the Emperor and his cronies ponder under what law they could get at Hai Rui who of course exercised a right and a duty by handing in a memorial. The contempt they show for the law and the frivolity with which the legal subsumption is handled shows them at their very worst. Eventually they sentence him to death under a law banning misbehaviour of a son towards his father.

[164] *Hai Rui shangshu, Shanghai jingju*, 1959. 2, p.38.

celebratory literature. The ubiquity of laudatory prose standing in for serious investigation is stressed in the play by having the entire senior officialdom appearing in court to submit their eulogies; their uniformity is represented in the fact that they can sing them in chorus; they are all the same. The pervasiveness of this kind of literature is further stressed through the confrontation with that single piece which is Hai Rui's memorial.

The play grants that the Prime Minister and probably others do not enjoy writing these panegyrics. That, however, is of little consequence. The question in the play is not whether they enjoy writing them but what their duty should be. In a polemical exchange with Xu Jie, Hai Rui takes up a metaphor from *Guan Hanqing* which had been used in nearly every critical new historical drama to characterize the writings of the 'hypocrites': namely the term *gancao*, licorice root, the sweet mild laxative.[165]

> Hai: Your student is full of hate – at these high officials and senior ministers who proffer these *qingci* and *hebiao*!
>
> Xu: Ah! – Where does your hatred come from?
>
> Hai: I have a good comparison for them.
>
> Xu: What is it?
>
> Hai: They are like the licorice root among the medicaments.
>
> Xu (feigning not to understand): Ah! Licorice root is a prescription, how can it compare to the senior ministers?
>
> Hai: The proverb says, words which grate the ear are bitter like *huanglian*, words which soothe the heart are no different from the sweet taste of licorice root. His majesty enjoys sweet things and loathes bitter things. Therefore when you high court ministers are together with the emperor, you utter all sorts of sweet words and honeyed statements. Is that not licorice root?
>
> Xu: Eh! Is your ridicule of the senior ministers not a bit exaggerated?
>
> Hai: Sadly enough, his majesty wants to become an immortal and seeks the Way. For over twenty years he has not once held court and taken care of political business. This has brought about internal disaster and external aggression, and the people cannot bear their lives any longer! Senior ministers have to speak straight words and remonstrate with the emperor. That is the correct principle (*zhengli*). But when they just babble what he wants to hear they are, in one word, hypocrites.

---

165 Compare the index of my *The Contemporary Chinese Historical Drama*, op.cit., sub 'licorice root' for the references.

To sum up, Hai Rui quotes another popular saying: 'The Son of Heaven ruthlessly uses his mighty powers; an open word is inviting disastrous consequences; all of them [officials] are a sorry lot; they only court the number one'.[166]

In this critical situation, the duty of remonstrance falls on a lowly fellow, Hai Rui of the sixth rank, far below the senior ministers. Hai Rui's 'literature' is of the 'realistic' kind. The play takes care to show him experiencing the real situation of the people when he happens to witness their eviction from their houses. In three scenes at the beginning of the Second Draft which were eventually cut for the performance because the play became too long, Hai Rui experiences the devastation in the countryside, the refugees, and the arrogance of the Daoist quacks on their way to court, who even requisition the horses of officials carrying urgent military messages. (It is a trope occurring in all of the critical historical plays such as *Guan Hanqing, Sun An dongben*, or *Xie Yaohuan*.) In one of these scenes, Hai Rui sang: 'On the entire way fields and villages were deserted and going to ruin, along the way many of the people had starved looks'.[167] The trope of the trip through the devastated countryside in the midst of the Great Leap famine often corresponded to actual trips by the authors to the countryside to familiarize themselves with the situation there. In the next draft, a few months later in 1960, the descriptions became even bleaker.

Hai Rui's lonely mission, matching the role of the play *Hai Rui Submits His Memorial* on the literary scene of 1959, is to do what all the high ministers fail to do. Hai Rui is explicit about the proposed functions of his prescription. 'A massive disease needs hefty drugs', he says. The emperor 'now has to take some *huanglian* and *batou*', 'so that His Majesty can make a major bowel movement and clean out his entrails'. When the Emperor reads the memorial, his reactions were appropriate, 'his body shakes, his eyes stare transfixed, his mouth is open with the tongue hanging out', the stage direction reads.[168] Eventually he spits blood, and never recovers from the onslaught. A short time thereafter he dies.

In Xu Jie and Hai Rui, two different approaches and functions of literature are discussed. Xu Jie's business is not the writing of *qingci*; he and the senior ministers are in charge of the government, and it is the accepted and correct principle (*zhengli*) that they should run the

---

[166] *Hai Rui shangshu*, *Shanghai jingju*, 1959.2, p.39.

[167] *Hai Rui – tianxie diyi shi*, p.8.

[168] ibid., p.47.

administration and correct the emperor where he fails. Instead they are writing assignment eulogies.

Obviously, we are dealing with two different functions; with Xu Jie the duties of the senior leaders are handled, while with Hai Rui the emergency function of literature is treated. Hai Rui, too, is an official, but literature in the PRC is a part of the state apparatus, and writers have quite regularly depicted the functions of literature through a minor official with access to both the Centre and the common people, which is exactly Hai Rui's position.[169]

Different models are provided for the two protagonists. When Hai Rui visits Xu Jie, he reminds him that 'peace in the empire depends upon a Yi Yin and a Gao Yao'.[170] Yi Yin was the minister of Tang, the founder of the Shang, and Gao Yao was minister under Shun. Even under kings who are sages, the fate of the empire depends on the top ministers. Both ministers are renowned for their administrative skill and wisdom, as well as their willingness to enforce laws. Yi Yin sent Tang's grandson into exile until the latter reformed. Through the historical paradigm, the themes of orderly government and legal protection against autocratic and tyrannical behaviour are once more stressed, with the ultimate solution coming not from 'revolution' but from the few correct officials who had survived in this political climate.

For Hai Rui, other models hold true. He finds satisfaction in the belief that 'history' will be written with material like his memorial, and though he may die, he will in fact be immortalized, as opposed to the Emperor who is being destroyed by his immortality drug. Far from being cowed by the fate of Yang Jisheng, he follows in his footsteps. In the first stage version Hai Rui refuses to be afraid of a similar fate; in the 1961 version, Hai Rui explicitly claims that his own enterprise is but the continuation of that of Yang Jisheng. He now quotes Yang's last poem before his execution:

> The breath of my life returns to the Great Void,
> but my red heart will glow through the ages.

---

[169] Compare my 'The Chinese Writer in his Own Mirror: Writer, State, and Society – The Literary Evidence', in Merle Goldman with T. Cheek and C.L. Hamrin (eds), *Chinese Intellectuals and the State: In Search of a New Relationship* (Harvard University Press, Cambridge, 1987), p.197 ff.

[170] *Hai Rui shangshu*, p.38.

Things I left unaccomplished in this life
I leave to the later born to achieve.[171]

Hai Rui's memorial claims to do exactly this, to achieve what has been left unfinished by earlier critics. In a further link, when Hai Rui is sent to the special prison for officials, which closely matches the special prison system for Party officials in the PRC, He Yishang decides to throw in his lot as well. Yang Jisheng did not sacrifice his life in vain, for Hai Rui took up the torch; Hai Rui will not lose his life in vain, for He Yishang follows him, and in this manner eventually things will have to change. He Yishang's reasoning merits attention. Where, he asks, 'would *zhengqi* be left between Heaven and Earth' if no one followed Hai Rui's path.[172] The term *zhengqi* had become famous through the poem by the Song loyalist Wen Tianxiang. There, it embodies all that is correct, orderly, lawful and propitious for the empire. In Tian Han's play, Guan Hanqing felt inspired by this poem in his own battle. Here it seems to signal once more the fact that *Hai Rui Submits His Memorial* inscribes itself politically as within the same tradition.[173]

The play does not envisage a particularly grand role for literature. Within the text, however, the sesame-seed official of the sixth rank that is critical literature, seems to embody the only institution with enough knowledge of the realities in the sidelanes of the cities, access to the top leaders, and guts to risk remonstrance in the face of massive threats. Through the direct confrontation with the Emperor, the critical role of this kind of literature is further stressed. The play does not advocate reckless sacrifice, but rather the use of all tactical and legal means to address the problems of the nation.

Two symbols, both introduced by Zhou Xinfang into the play, highlight the functions of literature; the coffin and the umbrella.

The coffin is brought by Hai Rui to the court when proffering his memorial. In the performance a real coffin was brought on stage. Zhou Xinfang wanted it to look like it was made from cheap wood to emphasize Hai Rui's failure to enrich himself during his tenure. Such a 'realistic' prop on a Peking Opera stage was highly unusual, and goes back to the influence of Stanislawski's realism on the Shanghai school. There seems to have been much opposition against this feature, and the workshop first made a sumptuous coffin, but Zhou Xinfang eventually

---

[171] *Jingju Hai Rui shangshu*, op.cit., p.72.

[172] *Hai Rui shangshu, Shanghai jingju*, 1959. 1, p.49.

[173] Compare my 'A Guide for the Perplexed', op.cit., p.45 ff.

had his way.174 The big coffin on stage during the key scene of the play on the day of the Grand Anniversary emphasized more than words could the treatment a critic could expect to receive from this court.

The play does not glorify writers in general; the opposite is true. One single piece of honest 'literature' is sneaked in among the pile of stale eulogies. True to the principle of the threefold elevation of Hai Rui and his memorial, Zhou Xinfang opted not for the tearful variant of meek pleading for the suffering populace, but for the manly variant of *ma huang*, cursing the Emperor to his face – much as did Zhou Xinfang's play. It shocks both friend and foe. The Premier does not deny the justification of Hai Rui's charges, but considers his plan to submit a memorial worthy of a 'madman' in its total disregard for the consequences.175 He Yishang in his turn concludes after reading the memorial that Hai Rui is beyond the pale of normal mankind (*lun wai de ren*).176

Much as Mao during and after the Lushan Plenum in 1959 denounced Peng Dehuai and his 'right opportunist' co-conspirators, the Emperor here instantly assumes that Hai Rui's memorial is a part of a planned political conspiracy 'with ulterior motives'. The charge that Hai Rui is part of a conspiracy engineered by hidden higher-ups enters the text for the first time in the Second Draft after the Lushan Plenum had ended. The Emperor daydreams about having Hai Rui sliced and torn apart by horses. Eventually, he accepts Xu Jie's sly suggestion that Hai Rui is only after immortal fame for having spoken out and having been killed. Thus the Emperor only is to have him tortured to ferret out his 'co-conspirators'.177 In the earlier versions, much of this was more fleshed out. In the first draft the Daoist Wang Jin chips in with the standard charge that Hai Rui 'is linked to foreign countries'178 and in the second, Hai Rui, when asked who was behind the memorial, claims with another trope that the true author is 'the suffering people'.179

Zhou Xinfang was aware of the implications of the coffin in terms of assessments of the Chairman. Late in 1961, his ensemble was invited

---

174 Jin Juyuan, 'Jiekai Zhou Xinfang', op.cit.

175 *Hai Rui shangshu, Shanghai xiju*, 1959. 2, p.40.

176 ibid., p.44. Hai Rui was in fact partly of foreign descent, his mother coming from a Muslim family from the Indian subcontinent.

177 ibid., p.48 f.

178 *Hai Rui shangshu chugao*, p.99.

179 *Hai Rui – Tianxia diyi shi*, p.91.

to perform the play in the Huairentang, the performance hall at Zhongnanhai, the quarters of the top Party leadership. The performance was attended by Mao Zedong, Jiang Qing, Kang Sheng, Qin Shengrong, Zhou Yang and a host of others. Zhou Xinfang was now confronting the Chairman with his play directly, as his Hai Rui had confronted the Emperor with his memorial. According to actors who were part of this performance, Zhou Xinfang caved in at the last moment and decided not to have the coffin brought on stage in this performance. He felt this was 'all too provocative' (*tai ciji*).[180]

An umbrella is a device designed to protect against inclement weather. As 'protective cover' (*baohusan*) it has a firm place in Chinese political vocabulary. The umbrella makes its first appearance in the First Outline where Hai Rui stands drenched in the rain to give support to the people who are being evicted from their homes; eventually, his servant holds an umbrella over him. In the First Draft, Hai Rui gives his umbrella to an old lady freezing in the snow and gets drenched himself. Symbolically, these gestures mean serving the people. In the last scene the people cheering Hai Rui when he is released from prison give his umbrella back. It begins to rain, and the people crowd under Hai Rui's umbrella. Hai Rui deplores that his umbrella is too small for so many people, but an old man claims: 'Even such a [small umbrella] is already hard to get hold of'. The umbrella represents the protection a person like Hai Rui can provide for the people against inclement political weather. To be sure, the weather has generally improved: it does not snow any more out of season, it just rains, but this also means that many problems and sufferings still persist although Jiajing is dead.

In the Second Draft the 'people break into a collective song in praise of Hai Rui' at the end, with a key line still providing the title for the play at this stage: 'straight words are the most important thing in the world – the Emperor does not matter, only the people are of importance'.[181] The finale was changed in the final draft used for the staging and continuing through the printed versions, with the last scene reaching its full symbolic maturity. Zhou Xinfang himself designed a new ending. After the scene with the small umbrella and the chorused song is over, the curtain goes down. Then suddenly it goes up again, and a huge umbrella held by Hai Rui and lit by multi-coloured lamps covers the entire stage and the 'people' on it, who sing the last line of their

---

[180] Interview with Li Zhonglin, Xu Xingye, Wang Zhengpin and Ma Ke, the assistant director of the play, Shanghai, 11 May 1989.

[181] *Hai Rui – tianxia diyi shi*, p.107.

paean: 'Praise be him [Hai Rui] for a thousand years to come, praise for a thousand years'. Apart from lifting Hai Rui to the highest possible peak, the scene with the large umbrella evidently is laden with symbolic freight. The 'unrealistic' size and colouring of the umbrella makes it part of the 'romantic' dream of future happiness. In this romantic ending of the play, the great umbrella unfolding in Hai Rui's hand over the heads of the 'people' symbolizes their protection from the onslaught of tyrannical government, and the institution of legal guarantees. The scene elevates Hai Rui from a sesame-seed official to an embodiment of the virtues necessary to secure the prosperity of the nation. It would be wonderful if people of Hai Rui's calibre and devotion would have some power, because then they could hold such a wonderfully protective umbrella over the Hundred Families, the common people. Even after the death of the Emperor, the Centre 'would still be' dominated by people like Xu Jie who lack a firm commitment to the people's interests. Hai Ruis will still be needed even in the hypothetical future, after the success of the memorial/play.

Conclusion

The play contains a fairly clear and explicit assessment of the contemporary political situation in the country and at the Party Centre in 1959 China, detailing how the authors saw the situation of the people, the main political problems, and the various roles of the Chairman, the Prime Minister, the senior ministers, and the dramatic intervention of the little official that is literature, which is saved in the romantic conclusion by Xu Jie's use of the good opportunity of His Majesty's death.

There was a sense of impending tragedy in the air. But Zhou Xinfang, writing in 1959, was still staring into an ill-lit future. By 1960, whatever might have been hypothetical in the play had become gruesome reality, and a few changes as well as the new experiences of the audience lent it more actuality than its authors might have wished for.

A last observation provides confirmation for the approach to theatrical interpretation that I have taken here. Communist historical drama operates on a base of class analysis. In this sense, Hai Rui is either a member of the landlord class and all of his actions are but attempts to forestall the inevitable popular rebellion, or he becomes a traitor to his class, and sides with the people for the cause of revolution. The emperor is but the representative of the ruling classes, and therefore by definition reactionary. The new historical drama of the critical variant (there are others) takes neither approach. Its heroes are from the ruling class, but they stand up for the common people. On the other hand, no one in these plays, not even in the romantic parts, threatens to overthrow the emperor. Kubilai Khan remains unscathed in *Guan Hanqing*, as does Wu Zetian in *Xie Yaohuan*.

This curious fact can only be explained in terms of the interaction of these plays with the present. If the new historical drama is to act out the conflicts in the Centre, the theme of overthrowing the emperor would have been bluntly 'counter-revolutionary', and as such highly dangerous. The change in the second printed version of *Hai Rui Submits His Memorial*, where Hai Rui vomits out all the good food and wine of his decapitation banquet in grief over the death of the very emperor who had ordered his decapitation, clearly was written after the events at the Lushan Plenum. The real Hai Rui, and those who continued to make propaganda for this hero figure in the midst of a frenzied 'campaign against right-wing opportunism', asserted deep loyalty to his majesty and never questioned his right to remain the emperor even when remonstrating with him that he should make orderly government the rule and stop wasting his time and the country's fortune in attempts to immortalize himself.

In the same manner, Hai Rui is depicted here and elsewhere as a real hero. The explicit reference to the Confucian bases of his commitment instead of some proto-revolutionary stance amounts to a rehabilitation of certain Confucian values at a time when in the name of cleaning out the dregs of the old society, simple principles of humanly acceptable behaviour were flouted as well. On the screen of the present, a class analytical approach would have eliminated for Tian Han, Wu Han or Zhou Xinfang the very potential of the new historical drama to speak to the political elite about the problems of the Centre in times of crisis when 'straight words' were certainly not possible.

The romantic part of the play was not to be fulfilled during the lifetime of Zhou Xinfang. He was criticized during the Cultural Revolution for directly attacking Chairman Mao in the figure of the Jiajing emperor,[182] and died in prison in 1975. His rehabilitation in 1979

---

[182] After Yao Wenyuan's attack on Wu Han's *Hai Rui is Dismissed from Office* had been published on 10 November 1965, Zhang Chunqiao gave orders on 30 November to Yang Yongzhi and Li Taicheng from the Shanghai Propaganda Department to attack *Hai Rui Submits His Memorial* simultaneously (*Shanghai wenyi liangtiao luxian douzheng dashiji*, Shanghai, 1967? p.63). On 26 December, Peng Zhen came to Shanghai and criticized local 'revolutionaries' for only focusing their attack on Wu Han's play *Hai Rui baguan* and not on *Hai Rui*

as the docile writer of political assignments might have done less honour to him than the better founded charges by his radical critics.

Submits His Memorial (ibid). After much haggling between leaders like Peng Zhen who tried to keep the debate 'academic', Xu Jingxian from the Shanghai city government [in summer 1989 still imprisoned for cooperation with the 'Gang of Four'] published the first attack against *Hai Rui Submits His Memorial* on 12 February 1966 in *Jiefang ribao* under the pen name Ding Xuelei. By mid-1966 the Shanghai papers were carrying many pages of excerpts from speeches against the play made by members of the ensemble as well as by 'workers, peasants and soldiers'.

THE STRANGE CASE OF *LIU ZHIDAN*

David Holm

> Writing novels is popular these days, isn't it? The use of novels for anti-Party activity is a great invention. Anyone wanting to overthrow a political regime must create public opinion and do some preparatory ideological work. This applies to counter-revolutionary as well as to revolutionary classes.

Thus spoke Mao Zedong at the Tenth Plenum of the Eighth Central Committee in September 1962,[1] a conference which marked a decisive swing to the left in Chinese politics. Oddly enough, it seems that for many years Mao's words were interpreted by foreign scholars as an attack on works such as Wu Han's *The Dismissal of Hai Rui* and Deng Tuo's *Evening Chats at Yanshan*.[2] The trouble is, neither of these two works is a novel, and Mao was attacking novels. It is only relatively recently that a better interpretation has been suggested, namely that Mao was referring to the novels *Defending Yan'an* (Baowei Yan'an) by Du Pengcheng and *Liu Zhidan* by Li Jiantong.[3] The former work is now quite well known, at least among Chinese readers, the latter much less so.[4] In fact *Liu Zhidan* became a *cause célèbre*, implicating eventually

---

[1] Stuart S. Schram, *Mao Tse-tung Unrehearsed* (Pelican Books, Harmondsworth, 1974), p.195.

[2] See Bill Brugger, *China: Radicalism to Revisionism 1962-1979* (Croom Helm, London, 1981), p.22. Wu Han and Deng Tuo were of course criticized for their plays and essays, not novels. As Brugger observes, 'The scope for scholarly interpretation in this period was...very wide'.

[3] Sylvia Chan, 'The Blooming of a "Hundred Flowers" and the Literature of the "Wounded Generation" ', in Bill Brugger (ed.), *China Since the 'Gang of Four'* (Croom Helm, London, 1980), p.176.

[4] Du Pengcheng's novel on the Civil War in North Shaanxi was first published in 1954, and quickly became a contemporary classic, selling almost a million copies. It went through a number of editions: the first was published in Beijing by Renmin wenxue chubanshe. English trans. Du Pengcheng, *Defend Yanan*

not just the author and her close associates, but also hundreds if not thousands of seasoned Party cadres. None of this was reported in the Party press at the time. It seems to be a case that merits further investigation.

Liu Zhidan is an historical novel about the life of the North Shaanxi guerrilla leader Liu Zhidan, a revolutionary martyr who reputedly died in battle on the Shanxi front in 1936.[5] It was finally published in three volumes in the late 1970s and early 1980s, almost twenty years after it was written.[6] At first glance it seems a most unlikely candidate for a literary inquisition. Not only is the subject matter of the novel impeccably revolutionary; the style and characterization were also in conformity with the then current norms of Socialist Realism and Socialist Romanticism.

The author, moreover, had an unassailable revolutionary background. Li Jiantong, far from being a troublesome intellectual, was a Party writer who had spent the war years in Yan'an engaged in Party organization work and later at the Lu Xun College of the Arts and the Northwest Literary Work Corps.[7] After 1949 she had worked in Beijing, first as the secretary of the Party committee in the Government Administration Council's Supervision Committee and, after 1954, as chief inspector in the Ministry of Supervision under the State Council.[8] Li also happened to be the wife of Liu Zhidan's younger brother Liu Jingfan.[9]

(Foreign Languages Press, Beijing, 1983). The novel was attacked because of its barely disguised adulation of Peng Dehuai.

[5] On the life of Liu Zhidan see Klein and Clark, *A Biographical Dictionary of Chinese Communism* (Harvard University Press, Cambridge, 1971), pp.585-88. For an official Chinese biography, see Li Zhenmin and Zhang Shouxian, 'Liu Zhidan', in Zhonggong dangshi renwu yanjiuhui (ed.), *Zhonggong dangshi renwu zhuan* (Shaanxi renmin chubanshe, Xi'an, vol.3, 1981), pp.191-228.

[6] The first volume was published in October 1979 by Beijing's Workers Publishing House (Gongren chubanshe). I also have to hand copies of the second and third volumes published in December 1984 and June 1985 by a Beijing publishing house directly under the control of the Ministry of Culture: Wenhua yishu chubanshe.

[7] See *Zhongguo wenxuejia cidian: Xiandai di'er fence* (Sichuan renmin wenxue chubanshe, Chengdu, 1982), pp.385-86. Li's extensive wartime reminiscences have been published in *Yan'an wenyi yanjiu*, 1985, nos.2-4, and 1986, no.1.

[8] *Zhongguo wenxuejia cidian*, loc.cit.

[9] *Renmin ribao*, 6 September 1979, p.4.

The initiative for the project, moreover, came not from Li herself but from the Workers' Publishing House in Beijing. As Li Jiantong explained the matter in her 1979 foreword to the novel, the Workers' Publishing House had the life of Liu Zhidan listed sometime before 1956 in their plan for literary production. This was in connection with a political assignment, namely to produce revolutionary memoirs and biographies of revolutionary martyrs in order to provide political education to factory workers.[10] Thus, if *Liu Zhidan* had been produced as originally planned it would have taken its place among the 'classics' of the late 1950s and early 1960s alongside Luo Guangbin and Yan Yiyan's *Red Crag* (Hongyan), Wu Qiang's *Red Sun* (Hongri), and Liang Bin's *Keep the Red Flag Flying* (Hongqi pu).[11]

The Workers' Press at any rate thought of approaching Li Jiantong. Based on her Yan'an experience and her connection with the Liu family, she had written on the subject of Liu Zhidan before – a short work called *Liu Zhidan at Qiaoshan* (Liu Zhidan zai Qiaoshan) which was published in 1957.[12] So it was natural that the Workers' Publishing House should press her to take on the project. She reports that she was at first quite reluctant to do so: 'Although I had heard people tell Liu Zhidan stories when I was in Yan'an, and had collected a few materials, yet in 1956 I had still not made up my mind to write. The subject was too vast, and I was not prepared for the task either ideologically or artistically…'[13] What concerned her especially was 'a period of highly complex political struggle' in which Liu Zhidan had been involved: 'Even if it were to be a novel, I would still not be able to avoid those incidents. And if I did keep silent about them, then that wouldn't be writing about Liu Zhidan'. Eventually, however, in spite of her misgivings, she gave in to the blandishments of the comrades from the Workers' Press, and agreed to write.

---

[10] Li Jiantong, 'Preface', *Liu Zhidan*, vol.1, p.1.

[11] Luo Guangbin and Yang Yiyan, *Hongyan* (Zhongguo qingnian chubanshe, Beijing, 1962; English trans. Foreign Languages Press, Beijing, 1978); Wu Qiang, *Hongri* (Zhongguo qingnian chubanshe, Beijing, 1959; English trans. Foreign Languages Press, Beijing, 1963); Liang Bin, *Hongqi pu* (Zhongguo qingnian chubanshe, Beijing, 1958; English trans. Foreign Languages Press, Beijing, 1963). All the above novels are discussed by Joe C. Huang in his *Heroes and Villains in Communist China* (reprinted by the University of Western Australia Press, Nedlands, 1974).

[12] Li Jiantong, 'Preface', *Liu Zhidan*, p.1.

[13] ibid.

Liu's worries were not without foundation. What she refers to, among other things, is a well-known incident in 1935, when Liu Zhidan and other leaders of the Shaanxi-Gansu Soviet were stripped of their posts and imprisoned by special representatives from Party Central on grounds of 'right-wing opportunism' and forming a 'feudal clique'. Many aspects of this incident are still quite obscure,[14] but in any case Liu and Gao Gang and others were quickly released after the arrival of Mao's First Army Corps in October 1935. The instigators, doctrinaire leftists in the Shaanxi Provincial Party Committee and in Xu Haidong's 25th Army, were criticized at the time by Mao and again in 1943 at the Higher Cadres Conference in Yan'an, but they continued in positions of authority in the Party and government both in Yan'an and after 1949. Regardless of the rights and wrongs of the case – and popular sentiment was definitely on Liu Zhidan's side – it would have been difficult to write about Liu Zhidan in detail without treading on some very powerful toes. The fact that Liu's close associate in the Shaan-Gan soviet, Gao Gang, had been purged from the Party in the wake of the 1954 Gao-Rao affair only intensified the problem.[15]

When Li agreed to write the biography of Liu Zhidan, it was in full awareness of the political difficulties; the comrades in the Workers' Publishing House were also aware of them. Li was, in fact, strongly discouraged by her husband, Liu Jingfan, and later also by Xi Zhongxun, a leading figure in the Shaan-Gan Soviet and a close comrade-in-arms of Liu Zhidan who had risen after 1949 to become secretary-general of the State Council.[16]

The actual writing process, which took from 1956 to 1962, conformed very closely to realist norms. The preparatory stage took almost two years, during which Li was accompanied by a female comrade from the Workers' Press. Together they travelled around collecting materials and conducting interviews, in the course of which they made several trips to North Shaanxi. Li finally started writing in 1958, and her second draft, completed in the spring of 1959, was still essentially a biography rather than a work of fiction. It was all still 'real

---

[14] The best account of the affair is still that of Mark Selden, 'The Guerrilla Movement in Northwest China: The Origins of the Shensi-Kansu-Ninghsia Border Region, Part II', *The China Quarterly*, no.29 (Spring 1967), pp.74-79. Selden identifies the chief instigators as Zhu Lizhi and Guo Hongtao.

[15] On the purge of Gao and Rao Shushi see Frederick C. Teiwes, *Politics in Mao's Court* (M.E. Sharpe, Inc., Armonk, 1990).

[16] Klein and Clark, p.314.

people and real events'. One result of this, from the artistic point of view, was that there were too many characters for the reader to keep track of. Further discussions ensued with the publishers, and it was decided to turn the book into a novel. The third draft then reflected this change in strategy. According to Li, the Press wanted to proceed immediately with publication, but she insisted on showing the draft to Xi Zhongxun first. As she put it, Xi had been the chairman of the Shaan-Gan Soviet government, a close comrade of Liu Zhidan, and had later been the secretary of the Party's Northwest Bureau. 'Not to have given him a chance to see it would have been a mistake on my part.'[17]

Xi did not finish reading the manuscript until the spring of 1960. His opinion was not favourable: the novel did not bring out the essential character of Liu Zhidan, and he did not wish to approve publication of the novel in its existing form. He did, however, make some suggestions for revision. This, as Li wrote afterwards, was entirely proper, and stemmed from Xi's feeling of responsibility for the revolution and its history.[18]

After this, Li returned once again to Shaanxi to conduct further interviews, and produced a fourth draft in the spring of 1961. This was a substantial re-writing, and Li went on to produce a more polished fifth draft by early 1962, which was printed in a limited trial edition and circulated to key officials in the cultural apparatus and to older cadres who had had experience working in North Shaanxi during the Land Revolution period. Zhou Yang was reportedly pleased with the project, and offered some judicious criticisms, but Li ran into serious trouble from another quarter:[19]

> A high official from a certain province came to Beijing for a meeting, and I also gave him a copy. This man had had policy disagreements with Liu Zhidan during the Land Revolution period, and when I interviewed him in 1956, we had had an argument then and there. But who would have thought that the day after I gave him the manuscript, and without even reading it, he would write a letter declaring that he could not agree to publication; as Party Central had made no resolution on some of the historical events in the book, I as the author could not assume responsibility for writing about them.

---

[17] 'Preface', *Liu Zhidan*, p.2.

[18] ibid. Also involved in consultation at this point were the editor-in-chief of the Workers' Publishing House, the chairman of the editing department, and Ma Xiwu, another veteran revolutionary who had served in the Shaan-Gan Soviet and in Shaan-Gan-Ning.

[19] ibid., p.3.

Party Central of course had already pronounced its verdict on the events of 1935 in the 1945 document 'Resolution on Certain Historical Problems',[20] and so Li's reaction at the time was simply to dismiss these objections out of hand. Publication of excerpts from the book proceeded in *Workers' Daily*, *China Youth* and *Guangming Daily* in the spring and summer of 1962.[21]

Serious trouble was soon to follow. In August of the same year there was a central work conference held at Beidaihe, prior to the meeting of the Tenth Plenum in September 1962. If at Lushan in 1959 it had been Peng Dehuai's letter to Mao that had been the catalyst for a sudden change in direction from anti-left to anti-rightist, at Beidaihe, according to one source, it was the Liu Zhidan affair that recharted the direction, from pragmatic discussions of economic policy matters to a hard new line in favour of renewed class struggle.[22] What apparently happened was that the 'certain high-level cadre' attended this meeting and was able to persuade Kang Sheng, an acquaintance of his, that the novel should be seen as a disguised attempt to 'reverse the verdict' on Gao Gang and, by extension, to exonerate Peng Dehuai. Kang Sheng, who by 1962 was head of the Ideology Steering Group (*Yishi xingtai xiaozu*) within the Central Committee, and again very much in Mao's favour, reportedly passed a note to Mao at the conference reading, 'Using novels to carry out anti-Party activities is a great invention'. Some days later Mao formally read the note out to the meeting, and a virulent struggle broke out, with Kang Sheng taking the lead in accusing Xi Zhongxun, Liu Jingfan and Li Jiantong of anti-Party activities.[23] As Kang Sheng clearly had Mao's backing, no-one was willing to speak up in opposition.

Shortly thereafter a directive was issued by the Central Propaganda Bureau, ordering publication of *Liu Zhidan* to cease. The source of the order was Kang Sheng. *People's Daily* and the monthly *People's*

---

[20] 'Guanyu ruogan lishi wenti de jueyi' (20 April 1945), in Mao, *Selected Works*, vol.4, p.341.

[21] See e.g., Li Jiantong, 'Xingxing zhi huo – changpian zhuanji xiaoshuo "Liu Zhidan" xuanzai', *Zhongguo qingnian* 1962, 15/16, pp.14-19. A short summary of volume 1 (Wen Jun, ' "Liu Zhidan" shangjuan neirong jieshao') was published in the same issue, pp.19-20.

[22] Lin Qingshan, *Kang Sheng waizhuan* (Zhongguo qingnian chubanshe, Beijing, 1988), p.193. This work, originally published in Hong Kong, was selling like hotcakes in China in late 1988 and early 1989.

[23] ibid., p.195.

Literature had no choice but to abandon their plans for serialization, which were already well advanced. Kang Sheng next wrote to the Party Central Office demanding that the novel be taken up as a political case. Here he met some initial opposition from the chairman of that office. Meanwhile he ordered the Workers' Publishing House to print 600 copies of the fifth draft and 300 copies of the third, to be sent to the Party Central Office for investigation.

At the Tenth Plenum in September Kang Sheng was able to press home his attack, and a special investigation team (*zhuan'an zu*) was set up to investigate *Liu Zhidan*, with Kang Sheng at its head. According to Kang Sheng's interpretation, there was an anti-Party group composed of Xi Zhongxun, Jia Tuofu, and Liu Jingfan, and the novel *Liu Zhidan* was their 'program' for 'taking over the Party and the country'.[24] In the next few months, the author of the novel, the three supposed principals, the officials of the Workers' Publishing House, and the old cadres Li Jiantong had visited were all blacklisted or brought under investigation. Between 1962 and 1966, large numbers of provincial-level cadres from the five northwestern provinces (Shaanxi, Gansu, Ningxia, Qinghai and Xinjiang) were transferred to Beijing for 'study'; and all were implicated in having taken part in an anti-Party group. The precise dimensions of this purge have yet to be examined in detail, but it clearly involved hundreds if not thousands of seasoned revolutionary cadres. Many of these cadres were at the level of provincial department head (*si-juzhang*) or above. In some provinces the provincial-level leadership was effectively hamstrung.

The author herself, for a start, was repeatedly asked to supply an account of how the novel had been written, and more ominously, her notebooks containing her records of interviews were confiscated. This meant that the investigators had a more or less complete record of all persons with whom Li had been in contact, and this was then used as evidence against people who might not otherwise have been involved, such as many basic-level cadres in the former guerrilla areas. Many of them were implicated for no other reason than that Li Jiantong had interviewed them.

Even people unconnected with Li's work came under suspicion. Most prominent among these was the poet Ke Zhongping. Ke, the self-styled 'Mayakovsky of the Chinese revolution', had been a prominent and powerful figure in the cultural scene in Yan'an, well-known for his declamatory verses and for his enthusiastic espousal of Mao's cultural

---

24   'Preface', p.4.

populism.[25] He was hardly a dissident writer, but rather an impassioned revolutionary romantic with considerable stomach for the less glamorous aspects of the Party's organizational work in cultural circles. Ke, too, had been inspired in Yan'an by stories of the great guerrilla leader Liu Zhidan, and in 1948 he had begun work on an epic poem about Liu, with the blessing of Mao Zedong and Liu Shaoqi. He was to spend the rest of his life on this unfinished and ill-fated project.

First, in 1953, the project was seriously affected by the Gao-Rao affair: Gao Gang had appeared as a character in the epic. Then, in December 1962, in the wake of the Liu Zhidan affair, Ke Zhongping's poem was attacked by the Shaanxi Provincial Party Committee at the instigation of Kang Sheng and labelled an 'Anti-Party epic poem'. Ke was 'struggled' for a month and was urged by his friends to give up the project, but he refused and continued to work on his manuscript under increasingly difficult conditions and in great personal stress, until his sudden collapse and death in October 1964. He was given a private funeral, and was only rehabilitated and re-buried at public expense in September 1979.[26]

Others fared as badly, or worse. Though no verdict was ever reached in this 'special case', the struggle against those under investigation intensified, if anything, during the early years of the Cultural Revolution. Yao Wenyuan added his considerable weight to the chorus of condemnation, and Kang Sheng, by this time an adviser to the Cultural Revolution Group, was able to ensure that the prosecution continued. Li Jiantong's and Liu Jingfan's work unit came under attack for having continued to employ them, and Red Guards from Tianjin and Beijing formed a 'Special Case 62 Unit' (*Liu'er zhuan'an bingtuan*), liaison offices of which were set up in Changsha and Yan'an. There was a big-character poster campaign, even in remote Zhidan County in north

---

25   See David Holm, *Art and Ideology in Revolutionary China* (Clarendon Press, Oxford, 1991), pp.48-49, 130-31.

26   Wang Lin, 'Hongxin si huo shuangxue zhong – Ke Zhongping de yi sheng', in Wang Lin (ed.), *Ke Zhongping shiwenji*, vol.4 (Wenhua yishu chubanshe, Beijing, 1984), pp.259-61. Ke Zhongping's own statement on the affair is his 'Guanyu wei wancheng changshi de jiancha fayan' (3 December 1962), ibid., pp.281-88.

Shaanxi, and many of the people under investigation since 1962 were 'nabbed' by Red Guards. Even local peasants who had served as Li's guides when she was travelling in North Shaanxi were 'struggled', and a number of them reportedly beaten to death by Red Guards.[27] Kang Sheng apparently turned all of the materials accumulated in four years of investigation, including Li's record of interviews, over to the student groups.[28]

Many of the victims suffered grievously. In 1967 Jia Tuofu died after struggle sessions in the outskirts of Beijing. In January 1968 Li Jiantong, her husband Liu Jingfan, and Ma Wenrui were all arrested at the same time. Ma Wenrui was to spend five years under military guard in a garrison near the capital, and Xi Zhongxun, who was also 'nabbed', was put away for eight years. Liu Jingfan, who refused to cooperate or furnish a statement, was dealt with as an active counter-revolutionary, was handcuffed and sent to prison for seven years. The author herself was detained in an underground bunker under the direct control of Kang Sheng, watched over by an armed guard, and in 1970 was expelled from the Party without notice and sent to undergo reform through labour.[29]

These verdicts were reversed only in late 1978, after the Third Plenum of the Eleventh Central Committee in December of that year. A low-level anonymous campaign against the by-now-deceased Kang Sheng, referred to only as 'that adviser' (*neige guwen*) or 'the authority in the realm of theory' (*lilun quanwei*), had started in the media in 1978.[30] In January 1979 a special joint meeting of the editorial boards of *Wenyibao* and *Wenxue pinglun* was held in Beijing: angry sessions were devoted in large part to denouncing the activities of Kang Sheng – still not as yet mentioned by name.[31] Among the many cases of writers and their works incarcerated in Kang's 'literary prison' (*wenziyu*) that were raised specifically at the meeting was that of Li Jiantong and

---

[27] ibid., p.11.

[28] ibid., p.6.

[29] ibid.

[30] See *Wenxue pinglun* for 1978. Kang Sheng had died in December 1975. Thinly veiled anonymity was maintained at this time probably because of Kang Sheng's close relationship to Mao.

[31] 'Jiefang sixiang, xunmeng qianjin', *Wenyibao* 1979, 1, p.3.

Liu Zhidan.[32] Approval for publication soon followed, and the first volume of *Liu Zhidan* subsequently appeared, in an austere grey and white cover design, in October of that year.

• • • •

So what was all the fuss about – if, that is, a 'special case' that took so many lives and hamstrung the senior Party cadres in five provinces can be called a 'fuss'? This is not easy to ascertain.

If we look at the text of the novel itself, there does not seem to be anything that remotely merits the treatment meted out to it. This is not an anti-Party novel, but rather a slightly fictionalized biography of a revolutionary hero who was also an exemplary member of the Chinese Communist Party. The attitude of the author towards her hero is entirely positive, and the virtues she extols are in conformity with the communist virtues and intra-Party norms as these were understood in the 1950s. There is in my mind no question of allegory here: *Liu Zhidan* simply does not fit into the ironical mould so evident in the Hai Rui plays and other historical dramas of the post-Leap period.[33] There is no latent satire of Mao Zedong. Rather, there are frequent passages in which Liu Zhidan, from 1928 onwards, is said to have drawn inspiration and understanding of correct revolutionary strategy from Mao's example.[34] The emphasis on armed struggle, on revolutionary base-building, and on revolutionary flexibility and adaptation to local rural conditions, as against the rigidity of urban-based left doctrinairism – all of these were standard ingredients in the Mao Zedong myth, and all of them find a prominent place in the story of Liu Zhidan. Thus Liu is presented essentially as a model for the application of Mao Zedong Thought. Liu, of course, was also safely dead, having been killed on campaign during the Red Army's brief foray into Shanxi in 1936. One would have thought he posed no threat to Mao. The content of the novel, then, is insufficient to explain the furore which overtook it in 1962. We must simply look elsewhere.

---

[32] Qi Xuan, 'Jiakuai luoshi zhengce de bufa, chedi jiefang wenyi de shengchanli', *Wenyibao* 1979, 1, p.5.

[33] On *Hai Rui baguan* and other historical plays see Rudolf G. Wagner, *The Contemporary Chinese Historical Drama: Four Studies* (University of California Press, Berkeley, 1990).

[34] *Liu Zhidan*, vols.1-3, passim.

One other avenue of approach is to look at the actual charges levelled against Li Jiantong and her associates. This is not entirely straightforward. Li was not actually told in 1962 or at the time of her arrest what the charges were, but she later heard indirectly about them from her guards. As relayed to Li, the charges can be summarized under five points:

1) that *Liu Zhidan* was an anti-Party novel;
2) that the author had 'appropriated' Mao Zedong Thought;
3) that she had made the Shaan-Gan Soviet look too good, in order to set it up in competition with the Central Soviet area in Jiangxi;
4) that Xi Zhongxun, who appeared in the book in the guise of an alias, had been portrayed as a young and vigorous leader, and that this was intended to serve as political capital for Xi's plans to take over the Party;
5) that Li had written about struggles in political line within the Party.

To take these points one by one, the argument that *Liu Zhidan* was an anti-Party novel was of course the most serious of these charges. According to Li, it rested primarily on an identification of a certain character Luo Yan with Gao Gang. Kang Sheng's argument presumably was that Gao as a disgraced leader should not appear at all. The reason given for this identification was that Gao Gang was known to have sent a letter at one point to the Zhaojin Soviet in 1932; in the novel Luo Yan is mentioned as sending a letter to the Zhaojin Soviet. Li pointed out, however, that many Party cadres had sent letters back and forth all the time. Furthermore, Luo Yan was a fiction, a composite character who took on the actions and characteristics of five historical persons. Thus even if there were some of Gao Gang in the character, logically this could not amount to more than 20 per cent. In any case, such circumstances did not constitute propaganda for Gao Gang.[35] This of course was to apply the logic of the late 1970s to the charges of the early 1960s, when very different discursive rules were in operation, but it is hard nevertheless not to agree that the prosecution's case was

---

35 'Preface', p.7. This explanation is consistent with the way in which she fictionalized an originally historical work, viz., names of living persons were changed, and the overall number of characters reduced by combining several historical personages into one fictional character.

exceedingly thin. On the more serious question of a 'Xi-Jia-Liu anti-Party group', more anon.

The second charge was that Li had appropriated ('plagiarized' – *piaoqie*) all of the central tenets of Mao Zedong Thought and conferred their discovery on Liu Zhidan. As we have seen, Li had gone to some lengths to avoid any suggestion that she was doing this. Li's angry rebuttal to this charge was to assure her accusers that her novel was full of praise for Mao Zedong Thought, and that it had been written to demonstrate how in the period of democratic revolution, right and left opportunism both led to the defeat of the revolutionary forces, and that it was only Mao Zedong's line that had led the revolution to victory.[36] Given the frequent cross-references in the novel to Mao and the Jinggangshan model, it is hard to find anything of substance in the charge against her. The radicals, of course, would and no doubt did retort that this homage was insincere, merely a smoke-screen to put vigilant proletarian revolutionaries off the scent.

The third charge, that she had made the Shaan-Gan Soviet look too good, is closely related to the second, and Li's response was to ask 'Where have I written anything that is contrary to history?' She further noted, 'When I began writing *Liu Zhidan*, my method was to understand ten parts and write only one part... It is all pure milk, with no water added to thin it down. At the most I added a bit of sugar to sweeten it up a bit so that people would find it easier to swallow'.[37] Again, it is hard to escape the conclusion that there was no genuine problem with the novel itself.

The fourth charge, that the novel made propaganda for Xi Zhongxun, is one that Li Jiantong answered again by referring to her creative method: 'In fact the characters in my novel are all fictitious, with the exception of a few revolutionary martyrs'. To have branded so many of the characters in the novel as 'bad people', moreover, was quite absurd: after all, they had managed to create a revolutionary base area – did Party Central want that or not?[38]

The fifth charge, that Li had written about 'line struggle', amounted to a charge that she had broken the rules regarding public discussion. If so, they were rules that had very recently been changed. Li reports that when her interrogators asked her why she had written about line struggle, she had replied, 'Chairman Mao tells us to write about it'.

---

36   'Preface', p.8.

37   ibid., p.9.

38   ibid.

Their response was, 'But Chairman Mao hasn't talked here about line struggle'.[39] What they meant to imply was that it was not permissible to write about issues or historical events on which there was as yet no definitive official pronouncement. This was clearly contrary to Li's understanding of the situation, for Mao had in fact written a great deal about political struggle with left-wing doctrinairism and right-wing opportunism in the Party, and the Party had also pronounced officially on the events of 1935. Again, thus, this strikes one as a trumped-up charge. Nevertheless, there is something that makes *Liu Zhidan* rather different from all other novels about the revolutionary period. Novels like Ding Ling's *The Sun Shines Over the Sanggan River* or Wu Qiang's *Red Sun* place the depiction of 'line struggle' within the Party in an entirely fictional, geographically localized context, and touch only incidentally on the main theatre of line struggle at Party Central. *Liu Zhidan* was different. Rather than a fictionalized appendix to history, *Liu Zhidan*, for all its rewriting, was still a novel that featured real historical people, and the main outline of its plot was provided by the history of the northwestern Shaan-Gan base area. Clearly it was this feature of the novel that made it such fertile grounds for the play of paranoid fantasies.

But was Kang Sheng really a paranoid? Let us turn to the question of a 'Xi-Jia-Liu anti-Party group'. After the death of Jia Tuofu in 1967, this epithet was changed to the 'Xi-Ma-Liu clique': 'With only two people left in the "Xi-Jia-Liu" group, they couldn't really constitute an anti-Party clique, so they added Ma Wenrui'. The sole reason why Ma Wenrui was included, according to Li Jiantong, was that he had been interviewed by the author and his name therefore appeared in her notebooks.[40] Later, the accusations upgraded the conspiracy to a 'Peng [Dehuai]-Gao [Gang]-Xi [Zhongxun] anti-Party group', and finally to a 'Northwestern anti-Party group'.[41] Clearly the accusations became more inflated as time went on.

What can we find then about those who were accused that might seem to merit the accusation levelled against them?

Xi Zhongxun, a native of Fuping county in Shaanxi, was one of the early leaders of the Communist guerrilla movement in Shaanxi, and from the 1920s onward worked closely with Liu Zhidan, Gao Gang, Li Zizhou and others. In early 1934 he was made chairman of the

---

[39] ibid., p.10.

[40] ibid., p.6.

[41] ibid., p.10.

Revolutionary Committee of the newly established Shaan-Gan Soviet, with Liu Zhidan as chairman of the Military Committee. Later, during the Civil War of 1946-49, Xi had worked together with He Long and Peng Dehuai in the military campaigns of the northwest. After 1949, he was one of the top officials in the Northwest Party Bureau and the Northwest Military and Administrative Committee. He was transferred to Beijing in 1952-53, where he soon rose to become secretary-general of the State Council and in 1956 a full member of the Party's Central Committee. By 1962 he was one of a handful of China's most prominent leaders.[42] His past associations with Gao Gang and Peng Dehuai may have made him vulnerable to attack, but there is no evidence to link him with any conspiracy.

Jia Tuofu was a native of Shenmu county in the far north of Shaanxi and, like Liu Zhidan and the rest of that generation, joined the Party through modern secondary schools such as the Yulin Middle School. Unlike the others, however, Jia spent the early 1930s in the Jiangxi Soviet, and returned to Shaanxi only with the Long March. In 1935 he had an important role as a liaison officer during the merging of the Jiangxi 15th Army Corps with the local 26th and 27th Armies – thus he was directly involved in the events of that year. The details of that involvement remain obscure. After war service in Shaan-Gan-Ning and the North China base, Jia returned to the northwest and, like Xi Zhongxun, served in the Northwest Military Affairs Commission from 1950 to 1952 under Peng Dehuai. He had been active in finance and economics, and after his transfer to Beijing he was made a vice-chairman of the State Planning Commission under the leadership of Gao Gang. Like Xi, Jia became a full member of the Central Committee after the Eighth Congress in 1956. There are some indications that he may have fallen from favour in 1959, as his name does not appear as expected in a number of key committees.[43] Like Xi, Jia would have been vulnerable because of his former close association with Gao Gang and Peng Dehuai.

Like his elder brother, Liu Jingfan had attended the Yulin Middle School, joined the Party, and had gone on to work in the Shaan-Gan-Ning government during the war, attaining a position of some prominence. He was transferred to Beijing in 1949, where he became vice-chairman of the People's Supervision Committee under the

---

[42] Klein and Clark, pp.312-14. Wolfgang Bartke, *Who's Who in the People's Republic of China*, 2nd edn. (K.G. Saur, Munich, 1987), pp.533-34.

[43] Klein and Clark, pp.171-72.

Government Administration Council. Thus he worked in the same office as his wife. In 1955 he was transferred to the Ministry of Geology, where he held the rank of vice-minister.[44]

Ma Wenrui, a native of Suide, was like the others actively involved in the Party in Shaanxi from an early date. Later, like the others, he held posts in the Shaan-Gan-Ning government. From 1947 to 1954 Ma served as the director of the Organization Department of the Party's Northwest Bureau, a position in which he was directly subordinate to Xi Zhongxun. He was transferred to Beijing in 1954 to head the Ministry of Labour, a post which he held at least until the mid-1960s.[45]

The careers of all these people follow a similar pattern, and there is no doubt that they (and others such as Liu Lantao, Wang Shitai and Ma Mingfang) comprised a group of high-ranking and experienced Party cadres with similar experience and outlook. In terms of Whitson's analysis of Chinese military elites, all of them were closely associated with the First Field Army elite.[46] In all cases their experience would have given them a strong antipathy toward the urban-based left-wing doctrinairism of people like Wang Ming and Kang Sheng, and a strong commitment to intra-Party norms as these were understood before 1959. There is no direct evidence of any conspiracy.

We might also investigate the identity of the 'high official from a certain province' who tipped off Kang Sheng in 1962. Who was he? Li Jiantong is reticent, as are all other published sources.[47] We know from Li's account that he had played an active part in the struggles during the 1930s between the guerrilla movement in Shaan-Gan and the urban-based Shaanxi Provincial Party Committee. We might have suspected that our mystery cadre was active on the side of the left-opportunists in the Provincial Party.

The identity of the official would remain a mystery, but for a private communication from a person who had been closely involved in the events of 1962. The 'high-level official' in question was Yan

---

[44] ibid., p.588.

[45] ibid.

[46] William Whitson, *The Chinese High Command* (Praeger, New York, 1973), pp.101-22.

[47] Lin Qingshan, who seems to have ferreted out the names of many of those purged in the Liu Zhidan affair, also fails to identify this key link, and refers to him merely as 'a trusty of Kang Sheng'. The official biography of Liu Zhidan is also careful not to reveal the names of any Party members who were involved in the 1935 action against Liu.

Hongyan, who in 1962 was based in Yunnan and had duties involving Party and military affairs. He had been elected an alternate member of the Central Committee at the Eighth Party Congress in 1956.[48] He was thus someone in a position to put a word in Kang Shang's ear.

What is there in the pattern of Yan's early career that would make him so sensitive about Liu Zhidan? Contrary to what one might have expected, Yan was not an urban-based doctrinaire revolutionary. He was a native of Shaanxi, and after military service under a local warlord he joined the Party in 1925. He then moved to Shanxi, where he was one of the main organizers of the Western Shanxi Guerrilla Detachment (*Jinxi youjidui*). This force was active in the Lüliang Mountains under Party leadership until it moved across the Yellow River to the North Shaanxi base in late 1931. Yan was one of its military commanders, with a reputation for considerable bravery in action.[49] The guerrilla detachment itself became an important component in the military forces of the North Shaanxi base, operating under the overall leadership of Xie Zichang.[50]

What is significant in all this for understanding the *Liu Zhidan* affair is that there was considerable friction between the leadership of the Party's two base areas in the Shaanxi-Gansu area. The Shaan-Gan base of Liu Zhidan and the North Shaanxi base of Xie Zichang were only amalgamated in 1934. Friction dated back to a notorious incident in late 1931, when the North Shaanxi Guerrilla Detachment, composed largely of troops from the former West Shanxi Detachment, forcibly disarmed and disbanded the Nanliang Guerrilla Detachment of Liu Zhidan, with some loss of life.[51] It is well known that during the 1940s many of the North Shaanxi faction, including Yan Hongyan, did not get on well with Gao Gang, who had become the leader of the Shaan-Gan faction after Liu Zhidan's death. Partly because the 'historical problems' were never definitively resolved, animosities carried over well into the post-Liberation period.[52]

---

[48] Klein and Clark, p.1018.

[49] See esp. Ma Peixun and Li Weijun, 'Bozhong Jinxi, jieguo Qin-Long – huiyi Jinxi youjidui diyi dadui de geming douzheng', *Shaanxi wenshi ziliao xuanji*, vol.6 (1979), pp.77-90.

[50] Wu Daifeng, Ma Peixun, and Ma Yunze, 'Huiyi Zhongguo gongnong hongjun Jinxi youjidui', *Shanxi wenshi ziliao*, vol.20 (1981), pp.1-35.

[51] 'Guanyu Xibei hongjun zhanzheng lishi zhong de jige wenti', *Dangshi tongxun* 1986 no.8, pp.3-4.

[52] They were still alive and bedevilling the work of Party historians in the early 1980s. For a discussion of some of the issues, see Li Zhongquan and Hu Minxin,

Why was Yan Hongyan particularly sensitive to the prospective publication of Li Jiantong's novel? The key to this further mystery is to be sought, almost certainly, in the events of 1935. The Sufan campaign remains to this day one of the least documented and least understood episodes in pre-1949 Party history. I cannot begin to investigate its complexities here, and I have as yet no information on the part Yan Hongyan or any of the other North Shaanxi leadership played in that movement. It is clear from the above, however, that the long-lasting antipathies generated by the incarceration of Liu Zhidan and the Shaan-Gan leadership had become entrenched by the 1950s within the very heart of the economic planning apparatus in Beijing, among other places.

In spite of our incomplete information, it does not seem likely that there actually was an anti-Party plot. Why then did Kang Sheng choose to act as if there were, and why did he get away with it? The answer will be found in the changed nature of the relationship between Kang and Mao in the wake of the Peng Dehuai affair. Previously, in the late 1940s and early 1950s, Kang Sheng's career had been in the doldrums. He was widely held responsible for the excesses of the Cadre Inspection and Forced Rescue Movements he had launched as head of the Social Bureau of the Party in 1943-44, and after Mao had intervened to stop the wave of imprisonments and forced confessions Kang Sheng had fallen from favour. After the Lushan conference, however, this changed, for it was Kang Sheng who, in his *Hongqi* article of October 1959, had provided the badly-needed theoretical justification for Mao's harsh treatment of Peng Dehuai.[53] Henceforth Kang was to be one of Mao's closest advisers on ideology. His activities in 1962 clearly set the stage for his ascent to national power in the Cultural Revolution.[54]

Who then were his real targets? It is not impossible that Xi Zhongxun, Jia Tuofu and Ma Wenrui, as powerful figures in the Party's Northwest Bureau at the time, had been in some way responsible for Kang Sheng's 1944 disgrace. If there is some truth in this, Kang's actions in 1962 would presumably have been motivated partly out of a

---

'Shaan-Gan geming genjudi shi yanjiu zongshu', *Dangshi tongxun* 1986 no.3, pp.27-31.

[53] *Hongqi*, 1 October 1959, 'A Communist should be a Marxist-Leninist, not a Fellow Traveller of the Party', mentioned in Klein and Clark, p.427.

[54] Kang emerged from the Tenth Plenum as a new member of the Party's Central Secretariat (Klein and Clark, p.428).

desire for personal revenge. Xi Zhongxun, given his office as secretary-general of the State Council, was clearly no small fry.

It was clearly Mao, however, whose changed state of mind allowed Kang Sheng to gather so much power into his hands. Mao's change of behaviour after the Peng Dehuai affair has often been remarked upon.[55] Whereas before, Mao had been content to operate within a framework of collective leadership and had been willing to tolerate the expression of diverse opinions, after Lushan he became increasingly suspicious, intolerant of others' opinions, and jealous of his prerogatives as Party leader and rightful proprietor of Mao Zedong Thought. Kang Sheng was quick to spot this change and sensed an opportunity for himself and for his previously discredited 'ruthless struggles and merciless blows' style of intra-party struggle. So one might say in a sense that the real target of Kang's attack on *Liu Zhidan* was Mao himself. By attacking *Liu Zhidan*, Kang could pander to Mao's vanity and his suspicions, and thereby create a new situation in which more firmly entrenched targets could be brought within striking distance.

Circumstances at the time would have helped to confirm Mao in his suspicions. Kang Sheng brought the *Liu Zhidan* novel to Mao's attention at the same time that Peng Dehuai was seeking to have his verdict reversed; and it also was well known that Xi Zhongxun had been close to Gao Gang before the latter's disgrace. Xi had even gone to see Gao after he had been named as the leader of an anti-Party clique. It seems he had made this visit as a friend, in order to try to prevent Gao's suicide, but Gao's widow, who maliciously started to name all of Gao's contacts, managed to put Xi in a bad light. Mao chose to believe Kang Sheng, who interpreted Xi's actions and his involvement with the *Liu Zhidan* novel as an attempt to reverse the verdict on Gao Gang.[56]

Regardless of Kang Sheng's motives, the consequences of the case for the development of the cult of personality and official ideology generally are crystal clear. Henceforth, only the revolutionary exploits of the great helmsman could be celebrated; the idea that anyone else could have reached similar conclusions about revolutionary strategy independently of Mao was rendered quite unthinkable. As Li Jiantong herself notes,

> The most ridiculous thing of all was that they monopolized the ideas of armed struggle, the peasant movement...such that before Mao Zedong pronounced on these questions, nobody was allowed to have said anything

---

[55] Teiwes, *Politics and Purges*, pp.439-40.
[56] Frederick C. Teiwes, personal communication, July 1989.

about them or put them into practice. Whoever did put them into practice was guilty of the most heinous of crimes.⁵⁷

Mao Zedong Thought henceforth was to be Mao's alone, and the contributions of other revolutionary leaders would be eclipsed. Thus in the area of Party history there was to be a shift from a relatively healthy pluralism to an historically untenable monism, and, we note also, a decisive shift in the direction of doctrinaire leftism. The *Liu Zhidan* affair was part of this process. Not Liu Zhidan but his enemies were vindicated. Essentially what this amounted to was an attempt to read back into the 1930s the position of absolute dominance that Mao occupied, or was persuaded he ought to occupy, in the 1960s. Kang Sheng and his secret police held this ideology in place until Kang's death in 1975. Subsequently, the decision by the Third Plenum in 1978 to release *Liu Zhidan* for publication should be seen not just as a measure to reverse an egregious case of injustice, but also as part of an overall plan to make Mao Zedong Thought and the Chinese revolution once again a collective creation.

What has this case to teach us about the politics of historiography and literature in China? The most important point is this: in Western studies on the relation between politics and literature, it is still all too often taken for granted that the principal contradiction was between 'the Party', on the one hand, and dissident intellectuals on the other. This case should make us pause and reflect. *Liu Zhidan* was not remotely a dissident historical novel. It was not, it seems, artistically innovative in any way, and it praises proletarian heroes like Liu Zhidan for their '*partiinost*' – their Party spirit. It obeyed all the tenets of Socialist Realism and reportage literature. And yet it was not only attacked, but attacked far more violently than anything since the Hu Feng campaign of 1955. At the very least, the history of literary politics of the 1960s will need to be re-written.⁵⁸

---

⁵⁷ Li Jiantong, 'Preface', p.8.

⁵⁸ One might even argue that the *Liu Zhidan* affair was just as important in its way as the criticism of Wu Han's play *Hai Rui baguan* in 1965. Its importance has been overlooked not only because it was 'in-house', and the purge conducted behind closed doors, but also because the victims were not prominent May Fourth-style intellectuals of the kind with whom foreign scholars usually like to identify themselves. The new information now available in the post-1979 flood of reminiscences has yet to be digested and incorporated in any systematic re-writing of the literary history of the 1960s in China.

The conflict in this case cannot even be seen in doctrinal terms, as a conflict between left doctrinairism of the Internationalist kind and the rural communist ideals of the guerrilla base areas. Not only is the principal contradiction to be located within the Party itself, but more particularly within the tangled nexus of personal relationships among veteran revolutionaries who had been friends and foes, patrons and clients since the 1930s.

Every Chinese writer of literature or of Party history needs a patron, or as the Chinese say, a *kaoshan*, a person as solid as a mountain on whom one can lean. Li Jiantong's relationship with Xi Zhongxun was clearly of this kind, and Xi in his turn doubtless had his own *kaoshan*. But in this case Peng Dehuai fell from power, and the mountains moved, conspiracy or no conspiracy. Li Jiantong became a victim, trapped between the task of commemorating a dead revolutionary hero and the bitter jealousies of powerful survivors.

QU YUAN AND THE ARTISTS: ANCIENT SYMBOLS AND MODERN POLITICS IN THE POST-MAO ERA

Ralph Croizier

For Chinese intellectuals, traditional and modern, Qu Yuan (338-278 BC) has been one of the most enduring symbols of moral rectitude and creative genius in the face of political oppression.

The remarkable posthumous career of the ancient poet-statesman has recently been described in Laurence Schneider's *A Madman of Ch'u: the Chinese Myth of Loyalty and Dissent*.[1] In this fascinating study, Schneider unravels the various layers and meanings of the Qu Yuan myth including its significance in the 20th century intellectual revolution. He ends with Qu Yuan in the 1970s firmly expropriated by the new historical orthodoxy of the Cultural Revolution which pictured the anti-Qin statesman of 2,300 years ago as just another defender of Legalist principles at that crucial juncture in ancient China when 'feudalism', the next stage in Marxist historiography, triumphed over 'slavery' and its Confucian defenders. There was a contemporary political moral behind this bizarre reinterpretation: the new stage of modern Chinese history, i.e., the 'new things of the Cultural Revolution', must prevail over conservative or restorationist forces, i.e., Confucius in ancient China, Zhou Enlai and his Party bureaucrats in the present.

It was a strange place to find Qu Yuan, eternal hero to centuries of Confucian scholars, as just another example of the Cultural Revolution turning traditional historical interpretations on their heads. But, significantly for our purposes, even the Cultural Revolution leftists wanted to appropriate Qu Yuan for their own cause.

---

[1] Laurence Schneider, *A Madman of Ch'u: The Chinese Myth of Loyalty and Dissent* (University of California Press, Berkeley, 1980).

This appropriation did not last for long. The ink was scarcely dry in Schneider's book before political and artistic events in China changed Qu Yuan's image over again. Just as the Maoist radicals had feared, 'ghosts and monsters' from China's historical past would not stay dead. With the repudiation of the Cultural Revolution at the end of the 1970s, Qu Yuan rose again, no longer confined in a pseudo-Marxist historiographical strait-jacket, but as a living symbol for present times. Partly, he represented the reconnection with China's past after the depredations of the Cultural Revolution. More specifically, he stood as a rebuke to political tyranny and a reassertion of the moral autonomy of the intellectuals.

This new Qu Yuan was more prominent in art than in literature, although there was one famous cinematic reference to him in Bai Hua's controversial screenplay, 'Ku Lian' (Bitter Love). But it was the artists, mainly traditional-style painters, who fleshed out the ancient poet's most recent reincarnation. The image they created spoke to more than just the art world.

There was good precedent for attaching contemporary significance to Qu Yuan both in earlier 20th century China and in the long Confucian past where scholars had grappled with the often conflicting demands of political loyalty versus moral integrity, social duty versus artistic expression. Qu Yuan, although not a Confucianist in his lifetime, was a natural choice for later Confucian scholars. In politics, his martyr's suicide (by drowning in the Milo River) made him a symbol of individual integrity, of persecution and neglect; in the arts, he was, in one sense, the father of Chinese poetry. There had been a long tradition of poetry before the 3rd century BC, but Qu Yuan was the first individual to have his name tied to a substantial body of surviving early poems. Moral duty (principled loyalty to the state) and personal expression (in poetry, the highest of the literati art forms) came together in this one historical symbol. And finally, to assert the individualistic and creative side of the Confucian personality, there was the freedom from social constraint and note of artistic wildness that was associated with 'the South'.[2] In Qu Yuan the tension between inner and outer, self-cultivation and social service, which Benjamin Schwartz identified

---

[2] Schneider, pp.80-81 for a discussion of literary and cultural associations with the South.

as a central polarity in Confucian thought,[3] was contained and, as Schneider so convincingly demonstrates, 'mediated'.[4]

Small wonder, then, that the poet-statesman of Chu became an increasingly common motif in literary and political discourse in the Confucian society of later times. And as painting emerged in the Song-Yuan period as a scholar class art form almost equal to poetry in prestige, small wonder that Qu Yuan and the body of poems attributed to him (The Chu Ci, 'Poems of Chu') became a frequent theme in literati painting.

The famous Song figure painter Li Gonglin (c. 1040-1106), established the convention of depicting Qu Yuan through multi-panel handscrolls illustrating the *Jiu Ge*, (Nine Songs), part of the *Chu Ci*.[5] The mountain spirits, river goddesses, and cloud deities in those poems – representations of this mystical shamanistic nature-worshipping religion of the ancient Chu area – are tamed by these later artists into rather restrained depictions of genteel scholarly figures [Illustration 1].[6] Qu Yuan himself appears as a quiet, dignified Confucian scholar, with little trace of the passionate emotionality that was traditionally associated with 'the South', or of the political implications behind his tragic death.

Yet as handscrolls of the 'Nine Songs' proliferated in the succeeding Yuan dynasty, generally following Li Gonglin's Confucianized iconography, there must have been some political edge on this literary symbol. Although the paintings themselves and texts or

---

[3] Benjamin Schwartz, 'Some Polarities in Confucian Thought', in Arthur Wright (ed.), *Confucianism and Chinese Civilization* (Atheneum, New York, 1964), pp.3-15.

[4] Schneider, pp.209-11.

[5] Deborah Del Gais Muller, 'Li Kung-lin's Chiu-kot'u: A Study of the Nine Songs Handscrolls in the Sung and Yuan Dynasties' (PhD diss., Yale University, 1981), 3 vols.

[6] Deborah Del Gais Muller, 'Chang Wu: Study of a Fourteenth Century Figure Painter', *Artibus Asiae*, vol. XLVII (1986), pp.5-50. Besides illustrations of three surviving Nine Songs handscrolls by Zhang Wu, an artist of only middling reputation, this article has portraits of Qu Yuan 'after' Li Gonglin and the very famous Yuan master Zhao Mengfu. Two Chinese publications from the late 1950s provide an even fuller collection of artistic images and literary references to them. *Chu Ci Huihua Ji* [Collected Paintings of the Chu Ci], (Beijing, 1958) and Ah Ying, 'Qu Yuan jiqishi pian zai meishu shang de fanying' [Qu Yuan and His Poems Reflected in the Fine Arts] in *Chu Ci Yanjiu Wen Ji* [Collected Research on the Chu Ci] (Beijing, 1957), pp.309-17.

1. After Zhao Meng-Fu, Portrait of Qu Yuan, one of ten album leaves in 'Nine Songs' album, ink on paper, The Metropolitan Museum of Art, New York.

inscriptions associated with them do not reveal it, the frequent visual references to Qu Yuan at the very least reminded viewers of a scholar-official who had sacrificed his life out of loyalty to a doomed ruling house. This could not help but be a source of consolation, if not inspiration, to the Song loyalists, scholars who refused to take office under the conquering Mongols.

Still, throughout the later Yuan and the Ming the sedate, scholarly depictions of Qu Yuan seemed to emphasize the literary, or perhaps generally cultural, side of the ancient poet-official rather than the political meaning of his actions. Only at the end of the Ming, when Confucian scholars and officials were again torn between loyalty to a fallen dynasty and service to effective new rulers, did the depiction of Qu Yuan change significantly.

The brilliant figure painter, Chen Hongshou, undertook a series of woodblock prints on the 'Nine Songs' which were completed by Xiao Yuncong around 1680. Most interesting is the portrait of Qu Yuan himself [Illustration 2]. Instead of the calm, dignified scholar who appears in the Song, Yuan and Ming renditions, a new Qu Yuan

2. Chen Hongshou, 'Qu Yuan', woodcut print, c.1680 from *Chuci Huihua Ji* [Collected Paintings of the Chuci] (Beijing, 1958).

emerges. The image is apparently no longer derived from Li Gonglin's prototype, but goes back to the description of Qu Yuan's last moments in Sima Qian's *Shi Ji* biography, which is the basic source for the historical Qu Yuan and emphasizes the moral and political meaning of his self-sacrifice. It shows a tall, grave figure slowly advancing in the wilderness, the 'walking and chanting' [of his tragic poetry] exactly as Sima Qian described his last moments. He wears the 'cloud towering cap' and 'long swinging sword' taken from his self-description in another of the *Chu ci* poems. His face is lined with grief, but there is also a sense of tragic dignity about him.

There is no direct evidence that this martyr portrait of Qu Yuan was intended as a comment on 17th century political events – the Qing conquest and the fall of the Ming – but 20th century Chinese nationalists have interpreted it that way.[7]

In fact, from the beginning of China's series of modern revolutions a new Qu Yuan started to emerge, one who could symbolize the patriotic and self-assertive qualities of China's new intellectuals.[8] Early in the 'New Culture Movement' he was invoked by Lu Xun, among others, but it was the left-wing historian, poet and playwright, Guo Moruo, who thrust Qu Yuan onto the centre stage of Chinese contemporary politics. In 1942, Guo created a sensation with his wartime drama, 'Qu Yuan'.[9] It was a Western-style spoken drama in which the ancient poet becomes a decidedly modern figure, an oppressed intellectual and frustrated nationalist who desperately struggles to save his country from an evil scheming empress and a stupidly arrogant king. In allusion to China's wartime politics, Guo Moruo substitutes Madame Chiang Kaishek as the bad woman and the Generalissimo as King Huai of Chu. The play also introduces a modern populist element by stressing the role of Qu Yuan's young maidservant, Zhan Juan, who, along with a wise and helpful fisherman, helps the hero in his struggle against corruption in high places.

At least two 'progressive' artists perpetuated this modern Qu Yuan in the visual realm during the tense years between the end of World War Two and the triumph of the Communist Party. Both were from the Canton-based 'Lingnan School'. Fang Rending, an innovative figure painter in the Chinese ink medium, painted a picture of Qu Yuan with

---

[7] Ah Ying, p.314.

[8] Analysed, mainly from literary sources, in Schneider, ch.3.

[9] Kuo Mo-jo (Guo Moruo), *Chu Yuan: A Play in Five Acts*, Yang Xianyi and Gladys Yang, trs., (Foreign Languages Press, Beijing, 1953).

the fisherman in October of 1946.¹⁰ It comes directly from the *Shi Ji* biography, as a haggard and sorrowful Qu Yuan explains to the sympathetic fisherman why a high court official is 'walking and chanting' in the wilderness. The painter's inscription closely follows Sima Qian's text, culminating in Qu Yuan's famous reply: 'The whole world is turbid and only I am pure; all are drunk and only I am awake. This is why you see me in exile'.¹¹ A traditional source, but a modern emphasis on the loneliness of the persecuted intellectual, somewhat alleviated by the sympathy of the common people.

Two years later, in 1948, a more famous Lingnan painter, Guan Shanyue, painted the same scene: Qu Yuan walking and chanting in deep grief just before his self-sacrifice [Illustration 3]. The inscription is almost identical with the *Shi Ji* text used by Fang Rending, but this time

3. Guan Shanyue, 'Qu Yuan', ink on paper, 1948, from *Guan Shanyue Hua Ji* [Collected Paintings of Guan Shanyue] (Guangdong Jenmin Chuban She, Canton, 1979).

---

10 Reproduced in *Fang Rending Hua Ji* [Collected Paintings of Fang Rending] (Lingnan Mei Shu chubanshe, Guangzhou, 1983), plate 14.

11 Sima Qian, *Shi Ji* liezhuan 24, vol.8 (Zhonghua Shu Ju, Hong Kong), p.2486.

the poet is painted completely alone in a simplified close-up portrait showing only his upper body with no background scenery. The face is even more haggard, with robes and beard blowing in the wind; the composition is stronger and simpler, with a single diagonal emphasizing movement and emotion. Here is the solitary genius and suffering martyr created by Guo Moruo and other modern intellectuals of the 'romantic generation'. The calm and dignified scholar of Yuan and Ming portraits has been replaced by the passionate patriot and untrammelled literary genius who calls to China's present-day intellectuals, in their country's hour of darkness.

After 1949, that particular hour of darkness was over for China's intellectuals and a Communist Party in power had less use for images of passionate and independent-minded scholars. Visual depictions of Qu Yuan in the 1950s proliferated, especially after the World Peace Congress selected him in 1953 as one of the 'four giants of human culture'.[12] But these tended to become standardized along two rather different lines. One was the heroic martyr, defiant and unafraid, who appeared in popular media such as comic book covers. The other, favoured in more serious art publications, looked more like the traditional image of the sober and dignified Confucian scholar. It is possible that some of the artists who depicted him in this way were making a subtle protest against the popularization and politicization of traditional art and culture. But that is very conjectural. In any event, both depictions shared one important factor. They lacked any sign of suffering, grief, or pathos – any implication of individualism and romantic rebellion. A safely historicized Qu Yuan had apparently been created as a standardized symbol for patriotism and pride in China's ancient cultural achievements. Significantly, the postage stamp portrait commemorating his selection as a 'giant of human culture' was taken from the sedate 14th century image.[13]

Amid this popularization and standardization of the hero in the mass media, there appeared one little publicized reference to the traditional image of Qu Yuan as the noble and pure-minded scholar. This was from the brush of Fu Baoshi, perhaps the most celebrated traditional-style painter in the People's Republic after Qi Baishi. Publicly, Fu was a model for Mao's slogan of 'making ancient [culture] serve the present' (*gu wei jin yung*). Privately, he interspersed his artistic references to the

---

[12] Commemoration of Ch'u Yuan, Nicholaus Copernicus, *François Rabelais José Marti* (Foreign Languages Press, Beijing, 1953).

[13] Reproduced in Schneider, p.163.

new socialist order with nostalgic portraits of traditional scholars. In 1953, he did a portrait of Qu Yuan which conveys a message rather different from his frequent works celebrating the new socialist order [Illustration 4]. But who could question the choice of subject when the World Peace Congress had just given the ancient poet the Communist world's official stamp of approval? In this painting, a sad and dignified scholar walked beside the fatal waters of the Milo River, anticipating the symbolic gesture of sacrifice and defiance that for 2,000 years Chinese scholars had seen as a reaffirmation of their moral autonomy in the face of political persecution. The romantic histrionics of Guo Moruo or Guan Shanyue's Qu Yuan have disappeared. So has the heroic posing of popular images and the blandness of more official portraits. Fu's Qu Yuan, walking and chanting beside his watery grave, conjures up a sense of tragedy as well as of calm dignity. It points to an abiding faith in those traditional cultural and intellectual values which were so much under attack in the new China.

4. Fu Baoshi 'Qu Yuan Walking and Chanting', detail, ink and colour on paper, 1953, from *Fu Baoshi Hua Ji* (Nanking, 1978).

During the relative relaxation of the mid-1950s, and again in the second 'Hundred Flowers Campaign' of the early Sixties, Fu Baoshi often turned to the *Chu ci* for inspiration. He was particularly fond of the Goddess of the Xiang River. In portraying her he invariably followed the literati tradition of showing a full-faced archaic Tang-period beauty, a convention which had first been established in the Yuan dynasty.[14] But Fu Baoshi went beyond his literati forebears in heightening the note of sadness by adding falling autumn leaves to his compositions. Sweet sadness and nostalgia for the past – worlds removed from the monumental landscape based on Mao's poem 'Snow' which, in collaboration with Guan Shanyue, Fu had done for the Great Hall of the People. In his private art, the painter said things that could not be voiced aloud. Of course, from what we now know about the covert criticisms of the Party by writers and historians in these years, it would be surprising not to find some hints of this in the fine arts.[15]

By 1966 (Fu conveniently had died the year before) no artist or writer dared to make this kind of allusion to traditional symbols and values. As Schneider concluded, Qu Yuan was simply not available as a symbol for any kind of criticism of the radical new order. But though out of sight for 'the ten bad years' (1966-76) he was not out of mind for the intellectuals who were trying to weather the latest, most severe, storms of political persecution. When, after the fall of the Gang of Four, a new Party leadership suddenly called on artists and writers to blossom forth with yet another Hundred Flowers, the painters – and Qu Yuan – were ready.

---

[14] See Muller, 'Chang Wu', plates 1,3,4,7,11,12 and 15. Compare with *Fu Baoshi Hua Ji* [Collected Paintings of Fu Baoshi] (Nanjing, 1980), pp.30,75,76,90.

[15] The historian Wu Han and his play on the loyal Ming official, Hai Rui, is best known. See James R. Pusey, *Wu Han: Attacking the Present Through the Past* (Harvard University Press, 1969). But there were also Mao's covert critics in the Peking press. For Deng Tuo, most prominent member of 'The Three Family Village', see Timothy Cheek, 'Deng Tuo, A Chinese Leninist Approach to Journalism', in Carol Lee Hamrin and Timothy Cheek (eds), *China's Establishment Intellectuals* (M. E. Sharpe, Armonk, N.Y., 1986), pp.92-123. And, finally, somewhat more comparable to the use of the Qu Yuan, image there was Tian Han's historical drama *Guan Hanqing* written in 1958. See Rudolph G. Wagner, 'The Chinese Writer in his Own Mirror: Writer, State, and Society – the Literary Evidence', in Merle Goldman, et.al. (eds), *China's Intellectuals and the State* (Harvard University Press, Cambridge, Massachusetts, 1987), pp.205-10. Also his book *The Contemporary Chinese Historical Drama: Four Studies*.

The new reincarnation of Qu Yuan in the late 1970s sprang from several sources. First, he was still a living presence for older intellectuals, especially those traditional-style painters who were deeply immersed in China's cultural tradition. Moreover, in the uncertain atmosphere before Deng Xiaoping firmly took control, it was still unclear how much criticism of the Party's cultural policies would be tolerated outside of personal vituperation of the Gang of Four. The old habit of criticism through historical allusion remained safer. Moreover, in the fine arts any experimentation with Western styles was problematic until the early Eighties, whereas anything traditional was officially welcomed as a relief from the cultural tyranny of the Gang of Four.[16] The fact that Jiang Qing had taken a personal interest in reforming traditional art, and had put some of its most famous practitioners on display as negative examples of 'black painting', ensured the prominence of traditional painting in the post-Gang backlash.[17]

In that context, Qu Yuan served even better than other commonly used symbols (Zhong Kui, Hai Rui, or Su Dongpo) as a vehicle for expressing intellectuals' ideals and their discontent with the present or near past. The distinction there – between protesting the liberalized, but still very real, restrictions on artists and intellectuals in the post-Mao era, or protesting the cultural and political tyranny of the safely-past Cultural Revolution – was, of course, absolutely crucial. But in practice the difference was not always so clear. That, too, was perfectly understandable when artists still had to respect the 'four basic principles', including support for Party leadership. However, when references to recent tyranny might also be applied to the current situation, another layer was added to the criticism by historical allusion and another twist to 'making the past serve the present'.

The interplay between deep historical symbols and recent historical references can be seen in an unusual portrait of Qu Yuan by the suddenly famous painter, Huang Yongyu [Illustration 5]. The earlier images of dignified scholar or popular folk hero have vanished. Instead, a dejected and forsaken poet hangs his head, while unkempt hair and dishevelled robes reinforce the image of gloom and suffering. The style

---

[16] Developments in Chinese painting during these years are covered by Joan Lebold Cohen, *The New Chinese Painting 1949-1986* (Harry Abrams, New York, 1987).

[17] Ellen Johnston Laing, *The Winking Owl: Art in the People's Republic of China* (University of California Press, Berkeley, 1988), pp.84-87 discusses the 'hotel school' and the 'black painting' exhibitions of the mid-1970s.

5. Huang Yongyu 'Qu Yuan Walking and Chanting', ink and colour on paper, 1978, from *Huang Yongyu Hua Ji* [Collected Paintings of Huang Yongyu].

might have come from the Western expressionism that was so influential with left-wing woodcut artists in the 1930s, for Huang started his career as a printmaker. But it could also reflect a Chinese pedigree coming from the eccentric tradition in literati painting. In any event, it is neither the traditional Confucian image nor the modern patriotic portrait of Qu Yuan. Huang Yongyu replaces the usual invocation of lines from Qu Yuan's own poetry with two lines from Lu Xun's 1932 poem on Qu Yuan:

> By the river bank someone chants his frustration
> In the autumn waves, vast and endless, the Ode to Sorrow ends.

What is the contemporary artist trying to say by painting an ancient symbol and citing a modern literary titan? Lu Xun had originally written the poem in the darkest period of Kuomintang suppression of intellectuals. Huang, one of the artists who drew the ire of Jiang Qing and ended up classified as a 'black painter', undoubtedly had more recent persecutions in mind. He was one of the earliest to come forward in the new Hundred Flowers with a boldly personal style not remotely resembling any kind of socialist realism or revolutionary romanticism.

In his private life, he was one of the intellectuals who was not content to forget or forgive what had happened to him and the arts in the Cultural Revolution. So perhaps his melancholy and unorthodox Qu Yuan can be taken as just a comment on that sad period. But it is painted in 1978 – the same year as the emergence of 'scar literature', the same year as the Party's official reversal of its verdict on the Tiananmen Incident, the same year that the officially sponsored cult of Zhou Enlai was expropriated by intellectuals to use in defending their rights against heavy-handed political harassment. There seems to be a connection between Qu Yuan, ancient martyr to political tyranny, and Zhou Enlai, modern exemplar of statesmanship and patriotism who, it could be claimed, was also martyred by the machinations of illegitimate power seekers and the foolishness of an arrogant ruler. Admittedly, there is considerable difference between dying in a Peking hospital cancer ward and drowning in a river in Hunan, but at this juncture the parallel served urgent artistic and political purposes.

The poet and screenwriter, Bai Hua, has his artist protagonist in 'Bitter Love' (also a painter) unfurl a large scroll at the Tiananmen Incident which reads, 'Qu Yuan Questions Heaven'. This echoes much of the 'Li Sao' questioning of how Heaven can permit such wrongs and more directly refers to another work attributed to Qu Yuan, *Tian Wen* (Questions to Heaven). In the visual arts, that same year the Shanghai figure painter, Cheng Shifa, composed a picture of Qu Yuan holding up an offering, 'Sacrifice to a Loyal Soul'. In late 1970s parlance the 'loyal soul' was unmistakably Zhou Enlai.[18] Thus, Qu Yuan, archetypical paragon of loyalty and principle, sacrifices to the modern communist paragon of those virtues. But in the process, Zhou Enlai also becomes identified with values of intellectual and artistic freedom. In celebrating the ancient hero, Chinese artists linked him to a modern source of

---

[18] As further, and more public, visual evidence, there is Wang Ximin's sculpture of martyrs of the Tiananmen Incident which shows a memorial to Zhou Enlai surrounded by his young supporters and is titled 'loyal soul'. Reproduced in *China Reconstructs*, no.5 (May 1980), p.23.

political legitimacy and used it to defend their cultural-intellectual independence and integrity.

So Huang Yongyu's neo-expressionist, neo-literati Qu Yuan was more than balm for past grievances. He also spoke to present issues.

One more reference to Zhou Enlai and Qu Yuan clinches the association. In September 1979, the leading art journal, *Mei Shu*, published a 'Western-style' pastel which showed Premier Zhou attending a rehearsal of Guo Moruo's famous play along with the playwright [Illustration 6]. The invocation of the staged version of Qu Yuan was obviously aimed at Jiang Qing's reign as cultural tzarina when, as another reincarnation of that stock Confucian morality-play figure of 'the bad empress', she brought the country to ruin, or nearly did so. In the post-Gang context, associating Zhou Enlai with the play also linked it to continuing issues of artistic freedom and the value, or dignity, of intellectuals. Whether it was also a sly dig at Guo Moruo,

6. Wang Ximin 'Premier Zhou and Guo Moruo Watch Rehearsal of the Play "Qu Yuan" ', pastel, from *Mei Shu*, September 1979.

whose talent for political survival contrasted so glaringly with Qu Yuan's sacrifice for principle, is beyond our ken. Not all the subtleties of Chinese intellectuals' and artists' internal discourse – the double or triple meanings, the ambiguous insider references – are readily apparent to the outside observer. Nor are they intended to be.

Subsequent issues of *Mei Shu* reinforced the revived image of Qu Yuan as a symbol of intellectual freedom against political tyranny and cultural sterility. In August 1980, Zhang Shengmo, a woodcut artist from Anhui, featured a dramatically posed Qu Yuan, beard and robes flowing in the wind, as he turns his back to the tempestuous waters of the Milo River.[19] The attitude is heroic and defiant rather than tragic. The next January there appeared a carved wooden statue by a graduate student of the Central Academy of Fine Arts, Sun Jiaben. The figure is less militantly heroic; it expresses deeper feelings of sorrow and tragedy. But most noteworthy is the style, which is elongated in the manner of German expressionism. Produced at a time when style as much as content was emerging as the new battleground for daring artists, it linked Qu Yuan to the emerging art issues of the 1980s while reaffirming him as a symbol for criticizing the crimes of the early 1970s. The same could be said of an ethereal oil portrait which has him rising wraith-like from the Milo River and is titled, 'The Nation's Soul: In Praise of Qu Yuan'.[20]

As stated earlier, however, the principal genre for praising the revived Qu Yuan was traditional-style Chinese painting. Among several ink portraitists, two prominent neo-literati figure painters stand out.

To take the younger first, Fan Zeng (b.1935) is a Beijing artist from a scholarly Jiangsu family background. He graduated from the Central Academy of Fine Arts in the early 1960s, produced hack illustrations for popular works on the history of class struggle during the Cultural Revolution, but also was an anti-leftist activist in the Tiananmen incident of 1976. Since the late Seventies he has been widely recognized as a specialist in historical portraiture which depicts China's famous literary and intellectual figures in dramatically heroic poses.

In 1979, the pivotal year for repudiating the Cultural Revolution's legacy and testing the limits of political dissent, Fan Zeng produced a series of Qu Yuan portraits. They all show the poet immersed in grief and anxiety about the fate of his country, and most of them use the

---

19 *Mei Shu*, no.8 (August 1980), p.25.

20 *Mei Shu*, no.10 (October 1984).

'walking and chanting by the riverbank' theme.[21] As with Huang Yongyu's melancholy portrait, they show the poet alone in the wilderness presumably just before his self-immolation.

But in most ways the younger artist shows a different Qu Yuan who apparently conveys a different message. Whereas Huang's Qu Yuan walks with head downcast and shoulders bowed by grief, Fan's Qu Yuan, whether shown sorrowing over the fall of the Chu capital in a painting which takes its title from the poem 'Ai Ying' (Lament for Ying) or in the more conventional 'walking and chanting', has his head erect, shoulders square, and an expression on his face that can be interpreted as determination, or defiance, perhaps sadness, but definitely not the beaten melancholy of defeat [Illustration 7 and 8]. Actually, it is the expression Fan Zeng gives to most of his portraits of heroic literati figures from China's past. Lofty, pure, unafraid, and unintimidated by persecution – these are symbols of moral integrity, independence of mind, and political courage that speak to China's present situation.

Although painted only one year later than Huang Yongyu's expression of grief over the horrors of the Cultural Revolution, Fan Zeng's Qu Yuan portraits already display a new confidence in the autonomy and value of intellectuals. Significantly, in all of them the ancient poet-statesman still prominently wears his 'long swinging sword', whereas in 1978 Huang showed him disarmed. For Fan Zeng, the bold and confident artist-activist who had stormed the barricades at the 'Tiananmen Incident' three years earlier, Qu Yuan was the perfect symbol for a heroic reassertion of intellectuals' values in 1979.

The other prominent traditional-style artist who used the Qu Yuan image to comment on current issues was the Shanghai figure painter, Cheng Shifa (b.1921). He represented both a different generation and a rather different artistic temperament. Cheng Shifa started his career in the 1950s, two decades before Fan Zeng. He too began as a book illustrator but by the 1960s was well known for lyrical portraits of young minority women, especially the exotic Dai of Yunnan province. He brought to these ink and colour paintings a freshness and spontaneity that made them attractive pictures of happiness in the new society. But at the same time, in his brushwork and compositions he exhibited a creative ability which showed him a worthy successor to the late 19th and early 20th century masters of the Shanghai school.

---

[21] Six of these are reproduced in *Fan Zeng Hua Ji* (Han Wenhua Fazhan Yu Xian Gongsi, Hong Kong, 1980).

7. Fan Zeng, 'Ai Ying', ink and colour on paper, 1979, from *Fan Zeng Hua Ji* [Collected Paintings of Fan Zeng] (Hong Kong, 1980).

8. Fan Zeng, 'Qu Yuan Walking and Chanting', ink and colour on paper, 1979, from *Fan Zenq Hua Ji*.

During the 'ten years' his art was too sweet and too traditional for approbation under Jiang Qing's canons of taste. But after 1976 his reputation soared again and he burst forth with a flurry of figure paintings drawn from China's literary, historical, and legendary past: Li Bo, Su Dongpo, Hai Rui, Zhou Bo, Zhong Kui, and especially Qu Yuan.[22]

---

[22] Most of Cheng Shifa's historical paintings from this period are conveniently collected in *Cheng Shifa Shu Hua: Lishi Renwu*, vol.5. (Xiling yinshe, Hangzhou, 1980)

As with Fan Zeng, Cheng's historical figures all symbolized or commented on issues coming out of the Cultural Revolution and its aftermath. Hai Rui, subject for the historical drama which had made the historian Wu Han one of the first intellectuals purged in 1966, was an obvious political symbol. Zhou Bo, venerable general who came out of retirement to frustrate the usurping schemes of the notorious Empress Lu in the Former Han, was a significant symbol in the late 1970s when the 'queen's party' (Gang of Four) had just been defeated. The poets Li Bo, Su Dongpo and others represented free and unfettered artistic genius transcending the trammels of the political world – an inspiration for writers and artists who had been tied to political propaganda work. Zhong Kui, the 'demon catcher' of popular mythology, was a dual-purpose symbol, representing stern justice towards those leftist demons and monsters who had plagued China for the last decade, but also, as a scholar wrongly treated by political authorities and a suicide too, he was yet another example of the persecuted intellectual.

Qu Yuan, however, was a much more powerful symbol of persecution. He also personified literary genius and the most pure-minded political rectitude. Therefore, it is not surprising that in the late 1970s Qu Yuan became Cheng Shifa's favourite subject for historical paintings.[23]

Actually, the modern painter's fascination with the ancient symbol had started during the last years of the Cultural Revolution decade (1966-76). Cheng's methods of depicting Qu Yuan drew on both ancient and modern sources. The first dated portrait is from 1972 [Illustration 9]. It shows a rather stern and austere Qu Yuan – stern in comparison with the more genial faces Cheng usually paints – who stands alone, hair and robes billowing in a fierce wind. The simple title is, 'Quzi [The master Qu] Walking and Chanting'. The prevailing mood here is one of defiance or high-minded adherence to principles rather than the tragedy of martyrdom. Although the brushwork is free and expressive in the usual Cheng Shifa manner, this is sterner or grimmer than his customary style, the closest of his paintings to Fan Zeng's heroic posturing. Cheng himself has confirmed the obvious references to the contemporary persecution of so many intellectuals in the Cultural Revolution. He is quoted in the preface to the volume on historical figure painting in his

---

23 There are seventeen paintings and sketches of Qu Yuan or figures from his poems in *Cheng Shifa Shu Hua*, vol.5. I have also seen several more paintings in the artist's possession.

9. Cheng Shifa, 'Qu Yuan Walking and Chanting, ink and paper, 1972, from *Cheng Shifa Shu Hua*, vol.5, [Painting and Calligraphy of Cheng Shifa] (Shanghai, 1980).

collected works as saying, 'Unjustly wronged, unjustly wronged – in my paintings that is the function of Qu Yuan'.[24]

The next dated picture, summer of 1973, appears to come from a modern version of the Qu Yuan story rather than the ancient *Shi Ji* biography [Illustration 10]. It shows the poet with a young female attendant, presumably the character Zhan Juan from Guo Moruo's 1942

---

[24] *Cheng Shifa Shu Hua*, vol.5, p.3.

10. Cheng Shifa, 'Qu Yuan', ink and colour on paper, 1973, from *Cheng Shifa Hua Ji* [Collected Paintings of Cheng Shifa] (Peking, 1980).

stage play, where she symbolizes the common people.[25] The implication here is that, just as the common people in the early 1940s had supported the progressive intellectuals who were persecuted by the Kuomintang dictatorship, in the Cultural Revolution the people and the intellectuals were still on the same side, suffering under a new dictatorship. In the painting a solemn but not quite so austere Qu Yuan, armed again with his 'cloud towering cap' and 'long swinging sword', stands proud and erect while the girl brings him that symbol of traditional scholarly

---

[25] Wagner, 'The Chinese Writer...', p.188. Here, as elsewhere, Wagner's interpretations of Guo Moruo's *Qu Yuan* seem both consistent and convincing.

11. Cheng Shifa, 'In Praise of the Orange Tree', ink and colour on paper, 1975, from *Cheng Shifa Shu Hua*, vol.5.

culture, the *gu qin*, Chinese zither. The classical musical instrument adds another symbol of the validity and continued worth of the traditional culture at a time when Jiang Qing's bastardized 'model plays' dominated official cultural policy.

Another painting, dated 'mid-autumn 1975', takes Qu Yuan's poem 'In Praise of the Orange Tree' as its inspiration [Illustration 11]. This particular poem was not only a personal favourite of Cheng Shifa, but also played a major part in Guo Moruo's drama, where the tree's purity and fruit-bearing capacity become metaphors for the intellectuals' duty

12. Cheng Shifa, 'Crossing the River', ink and colour on paper, 1976, from *Cheng Shifa Shu Hua*, vol.5.

to the people.[26] So when in 1975 the painter shows a still solemn-faced Qu Yuan and female attendant, partly obscured by a heavily laden orange tree, it is a reminder of the intellectuals' duty to persevere and, carrying with it, perhaps a note of optimism about the future.

When the leftist ascendancy ended in 1976, Cheng Shifa's Qu Yuan imagery abruptly changed. There is a painting from December 1976 that is dedicated to Marshall Ye Jianying [Illustration 12].[27] It again shows

---

[26] Wagner, p.187.

[27] This is not the only painting dedicated to the PLA general who was instrumental in ousting the Gang of Four. There are also several portraits of the elderly

the poet, solemn and dignified with his zither-bearing female attendant. But the setting has changed. He stands on jagged rocks above roiling waters gazing into the distance as his female disciple looks to him, presumably for guidance. The scene is similar to earlier 'walking and chanting' paintings, but here the text is taken from a somewhat more positive poem, 'She Jiang' (Crossing the River). In this selection from the Nine Declarations, the poet looks back in old age upon the perfidy of a corrupt world, but rather than ending it all in the beckoning waves, he resolves to go onward. It ends, probably here intended as reference to the Cultural Revolution:[28]

> For the Dark and Light have changed places: the times are out of joint.
> With true heart long I pondered; then suddenly I set forth.

In the context of the times, it could either be a flattering reference to Ye Jianying, suggesting comparison with Qu Yuan in the general's determination go on in old age, or it could be a self-reference to the artist's determination to preserve his own integrity. Or, most likely, it contained both messages, along with a more general reaffirmation of the dignity and worth of independent intellectuals.

Over the next few years Cheng completed a number of paintings based on Qu Yuan and his poems. There are at least three more that take 'In Praise of the Orange Tree' as inspiration. There is the portrait of Qu Yuan sacrificing to a 'loyal soul', previously referred to as part of the association between Qu Yuan and Zhou Enlai (see above p.37). And there are several illustrations of the female deities from the Nine Songs, presumably because Cheng likes to paint female figures, but also as an indication of more optimistic times.

For Cheng Shifa, Qu Yuan had been one of the most powerful and poignant symbols for expressing his distress about the Cultural Revolution, surreptitiously before the fall of the Gang of Four, and publicly after it.

By the end of the 1970s, he was joined by other artists in conveying the general message about the moral autonomy of intellectuals against the pressures of political tyranny. Neo-literati Chinese-style painters such as Cheng Shifa and Fan Zeng, more experimental artists like

---

general, Zhou Bo, who saved the Han dynasty from the usurping schemes of the Empress Lu. One dedicated to Ye Jianying was seen in Canton at the Academy of Fine Arts in December, 1982. Other pictures of Zhou Bo appear in *Cheng Shifa Hua Ji*, vol.5, pp.38 and 82.

[28] Translation from David Hawkes, *Ch'u Tz'u: The Songs of the South* (Beacon Press, Boston, 1962), p.65.

Huang Yongyu, or the younger woodcarvers and oil painters – all used the still potent symbol of Qu Yuan to make a statement about the political tyranny and cultural nihilism of the recent past and the need for intellectual freedom in the present. By appealing to pride in China's cultural legacy, moreover, they struck a responsive chord among more than their fellow intellectuals. Much of the general populace and many of the new Party leaders shared the artists' nationalistic feelings and revulsion against the crude political expropriation of culture in the previous decade.

In short, Qu Yuan was an effective symbol and rallying point during those few transitional years as China rehabilitated its past culture, restored intellectuals to a place of honour, and moved towards a more open society. By the early 1980s, the problems in art and culture generally were shifting towards new questions – how much direct political criticism would be tolerated, what new styles could be imported, should the state have any control over artistic expression? The battles of the Eighties would be fought less over traditional symbols than over abstract painting, ambiguous poetry, and amoral fiction. Although references to Qu Yuan and his poetry continued to appear in the fine arts, their political relevance was declining as they became more explorations of new styles than evocations of Qu Yuan's moral and political significance.[29] Still a potent symbol during the transition between the Mao and Deng eras, by the mid-Eighties the poet-patriot of Chu was no longer central to the concerns of a new generation.

We are not, however, quite ready to relegate Qu Yuan to history, even recent history. After the tumultuous student protest movement in 1989 and its tragic culmination in Tiananmen Square, at least one updated image of Qu Yuan reappeared directly commenting on current politics. It came from the brush of Huang Yongyu, one of the most prominent artists of the post-Mao period, whose painting of a grief-stricken Qu Yuan 'walking and chanting' marked the beginning of the ancient poet's visual revival at the end of the 1970s. Huang happened to be in Hong Kong on 4 June; after the massacre he did not go back to China. Outside the control of Chinese political authorities, he turned his creative talent to bluntly direct expressions of moral outrage.

---

[29] For an early example of this, part of the Eighties' trend towards using ancient folklore and legend to sanction stylistic departures inspired by modern Western art, see Li Shaowen's decorative and modernistic rendition of the Nine Songs cycle in *Mei Shu*, no.1 (January 1981).

Many of these were cartoon-like caricatures done with traditional-style techniques, ridiculing or castigating the leadership in Beijing.[30] Others were severely elegant paintings of lotuses, a symbol of purity and mourning which Huang had already used in the aftermath of the Cultural Revolution. Somewhere in between was a very unusual painting of Qu Yuan, quite unlike anything that had appeared earlier. Huang's 1978 version of Qu Yuan had shown him walking with head bowed, sunk in grief as he prepared for his final gesture of despair and defiance [Illustration 6]. But at least he was erect, and this 'walking and chanting' scene, taken from the well-known *Shi Ji* biography, would have reminded any Chinese viewer that ultimately Qu Yuan would be vindicated by history, that principle ultimately triumphs over persecution.

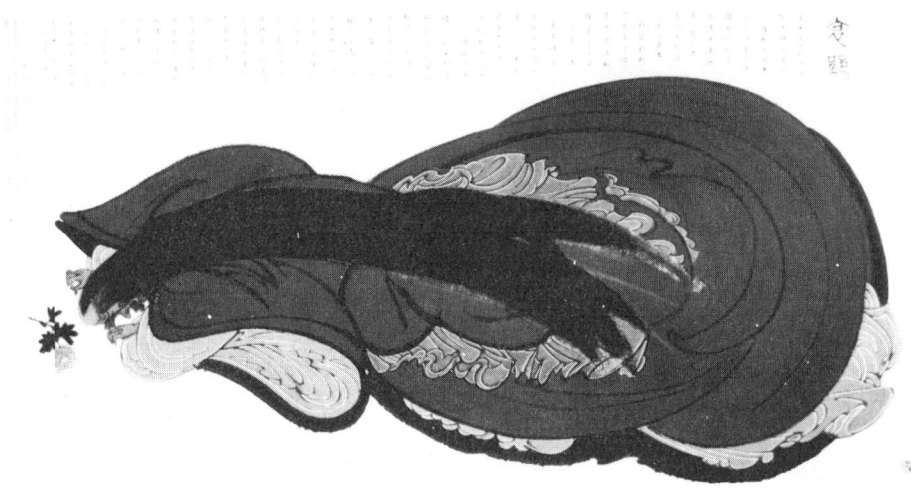

13. Huang Yongyu, Qu Yuan's 'Lament for Ying', photo by Kusada Yuen, courtesy of *The Nineties Monthly*.

---

30 Li Yi, 'Huang Yongyu: hua bi xia de xinjing' ['Huang Yongyu: Moods from his Painter's Brush'] *Jiushi niandai* [The Nineties], no.12, (December 1989), pp.83-87.

The 1989 version lacks that final consolation. The scene is taken from another poem attributed to Qu Yuan, 'Lament for Ying'. Here, too, the poet laments the collapse of the state, the suffering of the people, and his own unjust exile. In 1979, Fan Zeng had used part of that poem and its title for a portrait of a proudly erect Qu Yuan, hair dishevelled but hand firmly on his sword [Illustration 9]. In 1989, Huang Yongyu, in a highly unusual composition for a Chinese painting, shows Qu Yuan flat on the ground, robes billowing around him, a lined face and clutching fingers revealing his inner agony. Before him, a lone chrysanthemum, traditional symbol of the scholar's moral rectitude, has fallen from his hand [Illustration 13].

Although this is done in ink and the title is transcribed in antique characters, it is the most untraditional portrait of Qu Yuan to come from the hand of an artist from the People's Republic. Its message obviously is total grief and devastation at the state of affairs in China. This is mourning for current tragedy, not for the bygone atrocities of the Cultural Revolution era. Huang Yongyu casts aside the careful ambiguity about past or present reference which marked the paintings of the immediate post-Mao period. In Hong Kong, Huang did not worry about offending the power-holders in Beijing. As he explained in an interview with a reporter from *The Nineties* magazine (*Jiushi niandai*), he had originally done the painting in China, after the dismissal of Hu Yaobang, but it was only after 4 June, in Hong Kong, that he had copied on to it the entire 250 plus characters of the 'Lament for Ying', '...thereby completing the painting'.[31]

Perhaps the weight of the Maoist era, indeed the whole sad legacy of repression and frustrated hopes in modern Chinese history, still bore down upon the now-exiled artist in June of 1989. But this Qu Yuan really belongs to another era than the painted reincarnations of a decade earlier. Then, in an era of hope for the future as well as pain from the immediate past, even such a melancholy image as Huang's 1978 version could express hope as well as grief. In 1989, the picture of a prostrate Qu Yuan speaks simply of despair.

Yet is it ultimate despair, or does the very act of turning to a symbol possessing such deep historical associations with resistance to tyranny indicate, for this artist, some sense of confidence in the strength of Chinese culture?

At present we cannot know whether Huang Yongyu's Qu Yuan, finished and published in exile, is a solitary image testifying to the

---

31   Li Yi, p.83.

crushed hopes of 1989, or whether painters in China will also invoke Qu Yuan as a rebuke to oppressive rulers when, and if, it is possible to speak or paint on such issues. In some ways, the poet-statesman of Chu, paragon of dynastic loyalty, is a poor symbol for modern democracy. Yet his embodiment of independent judgement and individual conscience could serve the cause of intellectual pluralism and toleration that must be one of the foundations for building democracy in China.

As Schneider's detailed explication of the ancient poet's long posthumous career, or even this short exposé of recent images, should remind us, China's rulers will not easily keep Qu Yuan safely interned within the confines of the historical museum. The continued tension between political power and intellectual conscience suggests that his post-Cultural Revolution revival is not likely to be his last.

PARTY HISTORIOGRAPHY*

Susanne Weigelin-Schwiedrzik

Until the 1980s, the Party historiography produced in the PRC did not attract the serious attention of scholars in the West, who regarded it as stereotyped, monotonous and propagandistic. After Mao Zedong's death in 1976, this negative image quickly changed. Since 1979 Party historiography increasingly has become accepted as a serious contribution to the study of recent history by readers abroad as well as in China.

In this chapter, I shall challenge these views of Party historiography both before and after 1976. On the one hand, I shall argue that even though the pre-1976 Party historiography was largely stereotyped and monotonous, some publications have more value than one might think. On the other hand, while noting the greater liveliness of discussions of Party history after 1979, I will try to show that these discussions have followed patterns of argumentation and justification similar to those used in the pre-1976 era and thus can still be seen as stereotyped and monotonous.

In order to make this point clear, my analysis focuses first on the main characteristics of Party historiography in China as this developed between 1945 and 1981. Unlike the authors of the very few existing case-studies in this field,[1] I am not primarily interested in comparing

---

*   This chapter is based on my dissertation, *Parteigeschichtsschreibung in der VR China: Typen, Methoden, Themen und Funktionen* (Otto Harrassowitz, Weisbaden, 1984). I would like to thank Steven C. Averill, Timothy Cheek, Joseph W. Esherick, Frederick C. Teiwes, Rudolf G. Wagner, Frederick E. Wakeman, Jr., Andrew Watson, Peter Weber-Schäfer and Bodo Wiethoff for their comments and advice.

1   For examples, see John Israel, 'The December Ninth Movement: A Case Study in Chinese Communist Historiography', in Albert Feuerwerker (ed.), *History in Communist China* (MIT Press, Cambridge, Mass., 1968), pp.247 ff.; William F. Dorrill, 'Transfer of Legitimacy in the Chinese Communist Party: Origins of the Maoist Myth', *China Quarterly*, no.36, 1968, pp.45 ff.; W. Dorrill, 'The Fukien

different interpretations of Party history propagated in different phases of the political development of the PRC. Nor am I interested in comparing the different interpretations found in and outside China. My main interest is in the way Party history is written. I shall start by describing the organizational structure of Party historiography; I shall then look at its methodology, and finally try to explain the relationship between historiography, Mao Zedong (the person) and Mao Zedong Thought.

The study is based on an analysis of Party documents, textbooks, booklets and articles in journals and newspapers. In addition, during a research trip to China in 1980 I had the opportunity to interview thirteen Party historiographers living in Beijing,[3] and will draw on these in my discussion of historiography before that date.

The Historical Development of Party Historiography

Party historiography, in its institutionalized form, came into existence in 1945 when the Seventh Plenary Session of the Party's Sixth Central Committee passed a 'Resolution on Some Questions of History'.[4] Its origins lay in the Yan'an Rectification Campaign when Party history was officially discussed first by members of the Party Politburo and later by Central Committee members and other high ranking Party cadres.[5] A

Rebellion and the Chinese Communist Party: A Case of Maoist Revisionism', *China Quarterly*, no.37, 1969, pp.31 ff.

[3] Although most of my 13 interview subjects are prominent historiographers and must have had the Party's permission to give interviews, I have decided to quote them without giving their names. If any further information is needed, readers are asked to contact me directly. All interview quotations cite my dissertation, op.cit., in which the longer passages of the most important interviews are reproduced.

[4] 'Guanyu ruogan lishi wenti de jueyi'(April 1945), Mao Zedong, *Xuanji* [Selected Works], vol.III (Beijing, 1953), pp.975 ff.; English version: 'Resolution on Some Questions of History', Mao Tse-tung, *Selected Works* (New York, 1954-56), vol.4, pp.171 ff.

[5] See Wang Jianmin, *Zhongguo gongchandang shigao* [Outline History of the CCP] (Taibei, 1965), vol.3, pp.146 ff.; James P. Harrison, *The Long March to Power* (Praeger, New York, 1972), pp.342 ff.; Wang Ming, *Cultural Revolution or Counter-revolutionary Coup?* (Novosti Press Agency, Moscow, 1969), pp.46 ff.; Jacques Guillermaz, *Histoire du Parti Communiste Chinois (1921-1949)* (Payot, Paris, 1968), pp.353 ff.; Xu Xishan,'Dang de liujie qizhong quanhui yu "guanyu ruogan lishi wenti de jueyi"' [The Seventh Plenary Session of the Party's Sixth Central Committee and the 'Resolution on Some Questions of

committee was formed to compose the text of the 1945 'Resolution', originally intended for presentation to the Seventh Party Congress but eventually passed by the last plenary session of the Sixth Central Committee in April 1945.[6]

The next step in the development of Party historiography was the 'Resolution' passed by the Central Committee on the establishment of Huabei University. Hu Hua, who started teaching Party historiography in his youth, remembers:

The word 'Party history' [*dangshi*], as a name for a university course, was first mentioned in the 'Resolution on Huabei University' which the Chinese Communist Party formulated in May 1945. Before that time we had taught modern and contemporary history of the revolution [*gemingshi*], but there had not yet been a course called 'Party history'... We established a team of researchers under the leadership of Wu Yuzhang with me as the team leader. Comrade Wu Yuzhang and Comrade Cheng Fangwu...asked me to write a textbook on Party history. So I started teaching and at the same time wrote the teaching materials.[7]

After 1949, a Department for Party History was established at the Chinese People's University in Beijing where teachers who had taught Party history at Huabei University continued their work under the leadership of He Ganzhi. Their main task was to train a large number of teachers, since after the Communist take-over all universities were introducing courses on Party history and obliging their students to take political training classes.[8] At the same time, study courses were

---

History'], *Hongqi* [Red Flag], no.12, 1981, pp.32 ff. The discussions among Party leaders was assisted by two volumes of documents edited for this purpose: *Before the Sixth Party Congress* and *Since the Sixth Party Congress*. The former book was reprinted in 1980. See Zhonggong Zhongyang Shujichu, *Liuda yiqian dang de lishi cailiao* (Beijing, 1980). The latter book, too, has been reprinted, but I was not able to see the reprint or to obtain the original. Information about the book was given to me by Party historiographers.

6   According to a footnote in Mao Zedong, *Xuanji*, vol.III, p.975, the resolution was passed on 20 April 1945.

7   Interview VIII, in Weigelin-Schwiedrzik, op.cit., p.159.

8   At secondary schools students learn about the revolution in a course entitled 'History of the Modern Chinese Revolution'. At university level, Party history courses have been called into question several times since 1949. Some people have argued that these classes should concentrate on the 'history of the modern Chinese revolution' (see Li Zhengwen,'Dangshi ke shi daxue Makesi-Lieningzhuyi lilun jiaoyu de zhongyao zucheng bufen' [The Class on Party

established for Kuomintang personnel, retained in their posts by the Communists after 1949, and Party history became one of the most important items of study for them. In 1951, as the thirtieth anniversary of the founding of the CCP was celebrated with great fanfare, Hu Qiaomu wrote a work entitled *Thirty Years of the Chinese Communist Party*[9] which was declared to provide the most important text on Party history. This text, together with the (eventual) four volumes of Mao Zedong's *Selected Works*, in which the 1945 'Resolution' was published, were declared to provide the 'framework' for all publications on Party history written in the 1950s and early 1960s. Upon this foundation a growing number of textbooks appeared.

During the Cultural Revolution, Party history was cited in most of the political debates about China's present and future; but it ceased to exist in an institutionalized form. Party historiography had been closely linked to university political training classes, and since the universities were closed, there was no need for textbooks and articles on Party history. Instead, Red Guards compiled booklets with quotations from Mao's works to back their arguments on the 'struggle between the two lines'.[10] Party history writing only re-emerged after the universities had

---

History is an Important Part of a University's Theoretical Training in the Field of Marxism-Leninism], *Dangshi huiyi baogaoji* [Collection of Party History Meeting Reports] (1982), pp.317ff.; selected translations in S. Weigelin-Schwiedrzik (ed.), 'Party Historiography, Chinese Law and Government', vol.XIX, no.3 (Fall 1986), p.101. Comparing the textbooks, it is difficult to find any difference between those on the 'modern Chinese revolution' and those on Party history. Party historiographers have told me that the difference in the titles used for publications up to the early 1960s was due to the fact that authors did not want to challenge the final authority of the Party's Central Committee in writing Party history and were waiting for an official book-length text to come out. At the beginning of the 1980s, Party history was finally defined to include the content of the 'modern Chinese revolution' course supplemented by what is called 'Development of the Party *per se*' (*dang benshen de fazhan*) which includes inner-Party struggles and discussions. In the debate on what to teach at the university level some Party scholars argued that the content of the 'Development' course should only be taught to Party members and, accordingly, suggested that university courses could be retitled the 'History of the Modern Chinese Revolution'. Party historiographers told me that this suggestion was officially accepted in 1986.

9   Hu Qiaomu, *Zhongguo gongchandang de sanshi nian* [Thirty Years of the CCP] (Beijing, 1951).

10 See, for example, *Mao zhuxi lun dangnei liangtiao luxian douzheng* [Chairman Mao on the Struggle of the Two Lines in the Party] (1969); reprinted in Chinese

been reopened and new textbooks were required. These were based on what Lin Biao had said in his 'Political Report' to the Ninth Party Congress in 1969[11] and in the editorial written for the fiftieth anniversary of the founding of the CCP in 1971.[12] The authors of the latter toured a number of universities to lecture:

> These lectures exerted an enormous influence. The ideas expressed in the editorial and the lectures dominated Party history writing during the years 1971 to 1976 ... With regard to Lin Biao's 'Report', I remember that Party historiography had to follow his arguments on Liu Shaoqi, which meant that we had to follow the wording of Lin Biao's report to the Ninth Congress when writing our textbooks.[13]

While all textbooks edited during the Cultural Revolution were declared to be strictly for 'internal' use or even for 'use only within the university', after Mao's death and the fall of the 'Gang of Four' Party historiography gradually re-entered the public domain. Furthermore, after *People's Daily* published Li Honglin's article, 'Is the History of the Party Only the History of the Struggle of the Two Lines?',[14] the first open debate on questions of Party history began to develop. New textbooks could be bought openly at the bookstores. Articles appeared in university journals as well as in *Lishi yanjiu*. The newly established journal *Jindaishi yanjiu* (Modern History Research) appeared. So also did the Society for Research on Party History, its journal being the monthly periodical *Dangshi yanjiu* (Party History Research), published for 'internal use' from 1980 to 1982, but which can now be bought without restriction. A Society for Research on Personalities of Chinese

---

Research Materials, M 624 (Hong Kong, 1969) and *Mao zhuxi de geming luxian shengli wansui* [Long Live the Victory of Chairman Mao Zedong's Revolutionary Line] (Beijing, 1969).

[11] Lin Biao, 'Zai zhongguo gongchandang di jiu ci daibiao [Report to the Ninth National Congress of the CCP], *Hongqi*, no.5, 1969, pp.5ff.

[12] 'Jinian Zhongguo gongchandang wushi zhou nian' [In Commemoration of Fifty Years of the CCP] *Renmin ribao* [People's Daily], 1 July 1971, p.1.

[13] Interview I, in Weigelin-Schwiedrzik (1984), p.148.

[14] Li Honglin, 'Women dang de lishi jinjin shi liangtiao luxian douzheng shi ma?', *Renmin ribao*, 14 Dec. 1978, p.3. This was followed by a somewhat enlarged version of the same article under the title 'Smash the Taboos of Party History' (Dapo dangshi jinqu), *Lishi yanjiu* [Historical studies], no.1, 1979, pp.20 ff..

Communist Party History[14] was also established and decided to publish fifty volumes of biographies of leading members of the Party.

At the same time a Committee for Party History[16] was founded directly under the Central Committee to supervise the work of the Bureau for Research on Party History.[17] In this bureau, members of the Central Committee and prominent Party historiographers prepared the 'Resolution on Some Questions Concerning the History of the Party Since the Founding of the People's Republic of China'[18] which was officially passed by the Sixth Plenary Session of the Eleventh Central Committee of the Party in the summer of 1981.

The Organization of Party Historiography

Subsequent to the CCP's first attempt at determining the overall interpretation of Party history in 1945,[19] the organizational structure of Party historiography has developed a network, reaching from the Central Committee down to Party schools at the provincial and local levels and to the regional universities. To staff this, a large group of Party historiographers has been trained. Nevertheless, the Central Committee still plays the predominant role in deciding the official interpretation of events. This is then conveyed to lower levels through documents such as

---

14 Zhonggong dangshi renwu yanjiu xiehui. See Weigelin-Schwiedrzik (1984), pp.21, 78; see also the Society's Zhonggong dangshi rewu zhuan [Biographies of Historic Figures in the CCP], vol.1 ff. (Beijing, 1980), vol.1, pp.382 ff.

16 Dangshi Weiyuanhui. See Weigelin-Schwiedrzik (1984), p.24.

17 Dangshi Yanjiushi. See Weigelin-Schwiedrzik (1984), pp.4, 20.

18 'Guanyu jianguo yilai dang de ruogan lishi wenti de jueyi', *Renmin ribao*, 1 July 1981, pp.1 ff.

19 Before 1945, official interpretations of Party history were included in resolutions passed by Party congresses but they never covered more than the period since the last Party congress. Unofficial interpretations were given by individual Party leaders such as Mao Zedong, Liu Shaoqi, Li Lisan, Wang Ming, Qu Qiubai, Luo Fu et al. For an early and influential version of this kind, see Cai Hesen, 'Zhongguo gongchandang lishi de fazhan – Zhongguo gongchandang de fazhan jiqi shiming' [On the Historical Development of the CCP – the Development of the CCP and its Duties] in *Cai Hesen de shier pian wenzhang* [Twelve Essays by Cai Hesen] (Beijing, 1980), pp.1 ff.; and Cai Hesen, 'Jihuizhuyi shi' [History of Opportunism], in Wang Jianmin (1965), op.cit., vol.1, pp.483 ff.

the two 'Resolutions' discussed above.[20] The fact that Party historiographers have had to yield to these Central Committee documents accounts for the monotony confronting readers of textbooks on Party history.

Before the founding of the PRC, Party historiography had played its role as part of inner-Party struggles and related discussions. After 1949, its audience and functions changed. People either too young to know or politically not active inside the Communist Party had to be informed about Party history, and the interpretations had to be linked to a chronology of events in order to achieve plausibility. For this reason historiographers had to be trained both to teach relevant courses and to write the necessary textbooks.

Thus, there are Party functionaries in leading positions inside the CCP who decide how to interpret and evaluate Party history. Notwithstanding leaders like Mao Zedong and Deng Xiaoping, who exerted their influence directly, the most prominent member of the Central Committee working in this field has been Hu Qiaomu. As Mao Zedong's personal assistant, it was Hu who wrote the final draft of the 1945 'Resolution'. It was he who wrote the major text of the 1950s (*Thirty Years of the Chinese Communist Party*). And it was Hu who was asked to write the draft of the 1981 'Resolution'.[21] On the other hand, with the growing institutionalization of Party historiography after 1949, there developed also a hierarchy of Party historiographers who can be divided into three ranks reflecting differences in age, political background and training.

Party historiographers who are now in leading positions in the Academy of Social Sciences,[22] the Central Party School, and important

---

20 I only know of the two formal Party resolutions and I have the impression that no other Central Committee directives on Party historiography exist. In *Dangshi yanjiu*, however, there is a reprint of a speech by a member of the CCP Propaganda Bureau in which the new direction of Party historiography is explained. From information I gathered in Beijing I would suggest that this is an example of an alternative informal way of handing down directives on historiography. See Ma Jibin, 'Dangshi yanjiuzhong de jige wenti' [On Some Questions Regarding Research on Party History], *Dangshi yanjiu*, no.2, 1980, pp.29 ff.

21 For a biographical note on Hu Qiaomu, see Wolfgang Bartke, *Who's Who in the People's Republic of China* (Hamburg, 1981), pp.116 ff.

22 The Academy of Social Sciences system contributes to research in the field of Party history under the heading of 'modern Chinese history' (*jindaishi*), a term that refers to research within the period between 1840 and 1949. There is a

universities such as the Chinese People's University constitute the first rank in this hierarchy. Because of their age and their political experience as Party members since before the Liberation of 1949, they belong to the 'old generation of revolutionaries'. Most of them participate in policy making since they are not only historiographers but also influential members of the Party. They were delegated to become involved in Party historiography before 1949, and many of them taught at Yan'an or at Huabei University. Because of their experience and loyalty to the Party they have had a twofold task. They have been educators, writing the first textbooks on Party history[23] and training teachers for the universities, and at the same time have acted as advisers to the Central Committee on questions of Party history. In 1980 and 1981, as members of the Bureau for Research on Party History, they participated in drafting the 1981 'Resolution'. Subsequently, they drafted the first official book-length version of the history of the CCP, initially for classified (*neibu*) publication.

The second rank of Party historiographers consists of today's university professors of Party history. They were trained during the 1950s, mostly in the department of Party history at the Chinese People's University, and usually belong to the teaching bureaus of Marxism-Leninism, equivalent to university departments. They have been chosen

---

difference of opinion among historiographers in China on what to call 'contemporary' (*xiandai*) Chinese history. Up to the late 1970s, the majority held the opinion that, since the Russian October Revolution took place in 1917, the 'contemporary' period of Chinese history started in 1919 with the May Fourth Movement. Li Xin and a minority of historiographers, however, argue that 'contemporary' Chinese history only began after the new social system had been established. This is why they call the period between 1840 and 1949 *jindaishi* and after 1949 *xiandaishi*. See Li Xin, 'Guanyu jindaishi fenqi wenti de jianyi – wei "Zhongguo tongshi ban zhimindi ban fengjian shehui shidai (xia) jiaoxue da gang (chu gao)" suo xie de qian yan' [A Proposition Concerning the Periodization of Modern History – an Introduction Written for the Teaching Program on the Semi-colonial, Semi-feudal Period of General Chinese History (part 2, prelim. draft)], *Jiaoxue yu yanjiu*, vol.8, no.9 (1956), p.71.

[23] Publications from the first rank of Party historiographers are, for example: Hu Qiaomu (1951), op.cit.; Miao Chuhuang (1959), op.cit.; Liao Gailong, *Zhongguo renmin jiefang zhanzheng jianshi* [Short History of the War of Liberation of the Chinese People] (Beijing, 1952); Li Xin, Peng Ming, Sun Sibai and Chen Xulu, *Zhongguo xinminzhuzhuyi geming shiqi tongshi* [General History of the Period of the New Democratic Revolution in China] (Beijing, 1959-62), and Ye Huosheng, *Xiandai zhongguo gemingshi jianghua* [Lectures on the History of the Modern Chinese Revolution] (Beijing, 1951).

to become Party historiographers based on two criteria – not just their training in the field of Party history, but also their loyalty to the Party. They started writing textbooks at the end of the 1950s and the beginning of the 1960s[24] and today some of them are members of, or are associated with, the Bureau for Research on Party History at the Central Committee level.

The third rank of Party historiographers consists of today's younger generations of teachers, the oldest of whom were appointed after the universities were reopened at the beginning of the 1970s. Like the members of the second rank, they have gone through formal training in the field of Party history. They do most of the teaching at the university level and are the authors of many of the articles published in university journals in recent years, in which they are eager to show that they are able to 'liberate their thought' and 'smash the taboos of Party history'. At the same time, they are also obliged to edit new textbooks that are often published under the name of a Party historiographer in the second rank and which are strictly bound to the officially approved set of interpretations.

The Methodology of Party Historiography

In Party historiography, method is an extension of organization. This means that the method historiographers apply when writing Party history is a logical consequence of the position they occupy inside the hierarchy of Party historiography. This determines two important aspects of their work: the audience for which they are working and the access they have to so-called 'primary sources'. One Party historiographer told me about the importance of sources:

> I hold the opinion that research on Party history has to pay special attention to the newspapers inside and outside the Party as well as to newspapers that were published under the leadership of the Party. But it is not enough to spend a lot of time on this kind of material. And I am afraid that our problems are to be found here. The reminiscences [*huiyilu*] are also of some value to us, but they tend to contain mistakes, because of the length of time that has passed since the incident. As later ideas influence the narrative,

---

24 Publications from this second rank of Party historiographers are, for example: Wang Shi et al., op.cit.; Xu Yuandong, Ma Qingbo, Cong Xiaonan and Jiang Jue, *Zhongguo gongchandang lishi jianghua* [Lectures on the History of the CCP] (Beijing, 1962); Beijingshi gaodeng xuexiao dangshi jiangyi bianxie xiezuozu, op.cit.

things which only existed rudimentarily are later described as being already in mature existence. But still, they are of a certain value. Most important of all are the primary sources. There are primary sources of a propagandistic character and primary sources of an archival character. Of course, the latter are more valuable, but we very seldom have been able to consult archival material. Party historiography is a very young domain of history-writing. Many preconditions are not at hand yet. I myself hold the opinion that looking at it from a strict point of view, scientific research in the field of Party history has not yet really begun.[25]

The fact that most of the members of the second and third ranks of Party historiographers can only rely on propaganda material is closely connected with their role and the audience they are asked to write for. As they are mainly required to establish an official chronology of events and to link it to a given set of interpretations, newspapers normally are a 'sufficient' source of research. Only Party historiographers of the first rank need to be able to consult archival material, because their readers are the members of the Central Committee who interpret Party history. The power and authority of the first-rank Party historiographers thus relies heavily upon their access to what the second and third rank historiographers do not have access to. They act as advisers in preparing interpretations of Party history for the Central Committee, while the second and third rank historiographers specialize in disseminating officially approved interpretations, linking these to selected officially sanctioned data.

This functional division of labour underlines one of the key characteristics of Party historiography. That is to say, it can be divided into *shi* (meaning historical facts, *shishi*) and *lun* (meaning historical interpretation or evaluation, *pinglun*, and theories, *lilun*).[26] This division

---

[25] Interview I, in Weigelin-Schwiedrzik (1984), p.150.

[26] In using these terms, I am referring to a discussion on the relationship between 'theory' and 'facts' which was started by historiographers in China in the late 1950s and lasted up to the beginning of the Cultural Revolution. During the Great Leap Forward the discussion focused on the relationship of facts and theory as summarized in the official slogan 'theory has to take the lead over facts' (*yi lun dai shi*). But later on the discussion turned to the appropriate proportions of *lun* and *shi*. Fan Wenlan, Wu Han and Jian Bozan demanded that facts and theory should be combined appropriately, with Wu Han adopting the slogan 'interpretation evolves out of the facts' (*lun cong shi chu*). Starting in 1965 Wu Han, Jian Bozan and others were criticized by Yin Dei and Qi Benyu for overemphasizing facts. During the Cultural Revolution, the discussion on 'shi' and 'lun' stopped, but was reopened in the late Seventies, when the majority

corresponds to the organizational division between Party functionaries and Party historiographers. As a result, within the uniformity of Party historiography, we find texts which predominantly convey evaluations and theories alongside texts aimed at a detailed 'reconstruction of the past'.

The two 'Resolutions' on Party history of 1945 and 1981 are typical examples of the kind of historiography Party functionaries prefer. These are not aimed at 'reconstructing the past', but are to be conceived of as 'consensus papers', legitimizing the balance of power between different factions inside the CCP and defining the hierarchy of its leading members according to their 'contributions and mistakes' (*gong guo*) made in the course of Party history. They mostly contain, therefore, evaluations of historical events and accounts of the relevant persons involved and do not discuss the historical circumstances in detail. *Lun*, in this context, constitutes evaluations on the basis of pragmatic power politics and in accordance with the political philosophy of the dominant faction inside the CCP.

Most of the textbooks written before the Cultural Revolution are a combination of *shi* and *lun* inasmuch as they were written for propagandistic or, at least, didactic purposes. It was their task to disseminate the contents of Mao Zedong Thought, to reiterate the evaluations given in the Party 'Resolutions' and to link these to historical data in order to make them plausible to the reader. Here *lun* is Mao's theory on the Chinese Revolution as well as the evaluations of the 'Resolutions' on Party history. The point of departure is not 'reality in the past', but what Mao defined to be the essence of the historical process of 'the new democratic revolution'.

Whereas the many articles in historiographical journals before the Cultural Revolution, especially in *Jiaoxue yu yanjiu* (Education and Research) and *Lishi jiaoxue* (History Education) were written mostly to supplement the textbooks and therefore were pretty much of the same

---

seemed to favour the slogan 'combining theory and facts' (*shi lun jiehe*). Only a few articles chose to propagate Wu Han's slogan, while some in contrast emphasized the value of theory for historiography. See Jian Bozan, 'Shi yu lun' [On Historical Material and Historical Interpretation], in Jian Bozan, *Lishi lunwen xuanji* [Selected Historical Papers] (Beijing, 1980), pp.78 ff.; Jiang Dachun, 'Lun yu shi de guanxi kaocha' [Investigations on the Relationship Between Theory and Facts], *Lishi yanjiu*, no.4, 1982, pp.21-6; Xiong Deji, 'Lüe tan "shi" yu "lun" de guanxi' [Some Remarks on the Relation Between 'Historical Facts' and 'Interpretation'], *Guangming ribao* [Guangming Daily], 8 June 1981, p.4; Li Xin, 'Shi yu lun', *Lishi yanjiu*, no.4, 1984, pp.3 ff.

style, articles which appeared after 1979 exhibit a greater diversity of style and content.

Basically there are three different kinds of writing. First, there are texts whose authors are more interested in what they understand to be the *essence* of history than in details about events in the past. History does not constitute a value as such, but has to be related to the present and the future, thereby limiting the knowledge of the past to what is of interest to the present. In these texts we find that authors concentrate on establishing a logical chain of argument, referring to events in the past only to illustrate their own views. The credibility of the text, therefore, is not based on evidence derived from reconstructing the past, but on the inner logic of the argument.

The second kind of text is written with what I would call 'antiquarian' intentions. The authors of these texts define their task to be the reconstruction of past reality as the basis for intuitive understanding. They assume that the past must have been different from the present and therefore aim at preserving remembrance of it. Texts of this kind are extremely rare, but they can be found in the newly established scholarly magazines which circulate only internally.[27]

The third kind of text is a mixture of both the first and the second type. In articles belonging to this genre, authors convey both interpretations of the past and facts, with the result that they combine both 'antiquarian' interest and propagandistic goals. By measuring the amount of information given in the context of one set of interpretations, however, we can discover whether the text belongs more to the first or to the second category. Some authors, for example, refer to the official interpretation of an event at the beginning and the end of their article while most of the text is dedicated to their 'antiquarian' interests. Others are more informative than the normal textbooks on Party history but their data are still closely linked to pre-defined interpretations and evaluations. Thus, 'antiquarian' aims can be recognized by the amount of facts conveyed and the relative independence of the data from interpretations and evaluations, whereas power-legitimizing or propagandistic aims subordinate the facts to the interpretations and convey a relatively smaller amount of information. Texts of this latter

---

[27] For studies of Party historiography I have been able to consult two classified scholarly magazines – the *neibu* (internal distribution) version of *Dangshi yanjiu*, and *Dangshi yanjiu ziliao* (Material on Party Research), published by the archival section of the Museum on Revolutionary History in Beijing.

kind are extremely numerous and can readily be found in the academic periodicals produced by universities throughout China.

Discussions on evaluating Chen Duxiu, conducted in 1979 and 1980, provides a good example of the different types of balance between interpretation and information found in different articles at the beginning of the Dengist era. The main questions were whether Chen Duxiu could be conceived of as a Marxist; who it was who had been responsible for the defeat in 1927; and, finally, whether it is correct to say that Chen Duxiu had been a traitor. Articles dwelling on the first topic were mainly written by historiographers of the third rank and published in university journals. Although different answers were given to the question, a reader gets the impression that the authors were not discussing Chen Duxiu but were debating current political and theoretical issues.[28] Out of the enormous amount of material available they only selected those articles which served their own arguments without saying why these are more important than those other documents which other authors were citing to come to a different evaluation. They were obviously not trying to reconstruct the past, but were using the past to fight a battle in the present.

The second topic is very delicate, as it has to do with the evaluation of the role of Stalin and Comintern politics in China. Discussion of this question had to be mostly internal, since the Central Committee had not yet come to an official conclusion on how to interpret the issue. The discussion was confined to historiographers of the first and second rank because the main problem was to arrive at an evaluation which the majority of the Central Committee could agree upon. Finally, the question of whether it was right to say that Chen Duxiu was a 'traitor' (*hanjian*) was discussed in the classified (*neibu*) academic publications

---

[28] See Lin Mosheng, Wang Hongmo and Wang Shudi, 'Yingdang quanmian de lishi de pingjia Chen Duxiu' [We Should Evaluate Chen Duxiu Comprehensively and Historically], *Jiaoxue yu yanjiu*, no.3, 1979, pp.18 ff.; Wang Weili and Du Wenjun, 'Dui Chen Duxiu pingjia de pingjia – jian lun wusi shiqi Chen Duxiu de lishi diwei' [An Evaluation of the Evaluation of Chen Duxiu – On His Historical Position During the May Fourth Era), *Jilin daxue xuebao* [Jilin University Journal], no.2, 1979, pp.7 ff.; Sha Jiansun, 'Wusi houqi de Chen Duxiu shi bu shi Makesizhuyizhe? [Was Chen Duxiu a Marxist in the Later Phase of the May Fourth Movement?], *Beijing daxue xuebao* [Beijing University Journal], no.3, 1979, pp.21 ff.; Song Jingming and Ma Jianli, 'Ping Chen Duxiu zaoqi de lishi gongji' [Evaluation of the Historical Contributions of Chen Duxiu in his Early Phase], *Wuhan daxue xuebao* [Wuhan University Journal], no.6, 1979, pp.68 ff.

on Party history.²⁹ The aim was to challenge the verdict of the Sixth Party Congress at which Chen was accused of working for the Japanese and to criticize Kang Sheng for falsely calling Chen a 'traitor' and for making it impossible for him to re-enter the Party after Chen's release from prison in 1937. Party historiographers of the second rank combined 'antiquarian' and political aims by carefully reconstructing and re-interpreting past events, by making use of the political campaign in 1979 against Kang Sheng, a context in which 'leftist' tendencies could more easily be criticized. Even given this political context, however, in some of these articles, 'antiquarian' aims predominated, with the conveying of 'true' information in a dominant role and with interpretation only of secondary importance.

Party Historiography, Mao, and Mao Zedong Thought

Under Mao's rule, Party historiography was closely linked to Mao Zedong Thought and was defined as the 'history of the never-ending combination of the general truth of Marxism-Leninism with the concrete practice of the Chinese Revolution as represented by Mao Zedong Thought'.³⁰ That is, Party history was Mao Zedong Thought put into practice. In this respect, Party historiography in China followed the example set by the *Short Course on the History of the Communist Party of the Soviet Union*³¹ written under the personal supervision of Stalin

---

29 See Xia Liping, 'Chen Duxiu bei kaichu chu dang zhi hou' [Chen Duxiu After Being Expelled from the Party], *Dangshi yanjiu ziliao*, no.15, 1979, pp.13 ff.; Guo Xuyin, 'Ping Chen Duxiu gei dang zhongyang de san feng xin' [Evaluation of Chen Duxiu's Three Letters to the Party's Central Committee], *Shanghai shifan xueyuan xuebao* [Shanghai Normal College Journal], no.2, 1979, pp.14 ff.; Tang Baolin, 'Jiu an xin kao – guanyu Wang Ming Kang Sheng wuxian Chen Duxiu wei "hanjian" de wenti' [An Old Verdict Reinspected – On the Problem of Wang Ming's and Kang Sheng's Denunciation of Chen Duxiu as a 'Traitor'], *Dangshi yanjiu ziliao*, no.16, 1980, pp.19 ff.; Zhang Yongtong and Liu Chuanxue, 'Chen Duxiu zai kangri zhanzheng shiqi de zhengzhi yanlun' [Chen Duxiu's Expressions of his Political Ideas During the Period of the Anti-Japanese War], *Dangshi yanjiu ziliao*, no.16, 1980, pp.6 ff.

30 Hu Hua, 'Zenyang jiangshou Zhongguo xinminzhuzhuyi gemingshi' [How to Lecture on the History of the New Democratic Revolution], *Xin jianshe* [New Construction], no.1, 1953, pp.30 ff.

31 *History of the Communist Party of the Soviet Union, (Bolsheviks), Short Course* [Istoriia Vsesoiuznoi Kommunisticheskoi Partii (Bol'shevikov), Kratki Kurs] (Moscow, 1938).

and designated as representing the 'living history of Marxism-Leninism'.[32] But, whereas up to the end of the 1950s Mao Zedong Thought was propagated as the unifying ideology of the CCP, it was redefined to represent the correct ideology of the left wing of the Party on the eve of, and during, the Cultural Revolution. The coalition which had formulated the 1945 'Resolution' broke apart, and with it the evaluations of the 'Resolution' lost their importance. Instead, Mao's theory on the Chinese revolution was defined to constitute the main content of Party history. All allusions to theoretical contributions other

---

[32] 'Guanyu *Liangong (bu) dangshi jianming jiaocheng* chubanhou zenyang jinxing dang de xuanchuan' [On How to Conduct the Party's Propaganda After the Publication of the *History of the Communist Party of the Soviet Union (b) (Short Course)*], *Jiaoxue yu yanjiu*, no.2, 1954, pp.2 ff. When asked about the relationship between Chinese and Soviet Party historiography, my interview subjects stressed that there was no connection between the two whatsoever. They admitted having studied the *Short Course* in detail, but not as a model for their textbooks on Party history – only to understand the history of the Soviet Union and its efforts to build a socialist society. In all the articles written on how to write and study Party history the possibility of learning from the experience gained by other communist parties or socialist countries is never hinted at. See, for example, Li Da, 'Zenyang xuexi dangshi' [How to Study Party History], *Xin jianshi*, no.6, 1951, pp.2 ff.; Gu Chongshi, Li Fu and Li Mingqian, *Zenyang xuexi zhongguo gongchandang lishi?* [How to Study the History of the CCP] (Shanghai, 1951); Feng Wenbin, 'Jiaqiang jianguo sanshi nianlai dangshi de yanjiu' [Reinforce Research on the Thirty Years of Party History Since the Founding of the PRC], *Dangshi yanjiu*, no.1, 1980, pp.19 ff.; Fang Kongmu, 'Tan dangshi gongzuozhong de jigjfe wenti' [On Some Questions Concerning Work on Party History], *Dangshi yanjiu ziliao*, no.14, 1979, pp.7 ff.; Chen Wenbin, 'Yong kexue de taidu yanjiu dangshi' [Study Party History with a Scientific Attitude], *Dangshi yanjiu*, no.1, 1980, pp.36 ff.; Ma Jibin (1980), loc. cit. There is an interesting report on the Fourth International Conference on Party History in *Lishi yanjiu*, no.11, 1958, pp.74 ff. This says that international conferences on Party history had been organized by communist parties in power ever since 1955. China first participated in 1957 when the Communist Parties of Korea and Mongolia, as well as of some capitalist countries such as Austria, Italy and France, had been invited for the first time. Although the Chinese delegates gave reports on the state of Party historiography in China at the 1957 and 1958 conferences, they were satisfied to see that the emphasis of the 1958 conference had shifted increasingly towards understanding the history of the Communist International. The conference for 1959 was scheduled to take place in Romania and was supposed to discuss the question of how modern historical research could contribute to the struggle against 'modern revisionism'. No report on the 1959 conference can be found in *Lishi yanjiu*.

than those written by Mao himself, as well as quotations from Party documents, were deleted from textbooks on Party history, and increasingly detailed explanations of Mao's articles as published in the four volumes of his *Selected Works*[33] were introduced. A Party historiographer, remembering the formulations used at the time, told me:

> How did we formulate it then? When studying the history of the Chinese Communist Party, its history constituted a 'red thread', Mao Zedong Thought was the focus, and the works of Chairman Mao the 'basic teaching material'. This was formulated before the Cultural Revolution in 1964. I do not remember the exact situation, as this was a matter of the army, but I am afraid it had something to do with the fact that Lin Biao had been appointed Minister of Defence and had started to use wordings stressing unilaterally the study of Mao Zedong Thought. This way, studying Party history became identical with studying Mao Zedong Thought; it was studying the works of Chairman Mao.[34]

The growing Mao-centrism of Party historiography was reflected in the list of leading CCP members cited in different publications up to the beginning of the Cultural Revolution and the frequency with which they were mentioned. In the 1945 'Resolution' Mao was mentioned 49 times, Li Lisan, as the main target of criticism, 29 times, and all other leading members of the CCP were mentioned two to six times.[35] In Hu Qiaomu's *Thirty Years of the Chinese Communist Party*, which is a text of approximately double the length, Mao's name occurred 118 times, Chen Duxiu's 23 and Zhu De's seven times; the remaining 23 leading members of the CCP were mentioned one to five times.[36] A typical textbook of the 1960s containing 225,000 characters referred to Mao 370 times, to Chen Duxiu 65 times and Zhu De 12 times, with Li Lisan being mentioned 26 times. Even a Party politician as important as Liu Shaoqi was referred to only 13 times.[37] The only exception to this rule seems to have been the Party history written under the supervision of the Beijing municipal Party committee; here Mao and Liu were given equal space both in matters of practical politics and in theoretical

---

[33] See Mao Zedong, *Xuanji* (1969), vols.I-IV. The 1945 'Resolution' is not to be found in this edition.

[34] Interview II, in Weigelin-Schwiedrzik (1984), p.153.

[35] Mao Zedong, *Xuanji* (1953), Vol. III, pp.975 ff. For a more detailed comparison, see Weigelin-Schwiedrzik (1984), pp.174 ff.

[36] See Hu Qiaomu (1951), op.cit.; Weigelin-Schwiedrzik (1984), pp.174 ff.

[37] See Wang Shi et al., op.cit.; Weigelin-Schwiedrzik (1984), pp.174 ff.

contributions. But this volume did not come out until 1964 and was of highly restricted circulation.[38]

The Cultural Revolution, in its early phase, marked the negation of the conventions respected since the Seventh Party Congress and the total collapse of the coalition between Mao and Liu Shaoqi. Nevertheless, the textbooks written between 1971 and 1976 were not as different from the ones written before the Cultural Revolution as one might expect. Although the 'struggle between the two lines' was declared to be the main feature of Party history, very few of the textbooks I have been able to consult used a different pattern of periodization in order to depict Party history as the sequence of ten different struggles against the correct line represented by Mao Zedong.[39]

This relatively modest change relates to the power which the different factions inside the CCP held at the beginning of the 1970s. The 'leftists' were not strong enough to enforce upon the whole Party an interpretation of Party history which would legitimize their right to monopolize power.[40] Another factor lies in the political and ideological tasks of Party historiography. If we accept Max Weber's theory on charisma and routinization,[41] we must conclude that, in China, Party historiography had a dual role. On the one hand it was part-and-parcel of post-revolutionary routinization. On the other hand, it contributed to the perpetuation of Mao Zedong's charismatic leadership. Declaring Party history to be 'Mao Zedong Thought put into practice', and thus conventionalizing the understanding of Mao's writings, served the end of routinization. Declaring Mao to stand at the very centre of Party history was aimed at perpetuating his charisma. By redefining Mao

---

[38] See Beijingshi gaodeng xuexiao dangshi jiangyi bianxie xiezuozu, op.cit.

[39] An example of change is *Zhongguo gongchandang shici luxian douzheng shigao* [Outline History of the Ten Line-struggles of the CCP] (Beijing, 1976). For a mixture of the 'ten-line scheme' and the former pattern of periodization, see *Zhongguo gongchandangnei liang tiao luxian douzhengshi jiangyi* [Textbook on the History of the Two-line Struggle of the CCP] (Shanghai, 1972).

[40] In preparation for the 9th Party Congress of 1969, work was initiated to pass a resolution on Party history, but according to a document called 'Zhonggong zhongyang, zhongyang wenge xiaozu guanyu dui zhengxun zhaokai "jiu da" de yijian de tongbao [Zhangfa (67) 358 hao], the majority view held that the time was not yet ripe for this kind of Party resolution. See: *CCP Documents of the Great Proletarian Cultural Revolution 1966-1967* (Hong Kong 1968), p.609 ff.

[41] See Max Weber, *Wirtschaft und Gesellschaft, Grundrisse der Verstehenden Soziologie*, fifth revised edition (Mohr, Tübingen, 1980), pp.142 ff., 654 ff.

Zedong Thought to serve as the ideology of the Party's left wing and by declaring it to be Mao Zedong's personal contribution to the victory of the Revolution, the politicians of the Cultural Revolution attempted to use Mao's writings as the source of their own authority. Since they lacked historical legitimation for their claims to power and since Mao was their only root in history, Party historiography had to diminish the contributions of all the other leading members of the CCP who had been praised in the 1945 'Resolution'. The growing Mao-centrism of texts written in 1964 and 1965 thus prepared the ground for the texts of the early 1970s which combined Mao's theory with selected historical facts, pushing the evaluations of the 1945 'Resolution' aside.

The Mao-centrism of Party historiography, as observed between 1945 and 1976, was closely connected to today's main task in the field of Party history-writing – the dissemination of a restrictive view of Mao's role in history and the re-definition of Mao Zedong Thought as being the product of the CCP's collective wisdom. One way to fulfill this task has been to write articles on Mao's theoretical contributions during the pre-1949 era. These became incorporated into a political campaign but were also characterized by a shift toward providing more complete historical information.

Ma Yuqing and Chen Fengyi, for example, contributed a very detailed report on how the 'Resolution of the Gutian Conference', which defines the role of politics in the Red Army, came into being.[42] After examining the discussions leading up to the conference, they stressed that the Resolution:

> ...was the product of Comrade Mao Zedong's distillation of the wisdom of soldiers and officers in the Red Army, including the correct opinions of Comrade Zhu De and Comrade Chen Yi.

The main thrust of the article lies in the fact that it gives so many details on contributions made by people other than Mao that Mao's own role remains unclear. Other articles on this topic, such as Huang Shaoqun's, written in 1981,[43] have much the same characteristic: the greater the amount of data and details given (as compared to what Party historiographers would have said about the same incident in earlier

---

[42] Ma Yuqing and Chen Fengyi, 'Gutian huiyi jueyi shi zenyang chansheng de?' [How Did the Resolution of the Gutian Conference Come About?], *Guangming ribao*, 30 Dec. 1979, p.4.

[43] Huang Shaoqun, 'You guan Gutian huiyi liangge wenti de yanjiu' [A Study on Two Problems Concerning the Gutian Conference], *Jiaoxue yu yanjiu*, no.2, 1981, pp.62 ff.

times) the stronger the effect of reducing Mao's contribution to history – to a point where his leading position in the Party seemed almost unjustifiable.

Another example was Tian Yuan's discussion of Mao's attitude toward Li Lisan's 'left opportunism'.[44] In contrast to the textbooks, Tian Yuan stated that Mao's perspective on the Li Lisan line had passed through three phases. In the first phase, he had had the feeling that the line was incorrect but did not openly attack it. In the second phase he realized that the enemy was much stronger than the Red Army. And in the third phase he started to convince the soldiers to leave the city of Changsha as there was no use in occupying major cities unless one could hold them. Whereas Tian provided copious evidence for his explanation of the first and second phases in Mao's process of understanding, Tian did not quote from any documents nor give other proof of the correctness of his explanation of the third phase. The reader is left with the impression that Tian could demonstrate Mao's early acceptance of Li Lisan but cannot provide evidence of his later fight against Li's 'left' opportunism.

A response to Tian's paper, written by Lin Yunhui, criticized Tian for not following the interpretation of the 1945 'Resolution'.[45] Lin accused Tian of accepting the interpretation of the First Enlarged Plenary Session of the Central Committee Bureau for the Soviet Areas, thus implying that Tian's article was influenced by 'left' opportunist thinking. Lin put forth a further interesting argument against Tian's article; he does not agree with Tian's use of classified documents. As Mao's writings, as published in the four volumes, are for Lin the only reliable source of information, and as all of Mao's published articles touching upon the question of Li Lisan show his criticism of the Li Lisan line, he cannot follow Tian's argument that Mao submitted to Li Lisan in the beginning.

The major official pronouncements on Mao here leaned toward this second tack of not digging too rigorously into pre-1949 Party history. As

---

44 Tian Yuan, 'Lisan luxian shiqi de yi ge wenti – shilun Mao Zedong tongzhi dui Lisan luxian de renshi he dizhi' [A Problem Concerning the Period of the Li Lisan Line – On Comrade Mao Zedong's Knowledge of and Resistance to the Li Lisan Line], *Lishi yanjiu*, no.10, 1979, pp.13 ff.

45 Lin Yunhui, 'Lüe lun Mao Zedong tongzhi dui Lisan luxian de renshi he dizhi – yu Tian Yuan tongzhi shangque' [A Brief View of Comrade Mao Zedong's Understanding and Position Regarding the Li Lisan Line – A Discussion with Comrade Tian Yuan], *Dangshi yanjiu*, no.4, 1980, pp.51 ff.

the pre-eminent example, in the 1981 'Resolution on Some Questions Concerning the History of the Party Since the Founding of the People's Republic of China'[46] the validity of the 1945 'Resolution' was restated and Mao Zedong's contribution to the victory of the Chinese revolution was acknowledged to have been of major importance. In the second part, concerning the post-1949 period, Mao was criticized; but his contributions were still considered more positive than negative. With this evaluation, the Party leadership was trying to return to the strategy of the Seventh Party Congress. It was trying to unite as many different factions within the Party as possible; and, as all factions in one way or another were related to Mao Zedong, the evaluation of his contributions was equivalent to the evaluation of their own contributions. That is why, even though Mao had died in 1976, the 1981 'Resolution' still evoked the unifying force of his charismatic leadership. At the same time, the 'Resolution' also had to help stabilize the newly established collective leadership. One way of doing this was to define Mao Zedong Thought as 'the crystallization of the wisdom of the whole Party'.[47] Mao Zedong and Mao Zedong Thought were to be distinguished from each other, enabling the new leadership to criticize Mao personally but to hold onto Mao Zedong Thought as the agreed convention of the Party. By separating Mao Zedong from Mao Zedong Thought, all the aspects of Mao Zedong's ideas of which the new leadership did not approve could be excised while new content could be added. Every member of the new leadership was thus declared to have contributed to the creation of Mao Zedong Thought, which rendered the transfer of legitimacy and authority far easier.[48]

The 1981 'Resolution' illustrated aspects of both continuity and change. The new leadership tried to demonstrate continuity by declaring the 1945 'Resolution' to be correct for the evaluation of Party history up until the beginning of the third civil war. It emphasized change by criticizing Mao's post-1949 policies and by defining Mao Zedong Thought as having been created by the 'whole Party'. It relied on Mao Zedong's authority and, at the same time, tried to reduce it. Where his authority could be of use to the new leadership, that leadership tried to transfer it to itself. Where his authority undermined the stabilization of

---

[46] 'Guanyu jianguo yilai dang de ruogan lishi wenti de jueyi', loc.cit.

[47] Ye Jianying, 'Zai qingzhu Zhonghua renmin gongheguo chengli sanshi zhou nian dahuishang de jianghua' [Speech at the Conference Commemorating the Thirtieth Anniversary of the Founding of the PRC], *Hongqi*, no.10, 1979, p.3.

[48] See Weber, op.cit., pp.654 ff.

the new leadership's power, it declared his ideas to be false and, by criticizing them, gained credibility for itself among intellectuals.

The decisions made after Mao's death to establish a more restricted view of Mao's role in Party history gave historians more opportunity to pursue 'antiquarian' intentions. Whereas previously, as we have seen, persons or events which could not be related to Mao Zedong were directly or indirectly off-limits, now they could be examined if they could contribute to relativizing Mao's role in history. Party historiographers started doing research on the biographies of many leading members of the CCP, and they dug out material on its European branch, which had contributed so much to building the Party in the early years but which had hardly been mentioned in the official textbooks and articles.[49] Taking their lead from the 1981 'Resolution', historiographers started demonstrating to readers that Mao was not the only person able to make theoretical contributions to the strategy of the Chinese revolution. Thus the number of topics on which Party historiographers could undertake research grew considerably. Yet at the same time, the Central Committee was neither able nor willing to produce a single document on pre-1949 history in which all the questions raised by this new research could be answered.

However, the overall framework for Party historiography had not changed. The fact that the Central Committee passed the June 1981 'Resolution' shows that it still conceived of itself as being the only source of authoritative interpretations of Party history; and articles written by leading historiographers after the publication of the 'Resolution' show that they were still eager to demonstrate their loyalty to the Party's decisions.[50]

---

[49] See Zhang Jingru, Wang Chaomei, Wang Deqing and Huang Futong, *Zhongguo gongchandang de chuangli* [The Founding of the CCP] (Shijiazhuang, 1981), pp.119 ff., 171 ff. In this book there is a subsection on 'the help of the Communist International' as well as a subsection on Chinese Communist circles in France. In textbooks published before and during the Cultural Revolution neither issue was usually mentioned.

[50] See Li Xin, 'Qian shi bu wang hou shi zhi shi' [If You do not Forget Things Past, They will Lead You through the Future], *Guangming ribao*, 1 July 1981, p.3; Hu Hua, 'Dangshi shang xin de lichengbei' [A New Milestone in Party History], *Guangming ribao*, 9 July 1981, p.3.

Party History and Political Education

The close relationship between Party historiography and Mao Zedong Thought was evident in the examinations that students used to sit for. At every important step in their educational career, Chinese students have undertaken examinations in political studies which have included the study of Party history. Testing the students' knowledge of Party history is a way of checking their loyalty to the Party as well as their understanding of Mao Zedong Thought. Party historiography thus played a major role in the political training of future members of the bureaucracy, both of the government and Party. Since Party history was written as if it were Mao Zedong Thought put into practice, examining the students in it implied that their knowledge was being tested and not their *'Weltanschauung'*. The Communist Party seemed to be relying on experience derived from the Confucian examination system. A candidate being examined on his loyalty toward Confucianism was not asked to reveal his personal understanding of the Confucian Classics but was expected to know what the different commentators had said. The candidates were thus allowed to keep 'office' and 'personal life', 'inside' and 'outside', apart, and were accepted as members of the bureaucracy as long as they did not act counter to the conventions set by tradition.[51]

In the 1950s, the Chinese Communists followed this pattern in most respects. The students had to master the official version of Mao Zedong Thought and, in the tests, had to prove that they were able to think within the framework of set assumptions agreed upon by the Party leadership. By declaring Mao Zedong Thought to be the 'leading ideology' of the Party, it established a new code of thought and political behaviour for the bureaucracy, and by translating Mao Zedong Thought into Party history, it wrote the textbooks through which students could learn what Mao Zedong Thought was. The publication of the original four volumes of Mao Zedong's *Selected Works* canonized Mao Zedong

---

[51] The Chinese Communists, of course, also relied on the experience gained in the Soviet Union. But to my knowledge, there are no studies on Party historiography in the Soviet Union which could be compared with what I am doing here. That is why I am not able to trace back in detail the similarities and the differences between Chinese and Soviet Party historiography. The fact that Party history was part of political training in the Soviet Union and other socialist countries did not necessarily imply that the mechanisms that were applied in China were also to be found there.

Thought.[52] Party historiography conventionalized it. Learning about Party history meant learning to write in the way that the Party wanted future members of the bureaucracy to publicly think. The lack of Party historiography in the early stage of the Cultural Revolution had to be compensated for by having people learn Mao's texts and directives by heart. Before and after the Cultural Revolution, Party historiography, with its combination of facts (*shi*) and theory (*lun*), set the 'internal code' for China's new bureaucracy.

The predominance of theory over facts in the late 1950s and the Cultural Revolution period trained bureaucrats to look for 'ideological' solutions. By placing new emphasis on facts, Party historiography in the 1980s was striving to find a way of writing history that would encourage future bureaucrats to seek 'technocratic' rather than strictly 'ideological' solutions to China's problems.

---

[52] Helmut Martin, *Cult and Canon: The Origins and Development of State Maoism* (M.E. Sharpe, Armonk, N.Y., 1982).

THE CONTROVERSY OVER 'FEUDAL DESPOTISM': POLITICS AND HISTORIOGRAPHY IN CHINA, 1978-82

Lawrence R. Sullivan*

> From the Qin, monarchs have been bandits. (Tang Zhen)

Political conflict in the Chinese Communist Party (CCP) has often provoked critical commentary and debate over historiographical issues in China. Since the early 1950s, various intra-party factions have appealed to history to justify competing political and ideological positions, especially on the proper role of executive authority.[1] When Mao Zedong's arbitrary decisions produced the disastrous Great Leap Forward (1958-60), historical analogy was used to criticize the Chairman's actions with strong moralistic overtones. Zhou Xinfang thus questioned the Great Leap by portraying the efforts of the imperial official Hai Rui to appeal to a despotic and ill-informed emperor in the Ming dynasty [see Chapter Two of this book]. Condemning the

---

*   I thank Profs. Albert Feuerwerker, Noriko Kamachi, Kenneth Lieberthal, Michel Oksenberg, Barry Naughton, Martin Whyte, Ernest Young, and other members of the Faculty Seminar in Contemporary China Research, University of Michigan, and Paul A. Cohen (Wellesley College) and the anonymous referees of this article for their comments on earlier draft versions. Special thanks to Prof. Harriet C. Mills (University of Michigan), Prof. Timothy Cheek (The Colorado College), Virginia Chen (Harvard University), Huang Chin-shing (University of California, Berkeley), and Nancy Sweeney (Miami University, Oxford, Ohio) for their assistance.

1   Merle Goldman, 'The Role of History in Party Struggle, 1962-4', *The China Quarterly*, no.51, July-September 1972, p.500; Clifford Edmonds Jr., 'The Politics of Historiography: Jian Bozan's Historicism', in Merle Goldman (ed.), *China's Intellectuals and the State: In Search of a New Relationship* (Council on East Asian Studies, Cambridge, 1987), pp.69-85; and Arif Dirlik, 'Chinese Historians and the Marxist Concept of Capitalism: A Critical Examination', *Modern China*, vol.8, no.1 (1982), pp.105-32.

'tyrannical way' (*ba dao*) of ancient emperors, former *People's Daily* editor Deng Tuo voiced similar traditional arguments apparently to protest the purge of People's Liberation Army commander Peng Dehuai, who had openly challenged Mao at the 1959 Lushan Party Plenum.[2] During the struggle over Mao's succession in the mid-1970s, however, radical leftists, led by Jiang Qing, took the opposite tract by glorifying despots. In the 1973-75 Anti-Confucian campaign, the historian Shi Ting praised the imperial despotism and violent methods of China's first emperor Qin Shihuang (221-210 BC) to legitimize the Gang of Four's support of extreme autocracy.[3] Just as the creation of a unified empire and centralized state in the third century BC had justified Qin's 'burning of the books and burying of the scholars', so too, Shi Ting argued, was tyranny necessary to achieve radical political goals in the waning years of the Cultural Revolution.

Following the political victory of Deng Xiaoping at the December, 1978 3rd Plenum, Chinese historiography revived the anti-despotic themes voiced by Deng Tuo and Zhou Xinfang in the early 1960s. Despite the harm done to historians and history as a discipline by the Cultural Revolution (1966-76), many Chinese historians once again critically examined 'feudal despotism'.[4] Consistent with the CCP's post-1978 denunciation of Mao Zedong's 'patriarchal despotism' (*jiazhang zhuanzhi*), they drew parallels between Mao's degeneration into autocratic leadership after 1958 and similar experiences of emperors and leaders of peasant rebellions, such as Hong Xiuquan of the mid-nineteenth century Taipings.[5] But as this chapter demonstrates,

---

2   Deng Tuo, 'Wangdao he badao', [The Kingly Way and the Tyrannical Way], *Beijing wanbao* [Beijing Evening News], 25 February 1962, translated by Timothy Cheek in *Chinese Law and Government*, Winter 1983-84, pp.64-67.

3   Peter R. Moody, Jr., 'The New Anti-Confucian Campaign', *Asian Survey*, vol.14, no.4 (April 1974), p.321.

4   *Zhongguo lishixue nianjian* [Chinese Historical Studies Yearbook], (Lianhe Chubanshe, Beijing, 1979), pp.144-56. The spread of criticism of the Cultural Revolution as 'feudal-fascist', from Democracy Wall participants to the official ideology in 1979, opened the door to historians' examination of 'despotism'. John A. Rapp, 'The Fate of Marxist Democrats in Leninist Party States: China's Debate on the Asiatic Mode of Production', *Theory and Society*, no.16, 1987, p.711.

5   Mao Zedong's 'personal arbitrariness' became increasingly pronounced after 1958, according to the CCP's 1981 'Resolution on Certain Questions in the History of Our Party', when he systematically violated basic decision-making principles of 'collective leadership'. *Xinhua* [New China News Agency], 30 June

historiographical argument from 1978 to 1982 was not monolithic. Nor did it always serve the political and ideological views and interests of CCP leaders. In the midst of the debate over state structure and political authority raised in the post-Mao CCP and in popular protests such as the Democracy Wall Movement (1978-79), historians divided over basic interpretations of Chinese history. Variations in historiographical argument also reflected more esoteric disputes among historians over codifying China's past according to the prevailing Marxist criteria of historicism.

The dominant school of historiography, influenced by orthodox Marxism and Stalinist schemes of 'universal development' formulated in the 1920s, emphasized the deterministic role of impersonal economic forces to explain the persistence of despotic authority in China's imperial and modern history.[6] For these historians, referred to here as 'materialists', China had experienced a relatively unbroken *linear* formation of despotism (examined below) from Qin Shihuang to Mao Zedong, that reflected the eternal 'backwardness' of its agrarian economy and the 'feudal consciousness' of the peasantry. A minority of historians, in contrast, contested this orthodox Marxist paradigm by focusing on the autonomous role of the state and individual emperors in creating Chinese despotism. According to this 'political' school of historiography, despotism did not emerge from China's underdeveloped material conditions and 'backward' popular consciousness, but from unbridled state power and megalomaniacal leaders, whose awesome personal authority reflected inadequate institutional controls on rulers from late imperial times to the Communist era. Finally, an even smaller group of historians rejected the dominant anti-despotic theme of post-1978 historiography by praising the positive role powerful leaders have played in Chinese (and Western) history. Without sharing the extreme authoritarianism and leftist politics of Shi Ting and the Gang of Four, this 'great man' school of historiography believed China's past and future development required an 'enlightened despot' comparable to Qin Shihuang or Napoleon.[7]

1981, translated in US Foreign Broadcast Information Service, *Daily Report: China* (hereafter FBIS) 1 July 1981, pp.K1-K35.

6   Rapp, 'China's Debate on the Asiatic Mode of Production', p.716.

7   'Materialist', 'political', and 'great man' are terms assigned by this author to discrete schools of post-1978 historiography in China. The first and third groups usually published their views in the mainstream Party press, especially *Renmin ribao* [People's Daily], *Guangming ribao* [Enlightenment Daily], and *Hongqi*

Historiographical argument from 1978-1982 served immediate political ends just as Deng Tuo's and Shi Ting's earlier works had done. Although the political-ideological strait-jacket imposed on Chinese historians had loosened somewhat – with greater concomitant attention by historians to garnering evidence to illuminate the complexities of China's past – historiographical interpretation from 1978 to 1982 was still often related to contemporary policy controversies.[8] 'Materialist' historians thus analysed China's despotic traditions in terms consistent with Deng Xiaoping's agenda of promoting economic growth while limiting political reforms to moderate internal changes in the CCP. If economic backwardness created despotism from the Qin dynasty onward, then, it was argued, the Party must maintain its dictatorial control over Chinese society until economic and cultural development destroys the social basis of despotic politics, especially among the peasantry. In this basically conservative political prescription, supported by most central Party leaders, contemporary political reform should be limited to reinstituting 'collective leadership' (*jiti lingdao*) in the Communist Party, but without a fundamental democratizing of political authority. Since China's population is still overwhelmed by the same pro-despotic sentiments that sustained both two thousand years of imperial autocracy and the Mao cult, political liberalization would only produce another tyrannical 'popular god'.

'Political' historians, in contrast, formulated arguments diametrically opposed to the continuation of a one-party dictatorship. Reflecting the opinions of relatively liberal university intellectuals and political reformers in the Party, their interpretation of Chinese history pointed to institutional liberalization as the only permanent solution to China's despotic traditions. Unless a radical alteration of basic power relationships was effected between state and society, China could easily degenerate, they argued, into yet another despotism even after the death of Mao Zedong.

Finally, at the opposite end of the political spectrum, 'great man' historians evidently represented the views of politically conservative

---

[Red Flag], while the second group generally published in journals specializing in history, particularly *Lishi yanjiu* [Historical Research] and *Zhongguo shi yanjiu* [Research on Chinese History] and in various university-based publications.

[8] Paul A. Cohen and Merle Goldman, 'Modern History', in Anne F. Thurston and Jason H. Parker (eds), *Humanistic and Social Science Research in China: Recent History and Further Prospects* (Social Science Research Council, New York, 1980), pp.47-49. The drafting of the June 1981 6th Plenum Resolution, which began in March 1980, apparently helped spur the debate over despotism.

Party leaders, such as Chen Yun and Yang Shangkun, by favouring a strong single leader. Although opposed to the fanatical elements of the Mao cult, this school cited historical precedent to support one-man authority in the midst of China's great economic transformation under the reforms.

Historians in post-Mao China also confronted historiographical issues deeply rooted in Chinese Marxism and even classical historiography and philosophy that transcended immediate political conflicts. Competing interpretations of 'feudal despotism' in 1978-82 were not, in other words, simply an allegory for debating contemporary political reform, but a replay of sincere and long-standing arguments by professional historians on the origins of China's authoritarian political traditions and the role of the individual in history. Post-1978 criticisms of Chinese despotism recalled, in fact, the Social History controversy in the 1930s among Chinese Marxists over the 'Asiatic Mode of Production' and Karl Wittfogel's 'Oriental Despotism', and even seventeenth century critiques of imperial despotism by Huang Zongxi and Gu Yanwu.[9] 'Why China [had] established...centralized power and an emperor at the head of the state' was still the most compelling issue in Chinese historiography, a *Guangming ribao* article asserted.[10]

Yet considerable disagreement existed over the *source* of China's stagnation in the 'feudal' stage and the *pattern* of despotism's historical formation from the Qin dynasty (221-207 BC) to the contemporary era. 'Materialist' historians generally believed China's despotic traditions derived from the small-scale 'natural economy' (*ziran jingji*) that had shaped China's state structure in a *linear* formation of despotism over an unbroken two-thousand year period. From Qin Shihuang to Mao

---

[9] Clifford Edmonds Jr., 'The Politics of Historiography', in *China's Intellectuals and The State*, p.95; Timothy Brook, 'Theories of Traditional Chinese Society in Modern China and Japan', unpublished manuscript, pp.18-22; and William de Bary, 'Chinese Despotism and the Confucian Ideal: A Seventeenth Century View', in John K. Fairbank (ed.), *Chinese Thought and Institutions* (University of Chicago Press, Chicago, 1957), pp.163-203.

[10] *Guangming ribao*, 18 November 1980, p.4. This has been 'one of the most hotly debated questions among Chinese historians for the last 20 years', the same paper noted, as was clearly indicated by the open controversies voiced at history 'seminars' on 'feudalism' held in 1979 and 1980. *Guangming ribao*, November 1979, p.4. Some articles, such as an August 1980 series in *Renmin ribao* and *Guangming ribao* analysing 'eunuchs' dictatorial power' in Ming China, served purely political purposes, which in this case involved criticizing the leftist Wang Dongxing and his pro-Mao 'Whateverist' faction.

Zedong, economic backwardness had prevented China from breaking out of the despotic authority relationships which, based on the 'feudal' social order of the family and clan, permeated the state. 'Political' historians, however, contested this orthodox Marxist-Stalinist paradigm with a theory focusing on the autonomous role of political, ideological, and institutional forces. The state, not the economy or society, was the source of despotic values imposed on the Chinese people from above. Yet because emperors prior to the Song dynasty (960-1279 AD) had not pursued political absolutism, China had evolved in a *non-linear* pattern of political development. Full-blown despotism had emerged relatively late in history, with China's leaders, not the people, bearing ultimate responsibility for its creation. Finally, 'great man' historians rejected both these anti-despotic views by resurrecting the Carlylian theory of history that many Chinese intellectuals and political figures, such as Liang Qichao and Sun Yatsen, have found attractive since the late Qing dynasty.[11] Emphasizing the decisive historical role of the 'heroic' individual, these few historians were not concerned with explaining the origins of despotism, but rather with promoting the single leader's authority as the political means necessary to advance China's future development.

On the Material Basis of Despotism

> Having passed through millenia of authoritarian government, from Qin Shihuang to the Hongxian emperor...our people have fallen into the maze of wealth and position and have not become conscious of their situation. (Chen Duxiu, 1915)

The dominant historiographical argument supported by central Party leaders stressed the deterministic relationship between 'feudal small-scale production' (*fengjian xiao shengchan*) and 'patriarchal despotism'. Contrary to Yao Wenyuan's warning during the Cultural Revolution that 'capitalism' and 'bourgeois' interests threatened the CCP, post-1978 commentary considered the 'restoration' of 'feudalism' to be the primary problem in the Party and society.[12] The existence of the patriarchal leader in the CCP is inseparable from China's long history as

---

[11] Andrew J. Nathan, *Chinese Democracy* (Alfred A. Knopf, New York, 1985), pp.61-62.

[12] *Guangming ribao*, 21 January 1979, translated in FBIS, 6 February 1979, p.E3 and Deng Xiaoping, 'Reforming [the] Leadership System', *Beijing Review*, vol.29 (32) (11 August 1986), pp.15-19.

a 'feudal' society from the Qin dynasty to the present. Whereas the West experienced radical political change shaped by fundamental economic transformation, China had failed to produce mass revolutionary movements against the *ancien regime*. Without a comparable emergence of capitalism and bourgeois democracy, China had stagnated in a backward 'feudal mode of production' that 'materialist' historians suggested had created powerful despotic political forces from the third century BC to the present: 'In the Chinese feudal society that emerged during the Qin and Han Dynasties, the basic production units were small-scale peasant households under the landlord system'.[13] Their 'widespread, universal, and dispersed individual management, constituted the foundation for the system of feudal despotism in our country'.[14] Given the 'stubborn capability [of feudal society] to revive itself', China had suffered from a long line of 'emperors, generals, and ministers' who sustained the basic structure of despotic authority.[15]

Contrary to Karl Wittfogel's arguments, however, there was nothing uniquely 'Chinese' or 'Oriental' about the country's despotic traditions. Since 'political organization is inevitably conditioned by its corresponding economic base', many 'materialist' historians strongly criticized Wittfogel's 'hydraulic' theory on the intimate connection between irrigation and centralized autocracy. Reflecting Stalin's denigration of Marx's 'Asiatic Mode of Production' in favour of a view of Chinese history as 'feudal', they believed Wittfogel's theory denied the universal applicability of Marx's 'scientific' paradigm to all societies. Despotism was not specifically 'Chinese', for 'every state in its historical development must have a similar political form in correspondence to its respective economic base'. Nor was China's entire history characterized by despotic rule. On the contrary, China had enjoyed a long period of 'primitive' political formation preceding the imperial despotism of the Qin.[16]

---

[13] *Renmin ribao*, 11 July 1980, p.5.

[14] Li Yinhe and Lin Chun, 'Shilun woguo jianshe shehuizhuyi shiqi fan fengjian canyu de douzheng', [Tentative Discussion on the Struggle Against Vestiges of Feudalism in China During the Period of Building Socialism], *Lishi yanjiu*, no.9, 15 September 1979, pp.3-5.

[15] *Renmin ribao*, 11 July 1980, p.5.

[16] Liao Xuesheng, 'Guanyu dongfang zhuanzhizhuyi', [On Oriental Despotism], *Shijie lishi* [World History] no.1, 1980, pp.89-93. Liao argued further that 'the production force and its related economic and political system are not simply decided by the mode of irrigation' and that other great empires outside China had

This singular emphasis on the economic and social bases of the political superstructure led 'materialist' historians to blame the Chinese people for the long history of despotism. Repeating Marx's sociological analysis of Napoleon III's restoration in the *Eighteenth Brumaire of Louis Bonaparte*, Chinese historians singled out the peasantry as providing the critical support for both imperial and Maoist despotism.[17] China's 'small producers', like the French peasants described by Marx, have been overwhelmed for centuries by 'monarchist thought' (*huangquanzhuyi sixiang*) produced by backward material conditions and social isolation that remained relatively unchanged even during the Communist era. Unable to 'use their definitions (of reality) to protect their own economic position', Chinese peasants have suffered from a profound political dependency on both 'the authority of a God on high to

---

experienced despotism but without relying on irrigation. Similar Chinese criticisms of Wittfogel were voiced in the 1930s by Marxist historians heavily influenced by the theories of the Russian historian Pokrovsky, who, contrary to Wittfogel, saw a close causal relationship between commercial capitalism and despotism – an argument not repeated by Chinese historians in 1978-82. Anthropologists in the West have also concurred with Chinese criticisms of Wittfogel, such as K.C. Chang, who recently argued that 'the theory of water control as the primary basis of state power does not find support in the archaeology of the Three Dynasties', (2200-256 BC). Some contemporary historians in China, however, still adhere to a Wittfogelian analysis by stressing the unique social, political, and economic underpinnings for the long history of Chinese despotism. K.C. Chang, *Art, Myth, and Ritual: The Path to Political Authority in Ancient China* (Harvard University Press, Cambridge, 1983), p.128; Arif Dirlik, *Revolution and History: Origins of Marxist Historiography in China, 1919-1937* (University of California Press, Berkeley, 1978), pp.207-11; and Rapp, 'China's Debate on the Asiatic Mode of Production', pp.716-872, where Chinese distinctions between Marx and Wittfogel's theories are noted. The analysis of pre-Qin society described in the text is very similar to Guo Moruo's 1930 work, *Zhongguo gudai shehui yanjiu* [Studies of Ancient Chinese Society], while the view of the Qin to Qing period as an unbroken despotism also repeated the arguments of Wang Lixi and Hu Zhiyuan from the 1920s. Brook, 'Theories of Traditional Chinese Society', pp.25, 45.

17 Marx's analysis in the *Eighteenth Brumaire* of mid-nineteenth French society undergoing the tensions of capitalist development is not an especially appropriate explanatory framework for examining pre-modern Chinese history. But its focus on the restorational powers of monarchy and Marx's famous description of the peasantry as a 'sack of potatoes' has made the *Brumaire* very appealing among left-wing Chinese intellectuals ever since the May Fourth movement. Karl Marx and Frederick Engels, *Selected Works, Volume I* (Foreign Languages Press, Moscow, 1955), pp.247-355.

represent them' and the despotism of local clan heads who replicated imperial authority at the local level.[18] Rural China, like nineteenth century France, thus lacked the social cohesion characteristic of 'civil society' necessary to challenge state and clan power. 'Each household and each family produced most of its needs [so that] the ties bringing families together did not derive from economic relationships, but instead depended on a non-secular clan power'. As 'the organizers of social life', including 'ancestor worship', and as 'the leaders of production', the clan heads established the social foundations of imperial despotism by exercising absolute authority in the villages. Just as the 'clan heads were the representatives of a family and clan', so too did the emperor represent 'the authority of the entire nation and society'. 'Monarchism was simply the local patriarch writ large'. It was certainly true that the peasants' pro-monarchical sentiments reflected the economic oppression of 'feudal' society, where imperial authority helped sustain the economic interests of the landlord class.[19] But the primary reason for unbroken despotism in Chinese history, 'materialist' historians argued, was the peasants' limited consciousness, particularly their unshaken belief in the emperor's 'spiritual wisdom' (*shengming*) and in his purported 'transcendence of class interests'. 'Since the emperor was seen as a "true dragon" issuing imperial edicts', historian Li Guihai concluded that 'the peasants did not employ any standards to evaluate his behaviour, and nothing was allowed to shake their absolute defense of [his power] to decide all matters of right and wrong, justice or injustice'.

---

18 Li Guihai, 'Lun nongmin de huangquanzhuyi sixiang' [On the Peasants' Monarchical Thought], *Zhongguo shi yanjiu*, no.1 (January 1978), pp.44-50. K.C. Chang has argued, however, that 'Marx's formulation of a system of static, self-contained village communities' does not even apply to the Three Dynasties period in Chinese history – when there was a 'dynamic interaction within a constantly shifting, hierarchical economic and political system' – let alone to the later post-Qin dynastic era. Chang, *Art, Myth, and Ritual*, p.126.

19 The absence of 'flourishing relationships' among the people created, it was argued, the objective foundation for autocracy. Unlike Europe, China's infant textile industries in the Ming-Qing period lacked capitalist 'sprouts', which inhibited modern political development away from despotic traditions. *Renmin ribao*, 11 July 1980, p.5, translated in FBIS, 24 July 1980, pp.3-5. This is not necessarily an accurate picture of late imperial Chinese society, however, as recently described in Susan Naquin and Evelyn S. Rawski, *Chinese Society in the Eighteenth Century* (Yale University Press, New Haven, 1987).

This materialist reductionism essentially denied despotic emperors any fundamental causal autonomy in China's historical evolution. Rebutting the radical left's purported 'idealistic bias' in magnifying Qin Shihuang's personal role in the creation of the centralized empire in 221 BC, post-1978 historians redefined the character of the Qin emperor using both orthodox Marxist and traditional anti-despotic Confucian categories.[20] Radical leftists had praised Qin Shihuang's 'excellent leadership' and 'personal insights on historical trends' to bolster their purpose of 'creating a cult of personal worship'. In reality, it was the 'objective circumstances' of 'productive power' which had determined the revolutionary political and economic changes of the third century BC. Qin Shihuang had 'unconsciously' followed the historical trend, 'materialist' historians insisted, just as Marx had predicted all great leaders must do. The establishment of the centralized 'prefecture system' (*junxian zhi*) was not, as leftist historians had argued, the creation of the emperor's 'heroic' leadership, but resulted from a gradual process of institutional development beginning much earlier in the Spring and Autumn period (722-481 BC). Likewise, the radical alteration of land ownership did not demonstrate Qin Shihuang's personal initiative in benefiting the people directly. Rather, it was the culmination of historical forces that served the long-term economic interests of the emerging landlord class.[21] Finally, the emperor's victorious military tactics were not the product of 'his' genius, but resulted from the 'collective' contributions of the general staff. Although such characterizations imposed the leadership principles of the post-Mao CCP onto ancient history, 'materialist' historians dismissed the role of Qin Shihuang's 'personal will' and 'correct political line' in explaining his accomplishments. These fundamental changes reflected, instead, deeper socio-economic forces consistent with objective circumstances of the epoch.[22]

---

[20] Zhou Nianchang, Li Zude, and Xie Guihua, ' "Si Ren Bang" shenhua Qin Shihuang boyi' [Refuting the 'Gang of Four's' Mystification of Qin Shihuang], *Zhongguo shi yanjiu*, no.1 (January 1979), pp.16-28.

[21] Chinese historians in 1956 also argued that Qin's centralization served a newly emerging landlord class. A.F.P. Hulsewe, 'Chinese Communist Treatment of the Origins and the Foundation of the Chinese Empire', in Albert Feuerwerker (ed.), *History in Communist China* (The M.I.T. Press, Cambridge, 1968), p.125, and Arif Dirlik, *Revolution and History*, p.106.

[22] Hong Jiayi, 'Zhuanzhizhuyi de xingcheng ji qi weihai' [The Formation of Absolutism and Its Harmful Effects], *Nanjing daxue xuebao* [Nanjing University

A similar economic determinism was employed to revise the history of the Han dynasty (202 BC-220 AD), previously condemned by the Gang of Four purportedly for its attempted restoration of pre-Qin 'slave' society. According to the 'materialist' school's *linear* model of Chinese history (examined below), the Han had not retreated from Qin's 'progressive' centralization of authority, but 'fundamentally continued the political system of the Qin' consistent with the economic interests of the emerging feudal landlords.[23] Leftist polemical groups such as Liang Xiao had violated the basic tenets of Marxist materialism by denying 'the landlord class character of the Western Han feudal autocratic state' and by emphasizing, instead, a purported conflict between 'restorationist and anti-restorationist' forces among the imperial elite. The driving force in the Han was incorrectly seen to be 'the internal contradictions between the [old] ruling class and the landlord class [new] ruling position', while Liang Xiao misrepresented the early Han scholar Jia Yi as a 'young and powerful Legalist personality' opposed to the restoration of slavery. In reality, Jia Yi had actually favoured the 'concentration of authority' and 'loyalty to the emperor' not as an 'anti-restorationist' move to counter re-emergent slavery, but rather 'materialist' historians insisted, to give the emperor the authority to satisfy the economic needs of the new landlords by 'stabilizing the land system'.[24] Serving the 'progressive' economic interests of embryonic

---

Journal], no.1 (20 February 1981), pp.42-43. Although probably under-represented in my selection of historical journals, these university-based publications often provided alternative explanations to the historical phenomenon of despotism different from the more 'established' views of *Guangming ribao* and even *Lishi yanjiu*. See also, ff. no.24.

[23] Luo Dongsheng, 'Bo Liang Xiao dui Jia Yi "jiguan" sixiang de waiqu' [Repudiate Liang Xiao's Distortion of Jia Yi's Thinking on the 'Concentration of Authority'), *Xueshu yanjiu* [Academic Research], no.1 (20 May 1978), p.91.

[24] Many of these historiographical arguments paralleled contemporary debates in the CCP over political reform. Jia Yi's purported recommendation to 'concentrate power in the central government but not excessively in the person of the emperor' coincided with Deng Xiaoping's relatively conservative model of 'collective leadership'. Jia Yi's opposition to Qin's brutal treatment of ministers also supported contemporary proposals for restraining the single leader's authority over his immediate advisers. As author of the *Guo Qin lun* [Faults of the Qin], in the 2nd century BC, Jia Yi did, in fact, condemn Qin's unwillingness to 'trust ministers of proved ability' and exposed conditions under Qin rule which produced the great revolt, leading to the founding of the Han dynasty. Yet, like the dynasty he served, Jia Yi supported the centralization of political authority

'feudalism' was also the primary motive behind Dong Zhongshu's second century philosophy of the 'mandate of heaven' and his 'theory of heavenly portents'. Contrary to the Gang of Four's attack on Dong as a 'reactionary', the 'materialist' school declared Dong's theoretical constraints on imperial power to be part of the basic economic 'rationality' of the emerging feudal epoch.[25] Political thought in the Han was, in this post-1978 orthodox Marxist view, a mirror reflection of the basic production and class forces determining China's historical evolution. The Chinese state did not rule autonomously in its own interest, but served the dominant feudal class as 'every ranking official of the court in every dynasty was only a tool of the landlord class regardless of his background or nature'.[26]

The Linear Model of History

This uniform treatment of the Qin and Han dynasties reflected the linear view of Chinese history in 'materialist' historiography. From 221 BC to Mao's death, China had endured, these historians argued, an almost unbroken line of despotic leaders. 'After Qin Shihuang unified China, a centralized country under autocratic despotism was established. During the next 2,000 years, successive dynasties basically took over this

---

engineered by Qin's political revolution. C.P. Fitzgerald, *China: A Short Cultural History*, 3rd edition (Praeger, New York, 1965), p.149.

[25] Specifically, Dong's views were not, as the Gang of Four had argued, to 'frighten people into accepting the will of heaven', but rather to 'have the king under control' in the 'feudal' landlords' interest of preventing excessive taxation and 'over-exploitation of labour'. Such characterization of Dong's theories as a restraint on monarchs diverged, however, from the 'materialist' school's basic linear treatment of an unbroken development of despotism since the Qin. This is just another example of the contradictions produced in trying to impose a uniform Marxist determinism on Chinese history. For an alternative interpretation of Dong Zhongshu stressing his role in strengthening imperial absolutism, see Liu Yuhong, 'Cong "Wu Hua" dao "San Gang" ', [From the 'Five Relations' to the 'Three Bonds'], *Nanjing daxue xuebao*, no.1 (20 February 1981), p.41, and Zhang Chunbo, 'Lun Dong Zhongshu zhexue de lishi zuoyong' [On the Historical Utility of Dong Zhongshu's Philosophy], *Zhexue yanjiu* [Philosophical Research], no.9 (September 1979), pp.47-52.

[26] Lin Guanquan, 'The Asiatic Mode of Production and Ancient Chinese Society', *Shijie lishi*, no.3, 1981, cited in Rapp, 'China's Debate on the Asiatic Mode of Production', p.723.

system of feudal rule'.[27] Han, Tang, Song, Yuan, Ming, and Qing were all 'feudal autocracies' backed by a standard Confucian 'feudal ideology' which every dynasty exploited to 'deify emperors'.[28] Although some 'intelligent people' had periodically challenged autocratic principles (perhaps a reference to Huang Zongxi), 'they were invariably met with brutal persecution from the authorities' and failed to alter the system. Whereas 'European feudal society came about late and disappeared early', China's feudal period was longer and more profound in its political and social influence. The emperor 'embodied both imperial and divine power', while the 'patriarchal system, including familial nepotism, inevitably permeated the bureaucracy'.[29] This 'deep-rooted feudal consciousness', moreover, not only survived the 1911 Republican revolution, but continued to shape contemporary Chinese politics even after 'thirty years of socialist revolution'.

This resilience of despotic leadership was, indeed, a major theme in the 'materialist' school's analysis of modern Chinese history. Since the late nineteenth century, 'feudal' ideology and practice have consistently won out, their argument goes, in the struggle with emerging 'bourgeois'

---

[27] *Wen huibao* [Literary Gazette], 10 July 1980, p.3. This monolithic concept of Chinese history has its roots in the Marxist historiography of the 1930s and also predominated in the 1950s, when historians focused almost exclusively on the economic foundations of an 'unchanging' 'feudalism'. C.P. Fitzgerald, 'The Chinese Middle Ages in Communist Historiography', in Feuerwerker, *History in Communist China*, p.24.

[28] *Hongqi*, no.17 (1 September 1980), pp.25-30. The contradiction in 'materialist' historiography was evident in the treatment of Confucianism: while adhering to the orthodox Confucian rejection of Qin Shihuang's despotism, they still condemned Confucianism as the ideological foundation of the two thousand year despotic state.

[29] Pang Zhuoheng, 'Zhong-Xi fengjian zhuanzhi zhidu de bijiao yanjiu' [Comparative Analysis of the Chinese-Western Feudal Autocratic Systems], *Lishi yanjiu*, no.2 (February 1981), pp.3-13, and *Hongqi*, no.20 (16 October 1980), pp.32-35. Pang's article also linked superior agricultural productivity in the West to the relatively early emergence of social contract theory, which challenged monarchical authority, while in China the greater 'economic insecurity' of Chinese peasants – including 'free tenants and small landowners' – purportedly produced a 'vulnerability' to total state control. The absence in China of a general 'feudal crisis' – so critical to Western development – plus the country's long-term internal social peace, were also cited as major factors preventing China's break with 'feudalism'. *Renmin ribao*, 15 February 1980, p.5, and 11 July 1980, p.5; also, *Wen huibao*, 10 July 1980, p.3, and *Hongqi*, no.20 (16 October 1980), pp.32-35.

and 'proletarian' forces. Politically, the overwhelming power of China's despotic tradition has encouraged even the most progressive leaders to adopt a 'patriarchal' leadership style. The Taipings and Hong Xiuquan were praised for articulating 'anti-feudal thought' in their struggle against the social basis of imperial despotism, specifically the so-called 'four great ropes of feudal divine right, political power, clan authority, and the authority of the husband'.[30] But despite its initial opposition to despotic traditions, the Taiping movement, it was claimed, degenerated as Hong gradually embraced 'the religious thinking of the "divine right of kings" and the feudal theory of *"l'etat c'est moi"*' to solidify his political leadership. 'Hong's thinking emerged to serve the labouring people's revolution', one historian wrote, adding, in an apparent parallel to Mao, that Hong had reverted to tradition by becoming a 'personification of the sovereign god'. Such a contradiction between ideology and practice was not attributed, however, to Hong's personal political opportunism, but, in good Marxist fashion, to the inherent limitations of a political movement based in villages where the failure of capitalism to alter the local economy and social structure preserved pro-monarchist sentiments. 'Hong Xiuquan represented the peasants who as small producers [suffered] under inevitable historical limitations. They were unable to have a field of vision transcending the feudal system [and thus] the Taipings' ideology relied on religion to mobilize and organize the peasant'. Despite the best intentions, objective circumstances forced Hong (and by implication Mao) to adapt his leadership style to the 'backward' peasantry.[31]

Similar judgments were made of the 1898 Reform Movement, the Boxer Rebellion, the 1911 revolution, the May Fourth Movement, and even the Chinese Communist revolution. 'Materialist' historians described the Hundred Days of Reform as a 'fierce onslaught on feudal despotism' which had advocated 'the reform of feudal autocracy...and demanded "people's democratic rights"'. Yet the movement failed, they concluded, because it represented a 'national bourgeoisie' too weak to counter political feudalism.[32] Kang Youwei was also praised for

---

[30] *Guangming ribao*, 30 November 1979, p.4, and Su Shuangbi, *Jieji douzheng yu lishi kexue* [Class Struggle and Historical Science] (Renmin Chubanshe, Shanghai, 1982).

[31] Li Guihai, 'Lun nongmin de huangquanzhuyi sixiang', p.47, and *Renmin ribao*, 23 December 1980, p.5.

[32] *Guangming ribao*, 17 July 1979, p.4, 30 November 1979, p.4, and 16 December 1980, p.4.

attacking 'feudal despotism, demanding parliamentary rule and a constitutional monarchy' and, along with Yan Fu, promoting a 'bourgeois ideological enlightenment movement' which established the 'theoretical basis of his reform concepts'. 'For the first time in modern China', an article in *Guangming ribao* asserted, a movement arose to 'emancipate the mind, [which] created the conditions for the 1911 revolution'. But because this 'enlightenment' was restricted to intellectuals 'divorced from the masses', it was doomed to defeat by the Empress Dowager. Confronting the overwhelming power of feudalism, Kang ultimately abandoned his progressive political role and 'degenerated into a die-hard royalist'.[33] By 1911, the collapse of the monarchy and a purported 'equalization of land ownership' had weakened the political and economic underpinnings of the feudal system. But because the revolution 'did nothing about remaining feudal vestiges' – demonstrating the impossibility of 'eliminating feudal concepts overnight' – 'materialist' historians drew a negative conclusion on its overall political impact.[34] Even with fundamental political and economic changes in 1911-12, feudalism remained the dominant 'force' in Chinese society, exerting great pressure on the bourgeoisie whose ideology was ' "transformed" and "distorted" beyond recognition' from a 'progressive' to a 'reactionary' one.[35] 'Bourgeois' leaders, such as Sun Yatsen and Zhang Binglin, were not imperial despots, but they had assumed a 'feudal' leadership style which, 'based on the theory of innate genius' and 'regarding the broad masses as the "common herd"', rejected democracy and, like the Gang of Four, promoted rule by 'supermen of foresight'.

The regenerative power of feudalism was also evident in the persistence of despotic authority into the Republican and Communist eras. 'Materialist' historians praised the May Fourth Movement (1919-22), like the Hundred Days of Reform, for its iconoclastic assaults on despotic traditions, especially by intellectuals such as Wu Yu, whom the press eulogized in 1979 for his critiques of China's patriarchal family structure.[36] But since 'materialist' historians considered intellectual movements an insufficient transformative force in an overwhelmingly peasant society, the May Fourth Movement, they concluded, 'lost

---

[33] *Guangming ribao*, 8 May 1979, p.4.
[34] *Hongqi*, no.3 (6 March 1979), translated in FBIS, 13 April 1979, p.L6, and *Hongqi*, no.17 (1 September 1980), pp.25-30.
[35] *Renmin ribao*, 24 January 1980, p.5.
[36] *Wen huibao*, 15 September 1979.

momentum and petered out, existing only in name'.[37] Even the Chinese Communist Party, it was similarly argued, had made 'certain strategic compromises with feudal forces' during the 1921-49 period. The wars with Japan and the Kuomintang had, indeed, prevented the CCP from 'thoroughly eliminating the influence of 2,000 years of feudalism'.[38] The CCP was profoundly affected, 'materialists' argued, by the same 'small-scale production' and 'backward' consciousness which had inhibited previous political movements. The 'high ratio of comrades of petty bourgeois background' who believed that 'whoever conquers the world is entitled to dominate it' had created an especially strong basis for autocratic leaders in the Party.[39] Pessimistic about the CCP's capacity to inaugurate fundamental transformations of Chinese society, an article in *Renmin ribao* thus concluded: 'Even now we can only emphatically criticize feudalism, but are in no position to eliminate it'.[40]

In sum, 'materialist' historians interpreted Chinese history and the Chinese revolution in deterministic and linear terms. Beginning with the Qin dynasty, 'feudal production' became the objective force in shaping China's historical development into a despotic state. Tyrannical emperors dominated the entire dynastic era while the residual power of 'feudalism' has inhibited fundamental political reform ever since the Taiping Rebellion. Every revolutionary movement, including the Communists', thus degenerated into a despotism which could be 'traced to the material conditions of society'. Modern despots, from Hong Xiuquan to Mao Zedong, found a secure political base not only among the peasantry but even the industrial working class whose recent

---

[37] *Guangming ribao*, 21 January 1979, p.3.

[38] *Wen huibao*, 10 July 1980, p.3.

[39] Wang Xiaoqiang, 'Nongmin yu fan fengjian' [The Peasantry and the Struggle Against Feudalism], *Lishi yanjiu*, no.10 (15 October 1979), p.6. Li Guihai also argued that 'although the Chinese revolution has had a profound effect on the village through land reform and collectivization, because the technology in the village economy is still very limited and agricultural labour uses small-scale production techniques organized in one village or clan, [while] agricultural cadres rely on the patriarchal system to direct production... This provided the basis for Lin Biao's [power] and the feudal despotic system'. Li Guihai, 'Lun nongmin de huangquanzhuyi sixiang', p.50. That some Chinese historians saw a highly influential 'petty bourgeoisie' in a society they labelled as 'feudal', was just another example of the distortions produced by an excessively politicized historiography.

[40] *Renmin ribao*, 5 June 1979, translated in FBIS, 28 June 1979, p.L8.

'peasant origins' and labour-intensive production inclined them to 'superstitious practices' and 'monarchical thought'.[41] The lesson of Chinese history is that an underdeveloped society periodically gives rise to despots with considerable social support from peasants and workers. The only political solution then is for the CCP to exercise dictatorship according to 'collective leadership' principles until full-scale industrialization transforms the masses into a 'modern working class' supportive of non-despotic politics.

On the Political Basis of Despotism

> William the Conqueror especially ruled over [England] with a rod of iron...because he hoped...to test how far the powers of one man over other men can go. (Voltaire)

Historians in the alternative 'political' school of historiography argued that despotism was primarily the creation of the leader's pursuit of absolute power and the imposition of pro-despotic values on Chinese society by an authoritarian state. Despotic rule was not an inevitable result of the 'feudal' economy. Nor was it rooted in the 'backward' consciousness of the peasantry. Without explicitly denying the overall material basis of politics, these historians saw political leaders, ideology, and institutions as independent causes of Chinese despotism, which did not develop fully until the Song (960-1279) and even the Ming dynasty (1368-1644). From Ming Taizu onward, despots imposed their arbitrary rule on society through an increasingly powerful state apparatus, leaving the masses unprepared for democratic politics. Imperial 'will' and a coercive state, rather than 'small-scale production', accounted for the origins and development of Chinese despotism.

The Non-Linear Model of History

'Political' historians held a complex view of Chinese history in which imperial despotism matured relatively late in the series of dynastic

---

[41] Li Guihai, 'Lun nongmin de huangquanzhuyi sixiang', p.50; Jia Chunfeng and Wang Mengkui, 'Guanliaozhuyi, fengjian zhuanzhi yu xiao shengchan' [Bureaucraticism, Feudal Autocracy and Small-Scale Production], *Zhexue yanjiu*, no.3 (25 March 1979), p.14; *Fudan xuebao* [Fudan University Journal], no.5 (5 September 1979), pp.2-5; and Shao Yunrui and Ye Wuxi, 'Zhongguo de fengjian canzha shi zenyang fanqilaide' [How Remnant Feudalism in China Rose to the Surface Again], *Xueshu yuekan*, no.128 (20 January 1980), pp.46-49.

cycles.⁴² Before the Song, China lacked a 'full-fledged feudal autocracy', they argued, despite the existence of 'feudal' economic forces beginning in the Qin.⁴³ The authority of China's early emperors, including even Qin Shihuang, was circumscribed by the anti-despotic orthodoxy of Confucianism. Although Confucian maxims, such as 'the people can follow, but cannot know', contributed to the ideological basis of despotism, overall, 'political' historians suggested that the master's attitude toward 'loyalty (*zhong*) was not absolute and unconditional'.⁴⁴ Both Confucius and Mencius, in fact, stressed the mutual interdependence of political relations between the emperor, his ministers, and the people, which effectively prevented an excessive concentration of authority in a single ruler's hands for several centuries.⁴⁵ Such ideological constraints were, moreover, formalized in early institutional controls on imperial authority, such as the Han dynasty 'assessment system' (*guanli kao*), which, up to the Tang

---

42 The 'political' school of historiography does not include Chinese historians, such as Wu Dakun and Liu Chang, who have applied Marx's 'Asiatic Mode of Production' to Chinese history. Although sharing this school's emphasis on the autonomous role of political forces (and their general devotion to political reform in contemporary China), these historians see China's political history dominated by despotism since the Qin, which separates them from the 'political' school. Unlike 'materialists', however, Wu Dakun stresses the autonomy of China's despotic state, rather than as a mere agent of class interests. Rapp, 'China's Debate on the Asiatic Mode of Production'.

43 Chinese historians during the liberalization in the early 1960s also emphasized internal changes brought about by autonomous political forces in 'feudal' society, especially during the Six dynasties (222-589 AD) and the Tang (618-907) when, historians claimed, the positive role of enlightened emperors took precedence over deterministic material conditions. Fitzgerald, 'The Chinese Middle Ages', in *History in Communist China*, pp.126-30. The non-linear model described here is similar to the 'Kyoto School' of Sinology in Japan promoted by Naito Torajiro Konan. See Noriko Kamachi, 'Feudalism or Absolute Monarchy: Japanese Discourse on the Nature of the State and Society in Late Imperial China', unpublished manuscript.

44 Wang Cengyu, 'Zhongguo fengjian wenhua zhuanzhizhuyi pipan' [Criticism of China's Feudal Cultural Autocraticism], *Zhongguo shi yanjiu*, no.2 (February 1979), p.18.

45 Zhang Shancheng, 'Ping zhong jun daode' [Criticism of the Morality of Loyalty to the Master], *Zhexue yanjiu*, no.9 (September 1980), p.47 and Lin Zhichun, 'Kong-Meng shu suo fanying de gudai Zhongguo chengshi guojia zhidu' [Ancient Chinese City-States as Reflected in the Confucius-Mencius Books], *Lishi yanjiu*, no.3 (March 1980), pp.123-32.

dynasty (618-907), protected government officials willing to challenge errant emperors. After degenerating into sycophantic nepotism, the 'assessment system' fell into disuse as 'the Song, Yuan, Ming and Qing dynasties concentrated all power in the emperor while allowing officials to avoid their duties'.[46] But rather than reflecting any fundamental economic change, it was the recruitment of 'ignorant, incompetent and tyrannical people' after the Tang which fostered despotism.

The major cause of the increasing concentration of authority from the Song dynasty onward was the emperor's pursuit of absolute power. From the Han to the Tang, however, it was suggested that China's emperors did not manipulate institutions and ideologies to achieve total personal power. Reflecting the post-1978 'evaluation of personalities' in Chinese history, 'political' historians thus focused on the positive and negative roles of particular emperors in determining the course of China's non-linear historical evolution. Contrary to the period beginning with the Song (the major historical watershed in the development of despotism, according to the 'political' school's periodization), China's early rulers 'had a sense of self-confidence, and their minds were relatively flexible'. Even Qin Shihuang possessed positive characteristics: 'he was very much out in the open and frank [and] merely wanted to believe in law, rather than promoting benevolence' – a major tool of 'feudal' despotism, according to 'political' historians. Religion and government prior to the Song were 'basically separated', as emperors 'tolerated' different religious sects such as Buddhism and Taoism and willingly provided Confucian officials with 'a certain degree of freedom'.[47] But with their gradual loss of 'self-confidence' (*xin xin*), later emperors created a political and cultural autocracy by establishing imperial dominance over philosophical and religious thought, supported by increasingly subservient advisers. During the Song dynasty, Wang Anshi and Zhu Xi solidified despotism with rigid interpretations of Confucian doctrine, replacing the previously vigorous and creative approach to the classics that had existed since the Hundred Schools in the fourth century BC.

The greatest magnification of imperial authority came with Ming Taizu (1368-98), who imposed pervasive 'thought control' on the

---

[46] *Renmin ribao*, 13 November 1981, p.5 and 9 October 1980, translated in FBIS, 23 October 1980, p.L13. Assessments of government officials were, in fact, made every three years under this system prior to its corruption.

[47] Wang Cengyu, 'Zhongguo fengjian wenhua zhuanzhizhuyi pipan', pp.19 and 21, and *Renmin ribao*, 11 July 1980, p.5.

Chinese state and society by assuming the role of 'religious leader' and teacher.[48] Aware that Mencius' belief that 'the people are more valuable than the emperor' (*min gui jun qing*) was not in the interest of autocratic dictatorship, Ming Taizu quickly set about eliminating Mencius from the Confucian temple and ordered a revision of Mencius' compiled works'. The emperor Taizu used 'literary inquisitions' (*wenzi yu*) to crush autonomous thought and independent thinking, including scientific innovation. Contrary to China's basically secular tradition, he inextricably linked religion to politics for the sole purpose of absolutizing the emperor's personal power. Starting with the Ming, this excessive political centralization contributed, moreover, to China's rapid decline in comparison with the West.[49] The 'so-called "imperial compilation" drew selections from the classics to create a profound sense of literary slavishness, [subsequently] using the emperor's name to satisfy Kang Xi's and Qian Long's desire for self-aggrandizement as Confucian prophets. Intellectual and cultural debates [thus] became a plaything in the hands of imperial power...[while] these rulers exploited [fear of] spirits and ghosts to strengthen their dictatorship'. The Ming and Qing were China's 'worst' dynasties, as god-like emperors 'enslaved' both the people and scholar officials.[50]

The influence of Song-Ming Neo-Confucians on the increasingly despotic cast of the family and clan also helped to solidify the

---

[48] As a cruel emperor who exterminated his subordinates and tied the people to the land, Ming Taizu may have served as a surrogate for criticizing Mao. One article explained the emperor's transformation from a 'modest' to a 'brutal' leader in terms of 'personality' flaws that could also apply to Mao. Wang Hongjiang, 'Lun Ming chu huang zhuanzhi de jiaqiang' [On the Strengthening of Imperial Autocracy at the Beginning of the Ming], *Nankai xuebao* [Nankai University Journal], no.1 (January 1981), pp.44-50. Despite these possible allusions to Mao, the vast literature in China evaluating the Ming founder does contain varying opinions, indicating a genuine historical interest beyond mere political commentary.

[49] Wang Cengyu, 'Zhongguo wenhua zhuanzhizhuyi pipan', pp.19-21 and Hong Huanchun, 'Ming-Qing shiqi fengjian zhuanzhizhuyi de jiben tezheng' [Basic Traits of Feudal Autocraticism in the Ming-Qing Period], in *Nanjing daxue xuebao* (20 February 1981), p.45.

[50] Contemporary nationalist historians made similar arguments to debunk the 'alien' Qing dynasty. See Albert Feuerwerker, *State and Society in Eighteenth Century China: The Ch'ing Empire in Its Glory* (Michigan Papers in Chinese Studies no.27, Ann Arbor, 1976), p.72.

ideological and social basis of despotism.⁵¹ Whereas 'materialist' historians focused on the peasants' 'backward production and consciousness' as the basis of despotism at the local level, the 'political' school emphasized the primary role of the centralized state and its bureaucratic-ideological servants in imposing pro-despotic values on Chinese society from above. Zhu Xi's 'village covenants' (*xiang yue*) strengthened general social receptivity to imperial autocracy, it was claimed, by expanding the authority of clan and family heads to enforce arbitrary discipline. Despotic rule by local authorities was not a natural outgrowth of 'small-scale production' and the patriarchal peasant family, but a conscious creation of a centralized state devoted to instilling total subservience in the population. As the conventions of clan (lineage) organization gained acceptance among landlords, their promulgation through ancestral halls, clan registers, and family codes granted unprecedented discretionary authority to clan heads.

Thus the state had managed, without fundamental economic change, to transform local society into an apanage of centralized, monarchical authority by exploiting the quasi-legal nature of the village covenants. It also promulgated the Neo-Confucian theory that the five cardinal relationships were ordained in heaven and imbued with cosmological potency. The despotic character of local authority relations after the Song dynasty violated the traditional 'organic' unity of Chinese social organization. This was particularly evident in the increasing subordination of women to patriarchal control contrary to social practices since the Han. By the time of Wang Yangming (1472-1528) – whose own harsh village covenants further strengthened local family and clan despots – Chinese society, including the family, completely mirrored the state's absolutist structure.⁵² From this period onward, despotism permeated China's 'great' and 'little' traditions as local authorities willingly complied with the single ruler's will.

---

51   Qiu Hansheng, 'Song-Ming *Lixue* yu *zongfa* sixiang' [Song-Ming *Neo-Confucianism* and *Patriarchal* Thought], *Lishi yanjiu*, no.11 (November 1979), p.66.

52   ibid., pp.67 and 71. 'Materialist' historians, in contrast, located the roots of the patriarchal family much earlier in Chinese history during the Western Zhou. Western historians have also contrasted the horizontal social linkages created by Zhu Xi's community compacts with the more vertical and authoritarian covenants of Wang Yangming. *Hongqi*, no.20 (16 October 1980), and Timothy Cheek, 'Contracts and Ideological Control in Village Administration', unpublished manuscript.

In sum, 'political' historians did not consider despotism a mechanical reflection of China's 'natural' economy and the peasants' 'feudal' consciousness. Although underdeveloped material conditions determined the general authoritarian political context, it was the leaders' pursuit of absolute authority, backed by an increasingly intrusive and coercive centralized state, which had created the ideological and cultural conditions for mass obedience to the despot from Ming Taizu to Mao Zedong.

But just as relatively autonomous political and ideological forces created despotism, so too, in this formulation, could they be employed to eliminate despotic authority. Contesting the 'materialist' view that modern revolutionary leaders inevitably succumbed to popular pro-despotic sentiments, 'political' historians warned against 'underestimating' anti-feudal movements, such as the 1898 Reforms and especially the 1911 revolution.[53] The shift from an 'autocratic monarchy to a republican state' in 1911 had 'emancipated' the Chinese people from their submissive obedience to imperial authority, not because of basic changes in the economic base, but through ideological and political agitation against monarchism. Even in the midst of unchanging economic backwardness, intellectual and institutional assaults on despotism such as the May Fourth Movement profoundly affected popular attitudes toward the leader, which transformed basic authority relations between state and society. Although the feudal economy and the 'peasant mentality' provided a receptive audience for conservative political reaction such as Empress Dowager's obstruction of the 1898 Reform, the failure of progressive movements was not 'inevitable' as 'materialist' historians suggested. The defeat of anti-monarchical movements was, instead, largely a function of political forces generally independent of fundamental economic changes. Whenever conservative factions, such as the Dowager's, predominated and revolutionary

---

[53] *Renmin ribao*, 13 April 1981, p.5, and David B. Buck, 'Appraising the Revival of Historical Studies in China', *The China Quarterly*, no.105 (March 1986), p.140. An article in *Renmin ribao* also praised late nineteenth century 'constitutionalists' for 'enlightening the people' and criticized 'revolutionaries' (perhaps a surrogate for the CCP) for 'instigating armed uprisings' while neglecting education of the masses. Similar positive assessments were made of pro-Republican leaders such as Zou Rong, the 1898 Reforms, and even the Taipings, who, historian Liu Danian argued, had far more advanced 'ideas and organization' than previous rebellions and generally succeeded in subduing the 'feudal patrilineal system'. *Renmin ribao*, 22 September 1981, translated in FBIS, 8 October 1981, p.K13, and *Renmin ribao*, 11 January 1982, p.5.

movements suffered from 'incorrect leadership' (such as occurred during the later Cultural Revolution), popular opposition to despotism was correspondingly weakened.[54] But with the political victory of progressive leadership and democratic ideology, China could break its cycle of despotism without a concomitant economic revolution. Instituting constraints on political leaders in the direction of constitutional democracy does not, in other words, require basic materialist transformation postponed into the indeterminable future. Political reform and ideological liberalization could, instead, be achieved under contemporary economic conditions.

The Historiography of Chinese Democracy

China's only solution is free elections. (High level CCP official, 1986)[55]

'Political' historians reinforced their arguments for liberal reform in China by turning to the illustrious period of the Zhou dynasty (1028-221 BC) to discover 'democratic elements' (*minzhu zhengzhi de yinsu*) in Chinese history.[56] Appealing to ancient times as the primordial source of a democratic authority, they portrayed the 'city-state system' (*chengshi guojia zhidu*) of the Zhou in terms analogous to the democratic traditions and institutions of classical Athens and the Roman Republic.[57] From the Western Zhou to the Spring and Autumn period, 'ancient China had undergone the formation and development of city-states which, as described by Confucius and Mencius, were not despotic empires, but city-states with aristocratic and democratic polities'. Critical of both Wittfogel's theory of 'Oriental Despotism' and the 'materialists'' orthodox Marxist interpretation of ancient China as an autocratically ruled 'slave' society, 'political' historians saw not a 'trace of despotism' in the Zhou when, like the West, states were 'too small'

---

[54] *Renmin ribao*, 11 July 1980, p.5.

[55] Personal interview, December 1986, Beijing, China. Identity withheld.

[56] Such an argument challenges conventional defenders of the CCP dictatorship who consider democracy inappropriate for China because of its purely Western origins. It also rejects the orthodox Marxist periodization of the Zhou dynasty as 'slave', just as the earlier liberal historian Jian Bozan had done.

[57] Lin Zhichun, 'Kong-Meng shu suo fanying de gudai Zhongguo chengshi guojia zhidu', pp.123-24.

geographically to produce centralized political power.⁵⁸ Mencius' famous dictum that ' "the people are supreme, the state next, and the ruler least" reflected this reality and cannot be regarded as a utopia', argued the historian Ri Zhi.⁵⁹ Nor was the 'son of heaven' (*tian zi*) described by Mencius the powerful, despotic figure of later dynasties. Even the less democratically inclined Confucius accepted the severe limitations on imperial authority, which was an aspect of the master's orthodoxy that 'political' historians claimed historical revisionists subsequently distorted in pro-despotic terms during the late imperial era. Both Confucius and Mencius had, in fact, rejected 'personal loyalty to the lord', emphasizing, instead, 'the mutual ethics and responsibilities between the rulers and the ruled' that, if not completely democratic, expressed their opposition to despotic authority. In the Zhou city-states, the people were 'most important while gods and rulers could be replaced if they failed to perform their jobs adequately'.⁶⁰

The purported existence of 'assemblies' (*huiyi*) for both 'noblemen' (*zhudafu*) and 'commoners' (*pingmin jieji*) during the Zhou further substantiated China's democratic heritage.⁶¹ Such institutions reflected

---

58   ibid., p.124 and Xu Hongxiu, 'Zhou dai guizu zhuanzhi zhengti zhong de yuanshi minzhu yicun' [The Residue of Original Democracy in the Aristocratic Autocracy of the Zhou], *Zhongguo shehui kexue* [Chinese Social Science], no.2 (February 1981), pp.75-96.

59   Ri Zhi, 'Cong chun-qiu "chengren" zhi li zai lun yazhou gudai minzhu zhengzhi' [Using the Example of the 'Naming of Men' in the Spring-Autumn Period to Discuss Once Again Ancient Democratic Politics], *Lishi yanjiu*, no.3 (March 1981), p.6.

60   ibid.

61   ibid., pp.4-5. *Guoren* (Countrymen) was another name for the masses. Ri Zhi insisted that Chinese scholars have historically confused *guoren* with *zhudafu* (lords), which effectively overlooked the independent political role played by popular groups in the Zhou. Other historians argued that 'commoners' (*shuren*) possessed 'political and economic rights' in the Zhou, such as the 'right to participate in the important meetings involving interests of the state'. 'Materialist' historians, in contrast, asserted 'we cannot find [democratic assembly] political organs anywhere in Chinese history'. Ying Yongshen, 'Shuo "shuren"' [On 'Commoners'], *Zhongguo shehui yanjiu* [Chinese Social Research], no.2 (February 1981), pp.92-98 and Pang Zhuoheng, 'Zhong-Xi fengjian zhuanzhi zhidu de bijiao yanjiu', p.7. Similar debates between Feng Youlan and Guan Feng over the meaning of *ren* (the 'people') in Chinese history occurred in the early 1960s. The debates among Chinese 'political' historians on the mixed class composition of Zhou 'democracy' also parallel Western analyses

the importance of the common people as indicated in the *Shi Jing*: 'It is possible to have a corrupt ruler but it is impossible to have corrupt people'. The *Zhou Li* expressed similar 'democratic' concepts when instructing kings 'to gather people and consult them on state affairs'.[62] Although noblemen dominated politics from the Western Zhou to the Spring and Autumn period, 'political' historians claimed that 'countrymen [or commoners] had considerable influence in political, military, and diplomatic matters' as the assemblies 'dealt with the crucial affairs of the state, such as war, land reform, and selecting a new king' – issues similar to those confronting the post-Mao Chinese state. When kings committed errors, they 'could not avoid apologizing for their mistakes before the assemblies of noblemen and countrymen [and were required] to suggest their son or some other as a successor'. If the king did not respond to the commoners' 'mass opinions' brought to court, the people reserved the right, in good Rousseauian fashion, to rebel and even exile him.[63] In short, the Zhou dynasty exhibited a '"democracy" of some sort', which effectively shifted the roots of democratic principles from the 'alien' West to the very origins of Chinese political civilization that was itself described in highly positive terms.[64]

---

of Athenian democracy. Kam Louie, *Inheriting Tradition: Interpretations of the Classical Philosophers in Communist China, 1949-1966* (Oxford University Press, Oxford, 1986), p.69, and Perry Anderson, *Passages from Antiquity to Feudalism* (Verso, London, 1974), p.54.

[62] Ri Zhi, 'Cong chun-qiu "chengren" zhi li zai lun yazhou gudai minzhu zhengzhi', p.4.

[63] ibid., p.5, and Xu Hongxiu, 'Zhou dai guizu zhuanzhi zhengti zhong de yuanshi minzhu zhengzhi', p.8. Although noting the role of 'mass opinions in restraining the power of the king', Xu described the Zhou in less democratic terms, emphasizing the superior power of noblemen ministers to criticize and even 'refute' the orders of kings at the expense of the participatory role of commoner 'assemblies'.

[64] Contrast this historical optimism of the 'political' school with the 'materialists'' profoundly pessimistic treatment of China's ancient and fundamentally despotic political history, also recently evident in the PRC TV series 'River Dirge' (*He Shang*).

Historiographical Justification for Another 'Great Leader'

> This is the time when heroes should come forth. (Yang Xuqing, 1922)

'Materialist' and 'political' historians both opposed 'patriarchal despotism'. The former believed the depth of absolute authority in Chinese political culture reflected China's pervasive economic backwardness since the Qin, while the latter argued that despotic leaders, from Ming Taizu to Mao Zedong, had exploited the absence of institutional controls on the single leader. But not all historiography in post-1978 China followed this fundamentally anti-despotic line. Despite the CCP leadership's formal opposition to all forms of despotism, a few historians interpreted the Western and Chinese past in terms supporting the indispensability of the powerful single ruler for modernizing 'peasant' China. 'Collective leadership' in the CCP or a substantial liberalization of the political system were incapable of overcoming the enormous political-economic obstacles confronting the post-1978 reforms which only the absolute authority of another 'heroic' leader could overcome.

This historiographical view was espoused in an article praising Napoleon's 'personal military dictatorship' that appears as an allegory on post-1978 Chinese politics.[65] Criticizing recent negative judgements on Napoleon by Soviet historians, the author defended the French ruler's establishment of a 'dictatorial system' as 'entirely reasonable'. After winning power, Napoleon confronted a 'stage of consolidation' in the revolution when 'a stable political order and social peace' were

---

[65] Luo Rongqu, 'Lun Napolun zhuanzheng he Faguo zichanjieji qianghua guojia jiqi de lishi jiaoxun' [Historical Lessons on Napoleon's Dictatorship and the French Bourgeoisie's Strengthening of the State Apparatus], *Lishi yanjiu*, no.6, (June 1979), pp.76-87. The reference to Napoleon's 'military dictatorship' indicated perhaps that conservative military leaders in China, led by Yang Shangkun, supported a strong single leader. My interpretation of this article as an indirect political commentary may be a misreading since the author also criticizes Napoleon as a 'feudal ruler' and notes the French ruler's creation of a new aristocracy and the restoration of the Catholic church – changes hardly consistent with an appeal for 'enlightened despotism' in contemporary China. The primary significance of Luo's article may in fact, be a genuine historical analysis of French history in which several seminal French works are also used. Coming soon after Deng Xiaoping's rise to power, this article can, however, be read in part as an appeal for an assertive leader, though whether the author Luo Rongqu intended this meaning is questionable. This argument anticipated appeals for a 'new authoritarianism' made in 1988-89.

necessary. Describing conditions remarkably parallel to the post-1978 situation confronting Deng Xiaoping, the author lauded Napoleon's implementation of administrative and economic 'reforms' through 'the development of industry and agriculture'. 'According to the desires of the great majority of people', Napoleon used 'extreme means and methods' against 'royalist elements attempting to overthrow' the new system – strong measures, which, the article intimated, Deng should employ against opponents of reform in China. With French society fragmented like a 'plate of loose sand' (*yipan sansha*) – a phrase often used to describe China – Napoleon relied on 'a dictatorial system of unlimited personal authority' to create a 'new order' through the 'unification of laws' and the institutionalization of a rational and efficient administration. As the 'people's monarch' and a 'politician of steel will' – perhaps veiled references to Deng Xiaoping – Napoleon ended 'revolutionary chaos' (an allusion to the Cultural Revolution, I suspect) and replaced 'feudal dictatorialism' (perhaps the Maoist system) with a modern state apparatus. Napoleon's personal dictatorship was necessary to achieve political and economic modernization since the Directory had failed to accomplish its mission and English-type 'democratic assemblies' had proved unreliable. In China, neither democracy nor even the CCP under 'collective leadership' (symbolized by the Directory, I believe) had sufficient authority to bring about fundamental reforms, especially in the bureaucracy. Instead, only the 'steel willed' Deng Xiaoping could achieve economic reform through a temporary 'personal dictatorship'.

Articles highlighting the institutional changes introduced by 'enlightened' Chinese emperors and even Russian czars, such as Peter the Great, made similar appeals for a single leader to assume singular command of the reform process in contemporary China.[66] Qin Shihuang's unification of the empire and the institutionalization of a rational, meritocratic bureaucracy by powerful Han emperors were both strongly praised.[67] Notorious tyrants, such as Sui Yangdi the founder of the Sui dynasty (581-618), were similarly lauded for 'seizing the power to appoint and dismiss central and local...officials'. Such bold action undermined the monopoly of 'rich and powerful families' – perhaps a

---

[66] Sun Xiangxiu and Song Wenrong, 'Luelun Bide yishi de gaige' [On the Reforms of Peter the Great], *Sixiang zhanxian* [Ideological Battlefront], no.1, Yunnan University (1981), pp.13-15.

[67] *Guangming ribao*, 13 November 1979, p.4.

reference to the corrupt CCP bureaucracy – over candidate selection.[68] Without the personal intervention and authoritarian decrees of powerful emperors, local officials with their narrow special interests would have completely undermined the Confucian examination system.[69] Only the emperor, it was claimed, had the 'foresight' necessary to create a more rational political order. Thus, just before Deng Xiaoping engineered major personnel reductions in the state apparatus in 1982, an article in *Renmin ribao* praised similar actions by Tang Taizong – generally considered the most heroic ruler of China – in dramatically improving the imperial bureaucracy.[70] 'After reducing the number of officials, there were no more overlapping administrative organizations, official functions and powers were clearly defined...and various malpractices were eliminated, including that of creating personal patronage jobs...' Such achievements produced the kind of public adulation for the emperor which some historians and political commentators apparently hoped to replicate in the CCP: 'He checked the practice of eagerly pursuing official positions... He reduced the number of sycophants'.[71] Just as the single leader's 'decisive' actions had created a lean bureaucracy of assertive officials in the Tang dynasty, so too should Deng Xiaoping, it was implied, adopt the same leadership style to achieve comparable goals in the current reform process.

Conclusion

Chinese historiography from 1978 to 1982 offered radically different interpretations of the country's long experience with despotic rulers. Despite the enormous damage suffered during the Cultural Revolution, some historians reacted to post-1978 political developments by utilizing the Chinese tradition of using 'history as a mirror' to address current

---

[68] *Renmin ribao*, 28 December 1981, p.5.

[69] Such arguments anticipated Zhao Ziyang's 1987 proposal to establish a professional civil service in China, which also draws on institutional traditions from China's imperial past. John W. Dardess, *Confucianism and Autocracy: Professional Elites in the Founding of the Ming Dynasty* (University of California Press, Berkeley, 1983), p.90.

[70] *Renmin ribao*, 5 January 1982, p.5 and Charles O. Hucker, *China's Imperial Past: An Introduction to Chinese History and Culture* (Stanford University Press, Stanford, 1975), p.140.

[71] *Renmin ribao*, 5 January 1982, p.5.

controversies over reform.[72] 'Materialist' historians employed an orthodox Marxist paradigm – popular in China since the 1920s – to defend the CCP's continuing dictatorship over a potentially restorationist society by painting a generally pessimistic picture of China's institutional history and popular political consciousness since ancient times. 'Political' historians, however, countered with a more complex but basically optimistic view of Chinese history and the populace, including an embryonic 'democracy' during the Zhou dynasty, to justify a radical decentralization of political authority. 'Great man' historians, in contrast, apparently advocated a restoration of 'enlightened despotism' to impose the centralized dictatorship and administrative rationalism required by Deng's reforms. Despite similarities to the radical leftists' previous glorification of despotism, these few historians proposed that China's top leader should model his authority on Qin Shihuang or Napoleon to overcome the enormous obstacles to reform posed by a conservative peasant society and an entrenched party-state bureaucracy.

Beyond the political purposes of such historiographical arguments, this was also a sincere debate among professional historians over long-standing issues such as the nature of Chinese society, the periodization of China's political evolution, and the role of the individual in history. Western historians of China might question the scholarly quality of these analyses, which by trying to make China's past relevant to contemporary political issues produced inevitable distortions of historical reality. But this should not denigrate a controversy whose major themes have attracted Chinese intellectuals throughout this century and still remain central to the Marxist historicism dominating contemporary historiographical analysis and debate.

The most important issue, however, is whether this articulation of different historiographical views has had any real impact on the political reform process. The fact that Deng Xiaoping and the 'reform faction' (*gaige pai*) found it necessary to justify their limited reform proposals in historical terms indicates the resonance of historiographical issues in Chinese politics. In a system where Marxist historicism has reinforced the tradition of 'using history as a mirror', political leaders still rely on an interpretation of historical trend lines, bolstered by orthodox historians, as a guide or at least a rationalization for policy. Even as rural China's vigorous response to the economic reforms seemingly denies the image of a 'backward' and socially isolated peasantry, central

---

[72] Su Shuangbi, *Jieji douzheng yu lishi kexue*, p.53.

Party leaders draw on basic 'materialist' arguments, especially the purported role of economic 'underdevelopment' in shaping the masses' 'immature' political consciousness, to justify a continuing Party dictatorship that even historically-aware intellectuals often accept as politically necessary.[73]

Yet, given the 'materialist' school's conservative conclusion that any fundamental alteration of political and institutional power relations is totally dependent on gradual economic changes, the appeal of the two other historiographical schools may increase. This is especially true if China's current political structure proves increasingly ill-suited to grappling with current problems. The prominence of 'great men' in Chinese history – from Qin Shihuang to Mao Zedong – lends credence to historiographical interpretations which suggest that, to achieve reform, China should concentrate political authority in the hands of a single leader. Mikhail Gorbachev was initially admired by many Chinese, especially as Zhao Ziyang's prestige and authority faded in 1988 in the face of inflation and rampant corruption.[74] Although painfully aware of the political and economic catastrophes brought on by Mao's autocratic decision-making, the decisive role of 'great leaders' throughout Chinese history strengthens the view that the fundamental transformations of reform require greater centralization of authority, at least temporarily.[75]

For the supporters of 'democratization' in China, in contrast, an appeal to 'democratic elements' in China's golden age of the Zhou dynasty attempts to detach democratic principles from Western traditions. Although the Chinese leadership would reject such an

---

[73] Interviews, Summer 1988, Beijing, China. Identities withheld. That the masses are allegedly 'affected by a strong feudal patriarchal mentality' which prevents them from participating fully in the selection of leaders is an argument often voiced to oppose further democratization. 'Letter to the Editor', *Nanfang ribao* [Southern Daily], 21 February 1979, translated in John P. Burns and Stanley Rosen (eds), *Policy Conflicts in Post-Mao China: A Documentary Survey with Analysis* (M.E. Sharpe, Armonk, 1986), p.104.

[74] Gorbachev's assumption of the presidency and other structural reforms designed to strengthen his authority over a recalcitrant bureaucracy drew considerable interest in China in the late 1980s among people increasingly frustrated by their own leaders' inept response to economic problems.

[75] Shanghai's relatively 'liberal' paper, *World Economic Herald*, [Shijie jingji daobao] rejected this view: 'If only a certain person or a small number of people are granted the privilege to make decisions, the result is always disastrous'. Quoted in *New York Times*, 20 November 1988, p.E2.

esoteric interpretation of the country's past, events such as the 1976 political defeat of the radical leftists sustained the basic theme of the 'political' school that political and institutional change retain considerable autonomy in historical evolution.

By 1982, 'political' interpretations generally diminished as a major theme in Chinese historiography as Party conservatives, particularly Hu Qiaomu, prevented publication of works which implicitly supported radical political reform. Yet, the more that China's population have dispelled images of political and cultural 'backwardness', the more likely that a significant transformation towards political liberalization may shape China's response to the economic, scientific, and social demands of the modern world.

'THE SPIRITUAL HERITAGE OF CHINESE CAPITALISM': RECENT TRENDS IN THE HISTORIOGRAPHY OF CHINESE ENTERPRISE MANAGEMENT*

Tim Wright

The historiography of the pre-1949 Chinese economy has recently begun to take a new direction, as scholars in both China and the West emphasize the successes as well as the failures of China's early modern economic development. Quantitative studies are revealing that very considerable growth took place, especially in the modern sector, so that the old problematic of stagnation is no longer appropriate. China's organizational heritage, both state and private, is now also seen as having had a favourable rather than a purely negative impact on China's development.

One important facet of the new interpretation is the much more positive evaluation of the management practices of China's capitalist entrepreneurs up to 1937, and of the Western and Chinese theories that underlay those practices. This paper links the new studies of China's management history both to the current market-oriented economic

---

* This paper is based mainly on research done at the Institute of Economics, Nankai University. I would like to thank the staff members and students there for their friendship, help and encouragement. I also benefited from a library scholarship for research in Canberra granted by the Contemporary China Centre, Australian National University. Earlier versions were presented at seminars at Murdoch University and the Australian National University, and I am grateful for the comments and suggestions there. Beverley Hooper and two anonymous referees also made helpful suggestions which I would like to acknowledge.

reforms and to the attempt to develop a 'management with Chinese characteristics'. These two factors have led to the prewar capitalist entrepreneurs being used as positive models to inspire the managers of contemporary China's socialist enterprises.

The paper will begin by briefly outlining the old paradigm and considering the reasons for the shift. The central section will analyse the new evaluation of China's management history and theory, while the conclusion raises some problems in the academic interpretation of the recent studies. The main focus of the paper is on Chinese historiography, but it also notes that Western studies have undergone a similar change, if for somewhat different reasons.

The Paradigm of Failure

Any attempt to outline a pre-1976 paradigm on the history of Chinese capitalist management might easily end up creating a 'straw man', as it has to rely on relatively few general works. Moreover, some of the best work, both in China and in the West, has been on the late nineteenth century, so that there is a danger of incorrect extrapolation.[1] Nevertheless, it still appears that, until the late 1970s, studies of prewar Chinese enterprises were mostly concerned with explaining why they failed and why modern Chinese industry did not embark on a path of self-sustaining growth. Although the main reasons given for this related to factors external to the enterprises themselves, the early Chinese capitalists and their management methods also came in for criticism.

Chinese management tended to be bureaucratic rather than entrepreneurial. While the supply of entrepreneurial talent has not traditionally been a Marxist concern, and therefore was not prominent in Chinese studies, Western scholars argued that, in the words of Albert Feuerwerker, there was a 'relative absence of the entrepreneurial spirit

---

[1] For two recent treatments, see Qiao Huantian, 'Qiantan yangwu pai zai qiye guanli zhong de biduan' [A Brief Discussion of Malpractices of the Self-strengtheners in Enterprise Management], *Beifang luncong* [Essays From the North], no.5, 1981, pp.104-9, and Chen Yingfang, 'Jingying guanli yu yangwu qiye de pochan' [Business Management and the Bankruptcy of the Self-strengthening Enterprises], *Suzhou daxue xuebao, zhe she ban* [Suzhou University Journal, Philosophy and Social Sciences], no.1, 1986, pp.105-8, reprinted in *Baokan ziliao xuanhui, jingji shi* [Collected Materials from Newspapers and Periodicals, Economic History], no.3, 1986, pp.89-92.

among those men who led the industrialization effort of late Ch'ing China'.[2]

Chinese scholars have concentrated on showing that most business people before the First World War had their origins in the bureaucracy or politics rather than in private commerce or, still less, industry.[3] They were affected by habits rooted in these origins: the neglect of financial and commercial considerations, a liking for red tape and an avoidance of responsibility. Their motives for engaging in economic activity were often mainly concerned with furthering their own and their friends' official positions. Such characteristics both reflect and partially explain the social and political weakness of the Chinese bourgeoisie in the early twentieth century and hence its inability to fulfil its historic mission in the Chinese anti-feudal revolution.

These characteristics led to management methods which were backward in many respects. One recent article sums up this view: 'In pre-Communist China, the management of national capitalist enterprises was generally backward, using old-style accounting, using the foreman system in the workshop, and with no regular provision for the inspection or repair of machinery'.[4]

Most generally, instead of using universalistic criteria in staff selection, capital mobilization and economic transactions, the entrepreneurs were impelled by 'traditional' values to work mainly through particularistic criteria – especially familial ties, but also many other relationships, such as native place loyalties and teacher-pupil, school or institutional links.[5]

---

[2] Albert Feuerwerker, *China's Early Industrialization: Sheng Hsuan-huai (1844-1916) and Mandarin Enterprise* (Atheneum, New York, 1970), chs 1 and 2, quote from pp.58-59.

[3] See for example Yan Zhongping, *Zhongguo jindai jingji shi tongji ziliao xuanji* [A Collection of Statistical Materials on the Modern Economic History of China] (Kexue chubanshe, Beijing, 1955), pp.96-99, and Yan Zhongping, *Zhongguo mianfangzhi shi gao* [A Draft History of Chinese Cotton Spinning and Weaving] (Kexue chubanshe, Beijing, 1963), pp.139, 175. Also Editorial writing group, *Jiu Zhongguo de zibenzhuyi shengchan guanxi* [Capitalist Relations of Production in Pre-Communist China] (Renmin chubanshe, Beijing, 1977), ch.2.

[4] Chen Huixiong, 'Jiu Zhongguo Rong shi qiye de jingying guanli fangfa' [Business Management Methods in the Rong Enterprises in Pre-Communist China], *Jingying yu guanli* [Business and Management], no.1, 1986, p.44.

[5] Marion J. Levy, *The Rise of the Modern Chinese Business Class* (Institute of Pacific Relations, New York, 1949), pp.9-14; Albert Feuerwerker, *China's Early Industrialization*, ch.1; Wellington K. K. Chan, 'The Organizational Structure of

In staff appointments, enterprises were thus less concerned with choosing the best person for the job than with providing a sinecure for a friend or relative of the owner. Feuerwerker shows how family ties permeated the management of the China Merchants' Steamship Navigation Company in the late Qing,[6] and Wu Chengming points out the 'feudal' and 'familial' nature of twentieth-century Chinese industrial management, as most staff members were relatives of the capitalist and were paid at grossly inflated rates.[7] Huang Chengjing notes that the Nanyang Brothers Tobacco Company preferred to appoint first family members or relatives of the owners, and then fellow Cantonese.[8]

Similarly, the use of the contract labour system to recruit and supervise workers was a way of utilizing traditional 'feudal' personal relationships in the absence both of a modern labour market and of enough trained supervisors. In as far as the system recruited workers for reasons other than skill or ability, it impeded the progress of Chinese industry by holding down the quality of labour.[9]

Other aspects of the 'backward relations of production' characterized prewar Chinese industry: irrational wage systems exhibited either a lack of differentials or excessive differentials, while promotion was based on one's relationship to the capitalist.[10] There was, as a heritage of tradition, widespread use of apprentices, again often

---

the Traditional Chinese Firm and its Modern Reform', *Business History Review*, vol.56, no.2 (Summer 1982), pp.219-22.

[6] Albert Feuerwerker, *China's Early Industrialization*, pp.142, 145.

[7] Wu Chengming, 'Zhongguo minzu ziben de tedian' [The Characteristics of Chinese National Capital] (originally published in 1956), reprinted in Wu Chengming, *Zhongguo zibenzhuyi yu guonei shichang* [Chinese Capitalism and the Domestic Market] (Zhongguo shehui kexue chubanshe, Beijing, 1985), p.81.

[8] Huang Chengjing (Huang Yifeng), 'Cong Nanyang xiongdi yancao gongsi lai kan minzu zichanjieji de xingge' [An Examination of the Nature of the Chinese Bourgeoisie Through the History of the Nanyang Brothers Tobacco Company], *Xueshu yuekan* [Academic Monthly], no.10, 1958, p.39.

[9] Tim Wright, ' "A Method of Evading Management": Contract Labor in Chinese Coal Mines before 1937', *Comparative Studies in Society and History*, vol.23, no.4 (October 1981), pp.656-78. For an analysis which lays greater emphasis on the 'feudal' aspects of the system, see Nankai daxue jingji yanjiu suo jingji shi yanjiu shi [Economic History Unit, Institute of Economics, Nankai University], *Jiu Zhongguo Kailuan meikuang de gongzi zhidu he baogong zhidu* [The Wage System and the Contract Labour System at the Kailuan Coal Mine in Pre-Communist China] (Renmin chubanshe, Tianjin, 1983), Part 2.

[10] Wu Chengming, 'Zhongguo minzu ziben de tedian', p.82.

linked to the owners by familial or other ties.[11] Secondary studies laid great emphasis on the way work rules facilitated the ruthless exploitation of the workers, as authors warned against any 'beautification' of the national bourgeoisie.[12]

A further manifestation of the weakness of Chinese national capital was its technological backwardness and dependence. As Shannon Brown has shown, industrial enterprises in the late nineteenth century found it difficult to adapt to the demands of mechanized technology.[13] Although the twentieth century witnessed successful examples of the transfer of modern cement and cigarette technology,[14] many studies, such as that of Wu Chengming, still criticized the backwardness of Chinese industrial technology,[15] and the failure of Chinese industry to upgrade its increasingly obsolescent equipment.[16] A study of the Shanghai rubber industry described its technological level as very low, with continuing heavy reliance on manual methods.[17]

---

[11] Xu Daohe, 'Siying shangye qiye shehuizhuyi gaizao de dianxing diaocha – du "Beijing Ruifuxiang" ' [A Model Investigation of the Socialist Transformation of Private Commercial Enterprises – Reading 'Ruifuxiang in Beijing'], *Hongqi* [Red Flag] nos 17/18, 1964, p.48.

[12] *Jiu Zhongguo de zibenzhuyi shengchan guanxi*, p.104; Huang Chengjing, op. cit., p.36.

[13] Shannon R. Brown, 'The Transfer of Technology to China in the Nineteenth Century: The Role of Direct Foreign Investment', *Journal of Economic History*, vol.39, no.1 (March 1979), pp.181-97; Shannon R. Brown, 'The Ewo Filature: A Study in the Transfer of Technology to China in the 19th Century', *Technology and Culture*, vol.20, no.3 (July 1979), pp.550-68; Shannon R. Brown, 'Cakes and Oil: Technology Transfer and Chinese Soybean Processing, 1860-1895', *Comparative Studies in Society and History*, vol.23, no.3 (July 1981), pp.449-63.

[14] Albert Feuerwerker, 'Industrial Enterprise in Twentieth-Century China: The Chee Hsin Cement Co.', in Albert Feuerwerker et al., (eds), *Approaches to Modern Chinese History* (University of California Press, Berkeley and Los Angeles, 1967), p.312; Sherman Cochran, *Big Business in China: Sino-Foreign Rivalry in the Cigarette Industry, 1890-1930* (Harvard University Press, Cambridge, Mass., 1980), p.154.

[15] Wu Chengming, 'Zhongguo minzu ziben de tedian', p.80.

[16] Chen Huixiong, op. cit., p.44.

[17] Shiliao gongzuo zu [Historical Materials Work Group] of the Shanghai shi gongshang xingzheng guanli ju [Shanghai Bureau of Industrial and Commercial Management] and the Shanghai shi xiangjiao gongye gongsi [Shanghai Rubber Industry Company], *Shanghai minzu xiangjiao gongye* [Shanghai's National

Throughout the prewar period Chinese industry depended on foreign sources for technology. Especially in the initial stages, even the technical personnel were mostly foreign, for instance in the nineteenth-century coal industry or in the early twentieth-century Shanghai rubber industry.[18]

China's technological backwardness resulted in products of lower quality and higher cost than those of their foreign competitors in China or abroad. Comparisons of Chinese- and Japanese-owned cotton mills in China showed that production in the former during the 1930s was heavily concentrated in the lower quality coarser yarns and that greater investment per worker in the Japanese mills allowed production with fewer workers and contributed to lower costs.[19]

Naturally, the origins of this backwardness lay mainly in structural factors, and other early industrializing countries showed similar characteristics. But Chinese studies have also pointed to more immediate causes. Managerial personnel tended both to be ignorant technically and to share the traditional élite's disdain for manual labour, cutting them off from the actual production process.[20] The simple shortage of technical personnel was another limiting factor: even in 1953 there were only two engineers in 43 private steel-rolling factories in Shanghai, while only nine out of the three hundred technical personnel in the pharmaceutical industry were chemical engineers.[21]

Shortcomings in financial management plagued many Chinese enterprises. These may have resulted partly from inadequacies in the supply of capital to industry, though this is, in itself, a highly complex question.[22] 'Undercapitalization', whereby working capital was provided

---

Rubber Industry] (Zhonghua shuju, Beijing, 1979), p.78; though only published in 1979, the study was written in the 1960s.

[18] ibid. Also Shannon R. Brown and Tim Wright, 'Technology, Economics and Politics in the Modernization of China's Coal Industry, 1850-1895', *Explorations in Economic History*, vol.18, no.1 (January 1981), pp.60-83.

[19] Meng Xianzhang, *Zhongguo jindai jingji shi jiaocheng* [A Course in Modern Chinese Economic History] (Zhonghua shuju, Shanghai, 1951), p.183; Kang Chao, *The Development of Cotton Textile Production in China* (East Asian Research Center, Harvard University, Cambridge, Mass., 1977), ch.6.

[20] See Albert Feuerwerker, 'Economic Trends, 1912-49', in John K. Fairbank (ed.), *The Cambridge History of China, Volume 12: Republican China, 1912-1949, Part I* (Cambridge University Press, Cambridge, 1983), p.61.

[21] Wu Chengming, 'Zhongguo minzu ziben de tedian', p.80.

[22] Kang Chao, op. cit., pp.142-55.

by bank loans or even short-term high-interest advances from native banks, was a characteristic especially of small firms, but even of the largest companies in China, such as those of the Rong family.[23] Where the loans were from foreign companies, economic weakness also endangered sovereignty, and was judged even more severely.[24]

A related phenomenon was the excessive distribution of profits, which was enshrined institutionally in the guaranteed dividend (*guanli*) system. This practice was common in the early twentieth century,[25] but continued well into the 1920s and 1930s. Mishina's study of north Chinese flour mills shows that excessive distribution of profits left companies with no financial reserves against adversity,[26] while even in the Sino-British Kailuan Mining Administration there was much heavier pressure on the Chinese directors than on the British to pay large dividends.[27] As a result Chinese companies failed to build up reserves against a business downturn or even to make sufficient allowance for depreciation, which led to the growing obsolescence of their equipment in the 1930s.[28]

---

[23] Huang Yifeng, 'Jiu Zhongguo Rong jia ziben de fazhan' [The Development of the Capital of the Rong Family in Pre-Communist China] (originally published in 1964), reprinted in Huang Yifeng and Jiang Duo, *Zhongguo jindai jingji shi lunwen ji* [Collected Essays on Modern Chinese Economic History] (Jiangsu renmin chubanshe, Yangzhou, 1981), p.47.

[24] See for example Tianjin shi fangzhi gongye ju bian shi zu [History Writing Group of the Tianjin Textile Industry Bureau], 'Jiu Zhongguo shiqi de Tianjin fangzhi gongye' [The Textile Industry in Tianjin in the Pre-Communist Period], *Beiguo chunqiu* [Northern Annals], no.1, 1960, p.89.

[25] Albert Feuerwerker, *China's Early Industrialization*, pp.18,177-78; Yan Zhongping, *Zhongguo mianfangzhi shi gao*, pp.144-46. Kang Chao, on the other hand, points out that Japanese companies used the guaranteed dividend system, without the deleterious consequences attached to it in China, see Kang Chao, op. cit., p.146.

[26] Mishina Yoritada, *Hoku-Shi minzoku kogyo no hattatsu* [National Industrial Development in North China] (Chuo koronsha, Tokyo, 1942), pp.71-72.

[27] Nathan Papers, housed at the Bodleian Library, Oxford, Nathan to Turner, 13 December 1931, 10 February 1934, 28 December 1934.

[28] See Marie-Claire Bergère, *Capitalisme National et Impérialisme: La Crise des Filatures Chinoises en 1923* (Centre de Recherches et de Documentation sur la Chine Contemporaine, École des Hautes Études en Sciences Sociales, Paris, 1980), p.42; Albert Feuerwerker, 'Industrial Enterprise in Twentieth-Century China', p.325.

Finally, a widespread criticism of the prewar capitalists was that they engaged too much in speculation at the expense of productive activity, as part of a pro-commercial and anti-industrial bias.[29] A recent article attributes the exceptional success of Liu Guojun's Dacheng factory to his careful avoidance of the speculation indulged in by his competitors.[30]

This picture of Chinese capitalism does contain some elements of truth, but other factors possibly impelled scholars to adopt it to a degree beyond that warranted by the historical record. The urgency of Chinese nationalism meant that the primary materials were suffused with pessimism, even where a closer examination of the statistical picture would not justify that gloom. Moreover, Maoist class analysis for most of the period up to 1978 portrayed the prewar capitalists as unable to undertake the tasks of political state-building or rapid economic development, while at the same time brutally exploiting their workers. For their part, Western scholars were influenced both by the pessimism which suffused the Chinese materials, and by modernization theory, which compared Chinese practice with a number of 'ideal' characteristics for entrepreneurial behaviour, thus substantially exaggerating the negative aspects of the Chinese experience.[31]

Pressures for Change

On one level the academic debate moved according to its own autonomous dynamics. From the early 1980s onwards, scholars in China have re-examined the quantitative record and concluded that previous talk of economic crisis and stagnation was much exaggerated, especially for the 1920s and to a lesser extent for the 1930s.[32] Economic historians

---

29   Yan Zhongping, *Zhongguo mianfangzhi shi gao*, p.176.

30   Zhu Xiwu, 'Dacheng fang zhi ran gongsi yu Liu Guojun' [Liu Guojun and the Dacheng Spinning Weaving and Dyeing Company], *Gongshang shiliao 1* [Historical Materials on Industry and Commerce, no.1] (Wenshi ziliao chubanshe, Beijing, 1980), p.51.

31   Though Feuerwerker for one stresses that many of the characteristics shown by Chinese managers were also common in other countries, even America, in the early stages of industrialization; see Albert Feuerwerker, 'Economic Trends, 1912-49', p.61.

32   For a survey of recent developments in modern Chinese economic historiography, see Tim Wright, 'Introduction: Modern Chinese Economic History in a Period of Change', in Tim Wright (ed.), *The Chinese Economy in the*

in Shanghai, such as Huang Wei and Zhang Zhongli, have pioneered the new trend,[33] and this view has been largely, though not entirely, adopted in the most influential survey of the field, produced in 1985 by Wu Chengming.[34] The Institute of Economics at Nankai University also has plans for a thorough re-examination of modern Chinese economic history, which will include quantitative estimates for economic growth over different periods.

The change had come rather earlier in the West, where John Key Chang did much to systematize the evidence.[35] More recently the work of Thomas Rawski has challenged much of the old view of the prewar economy: his quantitative estimates of growth in the modern sector form the basis of a radically new perception of modern China's economic history.[36] In the field of enterprise management, Sherman Cochran has been particularly influential in arguing for the success of much Chinese entrepreneurship before the war, so that again a problematic of failure is inappropriate.[37] The decline of modernization theory and of its central idea of cultural convergence also allowed an examination of Chinese

---

Early Twentieth Century: Recent Chinese Studies (Macmillan, London, 1992), pp.1-28.

[33] Huang Wei, 'Zhongguo minzu zibenzhuyi jingji de fazhan he pochan wenti' [On the Question of the Development and Bankruptcy of the Chinese National Capitalist Economy], *Xueshu yuekan*, no.2, 1982, pp.21-26; Zhang Zhongli, 'Guanyu Zhongguo minzu ziben zai ershiniandai fazhan wenti' [On the Question of the Development of Chinese National Capital in the 1920s], *Shehui kexue* [Social Sciences] (Shanghai), no.10, 1983, pp.42-46 (translated in Wright, *The Chinese Economy*, pp.44-57).

[34] Wu Chengming, 'Zhongguo zibenzhuyi de fazhan shulüe' [An Outline of the Development of Chinese Capitalism], in Wu Chengming, *Zhongguo zibenzhuyi yu guonei shichang*, pp.128-33 (translated in Wright, *The Chinese Economy*, pp.37-42). See also Wang Yuru, 'Lun liangci shijie dazhan zhi jian Zhongguo jingji de fazhan' [On the Development of the Chinese Economy in the Period Between the Two World Wars], *Zhongguo jingji shi yanjiu* [Studies on Chinese Economic History], no.2, 1987, pp.97-109 (translated in Wright, *The Chinese Economy*, pp.58-77).

[35] John K. Chang, *Industrial Development in Pre-Communist China: A Quantitative Analysis* (Edinburgh University Press, Edinburgh, 1969).

[36] Thomas G. Rawski, *Economic Growth in Prewar China* (University of California Press, Berkeley and Los Angeles, 1989).

[37] Sherman Cochran, op. cit.

business practices more on their own terms and less through some Eurocentric ideal.[38]

With scholars in both China and the West demonstrating that very considerable economic growth did indeed take place, particularly in the modern sector, the question became: if industry was growing – relatively rapidly – why should we wish to ask why it was not growing? This in turn directed attention away from the failures of Chinese management.

Even in the West, academic discourse is not entirely autonomous. The production of quantitative evidence for the success of the pre-Communist Chinese economy partly reflects a general resurgence of faith in the efficacy of market forces. The new work shows that the prewar Chinese market economy was not working all that badly and maybe the massive injection of state control was not as clearly necessary as was previously thought.

In China the link between politics and academic discourse is much more direct, and the change in interpretation followed the re-emergence of a leadership concerned predominantly with economic results.[39] Specifically, the implementation of the reform policies led to a renewed interest in economic management, about which dozens of new periodicals have appeared. Most interest has centred on the macro problems of the relationship among enterprises or between enterprises and the state. These issues have also been raised to some extent in the historical literature.[40] But China's prewar capitalists operated in a very different macro environment and, for the moment at least, their experience has had limited relevance.

---

[38] Ramon H. Myers and Thomas A. Metzger, 'Sinological Shadows: The State of Modern China Studies in the US', *Australian Journal of Chinese Affairs*, no.4 (1980), pp.1-34, and Paul Cohen, *Discovering History in China: American Historical Writing on the Recent Chinese Past* (Columbia University Press, New York, 1984), pp.57-96.

[39] For an examination of the effects of this on academic economics, see Andrew Watson, 'Social Science Research and Economic Policy Formulation in China: the Academic Side of Economic Reform', in Michael Yahuda (ed.), *New Directions in the Social Sciences and Humanities in China* (St Martin's, New York, 1986), pp.67-88.

[40] As for instance in the injunction by Chen Bingfu to stress this aspect in historical research, see Chen Bingfu, 'Yingdang kaizhan Zhongguo guanli shi de yanjiu' [We Must Expand the Study of the History of Chinese Management], *Nankai xuebao* [Nankai Journal], no.4, 1984, p.54.

The inefficiency and lack of incentive within China's socialist enterprises has been seen as one cause of the country's economic problems. Thus China's literature on enterprise management has been redirected away from the earlier emphasis on worker participation towards a more output-oriented concern with efficiency and productivity: indeed this change is made quite specific, as the new literature stresses that industrial enterprises are production units and economic organizations, not (as the Gang of Four argued) tools of the dictatorship of the proletariat.[41] The new concerns can be seen not only in academic articles on management, but also in the literary expression of the new policies in the stories of Jiang Zilong, especially in 'Manager Qiao Assumes Office'.[42]

To improve enterprise management, China is looking not only to socialist but also to capitalist models and theories. It has been eager to learn from Western and Japanese management.[43] But another fruitful source of experience is the prewar management practices of China's capitalists, which can provide similar lessons to those learned from Japan or the West. The use of such models helps in the government's use of nationalism as a legitimizing force, at the same time making the lessons more familiar and easier to absorb.

This link with the economic reforms has been the most important factor behind the emergence of the new interpretation. Sometimes an article ostensibly solely historical has actually been written with a view

---

41 Fudan daxue jingji guanli jiaoyan shi [Economic Management Teaching and Research Unit of Fudan University], *Gongye qiye jingying guanli xue* [Business Management in Industrial Enterprises], vol. 1 (Fudan daxue chubanshe, Shanghai, 1982), p.46.

42 See Jiang Zilong, 'Qiao changzhang shang ren ji' [Manager Qiao Assumes Office] and 'Qiao changzhang houzhuan' [More About Manager Qiao], in Jiang Zilong, *Jiang Zilong duanpian xiaoshuo ji* [Collected Short Stories of Jiang Zilong] (Zhongguo qingnian chubanshe, Beijing, 1980), pp.1-52 and 53-101 (translated as 'Manager Qiao Assumes Office' and 'More About Manager Qiao', in Jiang Zilong, *All the Colours of the Rainbow* (Chinese Literature, Beijing, 1983), pp.130-78 and 179-224). For an interesting interpretation of Jiang's writings see Kam Louie, 'In Search of Socialist Capitalism and Chinese Modernisation: Jiang Zilong's Ideas on Industrial Management', *Australian Journal of Chinese Affairs*, no.12 (July 1984), pp.87-95.

43 '*Jingji guanli*' bianji bu [Editorial Department of 'Economic Management'], *Riben gongye qiye guanli kaocha* [An Investigation of the Management of Japanese Industrial Enterprises] (Zhongguo shehui kexue chubanshe, Beijing, 1979), pp.1-28.

to suggesting methods for contemporary management.[44] More often the connection is made explicit. As Zhu Yong concluded in 1985:

> Shanghai's national bourgeoisie, in the course of a struggle to promote its own interests, developed a capitalism which accorded with national interests, thus leaving us not only a material but also a spiritual heritage. Their experience of business management was an important part of that spiritual heritage. We must absorb the essence and reject the dross of that heritage, and so extract those things which are of use to us to accelerate the march of socialist construction.[45]

In management, as against historical, periodicals, the instrumentalism is even more direct. A survey of the management of department stores in pre-Communist China declared as its aim, 'to provide some lessons for present-day department stores'.[46]

Similarly a recent book on financial management makes its didactic purpose crystal clear:

> In order to meet the requirements of financial reform, to provide lessons from historical experience and to strengthen the business management of the financial sector, the People's Bank of China ... has developed research into the topic of the management of modern China's financial sector.[47]

Not only Chinese national capital but also foreign capital has been 'activated' in this way to support the current policies. Foreign capital is now regarded, according to Wu Chengming, as having been 'a component part of capitalism in [China's semi-colonial semi-feudal] society'.[48] Recently much work has been done on foreign enterprises in China, most importantly that of the Nankai Institute of Economics on

---

[44] As one author told me in China.

[45] Zhu Yong, 'Shanghai minzu ziben qiye zuzhi guanli jianlun' [A Brief Discussion of the Organization and Management of Shanghai's National Capitalist Enterprises], *Jingji lilun yu jingji guanli* [Economic Theory and Economic Management], no.3, 1985, p.71.

[46] Wu Guangyi, 'Woguo jindai minzu baihuo ye de jingying guanli' [Business Management in China's Modern National Department Stores], *Guanli shijie* [World of Management], no.6, 1989, p.192.

[47] Zhongguo renmin yinhang zonghang jinrong yanjiu suo jinrong lishi yanjiu shi [Financial History Unit, Institute of Finance, People's Bank of China], *Jindai Zhongguo jinrong ye guanli* [The Management of Modern China's Financial Sector] (Renmin chubanshe, Beijing, 1990), p.1

[48] Wu Chengming, 'Zhongguo zibenzhuyi de fazhan shulüe', p.114.

Kailuan,[49] and of the Shanghai Academy of Social Sciences on British American Tobacco and Sassoons.[50] Some of the articles attribute the success of the foreign companies partly to their superior service and management practices; thus Chen Zengnian wrote in an article on British American Tobacco:

> This essay will mainly examine the course of British American Tobacco's development in the context of its sales organization. This might have some reference value for the reform of our economic system and the improvement of our enterprise management.[51]

Bureaucratic capital is treated less kindly, for obvious reasons. Bureaucratic management is a central problem for current Chinese enterprises, and therefore bureaucratic capitalist enterprises are mostly cited as negative examples, exemplifying the faults that today's entrepreneurs have to avoid rather than the virtues they should emulate. Thus one article admitted:

> This article analysed the strongly feudal nature of official enterprises... Enterprises today cannot be said to be free from the influence of corrupt feudal thinking ...The directors and managers of enterprises must certainly struggle with this corrupt ideology, otherwise they will be wiped out in the competition of the commodity economy.[52]

---

[49] See especially Nankai daxue jingji yanjiu suo jingji shi yanjiu shi, op. cit., and Guo Shihao (ed.), *Jiu Zhongguo Kailuan meikuang gongren zhuangkuang* [The Situation of the Workers at the Kailuan Coal Mines in Pre-Communist China] (Renmin chubanshe, Beijing, 1985), and Ding Changqing, 'Kailuan meikuang de shichang jingying celüe' [Market Management Strategies of the Kailuan Coal Mines], *Nankai jingji yanjiu suo jikan* [Nankai Institute of Economics Quarterly], no.1, 1986, pp.54-61.

[50] See Shanghai shehui kexue yuan jingji yanjiu suo [Institute of Economics, Shanghai Academy of Social Sciences], *Ying-Mei yan gongsi zai Hua qiye ziliao huibian* [Materials on the British American Tobacco Enterprises in China] (Zhonghua shuju, Shanghai, 1983); and the series of articles published by Zhang Zhongli on Sassoons in *Shanghai jingji yanjiu* [Shanghai Economic Studies] and *Shanghai jingji kexue* [Shanghai Economic Science].

[51] Chen Zengnian, 'Ying-Mei yan gongsi zai Zhongguo de xiaoshou wang' [The Sales Network of British American Tobacco in China], *Xueshu yuekan*, no.1, 1981, p.16.

[52] Lin Daidai, 'Zhongguo jindai qiyejia he qiye guanli' [Entrepreneurs and Enterprise Management in Modern China], *Jingji wenti tansuo* [Inquiries into Economic Problems], no.4, 1987, p.56.

Nevertheless, in certain circumstances, even the performance of bureaucratic capitalists is being evaluated more positively. A notable example was a conference on the northern bureaucratic capitalist Zhou Xuexi, held under the auspices of the Tianjin Academy of Social Sciences in mid 1991. The fundamental thrust of the Conference was a revised evaluation of Zhou, moving away from an entirely negative judgement to one which also pointed to his achievements (and, specifically, the lessons that could be drawn from them); in part this re-evaluation consisted of redefining Zhou as a 'national' capitalist. Whatever his faults, Zhou is now seen to have made a contribution in a variety of areas, including development policy and education as well as management thought and practice.[53]

The New Interpretation

The verdict on the 'national' or 'private' bourgeoisie has been reversed or at least qualified, as Chinese historians seek to provide examples and lessons for the economic managers of the 1980s. This re-evaluation mostly entails a concentration on different aspects of the capitalist experience rather than diametrically opposite conclusions on a given issue. Some of the positive aspects were recognized in the earlier literature,[54] just as the negative aspects are today,[55] but there has clearly been a major shift in what can be published. Manuscripts from the 1950s and 1960s which could not be openly published at the time have recently seen the light of day in various series of *Wenshi ziliao* (Cultural and Historical Materials).

In place of the previous stress on the absence of entrepreneurial spirit, current scholarship points to many examples of successful Chinese capitalist entrepreneurs. In China, these examples are used to support Deng Xiaoping's concern for leadership, decision making and risk taking. New journals have appeared specifically to popularize entrepreneurship – for instance *Zhongguo qiyejia* (Chinese Entrepreneur) and *Qiyejia yuekan* (Entrepreneurial Monthly) – and, although their main focus is on the current scene, one section often deals

---

[53] This paragraph is based on a number of papers (not individually referenced here) which were presented at the Conference on Zhou Xuexi's Industrial and Commercial Group and Chinese Modernization, Tianjin, May 1991, as well as on discussions in the main sessions.

[54] As in Huang Yifeng, op. cit.

[55] Chen Huixiong, op. cit., p.44.

with the prewar Chinese capitalists. Paramount among these were the Rongs, the family of China's cotton and flour king, Rong Zongjing. Not only were members of the family – especially Rong Desheng, who survived to become a national capitalist after 1949 – praised in brief biographies in these magazines,[56] but in July 1986 Chinese leaders hosted a banquet in Beijing for the whole family, who were also received by Deng Xiaoping.[57] Other issues of *Chinese Entrepreneur* carried historical portraits, including even 'bureaucratic capitalists' such as Zhang Zhidong.[58]

In the West, too, Thomas Rawski has analysed the success of entrepreneurs in the engineering trades, where it was possible to start from small-scale operations,[59] and Sherman Cochran has provided the best picture yet of the operations of a Chinese enterprise – the Nanyang Brothers Tobacco Company – whose owners he saw as classical Schumpeterian entrepreneurs.[60]

Similarly, the new literature denies that the Chinese capitalists' management methods were as deficient as was earlier argued; especially from the 1920s they introduced aspects of scientific management from which present-day managers may have something to learn.[61] A recent article on contemporary management problems focuses on five problems, which form the basis for the following discussion of the historical literature: market consciousness, technical development, personnel and talent, social responsibility and management

---

[56] Xu Yin, 'Rongshi jiazu' [The Rong Family], *Zhongguo qiyejia*, no.1, 1986, pp.31-33. See also Lin Difei, 'Rongjia qiye de chuangye renwu – Li Guowei' [Li Guowei – An Entrepreneurial Figure in the Rong Enterprises], *Zhongguo qiyejia*, no.2, 1986, pp.32-34.

[57] See *China Daily*, 18 and 19 June 1986.

[58] In other issues in early 1986, *Zhongguo qiyejia* carried articles on Lu Zuofu, the shipping magnate (February), Zhang Zhidong (March), the Jians of Nanyang Brothers (April), and Li Zhuchen, the chemical industry pioneer (May).

[59] Thomas G. Rawski, 'The Growth of Producer Industries, 1900-1971', in Dwight H. Perkins (ed.), *China's Modern Economy in Historical Perspective* (Stanford University Press, Stanford, 1975), pp.207-13.

[60] Sherman Cochran, op. cit., p.214.

[61] Encyclopedia editorial department, *Zhongguo qiye guanli baike quanshu* [Chinese Enterprise Management Encyclopedia] (Qiye guanli chubanshe, Beijing, 1984), p.50.

philosophy.⁶² All these involve attitudinal change, which could be promoted by the citation of patriotic models.

Market consciousness, natural in a capitalist society, is one attitude the reformers wish to instil in socialist enterprises. The adjustment of products and output volumes to market demand has been a concept largely foreign to the socialist system; it was, however, stressed in Ma Hong's 1979 report to the State Economic Commission,⁶³ and in the stories about Manager Qiao.⁶⁴ Many prewar capitalists can be used as models in this respect. Wing On Cotton Mill adjusted its prices, products and packaging to meet market demand, carefully producing yarn of different counts for different markets – high quality yarn for Hong Kong, lower quality cheaper yarn for Chongqing and Thailand.⁶⁵ Similarly the Huacheng Tobacco Company carefully analysed the cigarette market and decided that there was a place for a product substantially cheaper than that of British American Tobacco; it later gradually moved up-market as boycott movements undermined the sales of the foreign company.⁶⁶

Market responsiveness depends on the collection of information about consumer demand.⁶⁷ In his analysis of the success of the Kailuan

---

62 Wang Anmin, 'Qiantan gongye qiye de jingying sixiang' [A Brief Discussion of Management Thought in Industrial Enterprises], *Lanzhou daxue xuebao, sheke ban* [Lanzhou University Journal, Social Sciences], no.1, 1986, pp.30-35, reprinted in *Baokan ziliao xuanhui, gongye qiye guanli* [Collected Materials from Periodicals and Newspapers, Industrial Enterprise Management], no.3, 1986, pp.35-40.

63 Ma Hong, 'Guanyu gongye jingji guanli wenti' [On the Question of Industrial Economic Management], in Ma Hong, et al., *Tigao qiye guanli shuiping* [Raise the Level of Enterprise Management] (Beijing, 1979), p.26. See also Liu Chunqin, 'Shichang tiaojie yinqi de qiye jingying guanli de bianhua' [Changes in Business Management of Enterprises Induced by Market Readjustment], in Yu Guangyuan, et al., *Gongye jingji yu qiye guanli* [The Industrial Economy and Enterprise Management] (Jixie gongye chubanshe, Beijing, 1983), pp.55-77.

64 Jiang Zilong, 'Qiao changzhang houzhuan', pp.56-57 ('More on Manager Qiao', pp.182-83).

65 Xu Dingxin, 'Minzu ziben qiye jingying guanli jingyan chutan' [An Initial Study of the Business Management Experience of National Capitalist Enterprises], *Shehui kexue* (Shanghai), no.3, 1980, pp.32-33.

66 Yi Wei, 'Jiu Zhongguo minzu qiye de jingying celüe' [Business Strategies of National Enterprises in Pre-Communist China], *Jingying yu guanli*, no.5, 1986, p.45.

67 Wang Anmin, op. cit., pp.37-38.

Mining Administration, Ding Changqing, while accepting the nefarious origins of the British company's control over the mines, is nevertheless concerned to analyse those reasons for its success which can still be of use to Chinese enterprises; he examines in some detail the intelligence network developed by Kailuan to inform it of changes in the market.[68] Similarly, Wing On used its knowledge of the vagaries of shipping on the Changjiang to develop an efficient distribution strategy to supply the Sichuan market.[69]

Quality control is vital in a consumer-oriented economy, and poor quality has been one of the most pervasive problems of Chinese industry.[70] In exemplary fashion the prewar capitalists are portrayed as having made great efforts to ensure a high quality product. Thus Fu Huaichen produced soap of a quality appreciated even by his British competitors, and the Wing On Cotton Mill ensured high quality by careful inspection at each stage of the production process.[71]

Quality control had to be accompanied by cost cutting in order to survive in the world of capitalist competition. In the contemporary situation, cost management and cost reduction is an important part of reforming enterprises to suit a more competitive environment.[72] Liu Hongsheng, China's 'match king', was especially noteworthy in this respect, even hiring an American-trained accountant to set up a system of detailed cost accounting,[73] which led to cost reductions in all areas.[74]

---

[68] Ding Changqing, 'Kailuan meikuang de shichang jingying celüe', *passim*.

[69] Xu Dingxin, 'Minzu ziben qiye', p.33.

[70] See for example the entries for quality control in *Zhongguo baike nianjian, 1983* [Chinese Encyclopedia Yearbook, 1983] (Zhongguo Da Baike Quanshu chubanshe, Beijing, 1983), p.338, and the stress in Manager Qiao on the issue, see Jiang Zilong, 'Qiao changzhang shang ren ji', p.43 ('Manager Qiao', p.169), also Wang Anmin, op. cit., pp.36-37, and Jiang Yiwei and Shen Hongsheng, *Gongye qiye guanli xue* [Industrial Enterprise Management] (Jingji Guanli chubanshe, Beijing, 1985), pp.205-33.

[71] Xu Dingxin, 'Minzu ziben qiye', p.31.

[72] Jiang Yiwei and Shen Hongsheng, op. cit., p.270.

[73] Ma Bohuang, 'Liu Hongsheng de qiye touzi yu jingying' [Liu Hongsheng's Enterprise Management and Investments], *Shehui kexue* (Shanghai), no.5, 1980, p.70 (translated in Wright, *The Chinese Economy*, p.92); Xu Dingxin, 'Minzu ziben qiye', p.32.

[74] Xu Dingxin, 'Zhongguo qiyejia zai jiu Shanghai de huodong zuji' [The 'Footprints' of the Activities of Chinese Entrepreneurs in Old Shanghai],

Even in America the practice of cost accounting had only been pioneered in the first decade of the century and generalized in the second, so Liu was following very recent trends.[75]

Chemical industry pioneer Wu Yunchu continually stressed raising quality and reducing costs and, when the Japanese dumped bleaching powder in China, he responded, after consulting his customers, by cutting his costs through the introduction of reusable galvanized iron drums instead of wooden cases to pack the powder.[76] Another entrepreneur who has had a good press recently is Chen Guangfu, head of the Shanghai Commercial and Savings Bank, who cut down on the use of paper, saving several thousand *yuan* in the early 1930s.[77]

A specific tactic which the reformers are keen to promote is that of increasing profits by boosting turnover even on small margins.[78] This was done by the Xiedaxiang Cloth Shop[79] and the Xinya Medicine Factory, which offered between 10 per cent and 40 per cent discounts for large customers paying in cash, thus accelerating the circulation of its capital, increasing its competitiveness and raising its profits.[80]

Customer service is a key aspect of market-consciousness.[81] The ethic of service is all too absent in China despite the slogans of 'Serve the People' and 'To Serve You'. There is much room to learn from the best of the prewar entrepreneurs, such as Chen Guangfu, who stressed that customers were the lifeline of his banking operations: any staff member who quarrelled with customers several times in one month was reported to the manager. When machines were introduced in the 1930s,

---

Shanghai jingji kexue, no.7, 1984, p.47 (translated in Wright, *The Chinese Economy*, p.109).

[75] Alfred Chandler, *The Visible Hand: The Managerial Revolution in American Business* (Harvard University Press, Cambridge, Mass., 1977), pp.278-79, 464-65.

[76] Wu Zhichao, 'Wu Yunchu ji qi huaxue shiye' [Wu Yunchu and His Chemical Factories], *Gongshang shiliao* 1, p.73.

[77] Xu Dingxin, 'Jiu Zhongguo Shanghai yinhang de jingying guanli' [Business Management in the Shanghai Bank in Pre-Communist China], *Xueshu yuekan*, no.9, 1981, pp.27-28.

[78] Wang Anmin, op. cit., p.37.

[79] Sun Zhaoming, 'Xiedaxiang zhoubu dian de "tebie zuofa"' [The 'Special Methods' of the Xiedaxiang Silk Cloth Shop], in *Gongshang shiliao* 2 (Wenshi ziliao chubanshe, Beijing, 1981), p.148.

[80] Yi Wei, op. cit., p.47.

[81] Wang Anmin, op. cit., p.37.

Chen warned lest they presage a decline in service.[82] Such attitudes were especially important for service industries, and the Minsheng Shipping Company put forward the slogan of 'Service Before Everything' in its competition with foreign companies. Anyone who has recently visited a state-run Chinese store will approve of the implied advice given when historical experience is described as follows: 'when a customer came to a counter, the attendant of their own accord greeted them and patiently introduced the nature and characteristics of the various goods on sale'.[83] For their part, the Guo brothers said that the need for politeness to customers ranked first among their ten lessons from experience, and their Wing On stores laid on transport for customers' purchases.[84]

Even productive enterprises needed to maintain good service. In the interest of maintaining long-term credibility with their customers, Kailuan passed up short-term profits, making sure to fulfil signed contracts even after the outbreak of war in 1937, when excess demand meant that the coal could have been sold more profitably elsewhere.[85]

A second current area of concern is technical development and for managers to be technically aware. So Du Mengrong draws attention to the way Liu Hongsheng overcame the traditional élite disdain for technical matters: when he set up a wool mill in Shanghai, he personally took an interest in the technology of wool production, and as a result turned out a product as good as imported wool.[86] Similarly Liu Guojun involved himself in Dacheng's experiments to establish a textile printing facility, and his studies of production technology made a major contribution to the company's success.[87]

Even managers less personally involved in technical matters could still give them high priority. Chen Huixiong contrasts the general state of technological obsolescence with the Rongs' constant quest for technical improvement:[88] when establishing the Shenxin No.8 mill in 1930 they insisted on the most up-to-date and productive British

---

[82] Xu Dingxin, 'Jiu Zhongguo Shanghai yinhang', pp.26-27.
[83] Wu Guangyi, op. cit. p.195.
[84] Xu Dingxin, 'Minzu ziben qiye', pp.34-35.
[85] Ding Changqing, 'Kailuan meikuang de shichang jingying celüe', p.59.
[86] Du Mengrong, 'Liu Hongsheng de jingying shu' [The Business Methods of Liu Hongsheng], Shanghai qiye [Shanghai Enterprises], no.5, 1982, p.43.
[87] Zhu Xiwu, op. cit., pp.51-52.
[88] Chen Huixiong, op. cit., p.44.

machinery,[89] although elsewhere much of their success was based on the improvement and maintenance of existing machinery.[90]

Adaptation of foreign models tempered the inevitable dependence of China's prewar industry on foreign sources for its technology.[91] The pioneer textile industrialist Mu Ouchu advocated the purchase of the most advanced machinery (American in this case), but also called for absorption and adaptation; the 'sinification' of machinery is something that is still relevant today.[92] By the end of the period an independent local machinery industry had begun to emerge. The Dalong Company's manufacture of cotton spinning machinery was much praised for producing high quality goods,[93] and for adapting foreign models to Chinese conditions, thus avoiding blind worship of foreign things.[94]

Personnel management, particularly the low quality and poor qualifications of both management and labour and the need to develop specialized and trained talent at all levels, has been the most pervasive concern of contemporary micro-level management literature in China.[95] Recent Chinese articles have stressed the degree to which prewar capitalists, in contrast to the warlords, rejected particularistic criteria in

---

[89] Xu Weiyong and Huang Hanmin, *Rong jia qiye fazhan shi* [History of the Development of the Rong Family Enterprises] (Renmin chubanshe, Beijing, 1985), p.78.

[90] ibid., also Xu Weiyong, 'Lüe tan jiu Zhongguo Shenxin fangzhi gongsi de guanli yu gaige' [A Brief Discussion of the Management and Reform of the Shenxin Textile Company in Pre-Communist China], *Jingji xueshu ziliao* [Materials on Economic Studies], no.5, 1982, p.34.

[91] See Yu Guoqiang, 'Lüe tan Zhongguo jindai minzu zibenzhuyi gongye qiye jingying de tedian' [A Brief Discussion of the Characteristics of Enterprise Management in National Capitalist Industry in Modern China], *Shanxi caijing xueyuan xuebao* [Journal of the Shanxi College of Finance and Economics], no.4, 1984, p.78.

[92] Chen Zhengshu, 'Ershiniandai Shanghai de qiye gaigejia Mu Ouchu' [Mu Ouchu, an Enterprise Reformer in Shanghai in the 1920s], *Shanghai jingji kexue*, no.11, 1984, p.39.

[93] Xu Dingxin, 'Minzu ziben qiye', p.31.

[94] Yi Wei, op. cit., p.46.

[95] See for example Guojia jingwei jingji ganbu peixun zhongxin [Economic Cadre Training Centre of the State Economic Commission] and Zhongguo qiye guanli xiehui [Chinese Enterprise Management Association], *Gongye qiye jingying guanli* [Business Management in Industrial Enterprises] (Jingji kexue chubanshe, Beijing, 1984), p.119-20; Fudan daxue, op. cit., p.47.

recruitment. Their slogan 'Empty bags cannot stand up straight' emphasized their desire for specialized skills and training.[96] Fan Xudong believed that 'the real basis of productive enterprises is talent',[97] and Liu Hongsheng also argued, 'One of the major reasons for the failure of enterprises is China's lack of management skills and trained personnel'.[98] Chen Guangfu is especially praised for insisting on qualifications and on continual upgrading of his staff, while the Rongs sought to replace the old 'feudal' foremen with trained personnel from the Hangzhou No. 1 Industrial School.[99] Kailuan also stressed both formal qualifications and work experience in its recruitment policies, with most top staff having had a tertiary education.[100]

Many units in China have now established formal criteria, including examinations, for recruiting personnel and even, as with Manager Qiao, to test existing staff. In 1936 the Minsheng Shipping Company had nineteen selection criteria for its recruitment scheme and chose only 80 out of 300 applicants, thereby strengthening its competitiveness. Ninety three per cent of its 3580 staff and workers in that year had been recruited through external examinations and competition.[101] The Jincheng Bank arranged with Nankai University to hold examinations for university and middle-school graduates; those passing were then taken on for a six-month probationary period.[102] Better qualified staff

---

[96] Xu Dingxin, 'Zhongguo qiyejia zai jiu Shanghai', p.44 (translated in Wright, *The Chinese Economy*), p.103.

[97] Li Zhichuan and Chen Xinwen, 'Zuguo, shiye, kexue, rencai: jinian shiyejia Fan Xudong dansheng yi bai zhounian' [Fatherland, Industry, Science, Talent: Recalling the Centenary of the Birth of the Industrialist Fan Xudong], *Gongshang jingji shiliao congkan, di er ji* [Collected Historical Materials on the Industrial and Commercial Economy, no.2] (Wenshi ziliao chubanshe, Beijing, 1983), p.12.

[98] Xu Dingxin, 'Minzu ziben qiye', p.31.

[99] Xu Dingxin, 'Jiu Zhongguo Shanghai yinhang', p.25; Xu Weiyong and Huang Hanmin, op. cit., p.76.

[100] Ding Changqing, 'Kailuan meikuang renshi guanli de lishi kaocha' [An Historical Investigation of Personnel Management at the Kailuan Coal Mines], *Nankai jingji yanjiu* [Nankai Economic Studies], no.4, 1986, pp.21, 24.

[101] Ling Yaolun et al, *Minsheng gongsi shi* [History of the Minsheng Company] (Renmin jiaotong chubanshe, Beijing, 1990), p.116.

[102] Tang Lizhong, Zhao Kuan and Lin Daidai, 'Lüe lun jiu Zhongguo minzu ziben qiye de laodong gongzi guanli' [A Brief Discussion of Labour and Wage Management in National Capitalist Enterprises in pre-Communist China], *Caijing yanjiu* [Studies in Finance and Economics], no.3, 1986, pp.54-55; Zhongguo

were more productive: output from the inferior equipment run by the Rongs' technically trained staff soon overtook that of the better machinery entrusted to the old, untrained foremen.[103]

Nepotism and the employment of relatives was one of the greatest barriers to appointment on merit. *'Guanxi'* (connections) and blood relationships have played and still do play a key role in China, though Western scholars no longer see this in an entirely negative light. Noting similar phenomena both in early European industrialization and among the highly successful overseas Chinese today, Marie-Claire Bergère argues that such connections were a source of dynamism for early Chinese capitalism.[104]

On the whole, Chinese writers have taken a standard 'modernization theory' position on this issue, and argued that such personal connections were incompatible with the demands of modernization, praising those capitalists who resisted this way of doing things. In running the Minsheng Company, Lu Zuofu believed that 'the traditional method of hiring people according to the introduction of friends and relatives was a product of the feudal small peasant economy and family system and should be thoroughly abolished'.[105] For his part, Wang Yunwu of the Commercial press forbade the hiring of any relatives of staff.[106] In practice, however, such commendable principles could at best be followed only partly: while Zhou Xuexi is praised for prohibiting the employment of relatives in the Beijing Water Company, in the more

---

renmin yinhang Shanghai shi fenhang jinrong yanjiu shi [Financial History Unit, Shanghai Branch, People's Bank of China], *Jincheng yinhang shiliao* [Materials on the History of the Jincheng Banking Corporation] (Renmin chubanshe, Shanghai, 1983), p.269.

[103] Xu Weiyong and Huang Hanmin, op. cit., p.76.

[104] Marie-Claire Bergère, 'Regional Loyalties and the Social Structures of Old Shanghai's New Business Class During the Republican Period (c. 1920-1927)', in Zhang Yufa (ed.), *Zhonghua minguo chuqi lishi yantaohui lunwen ji* [Proceedings of the Conference on the Early History of the Republic of China, 1912-27] (Zhongyang yanjiu yuan, Taibei, 1984), vol. 2, p.775.

[105] Ling Yaolun, op. cit., p.7.

[106] Xu Dingxin, 'Lun Zhongguo gudai guanli sixiang zai minzu ziben qiye zhong de yunyong' [On the Utilization of China's Ancient Management Thought in the National Capitalist Enterprises], *Shanghai jingji yanjiu* [Shanghai Economic Studies], no.3, 1986, pp.63-64.

important Qixin Cement Company, which Zhou also controlled, the staff was mostly selected according to particularistic criteria.[107]

On the other hand some scholars suggest that, while the unrestricted employment of relatives was clearly harmful, there may have been some virtue in their use under strict conditions, when the labour market was imperfectly formed. Thus the Leichongsheng medicine shop in Shanghai did employ relatives, but only where their ability was proved by having served three years' apprenticeship in another medicine shop.[108] Similarly several leading families, notably the Rongs and the Guos (Kwoks), sent their younger generation abroad to get a modern training so they would be worthy successors,[109] a practice which was 'more enlightened' than employing relatives with no ability.[110]

It is intriguing to speculate how we should read the 'real' message of this argument in the post-Mao period. Are the writers perhaps saying that since the use of *guanxi* is inevitable, it might be better to steer it in acceptable directions than to try, Canute-like, to stop the practice altogether? Do they implicitly support the controversial practice of China's leadership today, who send their children abroad, as an echo of the earlier situation?

On-the-job upgrading of employees is a key to raising the quality of enterprises, according to one current textbook,[111] and Manager Qiao argued that 'the main duty of those in charge of personnel is to see that no talents are wasted, to find and train promising workers and give them key jobs'.[112] Prewar capitalists used the apprynticeship system, short-

---

[107] Liu Gengsheng and Feng Dazhong, 'Lun Zhou Xuexi chuangban Jingshi zilai shui gongsi de jingying tese' [On the Management Characteristics of Zhou Xuexi's Beijing Water Company] (paper submitted to the Conference on Zhou Xuexi's Industrial and Commercial Group and Chinese Modernization, Tianjin, 1991), pp.9-10; Ouyang Yuefeng, 'Lun Qixin yanghui gongsi de jingying tedian' [On Management Characteristics of the Qixin Cement Company] (paper submitted to the Conference on Zhou Xuexi's Industrial and Commercial Group and Chinese Modernization, Tianjin, 1991), pp.3-4.

[108] Zhu Yong, op. cit., p.69.

[109] Huang Hanmin, 'Lüe tan Rong jia qiye de rencai peiyang wenti' [A Brief Discussion of the Question of Personnel Training in the Rong Family Enterprises], *Jingji xueshu ziliao*, no.2, 1982, p.27.

[110] Zhu Yong, op. cit., p.68.

[111] Jiang Yiwei and Shen Hongsheng, op. cit., p.312.

[112] Jiang Zilong, 'Qiao changzhang houzhuan', p.61 ('More about Manager Qiao', p.187).

term training schemes, specialized educational institutions, and study abroad to upgrade their staff.[113] Huang Hanmin describes the Rongs' efforts to train personnel at all levels, by setting up primary and middle schools in Wuxi, by instituting management training classes and later, during and after the war, by establishing institutions of higher education. Initially the main focus was on technical staff but, as the scale of Chinese enterprises grew from the 1920s, there was an increasing demand specifically for managers, and especially (then as in China today) middle-level managers.[114] Although the main emphasis was on staff training, the Rongs did try to train workers and institute general education.

Work rules and work discipline have been a major concern ever since the Cultural Revolution. Even from the late 1960s there was a fitful campaign to persuade the workers that not all work rules were oppressive. Now many scholars argue that, though the eventual aim of capitalists was to exploit workers and make profits, the rules they established to do this were at the same time necessary for the running of large-scale socialized enterprise. Thus Xu Dingxin, one of the most influential scholars in the new management history of China, describes the rules introduced at the Wing On mills to ensure workers obeyed orders, took care of equipment and improved productivity.[115] Another article distinguishes three areas covered by factory rules: time-keeping; obedience to instructions, for instance in not leaving the place of work; and avoidance of wastage of materials and damage to equipment.[116] Song Feiqing's factory rules were a reflection of 'scientific management', and covered many areas of private life as well as work: three small infractions were equivalent to one major infraction, and three major infractions meant dismissal.[117] Other studies have made similar points, while stressing more the element of exploitation.[118]

---

[113] Zhu Yong, op. cit., pp.68-69.
[114] Huang Hanmin, op. cit., pp.25-29.
[115] Xu Dingxin, 'Minzu ziben qiye', p.34.
[116] Tang Lizhong et al., op. cit., pp.54-55.
[117] Yang Tianshou and Li Jingshan, 'Tianjin Dongya gongsi yu Song Feiqing' [Song Feiqing and the Dongya Company in Tianjin], in *Gongshang shiliao 2*, p.118.
[118] For example Xu Weiyong, op. cit., p.35.

Material incentives, though highly controversial during the Cultural Revolution,[119] are now clearly favoured by the new leadership. There again useful historical precedents can be found. The Da Zhonghua match factory instituted bonuses of between 50 cents and Ch$3.00 per month for overfulfilling quotas, leading to a marked rise in productivity. Similarly the Xiedaxiang Cloth Shop in Shanghai introduced a bonus system, which resulted in the average sales per month per employee rising from Ch$3600 to Ch$4500.[120] One article drew a link between higher remuneration, higher productivity and higher profits, though the largest rewards went to the staff, not the workers.[121] Shenxin cut costs through a scheme of labour incentives, though Chen Huixiong also stresses the contribution of general welfare facilities.[122]

One of the ironies of Maoist 'moral' incentives in industry was their failure even to work on their own level and instil a corporate spirit among the workers.[123] The Chinese leadership has, however, not abandoned its interest in the creation of an 'enterprise spirit' similar to that commonly described in Japan. Interest has focused both on the content of such an enterprise spirit and on the methods by which it was inculcated.[124]

Patriotism was central to the content of 'enterprise spirit'. Many recent articles have stressed the patriotism of the early entrepreneurs: a tribute to Fan Xudong is entitled, 'Fatherland, Industry, Science, Talent',[125] and a survey article argues that, during the 'extreme left' periods in the PRC, historians overstressed the capitalists' search for wealth to the exclusion of their patriotic spirit.[126] Such patriotism was

---

[119] For one example see Carl Riskin, 'Maoism and Motivation: Work Incentives in China', *Bulletin of Concerned Asian Scholars*, vol.5, no.1 (July 1973), pp.10-24.

[120] Xu Dingxin, 'Minzu ziben qiye', p.34.

[121] Tang Lizhong et al., op. cit., p.56.

[122] Chen Huixiong, op. cit., p.45.

[123] Andrew Walder, 'Some Ironies of the Maoist Legacy in Industry', *Australian Journal of Chinese Affairs* no.5 (1981), p.26.

[124] Except where specifically noted, the next three paragraphs are based on Xiong Fu, 'Lun Zhongguo minzu ziben qiye de "qiye jingshen" ' [On the 'Enterprise Spirit' of Chinese National Capitalist Enterprises], *Sichuan daxue xuebao, zhe she ban* [Sichuan University Journal, Philosophy and Social Sciences], no.4, 1988, pp.3-10.

[125] Li Zhuchuan and Chen Xinwen, op cit., p.1.

[126] Lin Daidai, op. cit., p.55.

also a useful motivator for the workforce: many companies started their morning meetings for the workers with patriotic songs: the Minsheng Company even made a record out of its song 'Advance of the Army of Heroes', which was played constantly over the loudspeakers.

Service to society was a second major theme. The old family system was not appropriate for the developing commodity economy, and modernization required the development of groups which transcended particularistic relationships. While the profit motive was important, enterprises also had a broader social role: Song Feiqing's pamphlet on the 'Dongya Spirit' proclaims the company's intention to push forward the progress of society through production. By extrapolation, the Minsheng Company argued: 'the duty of the enterprise transcends economics, the work of the individual transcends the reward'. Finally, 'enterprise spirit' stressed diligence and thrift, the virtues of the Protestant ethic: Lu Zuofu suggested that 'diligence and thrift are the two precious virtues of the Chinese; they are two powerful fists, two sharp swords!'.

In order to inculcate such an 'enterprise spirit', the capitalists adopted several methods. They stressed the importance of propaganda work, and laid down a series of rules. On a material base, they introduced welfare facilities to care for the workers; such facilities both contributed to profits by improving the quality of labour and met the social responsibilities of the entrepreneurs.[127] Finally, pride in the enterprise and its success was encouraged as a way to motivate the workers to greater efforts, and the enterprise leaders were expected to set an example of selfless devotion to the enterprise. Such policies, one article concludes, left a legacy of useful experiences for present-day entrepreneurs.

The structure and organization of enterprises has been less prominent in recent Chinese studies than in Western business history. Most enterprises up to 1920 were small scale, and therefore could use a centralized management system focused on the chief manager. From the 1920s, as the scale of operations increased, and under the influence of the 'American management rationalization' movement, a more decentralized system emerged, with a greater division of labour. The new system was, however, implemented only unevenly: firms like Wing On adopted it from the start, others changed their system in that direction,

---

[127] See also Zhu Xiwu, op. cit., p.54.

and finally some, like Shenxin, which faced the opposition of vested interests in the form of the foremen,[128] made only partial changes.[129]

Again the economic reformers are stressing the role of organizational theory in management modernization, contending that 'continually improving the internal management structure of enterprises is an objective demand of the rapid development of the commodity economy and the rapid transformation of market forms'.[130] One perceived problem has been over-centralization in enterprise management,[131] which can be linked to the interest in more decentralized structures in prewar Chinese enterprise.

Central to the reform of urban enterprises in the mid and late 1980s has been the introduction of a so-called 'responsibility system'. Historians have also found parallels to this in the prewar period. The rapid expansion of the business in the early 1930s forced the Minsheng Company to introduce a much more structured management system, which centred on a clear devolution of specific responsibilities to individual members of staff. Handbooks laid down the scope and requirements of the responsibilities of each job, and each worker had to have thorough knowledge of the relevant regulations.[132]

The theoretical bases for the practice of the capitalists have also been a major focus of the recent literature. The most important source of management thought then and today has been modern, largely Western theory. Mu Ouchu is praised for studying Taylorism while in the United States and summing up management science under seven headings: strict planning; scientific recruitment; clear delineation of responsibilities; system of rewards and punishments; clear accounting as between departments; exchange between departments at market prices;

---

[128] Xu Weiyong and Huang Hanmin, op. cit., p.76.

[129] Zhu Yong, op. cit., pp.67-68.

[130] Ma Zhonghua, 'Xiandai qiye guanli zuzhi de bianhua qushi chutan' [A Preliminary Discussion of Trends in Changes in Modern Enterprise Management Organization], *Nankai jingji yanjiu*, no.5, 1985, p.24. Organizational theory plays a fairly prominent part in many of the management textbooks, such as Jiang Yiwei and Shen Hongsheng, op. cit., pp.17-33, 58-87, and Fudan daxue, op. cit., pp.76-105.

[131] See for example, Lin Ling, 'Reform of the Industrial Management System in Sichuan Province', in Xue Muqiao (chief ed.), *Almanac of China's Economy, 1981* (Modern Cultural Company Limited, Hong Kong, 1982), p.357, and Ma Zhonghua, op. cit., p.27.

[132] Ling Yaolun, op. cit., p.111.

and establishment of welfare facilities. On his return to China he wrote a translation of Taylor's work, the first systematic introduction in Chinese to modern management methods.[133] Later, Wang Yunwu of the Commercial Press and Lu Zuofu of the Minsheng Company were described as 'China's experts in scientific management'.[134] Liu Hongsheng also pioneered modern methods, especially in cost accounting.[135] Song Feiqing, like Mu Ouchu, studied management in the United States, and went on to found the Dongya Wool Company, which achieved success by stressing scientific management.[136]

At the same time, the capitalists drew on traditional Chinese management theory and practice. China has a long history of practical management experience, and Chen Bingfu outlines five major areas where traditional Chinese management has something to offer the contemporary world: the use of systems thought in management; games theory and policy making; business management thought; ideas on human psychology and behaviour; and the criteria for personnel recruitment.[137] Chen and others also assert that traditional China had progressed from perceptual to rational and theoretical knowledge in the field of management; Xu Dingxin argues the central idea has been that of '*zhi*', or control.[138] According to another article, Chinese accounting

---

[133] Chen Zhengshu, op. cit., pp.38-39.

[134] Jiang Duo, 'Lüe lun jiu Zhongguo Minsheng gongsi' [A Brief Discussion of the Minsheng Company in Pre-Communist China], *Shehui kexue zhanxian* [Social Science Front], no.2, 1990, p.218.

[135] Ma Bohuang, op. cit., pp.70-71 (translated in Wright, *The Chinese Economy*), pp.92-93.

[136] Mo Wu, 'Maofang dawang Song Feiqing de "kexue guanli"' [The 'Scientific Management' of Wool King Song Feiqing], *Qiyejia yuekan*, no.5, 1986, pp.30-31; Yang Tianshou and Li Jingshan, op. cit., pp.118-22.

[137] Chen Bingfu, 'Yingdang kaizhan Zhongguo guanli shi', pp.47-49; see also Chen Bingfu, 'Xiandaihua guanli yu Zhongguo gudai guanli sixiang' [Modernized Management and China's Ancient Management Thought], in Guojia jingwei jingji guanli yanjiu suo [Institute of Economic Management, State Economic Commission] (ed.), *Zhongguo gudai sixiang yu guanli xiandaihua* [Ancient Chinese Thought and the Modernization of Management] (Yunnan renmin chubanshe, Kunming, 1985), pp.29-37.

[138] Xu Dingxin, 'Zhongguo gudai guanli sixiang', p.59.

theory enjoyed two golden ages, in the pre-Qin period and the Song, when Chinese theory as well as practice was the world leader. [139]

Several scholars have gone on to argue that this theoretical tradition inspired China's modern capitalists. Mu Ouchu followed Sunzi's injunction to 'know thine enemy' in gaining intelligence about his Japanese competitors; he went on to translate a book on the Japanese cotton industry. Others used the story about Sunzi winning a horse race as the inspiration to make the best of limited resources to overcome their opposition.[140] Moreover, in their recruiting programs the capitalists used the Confucian tradition of picking able men, which dated from Confucius' conversations with Zilu.[141]

This interest in traditional Chinese management theory is explicitly linked to the development of socialism with Chinese characteristics. Management must be modern but also national. Although some discuss traditional management thought partly in the context of the survival of pre-modern economic forms, especially in the countryside,[142] others emphasize that it influenced not only Chinese but also Japanese management practices, which are acknowledged to be the most advanced in the world. One article linked Japan's success to its 'human-centred' (*ren*) management, and thence to the influence of Chinese Confucianism.[143] Whether or not that is a reasonable explanation for the rapid development of Japanese capitalism is far from certain, but its purpose is to suggest that Chinese characteristics are by no means

---

[139] Liu Jun, 'Tantan woguo lishi shang de kuaiji lilun' [On Accounting Theory in China's History], *Jilin caimao xueyuan xuebao* [Journal of the Jilin College of Finance and Trade], no.1, 1986, pp.48-49.

[140] See Sima Qian, *Shi ji* [Records of the Historian] (Zhonghua shuju, Hong Kong, 1969), vol. 7, p.2163. In a series of three races, Sunzi advised his employer to pit his weakest horses against his opponent's best, his best against his opponent's second best, and his second best against his opponent's weakest, thus winning two races and losing one.

[141] Xu Dingxin, 'Zhongguo gudai guanli sixiang', p.63.

[142] Zheng Shao, 'Qiantan Zhongguo gudai shangye jingying guanli sixiang' [A Brief Discussion of China's Ancient Commercial and Business Management Thought], *Shehui kexue* (Shanghai), no.2, 1985, p.20.

[143] Fang Yanming, 'Rujia de chuantong sixiang yu Riben de jingji fazhan' [Traditional Confucian Thought and Japanese Economic Development], *Shehui kexue* (Shanghai), no.2, 1985, pp.18-19, 37.

necessarily a sign of backwardness, though there is a need for selectivity in their adoption.[144]

Conclusion

Any evaluation of the recent Chinese literature is difficult because its message is at two levels. While on the surface it deals with the historical record, its real intention is to support the current economic reforms. Such an 'activation of the propaganda potential' of historical or literary figures has been the central feature of most academic writing in China, whether in the Maoist period or since;[145] indeed it was also common in Confucian historiography. The close link between the academic studies analysed in this paper and current policy concerns can also be found in most other areas of the humanities and social sciences in China. Thus a judgement on their quality as historiography may well miss the point.

Nevertheless, these articles do still confront historical issues. Moreover, the availability of company records in China is likely to mean that for some time overseas scholars will continue to be dependent on the Chinese literature to increase their knowledge of the internal workings of Chinese business.[146] So it is worthwhile asking how well that literature functions as historiography.

Several problems are evident, which result fundamentally from its dual purpose. One problem is a tendency towards a one-sided evaluation of prewar management practices. The slogan of 'let the past serve the present' has meant that most scholars aim (reasonably enough at one level) to provide positive – occasionally negative – examples for the edification of current readers rather than to arrive at a balanced judgement; this has been particularly true for some of the shorter articles

---

[144] Guo Jiguang, 'Zhongguo gudai guanli sixiang zuotanhui tantao jianli you Zhongguo tese de guanli kexue' [A Discussion on Establishing a Management Science with Chinese Characteristics at the Conference on China's Ancient Management Thought], *Jingjixue dongtai* [Developments in Economics], no.3, 1985, p.21.

[145] The phrase is Richard Taylor's, from his work on propaganda in Soviet Russia and Nazi Germany. See A. P. Foulkes, *Literature and Propaganda* (Methuen, London and New York, 1983), p.9.

[146] Western scholars gain access to some of this material through the publication of volumes of collected company documents, but they are likely to continue to use mainly original published sources such as *Yinhang zhoubao* (Bankers' weekly) and other important economic periodicals.

in management journals, but is often also the case in longer and more academic works.

This one-sidedness is exemplified in the reliance of most articles on examples rather than on the quantitative analysis necessary for a balanced judgement. This has been a general tendency in Chinese economic history and has been deplored by one of China's leading economists.[147] In some cases, such as that of the Rongs, the examples chosen may even belie the balance of the evidence. In the 1930s, Rong Zongjing and his enterprises were regarded as very traditional in their management methods. A foreign observer wrote:

> Mr Yung [Rong] is one of the older type Chinese, having something of a contempt for modern business methods and faith in doing things 'the Chinese way'.[148]

Nor was that opinion limited to foreigners. The banks believed that most of Rong's problems were of his own making and only agreed to lend him money if a nominated committee took over the management of his enterprises.[149]

This emphasis has been continued in a minority of recent writings. Thus Zhu Yong criticizes the Rongs for failing to implement a thorough-going structural reform,[150] and Yu Guoqiang argues that they maintained feudal links by investing in land.[151] Chen Huixiong notes the feudal environment within which they operated, and which limited their ability to reform accounting or supervisory systems.[152]

More typical, however, have been articles praising the Rongs' entrepreneurial spirit,[153] staff training policies,[154] and efforts to

---

[147] See Xu Dixin's introduction to Xu Dixin and Wu Chengming (chief eds), *Zhongguo zibenzhuyi de mengya* [The Sprouts of Capitalism in China], *Zhongguo zibenzhuyi fazhan shi* [History of the Development of Chinese Capitalism], vol. 1 (Renmin chubanshe, Beijing, 1985), p.27.

[148] A. Bland Calder, 'Report for the week ended July 21, 1934', in Papers of Julean Arnold, Hoover Institution Archives, Stanford University, Box 6.

[149] Chen Guangfu, 'The Reminiscences of Ch'en Kuang-fu (K. P. Chen)' as told to Julie Lien-ying How, 6 December 1960 – June 1961, translated into English, typescript, manuscript collection, Columbia University, New York, p.43; note however that the wily Rong managed to keep control in the end.

[150] Zhu Yong, op. cit., p.68.

[151] Yu Guoqiang, op. cit., p.78.

[152] Chen Huixiong, op. cit., p.45.

[153] Xu Yin, op. cit.

modernize their management.¹⁵⁵ Although the political preconditions for a more balanced treatment exist in the stress on the dual nature of Chinese national capital,¹⁵⁶ no article attempts to weigh modern and traditional elements in the management practices of the Rongs or other capitalists, or the advantages and disadvantages of each type of management.

Such a one-sided interpretation is not limited to those stressing the positive side of China's capitalists. The article by Yu Guoqiang swims against the tide by emphasizing their backward characteristics. While a welcome corrective to the uncritical praise in some articles, it is not a convincing overall evaluation. Most of the examples of backward traits are taken from before the First World War, and may not be typical of the later period.¹⁵⁷ In addition, Yu tends to cite a single trait – for instance, buying land – as evidence of 'feudal characteristics'. But many Western businesspeople have bought land without thereby being classified as 'feudal'. Nor is the indulgence of capitalists in speculation and the 'quick buck' in any way limited to the Chinese experience.¹⁵⁸ In so far as such activities are a rational response to the external environment, an 'objective' rather than a 'subjective' explanation is required.

One possible way to sidestep this judgemental problem would be to develop a more explicit comparative context in evaluating the progressive or negative features of Chinese management. Little has been done along these lines, however, although one 1988 article compared the nineteenth century performance of the China Merchants' Steamship Navigation Company with that of Japan's Nippon Yusen Kaisha.¹⁵⁹

Several difficulties plague the discussion of management theory. In tracing the history and content of traditional theories, both Chinese and Western writers face similar problems, in that management and accounting as independent disciplines are of very recent origin, as are

---

154 Huang Hanmin, op. cit.
155 Xu Weiyong, op. cit., p.34.
156 See for example Sun Shangqing, 'Guanyu qiye guanli wenti' [On the Question of Enterprise Management], in Ma Hong et al., *Tigao qiye guanli shuiping*, p.80.
157 Yu Guoqiang, op. cit., pp.77-78.
158 ibid., p.80.
159 Zhang Bozhao, 'Qiye jingying fangshi de jindaihua: Lunchuan zhaoshang ju yu Riben youchuan huishe de bijiao yanjiu' [The Modernization of Forms of Enterprise Management: a Comparative Study of the China Merchants' Steamship Navigation Company and the Nippon Yusen Kaisha], *Zhongguo jingji shi yanjiu* [Studies in Chinese Economic History], no.4, 1989, pp.104-19.

the large enterprises which make them necessary. Of course China has a long tradition of managing large-scale government projects (the Great Wall and the Grand Canal are the most obvious two examples), and of course that experience was to some extent theorized and generalized, though in a very piecemeal way. But the resulting theoretical statements are often so general that it is difficult to trace either their pedigree or their influence.

This problem of influence is a fundamental one in intellectual history. Xu Dingxin traces the way traditional management thought influenced Chinese capitalists.[160] But the injunctions of the sages were often too general or even commonsensical to enable one to judge their real influence. Were Chinese capitalists really following Sunzi in acquiring intelligence about their competitors, or was this merely a sensible thing to do in the circumstances? Even if they occasionally quoted Sunzi, was this not more likely an *ex post* rationalization for something done in response to an objective situation? Did they really need the advice of Zigong to formulate policies that had profitable results? For all that Rong Desheng proclaimed himself a disciple of Fan Li,[161] was that really why he reinvested capital within the enterprise? There may indeed have been some influence, but the exercise seems to be more an attempt to stake a case for 'management with Chinese characteristics' than a real explanation for the actions of the capitalists.[162]

There are a number of lesser and more narrowly academic problems with the recent Chinese literature, which might again stem both from the nature of the Chinese academic system and from the double purpose of writing articles. First, very little notice is taken of the work of other scholars either inside or outside China: Zhang Zhongli wrote his article on the Chinese economy of the 1920s without reference to Huang Wei's earlier article on a similar topic, although both articles were published in Shanghai. Nor do any of the articles dealing with the Rongs refer to each other. Thus there is considerable duplication. Second, the authors mostly

---

[160] See Xu Dingxin, 'Zhongguo gudai guanli sixiang'.

[161] On whom see Herbert Giles, *A Chinese Biographical Dictionary* (Paragon Books, New York, 1971), p.217, and Sima Qian, op. cit., vol. 10, p.3257.

[162] This problem exists in most areas of intellectual history, certainly not only in tracing Chinese influences on Chinese entrepreneurs. A similar case could be made against the influence of Western theories, but where those theories were more *specific*, then the likelihood of actually being able to trace influence increases.

develop isolated arguments on particular points, without really attempting to integrate them into a broader theoretical framework, whether Chinese or Western. This is linked to the failure to develop a comparative perspective or a quantitative approach.

Do these problems matter on the level of the 'real' message of the articles? In my opinion they do. A more systematic analysis of the strengths and weaknesses of prewar Chinese management would be a better base for intelligent use of that heritage, and for the creation of a management which is both 'modern and Chinese'.

The Maoist emphasis on the immediate practical use of academic scholarship is now discredited as having led to a serious poverty of theory. But narrowly instrumentalist views of education and research remain strong in both China and the West. At least in this case there seems to be a trade-off between immediate practical use and academic rigour. Unfortunately that lack of academic rigour itself may detract, possibly at one or two removes, from the practical use of the work.

SOCIALISM WITH CHINESE CHARACTERISTICS: SUN YATSEN AND THE INTERNATIONAL DEVELOPMENT OF CHINA

Michael R. Godley

> In a nutshell, it is my idea to make capitalism create socialism in China so that these two economic forces of human evolution will work side by side in future civilization.
>
> If we use existing foreign capital to build up a future communist society in China, half the work will bring double the results.
>
> Sun Yatsen

If and when the People's Republic of China (PRC) and Kuomintang remnants on Taiwan reach a *modus vivendi*, the 'Third United Front', like the First and Second, will surely give lip service to the 'Three People's Principles of Sun Yatsen' – nationalism, democracy and the people's livelihood. There has never been disagreement over the first, nationalism, and in regard to the second, one-party rule has proved problematic on both sides of the Strait, but for that very reason, for most of the past several decades, was not normally open to debate. It is the third of the Sunist trinity, the rather vague economic theory packaged as 'the people's livelihood' (*minsheng zhuyi*) that has fuelled ongoing argument.

On the off-shore island, the *minsheng* concept has – quite understandably – been touted as a far-sighted developmental model, one combining central planning and government regulation in a flexible export-oriented market economy stimulated by large inputs of foreign technology and investment, ideally suited for the modernization of the vast continent. But through much of the 1980s, Sun Yatsen's stock rose in the People's Republic, too. More than one prominent economist on the mainland likewise proposed that his ideas offered a sensible and balanced approach to the country's difficulties, pushing his rehabilitation further than any foreign observer might have thought possible. With the swing to the political left after the Beijing massacre of 1989, it may well be argued that fascination with the quintessential 'bourgeois idealist had 'bourgeois liberal' overtones.

As a non-economist I do not, in any case, wish to debate the nuts and bolts of development on either side of the Taiwan straits. Nor do I intend to discuss the blueprints as such, since what Sun, Marx, Lenin or Mao really meant to say is inevitably so politicized that debate is just as well left to partisans. Surely, as has been the case with Marxism-Leninism, part of the enduring legacy of 'Sunism' is the variety of possible interpretations.[1] Many good scholars have already noted that the *minsheng* ideal was never completely explained; its meaning was very much left to later generations. Nevertheless, as an exercise in the history of ideas, it can still be worthwhile to trace the exegesis – to see how, when circumstances change, founding fathers are reinterpreted.

The Changing 'Ism' of Sunnism

For a time (how long and with what conviction may always be debated) Sun Yatsen certainly seemed willing enough to equate his own socio-economic proposals with 'communism'. Rejection of the inevitability of class conflict and his awareness of some of the difficulties which brought about Lenin's New Economic Policy probably led him to back-pedal to 'socialism'. A sceptical Zinoviev once dismissed 'Sunism' as 'state capitalism', a term which was accepted by both Communist and Nationalist writers up to the 1960s. During the Sino-Japanese War and civil strife, the Kuomintang tended to play down the notion of 'land to the tiller'. Instead the economy was put on a militarized footing, giving great power to the state in a rightward-leaning interpretation of Sunnism. In contrast, the accomplished communist propagandist Chen Boda and leftist bookstores did more to popularize the more radical egalitarian dimensions of Sun's economic policies than the party he founded.

---

[1] Years ago, when the Kuomintang-inspired 'cult of Sun Yatsen' first emerged, Lyon Sharman observed that 'The Three Principles of the People is a very usable book for [such] purposes'. *Sun Yatsen: His Life and its Meaning* (Stanford University Press, 1934), p.274.

Under the influence of Tao Xisheng's increasingly nativist economic history, Chiang Kaishek tried to justify the heavy-handed state intervention required by wartime conditions with quasi-mercantilist notions pillaged from the Qin and Han and lumped awkwardly with Sun Yatsen's grandiose plan for the creation of a modern economic infrastructure. As a consequence, the strategies of capitalism were pushed aside, along with the goal of communism, in an interpretation which stressed traditional moral values and Sun's 'Chineseness', thus allowing for the rejection of both Marxism and the *laissez-faire* capitalist system. Thus the denunciations of Karl Marx in Chiang Kaishek's *China's Destiny* and *Chinese Economic Theory* were to be expected, and the virulent attack on Western imperialism understandable if embarrassing to American allies, but the emphasis on protectionism and home-grown economics nevertheless raised questions about just what course the country would take in the post-war period.

As the situation actually turned out in the island republic, large amounts of United States aid were utilized, and Kuomintang writers began to stress how Sunism combined the best features of capitalism and socialism. More recently, particularly after the mainland embarked on its 'four modernizations', Sun Yatsen's undeniably idiosyncratic amalgam of state controls and private initiative has been described in Taipei as a Chinese version of capitalism – a 'planned free economy' similar to Japan's.[2]

---

[2] See, for example, Hsu Yu-chu, 'Min-Sheng Chu-I and the Planned Free Economy', *China Forum*, vol.4, no.2 (July 1977), pp.123-37. Sun's ideas are regularly described in Taiwan as a far-sighted developmental model which combines central planning with individual enterprise in a flexible export-oriented market economy stimulated by large inputs of foreign technology and investment, ideally suited for the modernization of a vast continent. This point of view was argued at a Taiwan conference (Kauhsiung, 2-5 November 1985), in particular in the papers by Ramon H. Myers, 'Sunist Economic Thought and Chinese Economic Development'; Hou Chi-ming and Yin Nai-ping, 'Sun Yatsen and Economic Development in Taiwan'; A. James Gregor, 'Sun Yatsen, Dependency Theory and the Economic History of Taiwan'; and Wei Wu, 'Prospects of China's Economic Development in the Light of the Taiwan Experience'. Most of the ideas had been published elsewhere. See A. James Gregor et al., *Ideology and Development: Sun Yatsen and the Economic History of Taiwan* (University of California Press, Berkeley, 1981) or Shih Chien-sheng, 'The Min Sheng Chu-I and Economic Modernization in Taiwan', *China Forum*, vol.4, no.2 (July 1977), pp.79-100.

No doubt, the extent to which the so-called 'economic miracle' on Taiwan can be traced directly to Sun Yatsen could be hotly debated. (His name is rarely mentioned in serious economics journals or textbooks on Taiwan.)[3] But this academic truth only underscores the ironic convergence of factors which led to a revival of interest in Sun's ideas in the PRC, where they began to be cited, quite independently, to bolster policies otherwise considered Dengist. As one mainland writer observed in 1985:

> Opening China to the outside was the essential ingredient for accomplishing Sun Yatsen's ideal of modernization. He envisaged that after the revolution to establish a republic, the country should be opened up utilizing international capital, technology, equipment, and talent, in order to systematically establish commerce and industry, modernize the Chinese economy, and catch up to and surpass the advanced Western capitalist states.[4]

In historical perspective, of course, no dimension of Sun Yatsen's economic thought has been as controversial, or in such apparent contradiction to other fundamental goals of a 'nationalist' revolution, as his proposal to open the country to foreign capitalist penetration as a quick fix, a means to overcome the shortage of technology and wherewithal on the road to a modern yet just society. For years it was an embarrassment to those on both the left and right who wished to stress his 'anti-imperialism'. Nonetheless, the proposition that foreign capitalism can be used to build socialism has enjoyed something of a renaissance in the People's Republic.

---

[3] Samuel P. S. Ho, *Economic Development on Taiwan* (Yale University Press, New Haven, 1978), credits the $4.1 billion in United States aid in 1949-67 with allowing the Nationalists to stay in power on the island; but see also Neil H. Jacoby, *US Aid to Taiwan: A Study of Foreign Aid, Self-Help and Development* (Praeger, New York, 1966). To see how easy it is to explain the successful modernization of Taiwan without Sun Yatsen, consult Jason Shih, 'Taiwan: Model of Economic Development', *Chinese Culture: A Quarterly Review*, vol.20, no.3 (September 1979), pp.27-38.

[4] Cai Shan, 'Lun Sun Zhongshande duiwai kaifang sixiang' [On Sun Yatsen's Ideas about Opening the Country], in *Huanan shifan daxue xuebao* [Journal of South China Normal University], no.3 (1985), p.21.

Sun Yatsen and Foreign Investment

At the end of the Great War (1914-18), Sun hit upon the idea that the victorious Western powers could be induced to invest in China. Believing that their industries would need to shift to peacetime pursuits, he calculated that even a fourth of the total expenditures in the final year of conflagration would equal sixty million gold dollars a day. By early 1919, he had worked out where so mighty a sum could be invested – in a million miles of railways and in a multitude of other projects involving ports, mines, agriculture and industry.

Sun sent an outline to the American ambassador in Beijing; and the next month wrote directly to the US Department of Commerce. Although all the details are not known, he seems also to have written to other governments. He simultaneously carried on an enthusiastic correspondence with the international planner H. C. Anderson, who apparently passed on at least the gist of Sun's proposal to Woodrow Wilson in Paris. In order to reach the treaty-port audience, Sun published an introductory sketch in *The Far Eastern Review* (Shanghai) in March 1919 under the lengthy title: 'The International Development of China: A Project Designed to Assist the Readjustment of Post-bellum Industries, by Sun Yatsen, ex-President of the Republic of China'. Other proposals appeared in this journal as well as in the Kuomintang's new Chinese-language organ, *Jianshe zazhi* (Reconstruction Magazine). The assorted pieces were reassembled into Sun's well-known book *The International Development of China*, which ended with the words quoted at the beginning of this article.[5]

There seems no question that Sun was caught up in the general postwar enthusiasm for international co-operation; but the immediate catalyst was talk of a new Great Power Consortium. Nevertheless, when he finally had an opportunity to present his scheme to American banking interests in April 1920, he was decidedly an 'ex-president' – then on extended leave from his first Guangzhou government, and hardly in a position to negotiate for China. As C. Martin Wilbur has concluded, after describing this particular episode, the revolutionary physician was in the awkward situation of lobbying for his country's welfare whilst simultaneously looking for ways to destabilize the political order which continued to exclude him.[6]

---

[5] Taipei edition, 1953, p.208. The best English-language chronicle of the events leading up to the work can be found in C. Martin Wilbur, *Sun Yatsen: Frustrated Patriot* (Columbia University Press, New York, 1976), pp.97-100.

[6] Wilbur, op.cit., p.99.

Some writers have seen this stance as 'opportunism'. Although Sun had criticised the foreign loans negotiated first by the Qing authorities and then by Yuan Shikai, he eagerly sought foreign finance for his own cause and again when he was Minister of Railways. Later, he worked to undermine international support for that same republic whilst courting capitalist investors. In other incidents over many years, he was willing to strike a bargain with any foreign power which would agree to help his political ambitions. The Russians were perhaps the last.

There is no doubt that, as Mahatma Gandhi is reported to have said, 'consistency is a hobgoblin'; circumstances have forced even the most saintly of politicians to compromise and shift course. Sun, who never had an opportunity to put his prescriptions to any practical test until the second and third Guangzhou governments, was inevitably relegated to the role of 'schemer'. To be fair, what has been described as 'opportunism' could also be chalked up to 'idealism'. When he wrote the preface to *The International Development of China* in Guangzhou in mid-April 1921, he argued that 'international commercial war', and with it 'the internecine capitalist competition', might be avoided in China through a form of 'socialist' co-operation between labour and capital. The fact that this vision already clashed with Lenin's increasingly popular theory that imperialism was 'the highest stage of capitalism', and found less and less sympathy amongst youthful Chinese after the sell-out at Versailles, does not seem to have discouraged him. To his death, Sun retained the hope that China would find a way to harness the energy of capitalism to obtain the justice of socialism.

Marxists have traditionally argued that Sun failed to understand the nature of 'finance' or 'monopoly capital'. Even writers in the PRC, who began to use Sun Yatsen to support Deng's 'open door' and 'four modernizations' from the early 1980s onward, felt it necessary to repeat the criticism that the bourgeois revolutionary's generally 'progressive economic thought' was inevitably limited by his class outlook. Having failed to accept the 'scientific socialism' of Marxist-Leninism, his perspective was inevitably naive and would have led to an eventual capitalist take-over of China. That point has now become moot. Although authors in the PRC have agreed that foreign participation could not possibly have benefited the country when Sun was alive, because of the aggressive attitude of the imperialist powers which exploited Chinese weakness through unequal treaties, once the nation had become strong enough to control its own destiny the same previously foolhardy proposals suddenly came of age.[7]

Scholars working in Taiwan (and also some anti-communists in the West) prefer to argue that Sun Yatsen was more sophisticated – that he was willing to allow a measure of foreign economic domination because he foresaw its value to economic development. While he condemned the scramble for territories and gross exploitation, he accepted foreign intercourse and even developmental assistance for genuine net gain. Economic relations, even in the age of imperialism, could benefit all parties.[8]

This argument has important historical as well as contemporary significance since it intersects with that hoary debate over the extent and role of the earlier foreign economic stake in China – whether that presence was essential as a catalyst for economic growth or actually retarded growth. Was it exploitative, beneficial or, conceivably, both? In crude terms, was it a cure or a curse?

Many economic historians have begun to argue that, when all is said and done, the foreigners played a positive developmental role. As Robert F. Dernberger noted in 1975, the Chinese economy 'enjoyed significant absolute gains from trade and a gross transfer of productive capital and technology'.[9] Foreign investment in China has been estimated at US$788 million in 1902, doubling to $1610 million in 1914 and redoubling to $3243 million in 1930. By 1936, the per capita figure came to less than $8 a person. Hou Chi-ming has pushed the argument

---

[7] See Cai Shan, op.cit. For a slightly more cautious and traditionally Marxist assessment, see Wu Xizhao et al., 'Lun Sun Zhongshande weiwuzhuyi yuzhou fazhan jian' [On Sun Yatsen's Materialist Perspective – Past, Present and Future], *Zhongshan daxue xuebao* [Journal of Sun Yatsen University] (1979), pp.117-24. For a semi-official 'textbook' line, as of 1979-80, see *Zhongguo jindai jingji sixiang shi* [History of Modern Chinese Economic Thought] (Zhong Hua, Beijing, 1980), vol.2, pp.461-82.

[8] One of the most recent expressions of this line of argument is A. James Gregor and Maria Hsia Chang, 'Marxism, Sun Yatsen and the Concept of Imperialism', *Pacific Affairs*, vol.55, no.1 (Spring 1982), pp.54-79.

[9] 'The Role of the Foreigner in China's Economic Development, 1840-1949' in Dwight H. Perkins (ed.), *China's Modern Economy in Historical Perspective* (Stanford University Press, 1975), p.46. See also Chi-ming Hou and Tzong-shian Yu (eds), *Modern Chinese Economic History: Proceedings of the Conference on Modern Chinese Economic History* (Academia Sinica, Taipei, 1979), particularly Feng-hwa Mah, 'External Influence and Chinese Economic Development: A Re-Examination', pp.273-98.

that 'Although small in amount, foreign capital played a significant role in bringing about whatever economic modernization existed in China before 1937'.[10]

Nonetheless, such investment did not take place in a vacuum. In the context of unequal treaties and political weakness, the foreign stake in China – as direct investment and loans – became a symbol of alien invasion, an attack on sovereignty and national sentiment. Yet, as Tim Wright observed in the case of the coal industry:

> One cannot deduce even from the most outrageous piece of robbery practised against the Chinese people that the eventual net economic effect on China of foreign involvement in that particular case would necessarily be harmful.[11]

But that is not the way Chinese at the time tended to see the question of foreign investment or management.

In *China's Destiny*, Chiang Kaishek blamed the unfair tariff arrangements and other treaty provisions, including the right to open industries on Chinese soil, for the country's moral as well as economic difficulties.[12] Although Mao Zedong admitted that foreign penetration contributed to the expansion of the 'commodity economy', he too charged the outsiders with destroying traditional handicrafts, disrupting the natural order and retarding the independent development of Chinese capitalism.[13] As late as 1977, in the authoritative *Hongqi* (Red Flag), a Party writer confirmed: 'Ours is an independent and sovereign socialist state. We have never allowed, nor will we ever allow, foreign capitalists to invest in our country'.[14] The ink was barely dry before major policy changes were apparent.

A high-level decision to expand foreign trade and investigate possible sources of capital and technology had, in fact, probably been made as early as 1971 when the smoke first cleared after the Great

---

[10] Chi-ming Hou, *Foreign Investment and Economic Development in China 1840-1937* (Harvard University Press, Cambridge, Mass., 1965), p.216.

[11] *Coal Mining in China's Economy and Society 1895-1937* (Cambridge University Press, 1984), p.117.

[12] Available in English together with *Chinese Economic Theory* (Dennis Dobson, London, 1947).

[13] For more on Chinese Communist historiography, see Albert Feuerwerker (ed.), *History in Communist China* (M.I.T. Press, Cambridge, Mass., 1969), pp.216-46.

[14] *Hongqi*, no.4 (April 1977), as translated in *Chinese Economic Studies* (hereafter *CES*), vol.11, no.1 (Fall 1977), p.13.

Proletarian Cultural Revolution (despite the current rhetoric of its having lasted ten years). Yao Wenyuan reportedly protested that 'to trade our petroleum and coal for their equipment is to betray the nation'. According to post-'gang of four' reconstructions, the radicals favoured self-reliance and opposed opening the country. But, as Deng Xiaoping is known to have argued, 'no nation which wishes to develop today can remain closed to the outside'. By 1974, a new foreign trade magazine had been started, and although the minister in charge, Li Qiang, spoke out against the idea of importing capital, and though *Beijing Review* boasted that China still had no foreign debts in 1977, the die was cast the following year when the Bank of China began to solicit overseas deposits. Soon thereafter, Beijing asked for United Nations technical assistance, and subsequently joined the International Monetary Fund and the World Bank in the spring of 1980.[15]

In the meantime, the first draft law on joint ventures was approved in July 1979, and soon a Foreign Investment Control Commission was set up, headed by Vice-Premier Gu Mu. From then on, the door was obviously open to capital as well as trade. In the early 1980s, priority was placed on the development of energy resources, transport and communications along with smaller projects which could produce quick results for small investments. At first, it was strenuously argued that outside assistance was 'supplementary'. As one author in the journal *Jingji yanjiu* (Economic Research) explained, 'we will primarily draw upon our resources, while taking advantage of favourable international conditions whenever feasible, raising funds and importing advanced technology'.[16] By 1984, it was apparent to everyone that borrowing would be greatly expanded and controls on foreign capital relaxed.

One *Renmin ribao* (People's Daily) article put the question bluntly: 'do socialist countries need to utilize foreign capital?... Will relaxing

---

[15] The turn of events has been well studied. For background, see A. Doak Barnett, *China's Economy in Global Perspective* (Brookings Institution, Washington, DC, 1981) and the survey by Samuel P.S. Ho and Ralph W. Huenemann, *China's Open Door Policy: The Quest for Foreign Technology and Capital* (University of British Columbia Press, Vancouver, 1984). Also of special relevance are essays by Terry Cannon, 'Foreign Investment and Trade: Origins of the Modernization Policy', in S. Feuchtwang and A. Hussain (eds), *The Chinese Economic Reforms* (Croom Helm, London, 1983), pp.288-324; and Samuel S. Kim, 'Post-Mao China's Development Model in Global Perspective', in N. Maxwell and B. McFarlane (eds), *China's Changed Road to Development* (Pergamon Press, Oxford, 1984), pp.213-32.

[16] Translated in *CES*, vol.16, no.1 (Fall 1982), p.53.

the policy of utilizing foreign capital humiliate the nation and forfeit our sovereignty?' 'From a historical point of view', the author answered, 'we have had more failures than successes in our dealings with foreign countries... This makes some of our comrades worry... This feeling is understandable. And we should maintain vigilance. But the present is not the past'. 'How can you catch tiger cubs', he quoted from an old proverb, 'without entering the tiger's lair?'[17] Another author, five months later, continued the attack on protectionism and isolationism and concluded that 'socialism should not fear capitalism... The edifice of modernised socialism can be built only when we face the world... There simply cannot be a country stupid enough to refuse knowledge and technology from outside and to want instead to close its doors on everything and to do everything from scratch'. The author quoted Deng Xiaoping's claim that 'opening our doors to the world outside is a fundamental policy of our country. If there is to be change, it will be in the direction of even greater openness'.[18]

How tempting to argue that Sun's ideas had come full circle. In the second *minsheng* lecture of 10 August 1924, he observed that 'if we use existing foreign capital to build up a future communist society in China, half the work will bring double the results' – a proposition entirely consistent with the Deng Xiaoping line.

Sun Yatsen and Imperialism

Since the 1930s, when the rival parties first used Sun's words to bulldoze separate paths, anti-communists have tried to disprove Comintern influence by demonstrating that Sun rejected Lenin's judgement that imperialism was the 'highest stage of capitalism'. 'If Dr Sun had really adopted the Leninist analysis of imperialism, how could he welcome "the export of capital" from the capitalist nations to China for the purpose of her development?'[19] Or, as the American C. F. Remer

---

[17] 10 May 1984. Translated in *CES*, vol.18, no.4 (Summer 1985), pp.105-6.

[18] Citations from Li Honglin, 'Socialism and Opening up to the Outside World', *Renmin ribao* [People's Daily], 15 October 1984, translated in *CES*, vol.19, no.1 (Fall 1985), pp.26-39. For speculation on the attitudes of other officials, see David Bachman, 'Differing Visions of China's Post-Mao Economy: The Ideas of Chen Yun, Deng Xiaoping, and Zhao Ziyang', *Asian Survey*, vol.26, no.3 (March 1986), pp.292-321.

[19] See Tsui Shu-chin, 'The Influence of the Canton-Moscow Entente upon Sun Yatsen's Political Philosophy', Part II, *Chinese Social and Political Science Review* (*CSPSR*) (July 1934), pp.141-42. Originally a Harvard PhD dissertation

put it in 1959, when authorities in Taiwan had further sharpened this line of attack, 'it is important to see that Dr Sun could not have issued his proposals for the development of China if he had believed imperialism to be a necessary consequence of foreign investment in China'.[20] In only the latest restatement, A. James Gregor and Maria Hsia Chang have used Sun to attack 'dependency theorists' and propose that Sun, a perceptive Chinese politician, had realized back in the 1920s that his country's international weakness could be traced to its 'underdevelopment' rather than simply to foreign exploitation.[21]

As with so much of Sun's writings, the textual evidence for his attitude toward imperialism is ambiguous. Drawing upon only the *minzu* (nationalism) lectures, authors have had no difficulty in establishing outright hostility. Sun's sardonic description of China as a 'semi-colony' reinforced Lenin's thesis and influenced Mao Zedong. In *China's Destiny*, Chiang Kaishek quoted the same passages traditionally cited by communists, including:

> Oppression by economic power is more severe than oppression by political power. Oppression by political power is visible, but when one comes under oppression by economic powers, ordinarily one is not easily aware of it.[22]

Sun had stated in the second *minzu* lecture of 3 February 1924 that:

> We are being crushed by the economic strength of the Powers to a greater degree than if we were a full colony. China is not the colony of one nation but of all, and we are not the slaves of one country but of all. I think we ought to be called a 'hypo-colony'.

He continued:

> This economic control alone is worse than millions of soldiers ready to kill us. And while foreign imperialism backs up this economic subjugation, the living problems of the Chinese people are daily more pressing, the

---

(1933), republished in article form in *CSPSR* (1934-35), and then in Chinese; see *Sun Zhongshan yu gongchanzhuyi* [Sun Yatsen and Communism] (Hong Kong, 1954).

[20] *Three Essays on the International Economics of Communist China* (University of Michigan Press, Ann Arbor, 1959), pp.14-18.

[21] Gregor and Chang, op.cit.

[22] *China's Destiny and Chinese Economic Theory*, pp.83-84.

unemployed are daily increasing, and the country's power is, in consequence, steadily weakening.[23]

It is difficult to understand how he could chastise imperialists, express serious reservations about the self-interest of Western capitalists and then call for protective tariffs, when only a few years before he had tried to lure still more foreigners to China with the promise of greater profits. It becomes impossible, moreover, for the objective Western scholar to reconcile Sun's virulent attack on 'the vitiating influence of foreign economic control' in *minzu* lecture no. two with the recommendation six months later in *minsheng* lecture no. two that the country would need to borrow foreign funds. How could he believe, with any intellectual consistency, that international capitalist investment and bankers might help create state socialism?

In his conclusion to *The International Development of China*, Sun observed that his plan was:

> welcomed everywhere and by everyone in the country. So far there is not a word expressed in disfavour of my proposition. The only anxiety ever expressed regarding my scheme is where can we obtain such huge sums of money to carry out even a small part of this comprehensive project.[24]

As Lyon Sharman pointed out a little more than a decade later, when anti-imperialism was entrenched in the ideology called 'Sunism', 'improbable' as foreign co-operation had been in the original scheme, 'a more improbable feature was the enthusiastic support of the Chinese people and of the Chinese government'.[25] Even a cursory survey of economic works from the 1930s and 1940s shows how easy it was to drop from discussion all mention of the proposed 'international' origins of 'the development of China'. The convenient Chinese-language title, *Shiye jihua* (Plan for Industry and Commerce), encouraged sleight of hand. As Chiang Kaishek demonstrated in *China's Destiny* and *Chinese Economic Theory*, it was quite possible to maintain the dream of industrialization without ever mentioning the utility of foreign assistance. Sun Yatsen's own son, Sun Fo, expressed scepticism in a 1942 lecture in Chongqing that foreigners would continue to provide much comfort when the war was over: 'As we are going to carry out economic policies in conformity with *minsheng zhuyi*, foreign capitalists

---

[23] From the 1953 abridged edition of the Frank Price translation of the *San Min Chu I* (Taipei), p.10.

[24] p.204.

[25] Sharman, op.cit., p.289.

may feel that under the circumstances the profits are not attractive enough to induce their investments'.[26]

The proposition that Sun Yatsen had rejected Lenin's economics hinges on a belief that Sun did not see a connection between imperialism and capitalism – despite the presence of Comintern advisers and all the familiar quotations by Sun about the dangers of 'economic oppression' (including Sun's pessimistic prediction in the *sanmin zhuyi* that the country had already reached a state of bankruptcy and would be lost unless foreign domination was overcome). Sun's 'imperialism', as Tsui Shu-chin once insisted, was 'essentially political in nature'.[27] Its apparently deleterious effect on the Chinese economy could be overcome by nationalism. The Rosetta stone for such an interpretation is to be found in a preface to one of the Chinese-language translations of *The International Development of China*: 'If we hold the power of developing China, then we can exist; if others hold it, then we should die'.[28]

Be that as it may, once the unequal treaties had been abolished and the Kuomintang became ensconced in Taiwan, interpreters began to argue that the very attainment of political sovereignty made foreign participation possible. Thus, having leached Leninism from Kuomintang ideology, the party in power on the off-shore island opened the country to foreign capital and technology.[29]

Ironically, some would say, the same process is taking place today on the mainland, where the argument has clearly gained strength that a successful 'nationalist' revolution and economic modernization, not isolation, provide the means to de-fang imperialism. Indeed, it has been positively proposed in the PRC that Sun Yatsen's plan to 'use foreign

---

[26] *China Looks Forward* (Allen and Unwin, London, 1944), p.131.

[27] Tsui Shu-chin, op.cit., p.138.

[28] ibid., cited p.142.

[29] This process can be traced in Taiwan magazines which, though the course is a zigzag one, also shows the growing interest in the 'capitalist' dimension of Sun's writings. See *Zhongguo jingji* [The China Economist], *Shiyejia* [Entrepreneur], *Ziyou Zhongguo* [Free China] and *Zhengzhi pinglun* [The Political Review]. See also Gufu shiye jihua yanjiu hui [Research Committee on the Father of the Country's Plan for Industry], *Guofu shiye jihua yanjiu luncong* [Collected Research on Sun Yatsen's Industrial Plan] (Zhongyang Wenwu Gongying She, Taipei, 1956); or the arguments of Xu Gaoyuan collected in 1963 as *Zhongshan xianshengde quanmian liyong waizi zhengce* [(Sun) Yatsen's Strategy for the Comprehensive Utilization of Foreign Capital] (Taipei).

capitalism to construct Chinese socialism' was a 'visionary and courageous idea'.[30]

Sun Yatsen on Communism and Capitalism

Sun's great attractiveness to many mainland economists is, no doubt, his ambiguous treatment of both 'communism' and 'capitalism'. Although Kuomintang writers have devoted thousands of pages to a demonstration of his disillusionment, we will, in truth, never know his attitude toward communism. He was not well read on the subject and was easily swayed. Moreover, he had real practical problems in attracting support from the Soviet Union and from domestic leftists without totally alienating traditional friends, and could have changed his mind more than once.

Of course, the most efficient means to prove an argument has been to edit the text so as to eliminate offensive passages. The reference to 'half the work' leading to 'a future communist society' has been removed from some Taiwan editions. Other awkward moments still present in Frank W. Price's 1929 translation have had a similar fate:

> What is the Principle of Livelihood? It is communism and it is socialism. So not only should we not say that communism conflicts with the *Minsheng* Principle, but we should even claim communism as a good friend. The supporters of the *Minsheng* Principle should study communism thoughtfully. If communism is a good ally of the *Minsheng* Principle, why do members of the Kuomintang oppose the Communist Party? The reason may be that the members of the Communist Party themselves do not understand what communism is and have discoursed against the *San Min* Principles... Because they have not understood what the *Minsheng* Principle really is. They do not realize that our Principle of Livelihood is a form of communism.

Sun went on, it is quite true, to deny the need for class war or the confiscation of existing private property, but not before stating most succinctly that the distinction between *minsheng* and communism was that: 'communism is an ideal of livelihood, while the *minsheng* principle is practical communism. There is no real difference between the two principles – communism and *minsheng* – the difference lies in the methods by which they are applied'. To confuse matters more, Sun's 'communism' was 'a communism of the future, not the present'.

---

[30] Cai Shan, op.cit., p.21.

In his second *minsheng* lecture, Sun advised those 'scholars' who were putting their hopes in Marxism that they had failed to understand that 'China was suffering from poverty, not the unequal distribution of wealth'. What he proposed was a plan which could 'check the growth of large private capital and prevent the social disease of extreme inequality'. Only the barest suggestion of the mechanism he had in mind survives. It clearly involved 'regulation of capital'; but Sun implied that at the country's present stage of development, this would not mean confiscation of existing commercial or industrial wealth. The state would take the lead in the creation of an economic infrastructure, to include mining, manufacturing and communications, including transportation. He was never specific about the exact mixture of public and private.

If Sun Yatsen's attitude toward communism showed a certain ambivalence, so did his perspective on capitalism. In 1921, in *The International Development of China*, he told readers that:

> All matters that can be and are better carried out by private enterprise should be left to private hands, which should be encouraged and fully protected by liberal laws... All matters that cannot be taken up by private concerns and those that possess monopolistic character should be taken up as national undertakings.[31]

But three years later in the famous second *minsheng* lecture, he warned: 'if we do not use state power to build up these enterprises but leave them in the hands of private Chinese or of foreign businessmen, the result will be simply the expansion of private capital and the emergence of a great wealthy class with the consequent inequalities in society'. However, in 1925, he told an interviewer that, 'While there are many undertakings that can be conducted by the state with advantage, others cannot be conducted effectively except under competition... I have no hard and fast dogma. Much must be left to the lessons of experience'.[32]

These passages have been used to justify 'nationalization' by writers on both the left and right and, particularly since the Kuomintang moved to Taiwan, for a 'liberalization' of economic policy. In the past few years, the 'liberal' reading of Sun has led some economists to propose even further 'de-nationalization' and the 'internationalization' of the economy.

---

[31] See note 29.
[32] Cited in Tsui Shu-chin, Part III (October 1934), p.378.

Before the Kuomintang abandoned the mainland, the party's attitude toward capitalism had been much more critical. During the long war, when the National Resources Commission under the Ministry of Economic Affairs dominated planning, it was generally assumed that the peace-time era would see a 'socialization' of industry, both Chinese and foreign. Although the *minsheng* principle helped provide a rationale for the Nanjing government's emphasis on urban China, and allowed it to suggest that it protected the private sector at the same time as it was adding to the number of publicly owned enterprises, some theorists argued that private capital would have to be eliminated at some time in the future. Even Sun Fo argued in 1942 that 'when this war is over and victory finally won, there may still remain the economic victory which *sanmin zhuyi* must win over the forces of world capitalism'.[33] Thus, while the Kuomintang rejected communism, it also tended to reject capitalism. Anti-capitalist sentiments survived – tied closely to anti-imperialist ones – long after the Nationalist Party purged its Leninist members.

Elements of the Kuomintang 'left' like Tao Xisheng, who had been strongly influenced by Marxism, were more ambivalent. Tao argued that China had been 'proto-capitalist' since the early empire, but that 'commercial capital', which should have transformed the country had Western developmental rules applied, had been wasted because of the survival of 'feudal' ideology. This had allowed the landed gentry, in league with the imperial state and then militarists, to appropriate profits and restrain growth. The merchant class, as the well-worn argument went, was kept under the thumb of bureaucrats and never matured until the arrival of Western imperialists, who further distorted the situation and reinforced the exploitative tendencies of the old order. But precisely because capitalism was forced upon China from the outside, it was a political and not an economic problem. There was no need for class struggle. As Zhou Fuhai, another leftist who with Tao and Wang Jingwei would later swing far to the right, observed as he merged this argument with less articulated elements of 'Sunism', 'The method of *sanmin zhuyi* is to change politics through revolutionary means and use political means to change the economy'.[34]

Whatever Sun Yatsen actually had in mind, his words, with all their contradictions, perfectly suited a mixed or transitional economy. Back in

---

33 Sun Fo, op.cit., p.29.

34 *Sanmin zhuyizhi lilunde tixi* [The Theoretical System of the Three People's Principles] (Shanghai, 1928), p.232.

1940, when the 'Three People's Principles' were being pushed by the left as grounds for ideological compromise, He Ganzhi addressed the critical question: how could Sun talk about 'regulating capitalism' and 'developing socialism' at the same time? Granted that China was politically weak and had lost control over its own resources, there was an obvious need to protect its industry and capitalists. But would not 'capitalism' – even 'state capitalism' – invariably lead to more 'capitalism'? How could it ever produce 'socialism'? The answer was equivocal. Lenin had never said that state capitalism could not become socialism. It all depended on who controlled the state. Yes, fulfilment of the *minsheng* principle might well lead to the development of capitalism; but China did not necessarily have to follow the path taken by Europe or America. After removing the domestic and international obstacles to the rapid development of capitalism, a new political order might adopt selected Western technology to advance. After all, as He Ganzhi rather boldly proposed, the capitalism Sun advocated was not the same capitalism known in the West. There the goal was 'making money'; the *minsheng* ideal was to 'take care of the people', and its ambition was 'communism'. For having understood this distinction, He Ganzhi asserted, Sun Yatsen could be considered China's greatest political thinker.[35]

Although Mao Zedong might have had reason to disagree, his 1945 work 'On Coalition Government' used the very ambivalence found in Sun's writings to develop united front tactics:

> Some people fail to understand why, so far from fearing capitalism, Communists should advocate its development in certain conditions. Our answer is simple. The substitution of a certain degree of capitalist development for the oppression of foreign imperialism and domestic feudalism is not only an advance but an unavoidable process. It benefits the proletariat as well as the bourgeoisie, and the former perhaps more. It is not domestic capitalism but foreign imperialism and domestic feudalism which are superfluous in China today; indeed we have too little of capitalism. Strangely enough, some spokesmen of the Chinese bourgeoisie fight shy of openly advocating the development of capitalism, but refer to it obliquely. There are other people who flatly deny that China should permit a necessary degree of capitalist development and who talk about reaching socialism in one stride and 'accomplishing at one stroke' the tasks of the Three Principles of the People and socialism...we Communists clearly understand that under the state system of New Democracy in China it will be necessary in the interests of social progress to facilitate the development of the private

---

[35] He Ganzhi, *Sanmin zhuyi yanjiu* [Research on the Three People's Principles]

capitalist sector of the economy (provided it does not dominate the livelihood of the people) besides the development of the state sector and of the individual and co-operative sectors run by the labouring people.[36]

China scholars have long recognized that the same tensions between nationalism, capitalism and socialism which troubled Sun Yatsen and the Kuomintang also plagued the Communist Party. If foreign competition and unequal treaties arrested China's own native capitalist development, shouldn't the country find ways to protect them? If capitalism was what made the Western powers so strong, if according to Marxist-Leninist thinking capitalism and perhaps even imperialism were historically progressive, could China jump directly to 'socialism' or 'communism'? Because not only economic determinism but also nationalist sentiments were at stake, Guo Moruo and the Communists had immediately joined in the debate over the nature of Chinese society launched by Tao Xisheng. However, even as they argued that China preponderantly was still a 'feudal' society, they found it impossible to accept that their nation was so backward. As Mao was to write, 'China would of herself have developed slowly into capitalist society even if there had been no influence of foreign capitalism'. For their part, Kuomintang writers such as Sa Mengwu, who believed that Sun Yatsen had advocated the eventual absorption of all private capital by the state, nevertheless wrote that the government needed to 'protect Chinese capitalism because of China's unique society'.[37]

The argument that China was special – an ageless civilization, for which Sun Yatsen had produced a 'uniquely Chinese' economic philosophy – held a special appeal. Shortly after the founder's death in 1925, Dai Qitao first began to pull together what would become the 'conservative' reading of the *minsheng* principle, emphasising that Sun had not been inspired by Marxism but by ancient Chinese socio-economic thought. The very term 'the people's livelihood' was, according to this reading, chosen deliberately instead of the foreign word 'socialism'. As the controversial *minsheng* lecture number two ends: 'When the people share everything in the state, then will we truly reach the goal of the *minsheng* principle, which was Confucius' hope of a "great commonwealth" '.

(Xinchong chubanshe, 1940), pp.112-18 and 196-98.

36   *Selected Works of Mao Tse-tung* (Beijing, 1967), vol.3, p.233.

37   Cited by Robert E. Bedeski, 'The Tutelary State and National Revolution in Kuomintang Ideology, 1928-31', *The China Quarterly*, no.46 (April-June 1971), p.323.

When the Kuomintang arrived in Taiwan, it became an article of faith that Sun Yatsen had rejected both Marx and Adam Smith. However, in the early 1950s, under American influence, there was heated debate over how much 'public economic management' was consistent with a so-called 'free society'. In his 'Foreword' to the Taipei republication of *The International Development of China*, Jiang Menglin (who had helped with the original and did not hesitate in 1953 to note that Sun's plan was designed to allow 'capitalism...to work together hand and hand with socialism in one and the same country') asserted that Sun had once sought 'to strike a balance between private enterprise and state industry'. Before the end of the first decade off-shore, however, no one could doubt that the grounds for argument were shifting. As one writer proposed, Sun Yatsen 'adopted the strong points and rejected the defects of both systems in the light not only of the actual performance of the two systems in Europe and America but also the conditions of our own country'.[38] The proposition that *sanmin zhuyi* represented a 'third way', a 'middle path' uniquely 'appropriate' to China's economic problems, has had obvious emotional as well as intellectual appeal.

As the Kuomintang continued to distance itself from 'communism', it also drifted from 'socialism'. So, too, more and more writers in the PRC now suggest that Sun never really wanted state ownership of all the means of production but only those areas where monopoly power prevailed. Instead he favoured a government-managed free-market system with consumer sovereignty and private enterprise.[39] No one who has followed the changes which have taken place in China since the death of Mao can fail to see the similarity.

Without much in the way of acknowledgement to Sun, the term *minsheng* had already appeared in important speeches in China. The Special Economic Zones have been described as 'state capitalism within a socialist system', 'a composite capitalist economic form in which China's society is coupled with foreign capital'. 'Foreign capital', yet another high official proclaimed, 'speeds modernization'.[40]

The People's Republic of China, *Beijing Review* has reported, is 'developing a socialist planned commodity economy which is fundamentally different from the capitalist commodity economy'. Why? Among other reasons, because it is based on the *minsheng* idea, which

---

[38] K. Y. Yin, *Collection of Sources on Taiwan's Economy* (Taipei, 1960), pp.60-62.

[39] See *CES* (Winter 1985-86), p.45.

[40] *China Reconstructs* (June 1985), quoting Zhang Quan.

means 'public ownership of the means of production as the national economy's foundation', leaving room for a 'joint Chinese-foreign economy' and a 'solely foreign-owned economy' as well as the private sector.[41]

As might have been expected, one of the first detailed re-evaluations took place at Canton's Zhongshan (Sun Yatsen) University in 1979. When Chen Keqing published 'A Tentative Dissertation on Sun Yatsen's Thinking on Economic Construction' the following year in the prominent journal *Jingji yanjiu* (Economic Studies), it was clear that Sun's status as an economic theorist would receive serious reconsideration. Other authors soon outlined details of how he reportedly 'studied China's national conditions' to develop his plan for modern industry.[42] By 1986, Beijing-based economists were writing that Sun Yatsen was 'modern China's great revolutionary and a most brilliant thinker', someone who had left behind 'a priceless legacy of theoretical guidance on matters of economic management'.[43]

---

41 *Beijing Review*, vol.29, no.5 (3 February 1986), pp.16-17.

42 Chen Keqing, 'Shilun Sun Zhongshande jingji jianshe sixiang', *Jingji yanjiu*, no.2, February 1980, pp.45-51. See, too, Zhao Jing, 'Sun Zhongshan guanyu zai jingji fazhan fangmian ganchao shijie xianjin shuipingde lixiang' [Sun Yatsen's Ideal of Developing Aspects of the Economy to Surpass the Highest Global Standards], *Beijing daxue xuebao* [Beijing University Journal], no.3, 1979, pp.45-52. Duan Yunzhang, 'Sun Zhongshande Zhongguo jindaihua lixiang' [China's Modernization as Envisioned by Sun Yatsen] and Tang Zhaolian, 'Sun Zhongshande guanyu guomin jingji xiandaihua de sixiang' [Sun Yatsen's Ideas About the Modernization of China's Economy] – both articles in *Zhongshan daxue xuebao* (1979); Zhang Qicheng and Guo Zhikun, 'Lun Sun Zhongshan dui Zhongguo guoqingde yanjiu' [On Sun Yatsen's Study of China's National Conditions], *Fudan xuebao* [Fudan University Journal], no.5, September 1981, pp.48-53; Wang Gongan, 'Lun Sun Zhongshan jingji sixiang' [On Sun Yatsen's Economic Thinking], *Jingji yanjiu*, no.4, April 1982, pp.38-44; and Zhao Jing, 'Zhongguo jindai chenxing shiye sixiang de zongjie lun Sun Zhongshande "shiye jihua" ' [Generalization of Thoughts Regarding Modern China's Development of Industry and Commerce], *Jingji yanjiu*, no.7, July 1982, pp.64-71. See also the note below.

43 Zhao Jing, Chen Weimin and Zheng Xueyi, 'Zhongguo jindai jingji guanli lixiang yichan zhongde zhenpin – jinian Sun Zhongshan danchen 120 zhounian' [A Great Legacy to Thought on the Management of the Modern Chinese Economy – Remembering the 120th Anniversary of the Birth of Sun Yatsen], *Jingji yanjiu*, no.10, October 1986, pp.58-65, 71.

Conclusion

On the 70th anniversary of the 1911 Revolution, when Hu Yaobang invited the leader of Taiwan, Chiang Kaishek's son Jiang Jingguo, to visit the Chinese mainland, it was suggested that Sun would not rest in peace until the country was reunited. After all, he had proposed the first era of Kuomintang-Communist co-operation. Three years later, when the precedents for bi-party collaboration were again being praised, Zhou Enlai's widow Deng Yingchao recalled how Dr Sun 'let it be known that he was a friend of socialism; today, socialism is not only an ideal in China, but a reality'.[44] As a 1986 PRC publication patriotically observed, 'Since socialism and capitalism have inhabited the same planet for so long, why should they not be able to operate side by side in one country?'[45] Readers will already know that 'these two economic forces of human evolution' have long co-existed in the writings of Sun Yatsen.

---

[44] *Beijing Review*, no.42 (19 October 1981), pp.13-21 and no.27 (30 January 1984), pp.21-30.

[45] *Beijing Review*, vol.29, no.5 (3 February 1986), p.20.

HISTORY FOR THE MASSES

Geremie Barmé*

Every policy shift in recent Chinese history has involved the rehabilitation, re-evaluation and revision of history and historical figures.

The early stages of the Cultural Revolution were preoccupied with questions of political rehabilitation,[1] and even in the years following the Cultural Revolution political rehabilitation similarly affected virtually every aspect of society. Not only were older cadres who had been purged or maligned during the Cultural Revolution gradually restored to power or posthumously honoured, but entire historical epochs, figures, and even cultural forms, themes and styles were 'rehabilitated'.

From the late 1970s onward the Chinese leadership spoke of its work of righting past wrongs as 'bringing order out of chaos and returning to the rectitude (of the past)' (*boluan fanzheng*).[2] This was also described as 'giving things back their original appearance' or 'turning an inverted history on its head'. The rehabilitation process that began in the early 1970s and continued until the early 1980s[3] together with the 1981

---

* My thanks to Linda Jaivin and Jonathan Unger for their comments on this chapter.

[1] See, for example, Chen Boda, 'Wei shenma yao pingfan' [Why is Rehabilitation Necessary], in Luo Jicai, *Zhonggong wenge houde fan'an kuangfeng* [The Communist Party's Fierce Wind of Rehabilitations After the Cultural Revolution] (Youshi wenhua shiye gongsi, Taibei, 1983), pp.33-34. While the radicals had perceived suggestions that Peng Dehuai ought to be rehabilitated as a threat, for example, they pushed the rehabilitation of revolutionary rebels.

[2] Similar expressions that appeared in the preliminary phase of the reform era (which can be more accurately dated from 1974-75 rather than the Party's Third Plenum of December 1978) are *jiuzheng*, or 'putting [things] straight' and *zhengben qingyuan*, 'rectifying the root and cleansing the source'.

[3] A thorough study of these rehabilitations can be found in Ma Wencang's 'Lun xinshiqi dang zai zhidao sixiangshangde boluan fanzheng' [On Bringing Order

Party resolution on history formed a theoretical and practical background to the reform policies of the 1980s.

From the start, however, Deng Xiaoping and his fellows were concerned that the nation 'unite as one and look to the future'. They wished to avoid entanglement in historical minutiae and the settling of old scores. The Party therefore attempted to define the parameters of rehabilitation and debate rather than let the momentum of public, intellectual and academic pressure lead where they might, as was to happen, for example, in the Soviet Union under Gorbachev. In this context Deng Xiaoping's speech at the closing session of the month-long work meeting held in preparation for the Third Plenum of the 11th Congress of the CPC in December 1978 is of particular importance. The title of the speech itself was an indication of its basic tenor: 'Liberate Thinking, Seek Truth from Facts and Unite and Look to the Future'.[4]

Deng emphasized among other things that 'resolving questions left over from the past, clarifying the achievements and errors of certain people and correcting a number of major unfair, incorrect and false cases is essential for the liberation of thought as well as for stability and unity'.[5] Here the utilitarian dimension of the policy of rehabilitation is quite obvious. Deng also stole a march on his critics inside and outside the Party. He did this by emphasizing that the entire leadership and not Mao Zedong alone had to take responsibility for the errors of the 1950s and 1960s.[6]

---

out of Chaos in Regard to the Party's Directing Ideology in the New Age], *Dangshi tongxun* [Party History Newsletter], no.1, 1987, pp.14-24, and Fang Xiangan and Zeng Xiankai's 'Quanguo yuanjiacuoande fucha yu pingfan' [The Reinvestigation and Rehabilitation of Nationwide Unjust, False and Erroneous Cases], *Dangshi tongxun*, no.6, 1987, pp.20-25.

4 Deng Xiaoping, 'Jiefang sixiang, shishi qiushi, tuanjie yizhi xiangqian kan' [Liberate Thinking, Seek Truth from Facts and Unite and Look to the Future], 13 December 1978, in *Deng Xiaoping wenxuan, 1975-1982* [Selected Writings of Deng Xiaoping (1975-1982)] (Sanlian shudian, Hong Kong, 1983), pp.130-43, especially pp.137-39.

5 Deng Xiaoping, 'Liberate Thinking, Seek Truth from Facts and Unite and Look to the Future', p.137. This meeting set the line on the Tiananmen Incident of 5 April 1976, and re-evaluated the case of Peng Dehui and partially reassessed the Anti-Rightist Movement of the late 1950s.

6 See Deng's 'Opinions on the Drafting of the "Resolution on Certain Questions in the History of Our Party Since the Founding of the People's Republic of China"', 1 April 1980 (Dui qicao <<Guanyu jianguo yilai dangde ruogan lishi wentide jueyi>> de yijian), *Selected Writings of Deng Xiaoping (1975-1982)*, p.260.

One of the chief problems that the Chinese have had in coming to grips with the problem of Mao is that, unlike in the Soviet Union, there is no Stalin-Lenin dichotomy. Instead, a distinction is made between the early and late Mao. Deng's strategy, moreover, has been to create a collective body of 'Mao Zedong Thought' from which all unwanted theories can be excluded and into which any number of revisionist policies can be incorporated. As he stated in 1980, 'The banner of Mao Zedong Thought can never be discarded. To throw it away would be nothing less than to negate the glorious history of our Party... It would be ill-advised to say too much about Comrade Mao Zedong's errors. To say too much would be to blacken Comrade Mao, and that would blacken the country itself. That would go against history'.[7]

Since expediency and the immediate need for 'unity and stability' were the key motivations behind the late 1970s' Party revision of history, Deng stressed that 'it is impossible and unnecessary for [these questions] to be resolved to our complete satisfaction. We must consider the broader issues, we can afford to be sketchy; it's impossible to clear up every little detail, and unnecessary'.[8] Setting the basic line on the evaluation of both Mao and the Cultural Revolution, he made it quite clear that 'Mao Zedong Thought will eternally be our...most precious spiritual heritage'.[9] With such words, he avoided a repetition of the kind of political and ideological suicide committed by Khruschev when he launched his denunciation of Stalin.[10]

Developments in the Soviet Union have had a crucial impact on Chinese attitudes towards history. As Wen Yuankai, a leading Chinese thinker, said in January 1989:

> The bold measures which Gorbachev has taken since assuming office have had an extremely profound and subtle effect on China. Nearly all the reforming socialist nations are presently re-examining their own histories, including the great Stalinist purges. Every day new details are revealed, not

---

[7] These statements were made by Deng on 25 October 1980. See his 'Opinions on the Drafting of the "Resolution on Certain Questions in the History of Our Party Since the Founding of the People's Republic of China"', *Selected Writings of Deng Xiaoping (1975-1982)*, 1983, pp.262-63 and 266.

[8] Deng Xiaoping, 'Liberate Thinking, Seek Truth from Facts and Unite and Look to the Future', pp.137-38.

[9] ibid, p.139.

[10] See 'Rehabilitation, the Cultural Revolution and Chairman Mao', *Xinwanbao* [New Evening News], 20 November 1978.

only in the Soviet Union but in other countries as well, including China. This has made China reflect deeply on its own past.[11]

However, whereas Stalin and his henchmen are now readily used to personify evil in popular Soviet thought and culture, from the mid-1980s there has been a revival of the Mao Zedong cult in China. In addition to mass-released cassettes with fresh recordings of Cultural Revolution songs in praise of Mao and the mass-produced laminated portraits that went on sale starting in 1991, the most substantial expression of the revival has been in publishing, with numerous books on Mao authored by everyone from his last concubine (Zhang Yufeng) to his bodyguard (Li Yinqiao). Liu Yazhou's book of 1990 *The Square – Altar for an Idol*, altogether is sympathetic to Mao, depicting a great leader who finds that his people have failed him as much as he has failed them.[12] So, too, have the controversial reportage writers Jia Lusheng and Su Ya produced a remarkably obsequious and purple prose-laden 'study' of the Mao cult.[13]

Rather than allow the momentum built up during the rehabilitation process of the late 1970s to get out of hand, in 1981 Party leaders had ordered the writing of a new and supposedly final verdict on post-1949 historical questions that, theoretically, would end all debate on contentious major issues and ensure 'unity for the future'. (For an alternative perspective on this, see Suzanne Weigelin-Schweidrzik's chapter.) Hu Qiaomu, who had played a major role in the composition of the 1945 resolution describing the history of the Party from 1921 onward as a 'history of Mao Zedong'[14] – a resolution crucial in forming the basis of the Mao-cult from the 1950s – was assigned to oversee the writing of the 1981 resolution. Thus one of the leading and earliest architects of the Party's ideological mythology was put in charge of historical interpretation once more. (In the late 1980s, Hu led a group assigned to write the official history of the Party, while Deng Liqun,

---

[11] Zhang Weiguo, 'Ningjuli he xinxin wenti bi jingji xingshi geng yanjun: Wen Yuankai dui dangqian xingshide fenxi' [Cohesion and Confidence are more Crucial than the Economic Situation: Wen Yuankai's Analysis of the Current Situation], *Shijie jingji daobao* [World Economic Herald], 9 January 1989.

[12] Liu Yazhou, *Guangchang – ouxiangde shentan*, (Tiandi tushu youxiang gongsi, Hong Kong, 1990).

[13] Jia Lusheng and Su Ya, *Buluode taiyang* [The Sun Never Sets] (Zhongyuan nongmin chubanshe, Luoyang, 1992).

[14] See Laszlo Ladany, *The Communist Party of China and Marxism 1921-1985, A Self-Portrait* (C. Hurst & Company, London, 1988), p.60.

Hu's chief assistant in this project and a man who came to prominence as an underling of Chen Boda during the purge of Wang Shiwei in 1942, oversaw the composition of the first history of the People's Republic.)[15] The 1981 Party document gave what was intended to be the final word on Mao Zedong's errors, the nature of the political purges of the 1950s, and the Cultural Revolution. It would provide the theoretical basis for the 1987 purge of 'bourgeois liberalization' as well as the Party's interpretation of the events of 1989 and the justification for the post-Massacre purge.

The official limits imposed on the discussion of post-1949 history ran into opposition from the very outset. One of the first public objections came from the Shanghai-based veteran writer Ba Jin, who, in essays written in 1978-79, had appealed repeatedly for the 'right to remember'.[16] Despite the care taken by the leadership and Party ideologues, the official view of the Cultural Revolution as an historical 'blank spot' (*kongbai*), the call to 'liberate thought', the official stress on practice being the sole criterion of truth and particularly the 1981 document, all contributed in varying degrees to the creation of new ideological spaces in which writers and historians could pursue their work. In the late 1970s, the historian Li Shu, as the new editor of the major specialist journal *Historical Research* (Lishi yanjiu), called for a re-evaluation of major historical questions, as did the Party theoretician Li Honglin, who in 1978 demanded a lifting of taboos on Party history.[17]

However, while their work was highly significant, academic historians were not publicly prominent in the 1980s. They produced

---

[15] See Yang Shangkun, 'Xiwang jinkuai xiechu yibu wanzhengde Zhonggong dangshi' [Hoping to see a Complete Party History Produced as Soon as Possible], *Renmin ribao* [People's Daily] 1 July 1990, and 'Bianzuanhao Zhonghua renmin gongheguo shi' [Create a Good History of the People's Republic of China], *Renmin ribao*, 5 December 1990. Hu headed the drafting committee of the 'Resolution on Certain Questions', see the footnote on page 255 of *Selected Writings of Deng Xiaoping (1975-1982)*.

[16] These essays were part of his *Suixianglu* [Random Thoughts] which he wrote for publication in *Ta Kung Pao* in Hong Kong. Ba Jin chose this forum because the literary supplement of the paper, the *Ta Kung Yuan*, was not subject to the same level of censorship as the Mainland press, and the editor of the page, Pan Jijiong, was an old friend from the 1940s who had been sent to work in Hong Kong from Beijing in 1978.

[17] See Li Honglin's September 1978 article 'Dapo dangshi jinqu' [Break Into the Forbidden Zones of Party History], *Lilun fengyun* [Theoretical Storms] (Sanlian shudian, Beijing, 1985), pp.58-78.

important revelations on such subjects as the Chinese Trotskyites, the Cultural Revolution, and the Anti-Rightist Movement as well as on numerous other periods and incidents in the Party's history, material which has continued to appear in specialist journals, even since the June 1989 purge. But novelists, journalists and a few academics writing for the press, television or commercial publishers – despite what is often a more sensationalist or less rigorous approach – have had a more marked effect on the changing historical consciousness of the general population.

By the early to mid-1980s, pressure for further political rehabilitations reaching back to the 1950s and even earlier (first of Hu Feng, then Yu Pingbo, and later of the film 'The Life of Wu Xun' and Hu Shi) was threatening the legitimacy of the Party's entire post-1949 political and cultural line. Hu Yaobang, then Party General Secretary, advocated new cultural and political policies, allowing a higher degree of historical re-assessment than any other leader at the time. His stance can be interpreted either as a direct challenge to the Party's line on history as outlined in 1981, or as the inevitable outcome of the extraordinarily contradictory elements of the Party's new 'liberal Maoist' ideology. In 1986, Hu Qili, on behalf of Hu Yaobang, suggested a re-assessment of all the Party's major intellectual and cultural purges beginning with the 1940s (the denunciation of Wang Shiwei in Yan'an being a case in point).[18] When Hu Yaobang was later attacked for being indulgent toward 'bourgeois liberalization' and removed from office, his attitudes towards Party history and culture were among his crimes. It was the intellectual atmosphere he had helped create that resulted in the appearance of many of the works discussed below.

Having noted this, it should not be forgotten that Hu Yaobang also had had a key part in drafting the 1981 resolution on Party history and that in 1980 he had overseen the first (albeit mild) purge of the cultural world of the reform era, which included criticism of several popular works dealing with the Cultural Revolution. And despite his willingness in 1985 to confront the cases of Wang Shiwei and others, in 1986 he issued a directive warning that the depiction of historical events and figures in literary works must accord with Party policy: 'These are not

---

[18] See 'Hu Qili tongzhi guanyu gaige he jingshen wenming jianshe deng wentide tanhua [zhaiyao]' [Comrade Hu Qili's Remarks on the Questions of Reform and the Building of Spiritual Civilization (abstract)], *Dangshi tongxun*, no.10, 1986, p.3.

questions of artistic license, but issues of political import and rectitude'.[19]

The years 1985-88 were, nonetheless, something of a watershed in terms of media representations of history due in part to Hu Yaobang's pronouncements and the appointment in late 1985 of Zhu Houze as head of the Party's organs of propaganda. But if such political moves were opening up the past to political re-interpretation, economic reform opened up history to commercial exploitation as well.

One of the key catalysts of intellectual and cultural diversity in China from the early 1980s onwards was provided by the partial reform of the publishing industry. Encouraged to turn a profit, during each period of relative ideological relaxation publishers have learned that controversy and sensation sell books. Having been force-fed a unitary view of history for so long, many people had developed an insatiable appetite for alternative perspectives of any kind, no matter how ludicrous or fictional. This helped foster the boom in reportage and historical writing discussed below, as well as encouraging writers of serious literature to look into the hidden corners of pre-1949 history. Tabloids and monthly pulp magazines, meanwhile, have found the publication of historical revelations and scandal most profitable.

The ideological backlash of the post-Tiananmen period provided those who had been involved in prosecuting earlier purges with a convenient excuse to oppose further historiographical license.[20] The prospect of continued rehabilitations and re-evaluation of 1950s history posed a direct threat to leaders still in power who had participated in the past persecutions (including Deng himself, active in the Anti-Rightist Campaign of 1957).

So long as publishers must show a profit, however, controversial publications get produced, and the impact of such books can be massive. The official indexes of books banned after June 4 were carefully

---

[19] See 'Hu Yaobang guanyu chuangzuo dangshi ticai wenxue zuopinde yige zhongyao pishi' [Hu Yaobang's Important Instruction on Literary Works that Deal with Party History], *Dangshi tongxun*, no.3, 1986, p.1.

[20] This is most obvious in the case of Yu Pingbo, who died in 1990. Li Xifan, a scholar who came to prominence in the early 1950s' attacks on Yu, supported by Mao, was particularly energetic after 4 June 1989. He even denounced the veteran Party historian Hu Sheng for his attempts to set the record on Yu Pingbo straight. Interestingly, the preliminary 1986 rehabilitation of Sun Yu's film 'The Life of Wu Xun', denounced in 1951 in an incident that gave Mao's wife Jiang Qing (who then called herself Li Jin) an 'entré' into the world of post-'49 politics, was begun by Hu Qiaomu.

guarded so they would not fall into the hands of publishing entrepreneurs, as the government well knew that the temptation to produce pirate editions would be tremendous. Reading banned books traditionally is a popular form of opposing authority: in traditional China one of the great pleasures for a scholar-gentleman was described as 'shutting one's door, turning away guests and reading banned books' (*bimen xieke du jinshu*). Whatever the wishes of Party elders, revisionist writings on history continue to see the light of day.

Literature

In the post-Mao era, the first popular vehicle for historical re-awakening was the short story. Starting in 1978 a series of stories appeared dealing with the sufferings of individuals during the Cultural Revolution. They were called 'scar literature' or 'literature of the wounded' (*shanghen wenxue*).[21] There were also fleeting attempts in poetry and theatre directly to address problems created by the Mao personality cult. The most noteworthy example of such poetry is Sichuan poet Sun Jingxuan's 1980 'A Spectre Prowls Our Land', which equates Mao and feudalism.[22] The harsh criticisms to which Sun was subjected may have discouraged others from producing further works on this theme. The army poet and playwright Bai Hua's early Eighties play about the ancient kings of Wu and Yue is another example. (Bai Hua is best known for his screenplay 'Unrequited Love', which was denounced by Deng Xiaoping in March 1981. 'Unrequited Love' has, as a subtext, an attack on Mao, and pointedly ends with a symbolic setting sun.)[23] The suppression of attempts to deal, in fiction and other ways, with the historical problem of Mao set the stage in the late 1980s for a popular revival of the Mao cult.

In late 1985, following a seminar on new research options for modern literary studies, a group of Beijing University academics began

---

[21] The nomenclature is taken from the story 'Shanghen' [The Scar] by a Shanghai university student, Lu Xinhua, which was published in 1978. 'Scar literature' is, of course, a reference to the scars both physical and psychological left by the Cultural Revolution. A good review of the exposure literature of the late 1970s can be found in Kam Louie, *Between Fact and Fiction: Essays on Post-Mao Chinese Literature & Society* (Wild Peony, Sydney, 1989) pp.1-13.

[22] See Geremie Barmé and John Minford (eds), *Seeds of Fire* (Hill & Wang, New York, 1988), pp.121-28.

[23] 'Guanyu fandui cuowu sixiang qingxiang wenti' [On the Question of Opposing Incorrect Ideological Trends], 27 March 1981, *Selected Writings of Deng Xiaoping (1975-1982)*, p.337.

re-evaluating 20th-century Chinese literature.[24] They were building on the considerable work done in collecting, collating and publishing research materials in literary history from the early 1980s.

Ironically, it was the Party's invalidation of previous 'ultra-leftist' policies that not only provided researchers and writers the leeway to rewrite history in favour of the new dispensation, but to create new histories and styles of historical narrative as well. Younger scholars trained from the late 1970s onwards as well as middle-aged academics were the chief beneficiaries of the nascent pluralism, but it was not until mid-1988 that a concerted broad-based re-assessment of modern literature and the Party's literary canon began.

The new historiographical movement was launched from Shanghai. *Shanghai wenlun*, the arts journal of the Shanghai Academy of Social Sciences, published a series of articles beginning in August 1988, under the general title of 'Rewriting Literary History'. Edited by Mao Shian and the academics Chen Xihe and Wang Xiaoming, this series attempted a systematic critique of contemporary Chinese literature that questioned the cornerstones of the Party's literary canon. Chen remarked in the introduction to the series, which ran until late 1989:

> The aim of this section is to enliven literary criticism and to make an assault on the virtually immutable conclusions of our literary history. In the process it is also our hope to whet the reader's appetite for reconsidering the past. Of course, our aim is to have an impact on the present.[25]

From the mid-Eighties, individual critics like Liu Xiaobo in Beijing and Li Jie in Shanghai undertook independent analyses of literary history and the predicament of contemporary culture. For a while, Liu became a significant public figure, his views widely disseminated among university students. Li Jie was less of a firebrand.[26] Another academic, Xia Zhongyi, kept a low profile but launched one of the most

---

24 *Zhongguo xiandai wenxue yanjiu chuangxin zuotanhui*. See Wang Xiaoming, 'Zhuchirende hua' [A Comment from the Convener], *Shanghai wenlun* [Shanghai Literary Theory], no.6, 1988, p.4. The Beijing academics were Qian Liqun, Chen Pingyuan and Huang Ziping.

25 Chen Xihe and Wang Xiaoming, 'Zhuchirende hua' [A Comment from the Conveners], *Shanghai wenlun*, no.4, 1988, p.4. For an attack on the series, see Luo Shourang, 'Guanyu "Chongxie wenxueshi" de bianxi' [An Analysis of 'Rewriting Literary History'], *Wenyi lilun yu piping* [Literary Theory and Criticism], no.2, 1991, pp.95-109.

26 Li Jie's essays were published in the Anhui journal *Baijai*.

controversial attacks to date on Maoist literary theory, particularly as expressed at the Yan'an forum in 1942.[27]

In terms of elite literature, writers of the 'roots' (*xungen*) fiction of the mid-1980s can be seen as attempting to find an historical context and narrative for China's present state. From 1986 onwards many other novelists, including practitioners of the Chinese 'avant-garde' styles, also gradually developed an interest in historical themes. This has produced a rich body of works set in the Republican period, leading writers of such fiction being Su Tong, Ye Zhaoyan and Zhou Meisen.[28]

In early 1991, the Henan writer Liu Zhenyun published a novel which depicted the national character and tradition in a far more directly negative light than anyone else had to date. Liu's *Yellow Flowers*[29] opens in the early Republican period. It follows the internecine strife of a village near Kaifeng all the way into the early 1980s. It is a tale of personal alliances, betrayals, violence and mayhem woven into a 'meta-discourse' of early Republican politics, the anti-Japanese war, the strife between the Nationalists (KMT) and Communists and then the political struggles of post-1949 China. Published in the Nanjing literary journal *Zhongshan* as a prime example of 'new realism', *Yellow Flowers* goes beyond the pedestrian paradigms of the Anti-Japanese War, land reform and Cultural Revolution literature and deals instead with the group psychology of one village throughout seven decades of its history.[30] The result is both mordant and 'hyper-real'; it presents a historical landscape encompassing both gloom and humour that goes beyond the obstinately harrowing fictions of writers like Zhang Xianliang and Cong Weixi.

In terms of popular literature, however, the greatest commodification of history occurs in the pages of weekly tabloids and best-selling books about Cultural Revolution and Republican period scandals.

---

27 Xia Zhongyi, 'Lishi wuke bihui' [There is Nothing Taboo in History], *Wenxue pinglun* [Literary Review], no.4, 1989, pp.5-20.

28 See Chen Xiaoming, 'Lishi tuibaide yuyan – dangdai xiaoshuozhongde "hou lishi zhuyi" yixiang' [Allegories of Historical Decay – Post-Historical Intentions in Contemporary Fiction], *Zhongshan*, no.3, 1991, pp.144-56.

29 'Guxiang tianxia huanghua', *Zhongshan*, nos 1 & 2, 1991.

30 For three elucidating reviews of the novel, see Huang Yuhuang's 'True Life and Cultural Taste', He Zhiyun's Du *Guxiang tianxia huanghua* [Reading *Yellow Flowers*], both in *Dangdai zuojia pinglun* [Criticism of Contemporary Writers], no.5, 1991, pp. 17-25, and Sang Ye's 'Shuopo gouxiong jingsha ren', *Dushu* [Reading], no.12, 1991, pp. 107-9.

'Faction' and Mass Media Historians

The term 'mass media historian' is used by Stephen Wheatcroft to denote the journalist-historians, film-maker-historians and ideologues who helped awaken popular awareness of historical issues and whose works also gave an important thrust to the development of independent historiography in the Soviet Union in the mid- to late-1980s.[31]

Similarly, 'mass media historians' have played a crucially important role in China since the late 1970s. From the mid- to late-1980s, writers like Liu Binyan, Su Xiaokang, Dai Qing, Zhao Yu, Li Rui, Ye Yonglie, Quan Yanchi, Liu Yazhou, Yan Jiaqi, Gao Gao and many others have had a considerable popular impact. The works of many of these writers were subsequently banned, but this was more because of their activities in 1989 than inherent problems in their earlier writings.

These 'mass media historians' created a semi-official and at times even unofficial forum for the airing of controversial questions. While some have merely added footnotes to official history, or created wildly colourful fictional accounts of certain figures, periods and incidents, others have been involved in the creation of a 'parallel history' to that presented by the Party.

Here the term faction [factual fiction] is used as an equivalent of the Chinese term *jishi wenxue* which includes reportage (a generally heavily value-laden genre), biography, memoirs, special reports as well as new journalism.[32] The 'scar literature' and 'in memoriam literature' (*aisi wenxue*) of the late 1970s was, to a great extent, the precursor of certain styles of faction.[33] From 1985 onwards, faction, especially what was known as 'problem literature' (*wenti baogao wenxue*) and 'factual literature' (*jishi wenxue*), was increasingly directed at the mass audience. As the Shanghai critic Wu Liang put it, it satisfied the readers'

---

[31] Stephen Wheatcroft, 'Unleashing the Energy of History, Mentioning the Unmentionable and Reconstructing Soviet Historical Awareness: Moscow 1987', *Australian Slavonic and East European Studies*, vol.1, no.1 (1987), pp. 85-86, 97-105.

[32] See Cheng Can, 'Guanyu jishi wenxue erti' [Two Questions Concerning Faction], *Zhongguo wenxue yanjiu* [Research in Chinese Literature], no.4, 1989, p.103.

[33] He Zhiyun, 'Jishi wenxue zhege "zazhong"' ['Faction', a Literary Bastard], in *Yinxia zhizhua – He Zhiyun wenxue pinglunji* (Wenhua yishu chubanshe, Beijing, 1990), p.94.

natural curiosity and voyeurism in a way that serious literature or even pap novels never could.[34]

From the mid-1980s, of the two traditional strands of reportage in China – the social critique and the paean to socialism – the critical achieved a new popularity.[35] This was widely seen as an outcome of the increasing pressure within the society as a whole and among professionals in particular for greater freedom of the press: a desire for more untainted information about both historical and contemporary social questions. The repeated attacks on reportage writer Liu Binyan, and particularly his expulsion from the Party in early 1987 and subsequent attacks on his work, certainly would have encouraged more cautious writers to look for material which was topical yet sufficiently removed from sensitive political issues to ensure safe passage to publication. Younger writers, ranging in age from their twenties to forties, had fewer concerns for political propriety. They were less hesitant to reopen old debates or to discuss historical events and personalities from new angles. They have been motivated by a temptation to achieve fame through sensation as well as a desire to learn more about the past in order to come to grips with contemporary social and political reality.

Throughout 1986, the twentieth anniversary of the Cultural Revolution, numerous works on the 'ten years of chaos' were published, ushering in the first solid wave of Cultural Revolution nostalgia and also adumbrating the popularity of a new style of faction, historical journalism (*lishi jishi*).

During the Spring Festival of 1986, the official televised Spring Festival variety extravaganza featured arias from Beijing Revolutionary Operas of the Cultural Revolution era. Tapes of disco versions of the operas first produced in 1985, were sold nationwide. Similarly, fictionalized accounts of Cultural Revolution events became a minor industry. In 1985, Suo Guoxin, an army writer, published a popular trend-setter of this type, *Seventy-eight Days in 1967 – A Record of the 'February Countercurrent'*.[36] (Not a re-assessment of history, Suo's

---

34 Wu Liang, 'Guanyu jishi wenxue ji baogao wenxuede duanxiang' [Thoughts on Faction and Reportage], *Baogao wenxue* [Reportage], no.12, 1986, p.70.

35 Xie Yong, 'Shilun jinqi baogao wenxue zhutide zhuanyi' [A Tentative Discussion of the Shift in Reportage Themes], *Shanxi wenxue* [Shanxi Literature], no.4, 1988, p.67.

36 Suo Guoxin, *1967 niande 78 tian – 'eryue niliu' jishi* (Hunan wenyi chubanshe, Changsha, 1986). This book is written as a glorification of Chen Yi, Xu

book followed closely the official evaluation of the 'February Countercurrent'.[37])

'Yibairende shinian' (One Hundred Peoples' Ten Years), edited by Feng Jicai and published in major literary journals such as *Shiyue* and *Wenhui yuekan*, belongs to the so-called 'veritable record of oral statements' (*koushu shilu* or *jishi*) type of reportage popularized in China by Zhang Xinxin and Sang Ye in 1984 in their Studs Terkel-style 'Beijing ren' (Chinese Lives).[38] This form of oral history has been known in China for many years, and was used to record histories of families, factories, army units, and so on after 1949, with the purpose of illuminating the pain and suffering of the 'bad old days' before the revolution. In his work, Feng Jicai kept well within this tradition by adding at the conclusion of every account a moral aphorism, transforming them into a series of cautionary tales.[39]

Further publication of Feng's series was effectively stalled until 1989 by a Central Committee document issued by the Shanghai Publication Bureau on 18 October 1986, in compliance with a directive from the State Publication Bureau in Beijing which stated that all manuscripts dealing with the Cultural Revolution, sex and the Anti-Rightist Movement had to be submitted to the Bureau for approval before publication. This was taken to be equivalent to a ban, for it was understood that any manuscripts submitted would be confiscated. Naturally, none were sent to Beijing; and none were published for a time.[40]

Mud-raking *vis-à-vis* the past is not always a controversial task, though, and many clever writers have exploited Cultural Revolution

---

Xiangqian, Nie Rongzhen, Ye Jianying and Tan Zhenlin, as well as Zhu De and Chen Yun, with the dramatis personae divided into 'goodies' and 'baddies' at the beginning of text.

[37] See, for example, Deng Xiaoping on the subject in 'Opinions on the Drafting of "The Resolution on Certain Historical Questions Since the Founding of the People's Republic" ', *Selected Writings of Deng Xiaoping (1975-1982)*, p.267.

[38] Zhang Xinxin and Sang Ye, *Chinese Lives: An Oral History of Contemporary China* [edited by W.J.F. Jenner and Delia Davin] (The Macmillan Press, London, 1987).

[39] Feng Jicai, *Yibaige rende shinian (di yiji)* [One Hundred People's Ten Years], (Xiangjiang chuban gongsi, Hong Kong, 1987).

[40] The first volume of Feng's interviews was published on the Mainland in 1991. See Feng Jicai, *Yibaige rende 10 nian (shoujuan)* (Jiangsu wenyi chubanshe, Nanjing, 1991).

materials for their own political and economic profit. For example, during the summer months of 1986, before the above ban was supposed to take effect (not that it ever really did) Hu Yuewei and Ye Yonglie, two of the most prominent writers of such pulp history, published new works.[41] Their writings, while often quite sensational in tone, and allowing considerable license when it comes to reproducing the conversations and private thoughts of their protagonists, nonetheless keep well within the parameters of the politically acceptable.

This loose style of pop history is not limited to unabashed hacks like Hu and Ye: even the much-vaunted history of the period, Gao Gao and Yan Jiaqi's *The Ten Year 'Cultural Revolution'* suffers from such flaws.[42] It should be noted, however, that this book is not merely another pop history. It served definite functions within the context of the contemporary debates concerning political reform. Many similar works that 'used the past to serve the present' were produced by liberal- or reform-minded intellectuals around this time. An example is *Ten Years of Unjust Cases* published in December 1986, a volume of essays covering cases of unjust imprisonment during the Cultural Revolution produced by the Ministry of Public Security publishing house with a foreword by Yu Haocheng, a leading advocate of legal reform.[43] The

---

[41] See Hu Yuewei, *Fengkuangde Shanghai* [Shanghai Goes Crazy] (Sichuan wenyi chubanshe, Chengdu, 1986), the continuation of a work begun in 1983, and part of a trilogy on the Cultural Revolution in Shanghai. Also, Ye Yonglie, editor and writer, *Fu Lei yi jia* [The Fu Lei Family], (Tianjin renmin chubanshe, Tianjin, 1986). Ye's highly embellished version of the death of the famous translator of French literature and his wife was based on the account of the policeman in charge of the couple's household register. Ye has been one of the most prolific and politically cautious writers on the Cultural Revolution.

[42] First published in instalments over the summer months of 1986 by the Shanghai daily *Wenhuibao*, a book version of Gao and Yan's work appeared in Tianjin later in the year. Gao Gao and Yan Jiaqi, *'Wenhua da geming' shinian shi* (Tianjin renmin chubanshe, Tianjin, 1986, restricted circulation). First issued for public sale, it was suddenly reclassified for restricted circulation, with a stamp to that effect being affixed to the back of the books, ensuring a mass readership. For a thorough, albeit orthodox, review of the merits and faults of the book, see Wang Nianyi, 'Ping "Wenhua da geming" shinian shi' [Critique of *The Ten Year 'Cultural Revolution'*], *Dangshi tongxun*, no.4, 1987. A revised version of the book was published in Hong Kong in 1991.

[43] *Shinian qiyuanlu*, by the editors of *Falü zixun* [Legal Advice] magazine (Qunzhong chubanshe, Beijing, 1986). The contents, like those of an earlier volume (*Chunfeng huayuji* published in two volumes in 1981) were taken from

editors explained that the volume was produced to show the need for the rule of law and the protection of individual rights.

One of the first notable examples of a new strain of writing about the past, historical reportage (*lishi jishi*), was the *Liberation Daily* reporter Qian Gang's 'The Great Tangshan Earthquake' (Tangshan da dizhen), written for the tenth anniversary of the disaster in 1986. Using masses of documentary material and interviews, it attempted to go beyond superficial reporting to inform the reader not only what had happened and its political shock waves but also to point out its contemporary relevance. Also important and highly influential was Hu Ping and Zhang Shengyou's account of the tragic Red Guard link-up on Jinggang Mountain.[44]

Similarly significant was Ta Ying's 'Report on the War Prisoners of the Volunteer Army' (Zhiyuanjun zhanfu jishi), which revealed the previously unknown fates of Chinese soldiers on special missions who were taken prisoner in the Korean War and re-evaluated those involved. Such writing 'used history to see people afresh, to establish a new standard for judging people'. By discussing the fate of the prisoners it allowed readers to use the information to make their own assessment not only of the incidents depicted but the nature of China's socialist revolution and the relevance of the past to the present.[45] Zhao Yu's 'Dreams of Greatness' (Qiangguo meng) and Li Rui's 'The Deep Earth' (Houtu)[46] are both examples of works that dealt with unchanging traditions, the historical roots of present problems, and the national character.

---

official files. The earlier collection was based on the files of the Central Committee Letters and Complaints Office. This volume is written in the highly fictional style of reportage and contains twenty tales, mostly about famous people (Li Lisan, Deng Tuo, Wu Han, Ma Sicong, Ba Ren, Wen Jie, and so on) or famous incidents.

[44] Hu Ping and Zhang Shengyou, 'Lishi chensilu' [A Meditation on History], reprinted in Liu Yangdong, Meng Chao (eds), *Zhongguo chongjibo – dangdai shehui wenti baogao wenxue xuan* [China Shockwave – Selected Reportage on Contemporary Social Problems] (Zhongguo renmin daxue, Beijing, 1988), pp.5-82.

[45] See Wang Liya, 'Xin shiqi baogao wenxuede fei wenxuehua chuangzuo quxiang' [The Tendency Towards Non-fiction of Reportage Writing in the New Era], *Wenyi pinglun*, no.1, 1989, p.32.

[46] Zhao Yu's 'Dreams of Greatness' first appeared in *Dangdai*, no.2, 1988; reprinted in Liu Yangdong, et al., *China Shockwave*, pp.145-242. Li Rui's 'The Deep Earth' can be found serialized in *Shanxi wenxue* from 1986.

Such themes are particularly evident in the work of the journalist Dai Qing. Her research into the cases of Wang Shiwei and Chu Anping became part of a personal quest not only to investigate major historical incidents, but also to reveal how the Party systematically wiped out alternative schools of thought through its purges of intellectuals.[47]

Faction is generally regarded as having reached something of an apogee in 1988-89.[48] Zhang Shengyou, a leading writer of reportage for the *Guangming Daily*, remarked in March 1989 that Su Xiaokang's historical works (in particular his *On the Altar of 'Utopia' – Lushan in the Summer of 1959*)[49] comprised only a start: 'There is no way we can build a modern structure on the ruins of old ideology. We have to be like Gorbachev and engage in a large-scale reconsideration of history'.[50] He noted that the success of 'River Elegy' had prompted television stations to employ reportage writers to script new series. He thought this new mass medium held out great promise for historical investigations. In 1992, Zhang himself showed how reportage writers could also turn their talents to showing up the old ideology by scripting the sycophantic pro-Reform TV series 'Ten-year Tide' (Shinian chao).[51]

The Soviet writer Anatoli Rybakov's novel *Children of the Arbat* (published in 1987), about the Stalin era, was quickly introduced into China with excerpts, reviews and commentaries appearing in the literary press from early 1989.[52] In a comment on *Children of the Arbat*, Natalya Rubenshtein had remarked:

---

[47] For a detailed study of Dai's approach to history and an analysis of her work on the Wang Shiwei case, see G. Barmé, 'Using the Past to Save the Present: Dai Qing's Historiographical Dissent', *East Asian History*, no.1, June 1991, pp.141-81.

[48] One indicator of this was the increased subscriptions to the leading reportage journal *Baogao wenxue*. See Fu Xipeng's comments in 'Reportage: Attempting to Transcend Amidst both Success and Difficulties' (Baogao wenxue: zai fanrong he kunhuo zhong xunqiu chaoyue), *Baogao wenxue*, no.3, 1988, p.10.

[49] Su Xiaokang, Luo Shixu and Chen Zheng, '*Wutuobang' ji – 1959 Lushan zhi xia* (Zhongguo xinwen chubanshe, Beijing, 1988).

[50] 'Shehui wenti baobao wenxue: tansuo zhongde youlü' [Social Problem Reportage: Experimentation and Concerns], *Baogao wenxue*, no.5, 1989, p.55.

[51] For the text of the series, see Zhang Shengyou, *Shinian chao* (Zhongguo youyi chuban gongsi, 1992), pp.5-60.

[52] The debate over Rybakov's novel is discussed at some length by Natalya Rubinshtein in 'Glasnost Bestseller', *Index on Censorship*, no.9, 1988, pp.18-19, and Vazif Meilanov, 'Who'd Like to Speak?' on pages 19-21 of the same issue.

The revision of the past is a diverting pastime, but it has left the leaders and heroes of Soviet society naked. Ever since Herzen and Chernyshevsky the Russian novel has eagerly absorbed the social pamphlet and the sociological tract, bearing on its covers the evergreen questions 'Who is guilty?' and 'What is to be done?' These questions are still on the agenda today. But another question has been added to them: 'Was there another way?' In other words, was it inevitable that the dictatorship of the proletariat should have turned into a dictatorship of murderers? Was there, in history, another path which remained unused? The answer to this theoretical question has a practical significance. For on it depends the moral force – and staying power – of the present leaders' mandate.[53]

This is precisely the direction the writings of Dai Qing, Su Xiaokang and other relatively independent authors of 'historical investigative journalism' were taking in the late 1980s. As to the reason for the popularity of such writing, perhaps Rubenshtein's observation on Rybakov's marked success in the Soviet Union is relevant: 'he does give his readers a feeling of self-importance, by conducting serious conversations with them on society and history'. It can be argued that this is one of the reasons why Chinese writers like Liu Binyan, Su Xiaokang and even Cong Weixi, an author of 'prison reportage', and Zhang Zhenglong more recently[54] have achieved such extraordinary popularity. They have used the medium of popular – even purple – historical prose or investigative journalism to discuss issues of general interest and relevance in a language and style that can be tolerated, even sanctioned by the Party. They go a long way toward satisfying a popular appetite that remains unsatisfied by official communiqués.

Movies and Television Documentaries

Cinema was increasingly used in the last years of the Cultural Revolution to reflect the political policies of the day with considerable speed. In the mid-Seventies, films like *Chunmiao* (Spring Seedlings) and *Fanji* (Counterattack) had been prominent examples of radical Cultural Revolution policy and the fictional justification of it, while others, like

---

[53] Natalya Rubinshtein, op. cit., p.19.

[54] Zhang Zhenglong, a PLA writer in his forties, is the author of *Xuebai xiehong – Liaoshen zhanyi juan* [White Snow, Red Blood – the Liao-Shen Campaign], (Jiefangjun chubanshe, Beijing, 1989), an account of the Civil War in Northeast China which was banned in mid-1990. See Geremie Barmé, 'China: the Party has its Way with History', *Index on Censorship*, no.7, 1991, pp.12-14.

Chuangye (Pioneering), had been identified with the Zhou Enlai-Deng Xiaoping camp.

A hiatus in film production after Mao's death was soon followed by the production of cinematic works reflecting the new policies, including that of political rehabilitation itself. The most obvious examples include Xie Jin's 1979 *Tianyunshan chuanqi* (The Tale of Tianyun Mountain) and Yang Yanjin's *Kunaorende xiao* (Troubled Laughter). Another subgenre of rehabilitation cinema that received massive state funding were the films extolling 'revolutionary historical themes' (*geming lishi ticai*), consisting predominantly of tedious studies of the valour and achievements of Dead Revolutionary Males (DREMS) such as He Long, Chen Yi and other victims of the Cultural Revolution.[55] Even such products of a relatively strict Party line, however, revealed the contradictions, follies and tragedies created in the past by Party excesses and errors. While the aim of such cinema was, in the words of one critic, to 'revive the tradition of revolutionary realism and give history back its original mien',[56] it tended to further undermine the Party's monopoly over the past. The focus of such films remained educational and propagandistic but the tales they told, no matter how overwritten in favour of the *status quo*, could not help but warn audiences against putting too much faith in the Party and its evanescent policies. The more recent spate of revolutionary historical epics made between 1989-92 – ranging from the pro-Deng hagio-pic *Bose qiyi* (The Bo'se Rebellion) to a plethora of Mao movies – reflect a more deliberate policy of simply extolling leaders past and present, expurgating from the record as far as possible the irksome inconsistencies of historical fact.

A number of the earliest films of the 'fifth generation' directors who ushered in a new trend in Chinese cinema cast their stories in the historical past of the Party. This is true, for example, of Zhang Junzhao's *Yige he bage* (One and Eight) and Chen Kaige's *Huang tudi* (Yellow Earth), films that caused considerable controversy by reinterpreting elements of what can be called the Party's 'creation myth' of the Anti-Japanese War period and the Communist base in Yan'an. But they were not the only ones to engage in this project. At times changes in official

---

[55] Examples that come readily to mind are *Cong nuli dao jiangjun* [From Slave to General], *Shuguang* [Dawn] and *Chen Yi shizhang* [Mayor Chen Yi], made in the early 1980s.

[56] Ma Debo, *Dianying yishu zongheng tan* [Discursive Views of Film Art] (Huayue wenyi chubanshe, Xi'an, 1989), p.511.

policy have necessitated a recasting of history in ways that have had a mass impact.

Following the increasingly conciliatory line towards the KMT government in Taiwan during the mid-80s, films and publications were produced that gave a fuller picture of the Anti-Japanese War. *Taierzhuang zhi zhan* (The Battle of Taierzhuang) made in 1986 is an example. One of the most costly war epics made in China to date, it cast the KMT army in a positive, even heroic light in its battle with the Japanese. Prior to this, although specialist historical materials had gradually acknowledged that the Communists did not prosecute and win the war against Japan single-handedly, this was a watershed in terms of the mass media. Thus, although the film was part of a new propaganda strategy towards Taiwan it led the public to reconsider central elements of the Party's history, and one of the cornerstones of the Party's claim to historical legitimacy, in a new light – with unpredictable consequences.

The fate of films that attempted a re-evaluation of history before the Party was ready for it can be seen in the 1985 ban against Wu Ziniu's *Gezishu* (The Dove Tree). An anti-war film based on the Sino-Vietnam conflict of 1979, it reportedly deals sympathetically with the enemy. Production was stopped during filming. By the early 1990s, China's renewed friendship with Vietnam, on the other hand, forced one aspiring film-maker to cancel plans for an epic film portraying the Vietnamese in a negative light.

Many other films, particularly those dealing with the Japanese, have suffered from similar shifts in foreign policy. This is also true of documentary films; TV documentaries in 1985 of Japanese war atrocities, in particular the Nanjing Massacre, to some extent fired the first anti-government student protests of that time (the protests were initially aimed at Japan's 'new [economic] invasion' of China).

A number of Soviet films played a considerable role in popularizing historical debate from the mid-80s. Of these, the most often mentioned is Tengiz Abuladze's *Repentance*. A thinly veiled critique of Stalin, it had created a sensation in the Soviet Union. Chinese commentators were particularly interested in the fact that the film went beyond earlier works to delve 'deeply into the psychological make-up of the national culture so as to reveal the causes of the historical phenomenon of the personality cult'.[57]

---

57 Hu Rong, 'Dui Sidalin shidai beijude zai sikao – Sulian yinmushang luxu chuxian yipi zhengzhi baoluxing yingpian' [Rethinking the Tragedy of the Stalin Era – A Number of Political Exposés have Gradually Appeared on the Soviet Screen],

The discussion of historical themes and the nature of the Chinese national character (*guominxing*) became a central feature of TV documentaries in the late 1980s. In 1988, 'Heshang' (River Elegy), a six-part documentary, exploited the medium of television to present its own highly controversial view of Chinese history and its contemporary relevance. Seen by a number of critics as a natural corollary to the style of reportage and faction that had become increasingly popular since 1985,[58] 'River Elegy' also introduced to a mass audience some of the most unorthodox debates of the cloistered academy. This marriage of mass media and pop scholarship had an immense impact throughout China. Although the series was virulently denounced after June 4 1989, and its writers variously purged, detained or forced into exile, it has led to many imitations which in turn reflect a number of political and intellectual agendas.

The two most noteworthy post-1989 TV history documentaries are 'On the Road', screened in August 1990 and the final episode of 'Tiananmen', banned in early 1991. 'On the Road' (Shijixing – sixiang jiben yuanze zonghengtan) was produced by the Ministry of Propaganda as an obvious riposte to 'River Elegy'. The ideologue Deng Liqun acted as the series' general adviser.[59] One of the chief script writers was Qin Xiaoying, an historian and sometime 'liberal intellectual' formerly employed by the Academy of Social Sciences. Each of the four half-hour episodes highlights one of the Party's Four Basic Principles, with a commentary and images that interpret the history of the past 150 years as a process leading to inevitable socialist victory in China. The opening sequence uses a pop song over images of Marx, Lenin, Mao and Deng Xiaoping, affirming the apostolic succession within the historical enterprise of revolution. The pop star Liu Huan sings:

You are a seed of fire, igniting this slumbering land [image of Marx]

Dazhong dianying [Popular Cinema], no.4, 1989, p.8. The first Chinese review of the film was printed in the September 1987 issue of the same magazine. See Hu Rong's ' "Huiwu" – yiduan lishide huiyi', ['Repentance' – Remembering an Historical Period], *Dazhong dianying*, no.9, 1987, pp.10-11.

58 A slightly earlier work of 'TV Historical Reportage' was the 12-part *Rang lishi gaosu weilai* [Let History Tell the Future], produced for the 60th anniversary of the PLA in 1987. See Guo Shenzhi, *A History of Chinese Television* (Zhongguo dianshi shi) (Zhongguo renmin daxue, Beijing, 1991), pp.269-72.

59 See Deng Liqun, 'A Valuable Experiment – a speech at a seminar on "On the Road" ' (Yici keguide changshi – zai 'Shijixing' zuotanhuishangde jianghua), *Zhongliu*, no.10, 1990, pp.2-4.

You are a prophesy, describing the path for all human ideals [cut to a picture of Lenin]

You are a banner, fluttering in the wind to face all on-coming storms [portrait of Mao]

You spoke a truth, you are a banner, having fallen and risen, but emerging victorious [Deng Xiaoping, shown bobbing up and down in the water as he does the breast stroke].[60]

The opening sequence of the eight-part documentary 'Tiananmen', which was completed in May 1991, is radically different in both style and significance. It shows an artist retouching parts of the massive portrait of Mao Zedong that hangs on Tiananmen: a stroke to the eye, a brush to the nose, and then a caressing limning of the tell-tale mole on the chin. (Before 1 May and 1 October each year, the portrait is changed for a cleaned and retouched replica.)

'Tiananmen' was produced and directed by the young film-makers Shi Jian and Chen Jue who work for Chinese Central Television. Using the production name of 'The Structure, Wave, Youth, Cinema Experimental Group'[61] and availing themselves of the privileges and opportunities provided by their high-profile station, Shi and Chen spent some three years working on the project. 'Remembering Things Past' (Wangshi), the eighth and final episode of the series with a narration written by an academic, Guang Yi, is the most important in the context of 'using the past to serve the present'.

The episode is a meditation on the history of Beijing in the 20th Century, the subtext of which is a 'reflexive comment' on the events of 1989 by indirect reference to earlier historical events, dates and personalities. Following the official rewriting of the 1989 Protest Movement and the production of a plethora of books, articles and telespecials on 'the true mien' (*zhenxiang*) of what happened, it is easy for any alternative historical work to draw disquieting parallels between the past and the present. The narrator notes:

> This is a city that has inherited numerous written documents and oral tales from its past. No matter how people today wish to judge it all, the moment the gates of memory are opened, life, history and personal fate flow forth, demanding attention... History, like life itself, can be savoured.

---

[60] See Barmé, ' "Road" versus "River" ', *Far Eastern Economic Review*, 1990, p.32.

[61] *Zhongguo jiegou, langchao, qingnian, dianying shiyan xiaozu.*

When he lived in Beijing, Lu Xun commented on the Twenty Four Dynastic Histories: 'History records the soul of China, pointing out the future. Yet because it is overwritten and laden with rubbish, it is hard to see what is actually there. Like the moonlight seen reflected on moss through the leaves of a tree, all you can make out are shifting shadows'.[62]

The episode plays on the symbol and significance of May Fourth, the seventieth anniversary of which came in 1989. Images of the original patriotic movement are followed immediately by a commentary on its legacy and the December 9 Movement of 1935. (It should be recalled here that the first patriotic anti-government student demonstrations in the People's Republic occurred in 1985 as a commemoration of this movement). Film and photographic images of the police crushing the 1935 movement have a particularly strong resonance for those who experienced 4 June 1989:

> May 4, 1919: This is a date that has left a mark on modern Chinese history.
>
> December 9, 1935: This is another. Yu Xiu, a participant in the 9 December demonstrations recalled many years later: 'It was the middle of winter, and the streets were particularly cold that morning. The trams rattled past, as if to emphasize how empty the streets were... Suddenly from an alley near Gangwashi, a phalanx of students appeared. Waving their arms they shouted: 'Down with Japanese Imperialism!' 'Oppose Special Treatment for North China!' 'Stop the civil war, unite against Japan!' Then they sang the 'Song of the Volunteers'. This broke the morning silence of Xidan'.
>
> There are detailed written records, but the pictorial images we have are incomplete, making it hard to reconstruct the actual events of the day. The students proceeded to Xinhua Gate to present a petition. The authorities' response was unconvincing. Yu Xiu records: 'The leaders of the Beiping Student Union declared an end to the petitioning and called for the demonstration to begin. The students joined ranks behind their school flags. With written slogans leading the way they marched away from Xinhua Gate along the Avenue of Eternal Peace. They were blocked by armed police near Liubukou. When they forced their way through some students were beaten or hacked to death by bayonets. There was an uproar and the shouting of slogans could be heard from all quarters. A fire engine appeared and water cannon were aimed at the amassed students. They were dispersed for a time, but they soon regrouped and proceeded. Although their ranks had been broken, the demonstrators continued, arms linked'. It is a grim recollection,

---

[62] From Lu Xun's 'Huran xiangdao: si' [Sudden Realizations: IV], *Lu Xun quanji* [The Complete Works of Lu Xun] (Renmin wenxue chubanshe, Beijing, 1981, vol.III), p.17.

and the images are unclear. Yet the sensations and the details they present are undeniable... A new tradition was born, one that belongs to the young. Theirs is the voice of China's modern history.

This episode is studded with self-important yet powerful comments on the role of history. For example, a little further on comes the remark:

> Recollection is painful. But for the living, forgetfulness is more fearsome. These images and comments are all true. They are a harsh reality, one that lives on through the scattered remnants of passing time.

The episode ends with a few words about Tiananmen Square, the camera moving slowly over the heavily-scuffed paving stones ... stones also marked by the frantic wheeling of the tanks when they occupied the area and crushed tents on the morning of 4 June. The sequence following this shows a woman walking out of Tiananmen amidst a crowd of people. The commentary scrolls slowly over the last sepia-tinted shots:

> Sometimes the pace of history is rapid, at other times it is painfully slow. Regardless of this, with time the meaning of the past gradually gains clarity.
>
> It is impossible to say just how many people have walked over the stones of the square since they were first laid. If you have walked here, or if you return, stop and meditate for a moment. Many things from years past will gradually take shape in your mind's eye...
>
> Perhaps you will hear the events of a distant past recount to you some hope, long-born, and now clearly calling out to be heard. As life needs to be heard, as the months and days need to be heard. As time itself needs to be heard, in all of its detail...
>
> Today continues, every moment so very real.
>
> Our present travails will also be remembered and commented on.
> Today too is life, a witness...

Attempts to have the series screened at the 1992 Hong Kong International Film Festival were stymied by Beijing. As mentioned, an official TV version of the events of April-June 1989, with a contrary message, was produced for repeated screening in China and also for international consumption, the Chinese authorities even attempting to get this 'documentary' aired on foreign television. This too was a form of media history, a product that would be more familiar to Winston Smith and his colleagues in 1984's Ministry of Truth than any other produced in China in recent years.

Soap Operas

The recasting of history for mass consumption is not limited to propagandistic or art-cinema documentaries. TV soap operas also weave a mythology of the past for present-day audiences, influencing historical consciousness in many ways.

The fifty-part soap opera 'Aspirations' (Kewang), televised in late 1990, follows the fate of two families from the Cultural Revolution up to the 1980s. One of the most popular series of its kind, 'Aspirations' featured the loves and tragedies of a working-class urban family. Most Chinese commentators saw its immense success as due to nostalgia for the perceived simplicity and honesty of relationships in China before the introduction of mercantile competition and money-grubbing.[63] In terms of mass perceptions of history, there are a number of other noteworthy elements in the scenario.

The Party and its intrusive organizations are virtually absent, although the series' creators are careful to make one of their positive characters a workshop supervisor (Song Dacheng) and solid Party member. In the early episodes set during the Cultural Revolution, politics is kept in the background with the merest hint coming from the (background) 'red noise' of radio editorials, street broadcasts and tattered *dazibao*. Political language is only used in an ironic or sarcastic fashion; no street committees or their old ladies pry into the lives of a family that literally picks up a child on the street and fails to inform any authorities that they are keeping her. Nor are there any personnel files, Party committees or security offices; and there is no mention of the endless political campaigns that, if nothing else, would have impinged on lives through propaganda blackboards, meetings and study sessions. The intellectuals suffer as a result of vaguely defined Cultural Revolution policies, but none of the massive social and political prejudice aimed against them is ever verbalized. When the intellectual father is rehabilitated it is in vague terms. While this deprives the series of veracity, it makes it politically acceptable in these sensitive days and to an extent timeless as well.

One critic noted that the creators of the series had relinquished an ideal opportunity to attempt a mass media historical reflection on history from the 1960s to the 1980s. Instead they chose to play on emotion,

---

[63] For details, see Barmé, 'The Greying of China', in *China Review 1992* (Chinese University Press, Hong Kong, 1992), 13.4-8.

abandoning all but the bare bones of historical detail in favour a sentimental plot.[64]

Conclusion

In June 1986 Mikhail Gorbachev said that 'if we start trying to deal with the past, we will dissipate our energy' [65] However, by early 1987 his stance had changed, possibly as a result of the new historical consciousness fostered by the Soviet media. In February 1987, at a meeting with Soviet journalists, Gorbachev made the oft-quoted statement that 'there should be no forgotten names and blank pages [white spots] in Soviet history'.[66] Over the years the most extraordinary and wide-ranging re-evaluations of Soviet history have taken place. In China a similar process began in the late 1970s, and despite numerous political upheavals, it continues today.

The opposition to exposing and re-evaluating the past in both the former Soviet Union and China was summed up in the sentiments of the one-time Politburo member Igor Ligachev who cautioned against

---

[64] Ren Zhonglun, 'Yici wutiaozhande zhengfu' [A Victory without Challenge], *Shanghai wenlun*, no.2, 1991, p.8. See also Xu Jilin's comments in ' "Kewang" qishilu' [The Revelation of 'Aspirations'], *Wenhuibao*, 17 January 1991.

[65] 'Gorbachev Meets Soviet Writers: A *Samizdat* Account', *Radio Liberty Research*, 23 October 1986 (RL 399/86). Gorbachev's early statements on history, in particular Stalinism, are reviewed in R. W. Davies' *Soviet History in the Gorbachev Revolution*, (Macmillan, London, 1989), pp.129-31.

[66] Reported in *Pravda*, 14 February 1987, quoted in Vera Tolz, *'Glasnost'* and the Rewriting of Soviet History', *Radio Liberty Research*, 18 May 1987 (RL 189/87), p.2, also Stephen Wheatcroft, 'Unleashing the Energy of History, p.95, and Davies, *Soviet History in the Gorbachev Revolution*, p.130. Yuri Afanasyev and Aleksandr Samsonov are among the Soviet historians who, in 1986-87, called for the filling in of 'blank pages' or 'blank spots' in the country's history. See Vera Tolz, *'Glasnost'* and the Rewriting of Soviet History', pp.3-4. Elsewhere Tolz offers her definition of 'blank spots': '

1. Historical events that are never written about in the Soviet Union or are mentioned in the press only once or twice without any details.
2. Events that are treated with such bias that the facts are distorted.
3. Important historical documents whose publication is proscribed.

See ' "Blank Spots" in Soviet History', *Radio Liberty Research*, no.8, March, pp.2-3.

depicting the past as a 'chain of errors',[67] as well as historians who saw a crucial function of history as being to inculcate 'among the younger people a sense of historical responsibility for and pride in their homeland, in its heroic history and the present day'.[68]

In China, the elders in the post-1976 Party leadership belong to the original generation of revolutionaries who founded the People's Republic. Deng Xiaoping, Chen Yun, Peng Zhen, Li Xiannian, Bo Yibo, Yang Shangkun, Wang Zhen, and many others were participants in the major incidents and decisions in the Party's history, both before and after 1949. The interpretation of these incidents and decisions therefore often touches on questions related to the legitimacy of Party rule today. Even when their direct personal interests are not involved in an issue of 'classical Party history' (1920s, '30s or '40s), the Party leaders often have 'filial connections' or loyalties to deceased Party elders, former superiors or friends, and these hidden connections can still hinder a more frank and complete re-evaluation.

Against these factors stand the influence of the economic reforms on the publishing and media industry, as well as the work of foreign, emigré or dissident writers and historians. Available to specialists in journals or libraries, or translated and printed in tabloids and books for the general public, the introduction of independent views has continued to spread historical pluralism.

Moreover, as observed, the need to 'woo' Taiwan has helped spur a re-evaluation of Chiang Kaishek and the Nationalist Party, in particular with regard to their role in the war against the Japanese. Some of the Communist Party's most important claims to being the sole representative of nationalism are linked to that war. Until the mid-1980s the Nationalist war effort, which was considerable, was ignored or distorted. Since then books and films in which the Nationalists are portrayed as patriotic heroes have abounded.[69] This has led to radical changes in popular perceptions of the past and therefore helped clear the way to creating a positive view of Taiwan today, and of everything the

---

[67] Tolz, '*Glasnost*' and the Rewriting of Soviet History', p.3.

[68] From a letter from Party historians criticizing Afanasyev's 'revisionism'. Quoted in Wheatcroft, 'Unleashing the Energy of History', p.120. For similar statements by Hu Qiaomu, see Barmé, 'China: The Party has its Way with History', p.14.

[69] The most stunning example of this historical re-evaluation is the former PLA writer Sun Tingxin's *Zhongri Changjiang da juezhan* [China-Japan: The Final Conflict] (Chengdu chubanshe, Chengdu, 1991), released in early 1992 amidst great controversy.

island represents: democratization, a market economy, and so on. What essentially originated in the early 1980s as a political ploy to bring the Nationalists to the negotiating table has had an unexpected and unsettling effect on the Mainland.

In preparation for the reunification of Hong Kong with the Mainland in 1997, there are indications that the Chinese authorities are going to launch a propaganda offensive that will justify in historical terms the steps they want to take with Hong Kong. In late 1990, for example, the British authorities in the territory were cautioned to be careful as to how they commemorated the ceding of Hong Kong in the 19th century, and much was made in the Mainland media of the 150th anniversary of the Opium War.

During the 1989 Protest Movement, one group of writers in Shanghai called directly for an independent right to history. In a petition in support of the students in Beijing signed on 13 May, they said:

> Writers must have the freedom to analyse, explain and publish their views on all aspects of Chinese reality both historical and present, in particular political incidents. For a Party official to use his position or administrative powers to restrict or interfere with writers or deprive them of their freedom of expression or of publication is not only an abuse of power, but illegal.[70]

While the sprouts of independent historiography have appeared in China, both in specialized and public forums, the approach of most writers is still influenced by the dictum of 'using the past to serve the present'. Various schools of thought, factions and lobbies tend to see their writings in terms of how it can reflect and influence their contemporaries. It may still be some time before we see the emergence of a school of historiography – either academic or popular – devoted to 'history for history's sake'. In the meantime, most writers of popular history are consoling themselves with making a fast buck.

---

[70] 'Human Rights for Chinese Writers', a handbill drafted by Zhu Dake, Song Lin, Li Jie, et al. For a translation of this petition, see Barmé and Jaivin (eds), *New Ghosts, Old Dreams* (Times Books, New York, 1992), p.60.

INDEX

Agrarian economy, and materialist historians, 176
Anderson, H.C., and Sun Yatsen, 243
Anti-Confucian campaign, 175
Anti-Rightist Campaign, 47-49, 54-58, 68-69, 78, 92; cadres' discretionary powers, 80; resulting political pressure from, 68
Apprenticeship system, industry, 208-209, 227-28
Artists, restrictions imposed on, 5

Bai Hua, poet and screenwriter, 125, 136
Bank of China, 216, 247
Bao Cheng, Song Dynasty judge, 49, 53-54, 56-57, 80
Beijing massacre of 1989, 147, 240
Bi Gan, 51, 57
Bourgeoisie, 7, 14, 179, 186-88, 207; historians, 2
Boxer Rebellion, 187
Buck, David, historian, 7
Buddhist scriptures, 43

Cao Cao, 29, 32, 33, 40, 54-55
Cao Yu, writer, 40, 59, 77
Capitalism, 3, 6-7, 179, 205-238, 239-259 passim
Carlyle, theory of history, 179
Censorship, 28-29, 61; and Dai Fengxiang, 21
Ch'ing period, writings on Hai Rui, 23
Chang, John Key, economic historian, 213
Chen Boda, 240
Chen Duxiu, 166; and Marxism, 163-64
Chen Fengyi, and the Red Army, 168
Chen Hongshou, figure painter, 128
Chen Xiting, writer, 66
Chen Yi, 58

Chen Yun, Party leader, 178
Chen Zilong (1608-67), writer, 38
Cheng Fangwu, researcher, 153
Cheng Shifa, Shanghai figure painter (b.1921), 139-46
Chiang Kaishek, 241, 246, 249-50; Madame, 129
China Merchants' Steamship Navigation Company, 208
Chinese Communist Party (CCP), 3, 9-10, 44-45; historiography, 3, 6, 151-73, 174-204; leadership of, 2-3, 32, 46-48, 175, 179; collective leadership (*jiti lingdao*), 177; leadership and despotism, 175, 199; fiftieth anniversary of, 155; resolutions on Party history, 6, 151-173, 260-286 passim; tenth anniversary, 55, 64, 68, 70, 95; congratulatory odes, 76; thirtieth anniversary of, 154
Chinese Communist revolution, 187
Chinese People's University, Beijing, 153-54, 158-59
Chinese press, 9; see People's Daily, Renmin ribao
Class struggle, 2-3
Cochran, Sherman, 213, 219
Cohen, Paul, historian, 7
Collectivization, 47-48, 90, 92-93
Comintern politics, and Stalin, 163-64
Common people, portrayal of, 79, 102
Communes, see People's Communes
Communist critics (Hu Feng), campaigns against, 73
Communist historical drama and class analysis, 2-3, 9-45, 46-103 passim
Communist Party, see Chinese Communist Party
Communist Youth League, 47-48
Confucian doctrine, 1-2, 13, 29, 124

Congratulatory messages, dramatic genre under the Jiajing Emperor, 46-103 passim
Contemporary Theatre, context, 39-44
Contract labour, *see* Recruitment programs
Cultural Revolution, 4, 6-7, 9-10, 12-14, 17, 19-22, 24, 35-36, 45-47, 56, 58, 61, 66, 68, 71, 76, 80, 102, 111, 120, 124, 133-34, 136, 138, 140-150 passim, 154-55, 165-68, 173, 175, 179, 196, 228, 229, 247; rebels, 56, 66, 67; damage suffered during, 175, 201; historical orthodoxy of, 124

Dai Fengxiang, censor, 21-22
Dai Qitao, 256
Democracy Wall Movement (1978-79), 176
Deng Tuo, essayist, 18, 46, 175, 177
Deng Xiaoping, 4, 6, 7, 134, 157, 175, 177, 199-202, 218-19, 247-48; and Napoleon, 200; and entrepreneurship, 218; use of Sun Yatsen's support, 244; Dengist policies, 242
Dernberger, Robert F., 245
Despotism in Chinese history, 8, 174-204
Dividend (*guanli*) system, 211
Dong Zhongshu, and the 'mandate of heaven', 185
Dragon Boat Festival, 5
Du Pengcheng, novelist, 104

Economic backwardness, and authoritarianism, 179
Emperors, 1-2; Jiajing, 52-102 passsim; obsession with longevity, 82; pursuit of absolute power, 192
Empress Lu, 4
Empress Wu (r. 690-705), 29-32, 40, 71, 73
Engels, F., 3
Entrepreneurs, 205-238 passim
Eunuch officials, 1

Famine, 68, 85, 90, 96
Fan Zeng, artist, 138

Fang Rending, figure painter, 129-30
Feudalism, 3, 174-204 passim; ideology, survival of, 254; ruling class, 44
Feuerwerker, Albert, historian, 4, 206, 208
Financial management, 205-38 passim
Foreign investment, 243-47
Foreign trade, 246
Fu Baoshi, traditional-style painter, 131, 133

Gang of Four, 4, 9, 133-34, 141, 146, 155, 175-76, 184-85, 188, 215; fall of, 133; *see also* Jiang Qing *and* Yao Wenyuan
Gao Gang, 107, 109, 114, 116-17, 119, 121
Gao Gong (1512-78), head of the ministry of personnel, 21-22
Gao-Rao affair (1954), 107, 111
Gao Xiaosheng, writer, 47
Geertz, Clifford, 44
Goldman, Merle, 7
Gorbachev, 203
Great Leap Forward (1958-60), 5, 11, 25-31, 44-48, 51-52, 54, 69, 71-72, 76, 85, 88-89, 92, 96, 160, 174; and Peng Dehuai, 26; production targets, 48; popular songs, hyperbole, 72, 85; commune programme, 11; dissatisfaction with, 46; published eulogies on, 76; reform-minded officials, 88
Great Power Consortium, and Sun Yatsen, 243
Gu Mu, Vice-Premier, 247
Guan Feng, 37-39
Guan Hanqing, Yuan dynasty playwright, 41, 50, 52
Guan Shanyue, Lingnan painter, 130-32
Guanxi (connections), 226-27; *see also* Nepotism
Guo Moruo, historian, poet, playwright, 48-49, 51, 55, 70-73, 129-32, 137, 142, 144-45, 256; President, Academy of Sciences, 40
Guomindang, see Kuomintang

Harrison, James P., historian, 3

He Long, 117
He Qiaoyuan (1558-1632), Ming scholar, 37-39
Hong Xiuquan, and the Taiping movement, 175, 187, 189
Hongqi [Red Flag], 37, 120, 176
Hu Hua, teacher of Party historiography, 153
Hu Qiaomu, 34, 64, 166, 204; as Mao Zedong's personal assistant, 157; as secretary of Central Committee secretariat, 28
Hu Yaobang, 259
Huabei University, establishment of, 153
Huang Shaoqun, 168
Huang Wei, economic historian, 213
Huang Yongyu, painter, 5, 134
Huangpu Peking Opera Troupe, 53
Hundred Days of Reform, 188
Hundred Flowers period, 49, 50, 77-78, 133-34, 136; and the bureaucrats, 77

Industrial technology, backwardness of, 209-10
Intellectuals, 5, 47, 85, 124; and popular thought, 2; victims of the Cultural Revolution, 46; in China and the West, 214
International financiers, 7
International Monetary Fund, joining of, 247

Japan, 3
Jia Tuofu, 112, 116-17, 120
Jiajing period, 9-45 passim, 46-103 passim
Jian Bozan, scholar, 41
Jiang Jingguo, son of Chiang Kaishek, 259
Jiang Menglin, 257
Jiang Qing, 4, 9, 13, 20, 39, 45, 100, 134, 136-37, 140, 144, 175, 266; 'May Sixteenth Circular', 26
Jiang Xingyu, Ming historian, 49, 50, 54, 59, 62-63, 67, 74, 85
Jiefang ribao [Liberation Daily], 62

Kailuan Mining Administration (Sino-British), 211, 217, 220-21, 223, 225

Kang Sheng, 46, 72, 77, 100, 109-122
Kang Youwei, 187-88
Ke Qingshi, 58
Ke Zhongping, poet, 110-11
Khruschev, and the internal affairs of the CCP, 26
Kuomintang, 49, 143, 153-54, 189, 239-59 passim; policies concerning Communist critics, 73; writers, 241, 252, 256

Law and legality, 80, 91, 93, 98
Leading families, Rongs and the Guos (Kwoks), 227
Lenin, 240, 244, 248-49, 251, 254-6; New Economic Policy, 240; Leninist/Stalinist doctrine, 2
Li Gonglin (c. 1040-1106), Song figure painter, 126-29; Confucianized iconography, 126
Li Guihai, historian, 182
Li Honglin, 155, 264
Li Jiantong, 104-23 passsim
Li Lisan, 166, 169
Li Qiang, foreign trade minister, 247
Li Taicheng, head of the Cultural Affairs Bureau, 59, 67
Li Zhi, 38
Liang Qichao, 179
Liang Xiao, 184
Liao Mosha, Beijing literary figure, 15, 19
Lin Biao, 63, 155, 166
Lin Jie, 37-39
Lishi yanjiu, historical journal, 29, 30, 155, 177, 264
Literature, role in addressing problems, 40, 46-103 passim; part of the state apparatus, 97
Liu Binyan, writer, 47, 78, 270-71, 276
Liu Hongsheng, China's 'match king', 221
Liu Housheng, Shanghai Cultural Office, 55, 59
Liu Jingfan, 105, 107, 109-12, 117
Liu Shaoqi, 15, 111, 155, 166; coalition with Mao, 167
Liu Shaotang, writer, 47

Liu Zhidan, 5, 104-23
Lu Zhenqu, historian, 40
Luo Longji, Democratic League leader, 17
Lushan Party Plenum, 25-26, 28, 53, 60, 63, 85, 91, 99, 102, 109, 120-21, 175, 275

Ma Lianliang, Beijing Opera Troupe, 19
Ma Wenrui, 112, 116, 118, 120
Ma Yuqing, 168
Mao Dun, 77
Mao Zedong, and Maoism, 1-8, 10-15, 27-34, 44-47, 51-55, 63-64, 70-72, 77, 82, 89, 94, 99-100, 102, 104, 107, 109-16, 120-22, 125, 151-173 passim, 174-79, 181, 183, 186-87, 189, 195, 198, 203, 212, 227, 229, 234, 238, 240, 246, 249, 255-57, 261-65, 269, 277-80; and Liu Shaoqi, 167; change of behaviour after the Peng Dehuai affair, 121; autocratic leadership after 1958, 175; Mao cult, 121, 177-78, 263, 267; 'make the past serve the present', 29; harsh treatment of Peng Dehuai, 120; Mao's poems 32
Mao Zedong Thought, 113, 115, 121, 152, 164-72, 262-63; as Mao's alone, 122; as the ideology of the Party's left wing, 167; as the unifying ideology of the CCP, 161
Marx, and Marxism, 3, 72, 176, 179, 196, 240, 241, 253, 254, 257; his writings on capitalism, 7; 'Asiatic Mode of Production', 178; historiography, 2, 3; criteria of historicism, 176; depiction of leaders, 72; Marxist-Leninist classics, 72
May Fourth Movement (1919-22), 187, 188, 195; historians of, 2
Mei Lanfang, 52
Meng Chao, dramatist, 46-49
Ming dynasty, 4, 9; symbolism of, 29; historian Jiang Xingyu, 62; Ming history, 16; Ming land-holdings patterns, 14
Ming Taizu (1368-98), 27, 192-93
Minsheng Principle, 239-59 passim

Nankai Institute of Economics, 216-17
Napoleon, 181, 199-200
Nepotism, 208, 226; *see also Guanxi*
Ninth Party Congress, 155
Northwest Military Affairs Commission, under Peng Dehuai, 117

Party, *see* Chinese Communist Party
Patriotism, and 'enterprise spirit', 229
Peasantry, 3-4, 7, 14, 20-27, 32, 43, 48, 50, 92, 102, 112, 122, 176-77, 180-82, 187, 189, 194, 196, 199, 202-203, 226; and imperial and Maoist despotism, 181
Peking Opera, 1, 19, 26, 48-49, 51, 53, 55-56, 58-63, 66-67, 77, 79, 80-84, 86-87, 99; development of, 58
Peng Dehuai, 10-11, 13, 15, 26-27, 45, 52-53, 63, 72, 84, 91, 99, 109, 117, 120-21, 123, 175; as Hai Rui, 15; return of from Europe and the USSR, 27
Peng Zhen, Beijing mayor, 15, 58
People's communes, 11, 14, 47, 80, 89, 92-93; introduction to during the Great Leap, 80, 89
People's Daily, 9, 15, 27, 34, 37-39, 109-10, 155, 175, 247-48; *see also Renmin ribao*
Plays, affects popular behaviour and thought, 40; *see* Literature
Pre-Liberation period, 13, 30
Prison system, for Party officials in the PRC, 98
Propagandists, Party, 3; Propaganda Department, 55, 109; Shanghai, 67
Pu Songling, 54
Public criticism, suppression of, 91; *see* Censorship

Qi Benyu, 11, 38
Qi Yanming, Secr to Zhou Enlai and a Vice-Minister of Culture, 59
Qian Junrui, a Vice-Minister of Culture, 53, 55

INDEX 291

Qin Shengrong, 100
Qin Shihuang (221-210 BC), China's first emperor, 175-76, 178-79, 183, 185, 191-92; unification of the empire, 200; Qin Shihuang and Napoleon, 200, 202
Qingguan, pure officials, 49
Qu Yuan, 4-6; expression about the Cultural Revolution, 124-50 passim

Rawski, Thomas, 213, 219
Realism, 70, 98
Recruitment programs, 78, 91, 192, 208, 225, 231-32
Red Guard, 46, 56, 111-13, 154; critics 82; sources, 28, 55, 61, 63
Reform Movement of 1898, 187, 195
Renmin ribao, 35-36, 189, 201, 247-48; *see also People's Daily* and Chinese Press
Revolution of 1911, 187, 188, 195; seventieth anniversary, 259
Ri Zhi, historian, 197
Right Opportunists, campaigns against, 85
Romanticism, 70, 84, 93, 103, 131
Rong Desheng, 237
Rongs, family of China's cotton and flour king, 219, 225-26, 235; efforts to train personnel, 223, 228
Rubber industry, Shanghai, 209

Seventh Party Congress, 167
Shaan-Gan Soviet, 107-108, 114-15, 117
Shang dynasty, 51
Shang Yue, scholar, 40
Shanghai Academy of Social Sciences, 217
Shanghai Cultural Office, 49, 6; Central Work Conference, 34
Shanghai Municipal Committee, 67
Shanghai Work Conference, 52, 55
Shanghai xiju, 64, 66
Shi Ting, 175-77
Shi Ximin, 59
Shu Hua, 21-22

Sino-British Kailuan Mining Administration, 211; *see also* Kuailuan
Sino-Japanese War (1894-95), 41, 240
Sino-Soviet relations, 26
Skinner, Quentin, historian, 12, 45
Slogans, 11, 29, 55, 65, 79, 131, 222, 225, 234
Socialist realism or revolutionary romanticism, 105, 122, 136
Soviet historians, and Napoleon, 199-200
Soviet Thaw, journalistic writers from, 47
Soviet Union, 71, 252; relations with China, 41
Special police, 54
Stalin, 71; Stalinist schemes of 'universal development', 176; and Marx's 'Asiatic Mode of Production', 180; role of, 163; death of, 72
Sui Yangdi (581-618), 200
Sun Fo, son of Sun Yatsen, 250, 254
Sun Jun, Party secretary of the Shanghai Peking Opera Ensemble, 59, 67
Sun Pengzhi, 57
Sun Yatsen, 179, 188, 239-59; and foreign investment, 7, 243; and imperialism, 248; on communism and capitalism, 252

Taiping movement, 187, 189
Taiwan straits crisis, 91
Taiwan, 242
Tang Taizong, 201
Tao Xiong, 56, 59, 61-62
Tao Xisheng, 241, 254, 256
Tao Zhu, and the Great Leap, 27
Technical development, 209, 223
Tenth Plenum, 27
Tian Han, dramatist, 41-42, 46, 48-50, 52, 59, 62, 72, 74, 79, 94, 98, 103
Tian Yuan, 169
Tiananmen incident of 1976, 136, 138
Tiananmen Square, 1989, 147, 240
Tobacco Companies, Nanyang and Huacheng, 208, 219-20

United Nations, 247
United States aid, 241

Wang Meng, writer, 47, 58
Wang Yangming (1472-1528), 194
Wars, with Japan and the Kuomintang, 189
Warsaw Pact countries, 26
Wei Zheng, the minister under Li Shimin, 53
Wen Tianxiang, Song loyalist, 98
Wenhuibao, 13, 57
West, 3, 29, 180, 193, 196, 199, 205, 219, 231, 238; businesspeople, 236; capitalists, 250; expressionism, 135; historians, 2; imperialism, 241, 254; observers of China, 16; political analysts, 10; scholars, 11, 206, 212, 226; technology, 255; studies on politics and literature, 122; experimentation with, 134
Western and Japanese management, 215
Wilson, Woodrow, 243
Wing On, 230; Wing On Cotton Mill, 220-21, 228
Wittfogel, Karl, and 'Oriental Despotism', 178, 180
World Bank, joining of, 247
Wu Han, historian, 4, 9-45 passim, 49;
Wu Shijian, 59
Wu Yu, intellectual, 188
Wu Yunchu, chemical industry pioneer, 222
Wu Yuzhang, of Huabei University, 153
Wusong River and the Baimao River, dredging of, 21

Xi Zhongxun, of Shaan-Gan Soviet, 107, 109, 112, 114-16, 121, 123
Xijubao, leading theatre journal 1959, 41
Xu Dingxin, scholar, 228
Xu Hongzu (1586-1641), geographical explorer, 44
Xu Jie (1503-83), Grand Secretary, 20-25, 34, 62, 65, 73-79, 83-103 passim
Xu Siyan, 56, 59-67

Xuan Zang (602-664), Tang monk, 44

Yan Fu, 188
Yan Hongyan, Party official, 118-20
Yan Song, 52, 73
Yan'an Rectification Campaign, 152
Yang Jisheng, 73, 75; fate at the hands of Yan Song, 78
Yang Shangkun, Party leader, 178
Yao Wenyuan, 10, 13-14, 27, 111, 179, 247
Yellow Turban popular uprising, 33
Yuan court, 50
Yuan Shikai, 244
Yue Fei (1104-42), Song General, 41, 44

Zhang Bingkun (Wei Ming), 59
Zhang Binglin, 188
Zhang Zhidong, entrepreneur, 219
Zhang Zhongli, economic historian, 213, 237
Zhao Ziyang, 203
Zhou Enlai, 55, 59, 66-67, 76-77, 80, 85, 87, 95, 137; and his Party bureaucrats, 124; cult of, 136
Zhou Xinfang, actor, 5, 27, 46, 48-49, 54-60, 63, 66, 71, 174-75; his status in the opera world, 51, 79
Zhou Xuexi, Northern bureaucratic capitalist, 218
Zhou Yang, Propaganda Department, 55-59, 70, 88, 100; and the Anti-Rightist Campaign, 75
Zhu De, 166
Zhu Yong, 216
Zhu Yuanzhang, biography of, 16